Fateful Shapes of Human Freedom

THE VANDERBILT LIBRARY OF AMERICAN PHILOSOPHY
offers interpretive perspectives on the historical roots of American
philosophy and on present innovative developments in American
thought, including studies of values, naturalism, social philosophy, cultural criticism, and applied ethics.

Series Editors
Herman J. Saatkamp, Jr., General Editor
    (Indiana University Purdue University Indianapolis)
Cornelis de Waal, Associate Editor
    (Indiana University Purdue University Indianapolis)

Editorial Advisory Board
Kwame Anthony Appiah (Harvard)
Larry Hickman (Southern Illinois University)
John Lachs (Vanderbilt)
John J. McDermott (Texas A&M)
Joel Porte (Cornell)
Hilary Putnam (Harvard)
Ruth Anna Putnam (Wellesley)
Beth J. Singer (Brooklyn College)
John J. Stuhr (Pennsylvania State)

Fateful Shapes of Human Freedom

JOHN WILLIAM MILLER AND THE CRISES OF MODERNITY

Vincent Colapietro

Vanderbilt University Press • Nashville

© 2003 Vanderbilt University Press
All rights reserved
First Edition 2003

This book is printed on acid-free paper.

Library of Congress Cataloging-in-Publication Data

Colapietro, Vincent Michael, 1950–
Fateful shapes of human freedom : John William Miller and the crises of modernity / Vincent Colapietro.— 1st ed.
    p. cm. — (The Vanderbilt library of American philosophy).
Includes bibliographical references and indexes.
    ISBN 0-8265-1409-X (alk. paper)
    ISBN 0-8265-1433-2 (pbk. : alk. paper)
    1. Miller, John William. I. Title. II. Series.
B945.M4764 C65 2003
191—dc21
                                             2002153469

To John E. Smith
and John J. McDermott

Whose example and friendship have been
for me a constant invitation
To look anew at our defining histories
And at the actual shapes of our fragile freedom

Contents

Acknowledgments ix

Abbreviations xi

Preface xiii

1 Crises of Modernity 1

2 Revision of Philosophy 29

3 The Midworld 86

4 Historical Displacements and
   Situated Narratives: Locating Responsibility 133

5 Critique, Narration, and Revelation 187

Notes 273

References 299

Name Index 311

Subject Index 315

Acknowledgments

There are of course far too many debts to acknowledge here. But the personal and intellectual support and encouragement of certain friends and colleagues have been, without exaggeration, indispensable. I owe deep gratitude to Doug Anderson, Bob Ashmore, Dom Balestra, Richard J. Bernstein, H. Patrick Costello, John Greco, Peter H. Hare, John Lachs, the late Henry W. Johnstone Jr., Jude Jones, Peter T. Manicas, John J. McDermott, Richard S. Robin, Beth J. Singer, Ken Stikkers, John E. Smith, and John J. Stuhr, and Stephen Tyman. I am also grateful to Michael Ames, director of Vanderbilt University Press, and to Herman J. Saatkamp, Jr., Cornelis de Waal, Dariel Mayer, and Deborah Stuart Smith.

Kory Spencer Sorrell and Michael J. McGandy are close intellectual companions who have subjected to painstaking attention an earlier draft of this study.

John William Miller's two sons, Eugene and Paul, have in different ways been very helpful, as was his widow, Catherine (Gisel) Miller.

Joseph P. Fell and the late George P. Brockway read various drafts, offering numerous suggestions, insightful criticism, and unceasing encouragement. My deepest regret regarding this project is that George did not live to see the publication of this book. My deepest satisfaction is that Joe's assistance will not have been squandered!

Others who also knew John William Miller were very generous with their time, above all, Robert H. Elias, Robert E. Gahringer, and Cushing Strout. Along with letters from George Brockway and Joe Fell, my correspondence with these three individuals provided invaluable clarifications, corrections, and criticisms.

I am grateful for both the very generous financial support of the John William Fellowship Fund and an array of resources at Williams College.

My sons Peter Carlo and Vincenzo as well as Doug Glorie and Michele Glorie Palmer have been helpful in ways they might not even imagine, often by simply being welcome distractions, but also by being such thoughtful, curious individuals in their very different ways. My wife, Jo Carubia, proved, once again, to be an editorial genius, fierce ally, and steadying presence.

Abbreviations

Abbreviations are used to cite the writings of John William Miller, published and unpublished, as well as Joseph P. Fell's transcriptions of his notes from four of his courses at Williams College with John William Miller and Eugene R. Miller's collection of his father's papers and letters.

The unpublished writings of John William Miller housed at Williams College are identified by the following abbreviation. Citations include box number followed by folder number:

JWM   Williamsiana Collection of John William Miller Papers. Williams College, Williamstown, Mass.

The published writings are identified by the following abbreviations:

AW   Afterword to *History as System and Other Essays: Toward a Philosophy of History* by José Ortega y Gasset. New York: W. W. Norton, 1961.
DP   *In Defense of the Psychological*. New York: W. W. Norton, 1983.
DT   *The Definition of the Thing*. New York: W. W. Norton, 1980.
FI   "For Idealism." *Journal of Speculative Philosophy* 1 (4) (1987): 260–69.
ME   "Motives to Existentialism." *Comment* (Williams College) 1 (spring 1948): 3–7.
MS   *The Midworld of Symbols and Functioning Objects*. New York: W. W. Norton, 1983.
OM   "The Owl of Minerva." In *The Transactions of the Charles S. Peirce Society* 24 (3) (1988): 399–407.
PC   *The Paradox of Cause and Other Essays*. New York: W. W. Norton, 1978.

PH   *The Philosophy of History with Reflections and Aphorisms.* New York: W. W. Norton, 1981.

Joseph P. Fell's transcriptions of his notes from his courses at Williams College with John William Miller are identified by the following abbreviations:

PH 1-2   Philosophy 1-2: Types of Philosophy. Williams College, fall and spring semesters 1950–51. " 1991 by Joseph P. Fell.
PH 7   Philosophy 7: Philosophy of History. Williams College; fall semester 1951. " 1991 by Joseph P. Fell.
PH 8   Philosophy 8: American Philosophy. Williams College, spring semester 1952. " 1997 by Joseph P. Fell.
PH 19 –20 Philosophy 19–20: Senior seminar. Williams College; fall and spring semesters 1952–53). " 1998 by Joseph P. Fell.

The "Papers and Letters of John William Miller" includes a brief introduction by Eugene R. Miller to each of the 186 items in this collection of almost one thousand pages of his father's writings. Page numbers refer to those in Eugene Miller's typescript.

PL   "Papers and Letters of John William Miller." Edited and transcribed by Eugene R. Miller.

Preface

John William Miller (1895–1978) was an American philosopher who exerted a tremendous personal influence on his many students but, because he published very little during his career, had little impact on professional philosophy during his lifetime, beyond the circles of his acquaintances.[1] In this regard, he was like many other academic philosophers. One crucial difference between Miller and other teachers who have also exemplified the Socratic life in an unforgettable way, however, is his noteworthy achievement: primarily in conversations and in letters, notes for lectures, and drafts of essays, Miller fashioned a unique philosophical perspective worthy of the most serious consideration.

Miller studied at Harvard, receiving his baccalaureate in 1916 and, after serving in the ambulance corps during World War I, his doctorate in 1922. As a graduate student, he took courses with Ralph Barton Perry, E. B. Holt, William Ernest Hocking, and C. I. Lewis (Fell 1990a, 21). Thus, he was party to the disputes between advocates of objective idealism and champions of the new realism. Miller taught at Connecticut College for Women (New London, Connecticut) for a very short while and, immediately after, at Williams College from 1924 until 1960, with one year's interruption (during which he taught at the University of Minnesota). His senior colleague at Williams was James Bissett Pratt, an able defender of what Pratt called personal realism. For most of his professional life, Miller was never far from individuals hostile to his own outlook. From 1960, the year of his retirement, to that of his death eighteen years later, Miller continued exploring, mostly through conversations and letters, several topics that had been the focus of concern during his years as a teacher. Some of the letters are over a hundred pages long. Miller wrote countless pages both before and after his retirement. Nevertheless, he published few articles until near the very end of his life.[2] In 1978, however, *The Paradox of Cause and Other Essays* appeared several months before his death on December 25. Four other volumes have been published posthumously.[3] George P. Brockway, the editor of these volumes and a lifelong student of Bill Miller's, celebrated the career of his teacher in a memoir included in Joseph Epstein's *Masters: Portraits of Great Teachers* (Brockway 1981). This anthology puts Miller in the company of (among others) Morris Raphael Cohen, Alfred North Whitehead, John Crowe Ransom, I. A. Richards, C. S. Lewis, Hannah Arendt, and Margaret Mead. Brockway's memoir concludes by offering the highest praise a student can give to a teacher: "Of all the men of his time whom I have known, he was the wisest, and justest, and best" (64).

A volume of essays edited by Joseph P. Fell (1990b) offers an exquisite portrait of the man and insightful studies of various aspects of his unique perspective. A book by Stephen Tyman, *Descrying the Ideal: The Philosophy of John William Miller* (1993), aims to make the writings of this philosopher "accessible and to advertise their contemporary relevance and vital importance" (xi). It succeeds admirably in realizing this objective, though Tyman tends to neglect the distinctively American character of Miller's radical revision of German idealism. He reads Miller in reference to such figures as Fichte and Hegel, but not Emerson and Thoreau, or Peirce and James, or Dewey and Santayana. Much is to be gained by interpreting Miller's project as a development of "a certain stand of post-Kantian thought" (xi). But Miller's creative appropriation of German idealism was mediated by his personal association with Josiah Royce and William Ernest Hocking. It was also colored by his antipathy toward American pragmatism and his ambivalence toward American transcendentalism.[4] Hence, as far as Tyman's study goes in exhibiting the relevance and significance of Miller's project, it fails to situate Miller in the cross currents of American thought.[5] In a doctoral dissertation, Michael J. McGandy (2000) strives to present "a detailed and systematic articulation of John William Miller's philosophy understood in relation to Walt Whitman's challenge to forge 'a new Literature, perhaps a new Metaphysics,'" worthy of American democracy (vii).[6] Anyone who is interested in seriously exploring Miller's philosophy must not only consult but also study this superb exposition of the intricate weave of philosophical texts still unknown even to most of the best-informed students of American thought. It amply rewards rereading. Moreover, it is deeply informed by the arguments and orientation of Miller's own dissertation, "The Definition of the Thing" *(DT)*. In my reading of Miller, *The Definition of the Thing* is accorded less significance. Thus, in Michael McGandy's interpretation, Miller is more of a transcendental philosopher than he is in my interpretation. For me, the emphasis on historicity is central.

In a letter dated September 5, 1955, to Alburey Castell (a student who became a professional philosopher), Miller confesses: "I have been fussing with the idea of history, and find it vast and difficult" (JWM 21:1). He continued to explore this topic until his death (see Brockway 1981, 164). Despite its vastness and difficulty, Miller gave the idea of history an articulate shape and authoritative status. In doing so, he made a significant contribution to philosophical reflection. Such, at least, is what I strive to show in this book.

Fateful Shapes of Human Freedom

1

Crises of Modernity

> The chaos of today is the historical consequence of a metaphysical lapse. But it is historical and fateful, as is any historical identity.[1]
> — John William Miller, *In Defense of the Psychological*

Karl Marx claimed humans make history but not in circumstances of their own choosing.[2] The circumstances in which we live, however, are ineluctably maintained by our efforts to make a life for ourselves. Yet they are of such a character and complexity that they cannot be maintained without being revised: conservation requires innovation. In any event, our circumstances are not simply forced upon us by the inertia of the past. These circumstances are as much incorporated in our mode of existence as we are enveloped in these circumstances.[3] In other words, they contribute greatly to our agency and thus our identity (see Taylor 1993; Macmurray 1957). We are what we have made of ourselves in circumstances we have maintained by our very efforts to shape a singular life from an inchoate inheritance.[4] In addition, we are what we can yet make of ourselves. Our achievements cannot be gainsaid, but neither can our capacity for alteration. It may even be that what we are not yet is far more important than what we now are (cf. Hocking 1942, 4). Yet, just as all of our achievements are precarious (cf. Ortega 1957, 25–26), any determinate form of human life is transitional. We are continuously becoming other than we have been (Conrad [1900] 1961, 204–5), often only imperceptibly but occasionally in a dramatic and arresting manner.

Even in "epochs of revolutionary crisis," we are like those who in the process of learning a new language begin by translating the unfamiliar medium into our native tongue (Marx 1978, 595). We spontaneously translate the unfamiliar into the familiar. But the opposite of this is equally noteworthy: even in times of historical continuity, we are, apart from intention or awareness, contributors to novelty. We inevitably transform the familiar into the unfamiliar, the structures of our historical inheritances into resources of historical improvisation. Though transformation is inescapable, progress is not guaranteed.

History is, however, neither a tragedy nor a farce.[5] The literary genre of the novel is distinctively modern not only in origin but also in sensibility. It is nothing less than a vital expression of modern consciousness, without which modernity would be largely ignorant of itself. It encompasses the tragic and the farcical, as well as much else, but it is not reducible to these. The novel tends to depict human beings as simultaneously unwitting and knowledgeable actors, fated to be exiled from the commonplace and (wherever successful) to become reconciled with the foreign (cf. Rieff 1993). The novel is a form of historiography in which historicity and place are reclaimed as part of the everyday lives of ordinary people, caught up in the momentous task of holding themselves and their worlds together.[6] It is a way of telling time—not the uniform regularity measured by clocks but the dramatic displacements, ironic reversals, and other reconfigurations only discernible by means of narration (Bradford 1997). As such, this genre concerns our struggles for self-possession and thus our phases of self-dissolution and our acts of self-annihilation.

Despite our denials and evasions, our fate is of our own making, whereas the form of our freedom is initially the consequence not of our own private choices but of our shared circumstances (cf. Brockway 1985, 34–42; Burckhardt 1943). This form is part of our inheritance; the appropriation of this inheritance is our first exercise of autonomy, wherein human agency alone takes recognizable form. Accordingly, the fateful shapes of human freedom are, at every turn, due to the exercise of freedom, even when this exercise takes the form of acquiescence or resignation. The choices we make are ultimately irresponsible if they do not extend to the circumstances in which we exercise our autonomy. The totality of these circumstances, actual and imagined, makes up our world. Our responsibility, consequently, extends to nothing less than our world.[7]

But our world is one in which we are fated to build amid the ruins of worlds we have often had a hand in destroying (cf. Hodges and Lachs 1999).[8] How are we to rebuild our world amid ruins? Indeed, what are we to do with the ruins of worlds either not our own or, apparently, no longer ours?[9] How are we to understand the circumstances in which we are fatefully compelled to assume responsibility for this task?

My purpose here is to address these and related questions in the light of John William Miller's contribution to philosophy. Part of my hope is to make his contribution known to those who take such questions seriously; a larger part is, in the spirit of Miller himself, to put forth liberating responses to fateful questions. Miller does not free us from our past but rather liberates us from impoverished and, indeed, impoverishing ways of conceiving the overlapping histories in which our singular identities are rooted and by which our defining commitments are sustained. That is, he frees us of the illusion that we could ever free ourselves from the past, by exposing the error that the acquisition of genuine freedom entails an annihilation of an authoritative history. Miller does so also by compelling us to come to terms with the fateful shapes of human freedom, at a critical juncture in human history. Freedom encompasses the capacity of owning up to what is ours and owning up to what owns us despite our disclaimers and denials (Allan 1986). We come to acknowledge, at the heart of freedom, the capacity to confront a unique form of human compulsion and to make of this compulsion what we can[10]—or, evading such confrontation, the tendency to empty freedom of all force and hence all meaning. Freedom contains within itself the capacity to negate itself no less than the potential to enlarge its scope and to redefine its meaning.[11]

Miller recovers autonomy by reclaiming history. But the reclamation of history here means a confrontation with those unique forms of human compulsion, including the inherited shapes of human freedom themselves, in and through which human lives acquire their singular significance.[12] It may be that history owns us before we own it. But our ability to own up to the exigencies of our past and, indeed, even our tendency to disown history—above all, its imperatives and authority—result from our incorporation (in effect, our appropriation) of skills and competencies already in place at the time we were born. The disavowal of history was a historical act having fateful consequences.[13] So, too, is its reclamation. But, historically, what prompts this turn toward history?

Moving Beyond Modernity

Part of the self-image of our age is a sense of radical reorientation and even of absolute rupture.[14] We feel ourselves to be in the midst of a profound upheaval and this feeling colors our image of ourselves, suggesting—at least, to some cultural critics—a revision of outlook no less dramatic than the transition from the medieval to the modern worldview (see, e.g., Ortega 1961; also Westphal 1990, 155; Cahoone 1988, xi). The pervasiveness of this sense is evident in how much attention is being paid today to postmodernism. The term *postmodern* implies a movement beyond modernity[15]—an eclipse of the ideals, assumptions, and attitudes that have become ever more deeply characteristic of postmedieval institutions, practices, and discourses. For some, this movement involves, within philosophy, the movement beyond epistemology-centered reflections and, more broadly, the movement beyond Eurocentric concerns.[16] In general, what has been central is becoming peripheral and what has been marginal is becoming focal. The metaphor of marginality has become central and the unqualified celebration of heterogeneity and alterity threatens to undermine any effective ideal of integration or community. The situation William James noted in the opening decade of the twentieth century appears only to have intensified in the closing one: "It is difficult not to notice a curious unrest in the philosophic atmosphere of the time, a loosening of old landmarks, a softening of oppositions, a mutual borrowing from one another on the part of systems anciently closed, and an interest in new suggestions, however vague, as if the one thing sure were the inadequacy of the extant school-solutions" ([1912] 1976, 23). What is today being judged inadequate, however, is not something so limited as "the extant school-solutions"; it is the entire Western tradition. In our colleges and universities, there rage bitter controversies regarding curricular revisions. These are best seen as symptomatic of a deep division regarding the enduring validity of the ideals constitutive of Western culture.

Just as early modern authors used the term "medieval" to disparage the epoch from which they were disentangling themselves (Pieper 1964, 15), so in our own time the term "modernity" is being used with increasing frequency to designate a cluster of ideals allegedly discredited by the actual course of recent history. These ideals are supposed by a growing number of persons to have been refuted not so much by arguments as by events. In order to secure a basis for certain knowledge of and thereby effective control over the natural world, Francis Bacon, René Descartes, and others self-consciously broke with the dominant intellectual tradition of their own time. Modernity began with an assault on tradition, thus sowing the seeds for one of the more paradoxical parts of our cultural inheritance, the tradition of antitraditionalism. In order to avoid being unwitting ideologues for the dehumanizing practices of such forces as capitalistic oligarchies and Western technology, Jean-François Lyotard, Michel Foucault, Jacques Derrida, Paul Feyerabend, and countless others have been launching an assault on the very ideals of the Enlightenment.

In particular, the ideals of impartial reason, human domination, and unlimited progress are treated with extreme suspicion and even outright scorn. The task of our time is to unmask these "universal" ideals, to show them to be merely the ideological props of a particular class: their professedly universal character is a sham needing to be exposed, their purely ideological function a truth needing to be accepted. The light of reason has cast dark and long shadows. The desire for domination has led to a growing sense of impotence no less than to a widening circle of crisis. The lure of progress has undermined the authority of the values by which progress can be distinguished from retrogression, so we settle for change and hope it is, on balance, more beneficial than harmful (Hocking 1942, 10–12; see, however, Lachs 2001). But there is no authoritative way in which *we* in an inclusive sense of this term can decide whether the benefits do outweigh the drawbacks; and thus we settle for change because we do not know what else to do or even how to resist the seductions of novelty.

So, just as early modern figures defined their projects in opposition to the dominant intellectual traditions of their time and, in effect, to the very notion of an authoritative intellectual tradition to which an isolated human consciousness should submit, postmodern writers are defining themselves through their opposition to any form of reason which pretends to operate apart from a particular historical tradition (Schmitz 1995). For the early moderns, the task was to liberate human reason from the disfiguring constraints of tyrannical traditions; for postmoderns, the task is to protect the plurality of humanizing traditions from being homogenized by an abstract reason.[17] On one side, we witness the struggle against traditions inherently hostile to individual conscience and conceptual novelty; on the other, the attack on a form of rationality systematically blind to its own indebtedness, above all, its indebtedness to various and even incompatible traditions.[18] The conception of rationality inherited from the Enlightenment is that of a form of reason systematically unable to come to terms with its own historical rootedness and political complicity. The capacity of reason to abstract itself entirely from its historical circumstances and, thereby, from the actual political struggles of its unique historical moment is the capacity of reason to be beside itself, to be even its opposite, antireason. The irrationality of this form of reason—abstracted reason—resides in taking its fatal flaw as its principal strength: its alleged impartiality is simply a systematic blindness to its own contingent commitments and ideological role.

It has now become imperative to conceive abstracted reason in concrete terms, to portray it in the manner it most strenuously resists. This means depicting it in terms of the actual institutions, practices, and discourses in which it is embedded and by which it is sustained. An abstract portrait of abstracted reason is, in essence, a form of homage to a tyrant that deserves to be deposed, not honored. In contrast, a concrete depiction contributes to a conceptual rebellion against the tyrannical reign of Enlightenment reason.

The historical institutions actually served by the discursive practices of modern speakers and writers are being challenged today by postmodern authors just as medieval institutions were contested by early modern figures. The challenge extends to the forms no less than to the substance of discourse. Experimentation with genres is essential if we are to be successful in freeing ourselves from the crippling limitations and destructive illusions of the modern epoch. Just as the *summae* so closely linked to the public, oral disputes became in time a discredited literary form, so the genres of our own day are destined to become obsolete. Thought is inseparable from expression: a form of thinking not completely undermined by these limitations and illusions demands a form of expression free from the rhetorical ideals of modern discourse—clarity, coherence, hierarchy—or more accurately, demands forms creatively and playfully freeing themselves from these ideals. Complete freedom from these rhetorical ideals and forms is unattainable. The best we as speakers and writers, always already inscribed in the discursive practices of the postmedieval world, can do is contest these practices from within, turning texts against themselves. In the process, the understanding of text as an integral unity is shown to be an illusion; so too is the author envisioned as the real source of the artistic product determined to be illusory. The reader replaces the author, just as polysemous and fragmented discourse replaces the integral and coherent text (see, e.g., Barthes 1977, also Derrida 1974, pt. 1).

These tendencies are clearly apparent in a variety of contemporary movements and concerns, ones too often and too indiscriminately lumped together under such terms as "deconstruction" and "postmodernism." Deconstruction is, at the very least, a concerted effort to contest in a radical fashion the forms and presuppositions of modern discourse, including the presuppositions that authorial intent and textual coherence are helpful, let alone necessary. But deconstruction is an effort by those who know that the only place from which these discourses could be contested is within these discourses themselves. As Derrida noted in an interview, it is not a question of simply junking the concepts we have inherited; rather, it is necessary to transform these concepts:

> [T]o displace them, to turn them against their presuppositions, to reinscribe them in other chains, and little by little to modify the terrain of our work and thereby produce new configurations; I do not believe in decisive ruptures. . . . Breaks are always, and fatally, reinscribed in an old cloth that must continually, interminably be undone. This interminability is not an accident or contingency; it is essential, systematic, and theoretical. (1981, 24)

There is, in general, no possibility of occupying a vantage point beyond these historically conditioned discourses from which to issue a critique. Indeed, the belief that there is a point from which a transhistorical perspective is obtainable is one of the illusions that needs to be exposed. It is an illusion connected with a mistaken conception of human reason. According to this conception, reason is the power of grasping the essence of things, where the essence of things is construed as not only universal but also invariant, that is, ahistorical. For those who oppose this conception, reason—if, indeed, this term is even retained—is the power to see through our pretensions of ever grasping timeless essences or eternal natures; more fundamentally, it is the power to see the search for such essences or natures as itself chimerical. The focus shifts from invariant natures to historical variations, from eternally immutable essences to temporally improvised deeds.

Jean-François Lyotard has defined postmodern as "incredulity toward metanarratives" (1984, xxiv). Such incredulity fosters what Paul Ricoeur has called a "hermeneutics of suspicion," those strategies of interpretation aimed at unmasking "the illusions and lies of consciousness" (1970, 32). While interpretation can be undertaken as an explication of meaning, of what someone utters in some form, it can also be undertaken as an exposure of what someone does not utter and even resists uttering. In the former case, the ideal is radical openness to whatever is actually uttered; in the latter, it is radical suspicion of whatever is manifest, a suspicion enlisted in the service of bringing to light the latent meaning of some human utterance. To anyone adopting a hermeneutic of explication, the text is to be respected; this means, among other things, it is to be taken on its own terms. To anyone espousing a hermeneutic of suspicion, the text is to be contested, to be taken on the very terms it itself suppresses.

A metanarrative is an overarching narrative in which the disparate events of human history (the plurality of stories of our acts and their consequences) can be encompassed. For those committed to constructing a metanarrative, the drive for a coherent and comprehensive story does not violate the character of the multifarious and particular stories we so irrepressibly tell. For those suspicious of this form of narrative, however, this drive leads to nothing less than such a violation. Frequently, it also leads to violence or at least to the justification of sacrificing concrete human beings on the altar of abstract categories, such as "individual freedoms" or a "classless society."

The radical suspicion of metanarratives has emerged alongside a deepening appreciation of narratives. The appreciation of narrative as an irreducible mode of human knowing is not necessarily tied to projects of wholesale debunking or "radical" critique. While certainly not eschewing the necessity of critique, some of those who are insistent upon granting narrative such a status are doing so primarily as a way of making sense out of ourselves and our world, including our various ways of making sense of things—for instance, science, art, religion, and philosophy.

John William Miller's project shows many and deep affinities with those of R. G. Collingwood, Benedetto Croce,[19] and José Ortega y Gasset.[20] Moreover, it anticipated the main thrust of views defended by Paul Ricoeur (1965, 1970, 1974, 1984, 1988, 1989), Louis Mink (1969, 1997), Alasdair MacIntyre (1980), Joseph Margolis (1991, 1993, 1995), David Carr (1986, 1994), and what are by now numerous others on the contemporary scene. From a different cultural location, Miller undertook what his slightly older contemporary tried to accomplish across the Atlantic Ocean: "The chief business of twentieth century philosophy is," according to Collingwood, "to reckon with twentieth-century history" (Collingwood 1939, 79; see Strout 1990b, 154). To make of twentieth-century history in its historical actuality the focal concern of philosophical reflection, to take his own actual time and place with the utmost seriousness, is one way of describing John William Miller's overarching concern. While later chapters examine in detail how he carried out this project, our purpose first is to indicate how Miller's historicist preoccupations are relevant to our contemporary scene.

The contemporary or postmodern debate over modernity is bewildering in its complexity. Given the unbridled spirit of playfulness and the novel forms of contestation, it is often not easy to ascertain precisely what is being disputed. One point at issue is, however, clear. There are some thinkers, the most prominent among them being Jürgen Habermas, who argue for an acceptance of our inheritance from the Enlightenment. In his Introduction to *Habermas and Modernity*, Richard J. Bernstein maintains: "One might epitomize Habermas's entire intellectual project and his fundamental stance as writing a new *Dialectic of Enlightenment*—one which does full justice to the dark side of the Enlightenment legacy, explains its causes but nevertheless redeems and justifies the hope of freedom, justice, and happiness which still stubbornly speaks to us" (Bernstein 1985, 31). For Habermas, then, the project of modernity "is not a bitter illusion, not a naive ideology that turns into violence and terror, but a practical task which has not yet been realized and which can still orient and guide our actions" (ibid.). This acceptance cannot be uncritical; indeed, the inheritance itself demands a critique of all things, including the traditional forms of cultural criticism and even the very ideal of critical consciousness. There are, however, others who are far more ambivalent in their attitude toward this inheritance. The point is not to do better what our predecessors tried to do but to do something completely different. On one side, we encounter writers who advocate reconciliation with the deepest ideals of the Western tradition, including the philosophic tradition; on the other, we encounter authors who celebrate the rupture now taking place between the definitive concerns of this tradition and the focal preoccupations of the present.

The reflections of Miller are relevant to the contemporary debate over modernity and, even more specifically, to the facet of this debate concerning reconciliation versus rupture. In order to be in a position to appreciate this relevance, however, it is necessary to explain fully and systematically one of Miller's most basic concepts, that of "constitutional conflict." (Here we can only begin such an explication; in later chapters, this task is rejoined.) Not all conflicts are on the same level: some take place within an unproblematic context, while others are so deep and disruptive that they are nothing less than threats to the very context in which the conflicts are taking place. The debate between Thomas and Duns Scotus on the nature of universals is an example of the former, while the debate between the early modern thinkers—most dramatically, Francis Bacon and René Descartes—and their medieval predecessors is an illustration of the latter. The debate between Thomas and Scotus contributed to the articulation of a novel outlook, rendering this outlook more nuanced and defensible. The assault of Bacon, Descartes, and others on the schoolmen—a decisive moment in giving "academic" the pejorative connotation it still possesses—contributed, in contrast, to the revision of the existing and indeed authoritative outlook. Two fateful consequences of this constitutional revision need to be noted here: nature was stripped of its sacramental character and the self of its essential sociality (cf. Hocking 1959, vi).

But this is to state the matter negatively, in terms of what was lost and, moreover, with not even a suggestion of what was gained. The quantification of natural phenomena by those who followed the early modern "revisionists" made possible a control of natural processes previously only dreamed. In addition, the sense of personal identity secured by a consciousness refusing to accept the inevitability of traditional roles eventually made possible a control over one's own existence previously not even imagined. Nature came more and more to be conceived of as an absolutely impersonal order; no longer a perceptible sign of divine graciousness, it became the raw material for human ingenuity. At the same time, the self came more and more to be seen in terms of a completely inner drama (cf. Dewey [1925] 1988, 175–80).

On the stage of nature so conceived, no actor can appear, no person could ever be present.[21] So the drama shifts from the public to a private setting. In this essentially inner drama, the relationship of the self to itself is primary and the relationship of the self to all other actual selves becomes a matter of purely voluntary association—a matter of what the self, with an ever-decreasing sense of obligation to the past, including its own past commitments, freely chooses at this moment. For this reason, narcissism is part and parcel of modernity;[22] and since narcissism undermines the very reality of the individual self as an integral presence upon which it is fixated, nihilism is also part and parcel of modernity. For narcissism not only negates the reality upon which it fixates; it also negates any possibility of authoritative values apart from the arbitrary preferences of isolated individuals. But such preferences can neither sustain nor guide historical agents in their struggles to forge a unique identity. For the values to which the self-absorbed or narcissistic self is committed come to be felt, by this self, as hollow and insignificant, in short, as valueless; the meanings around which such a self structures its life become for this self meaningless, if not also demeaning. The more successful the narcissistic self is in its essential project—defining itself exclusively in terms of itself and thus in disregard of all others—the more impoverished is its vision of the worthwhile and the more dissipated are the sources of its morale.[23]

We, who have made or are able to make the pilgrimage from Descartes and Bacon to our ravaged natural environment and our radically insecure identities, know the price to be paid for the disenchantment of nature and the uprooting of the self.[24] Nature, quantitatively conceived, eclipses the personal; the self, essentially deracinated, eclipses the other. Our natural no less than our social chaos needs to be grasped by its roots. To do so, the chaos confronting us today must be seen not as a purely adventitious but as our unique historical fate. Given our outlook as it effectively informs our appropriation of nature and our encounters with persons, such chaos was inevitable. To comprehend this inevitability, it is necessary first to see the chaos and, indeed, the violence so characteristic of our times as occasioned by the "radical conflicts over the controls of our reason, and so of our commitments" (*PC*, 191), in short, by constitutional conflicts. This itself requires a fuller understanding of what Miller means by "constitutional conflicts."

Constitutional Conflicts

We live in a common world insofar as we have mastered common forms of human action such as perceiving, counting, measuring, speaking, promising, and voting. This is in part what Miller means when he asserts: "In so far as I have another man's problems of form, I am not analogous but actually identical [with that man]. It is this identity of actuality that is also our only community" (*PH*, 129). To have another person's problems of form involves sharing not only mastery of the same forms of action but also the conflicts generated by this mastery. For example, American citizens during the Civil War were united, on one side, by taking the abolition of slavery as the immanent moral trajectory of our actual political past and, on the other, by proclaiming the primacy of states' rights as the trajectory of this same past. "There can be no urge to community where there is no division" (*PC*, 175). In a sense, both Southerners and Northerners were Americans insofar as they actually shared the problem of determining what form the Constitution must take in order to preserve the integrity of the nation. This is the sense in which the United States was a nation divided against itself (see, e.g., *PH*, 150).

The world of so-called common sense is more accurately designated as the world of shared action. This is the actual world, the world insofar as it is maintained, established, and revised by our actions. Perception must itself be conceived of as a shared form of human activity: you and I can perceive the same objects because we can perform the same functions. The most immediate aspect of the world of "common sense"—the insistent presence of tangible objects with determinate characters—is not revealed to a disengaged, solitary spectator but only to a finite person implicated in the ongoing activities making up various social practices. Apart from these activities, nothing is given, least of all the palpable presence of physical objects. The secure status of these objects is, accordingly, one with our unhesitating command of and our fluid control over our own embodied agency, including, of course, our organs of perception and manipulation. As the words "tangible" and "palpable" themselves suggest, there is here an essential connection between the presence of such actions and the power of the hand to grasp or merely to touch what is immediately present.

So, too, the word "object" etymologically means that which is thrown in our way; however, apart from agents who have the capacity to be in transit in some fashion, there are no objects.[25] Without assertions, there can be no objections; likewise, independent of a self-assertive presence, there can be no "external" objects. Even Dr. Samuel Johnson had to kick a stone in order to "refute" Bishop George Berkeley's idealism ("I refute him thus"), the contention that *esse est percipi* (the claim that the being of an object is nothing other than its being perceived). Johnson was thereby caught in the act: the thereness of the stone was established in the very act of kicking. Apart from this or some other act, neither subject nor object is truly present. The forms of action make possible a world of common objects because they make possible continua of shared actions. As a self- and world-declaring utterance, the act of kicking is part of a continuum. Its continuity with both prior and subsequent acts allows the act to be an articulate exertion rather than simply a brute effort: it allows, in short, the act to be an utterance.[26]

The continua of shared actions make possible the world of our shared experience. Accordingly, the actual world is truly a common world. It is, however, also a confused world, though the confusions inherent in this world are not ordinarily the focus of attention. As Miller puts it, the "actual world of common sense is confused. As a rule we are content to let this confusion rule, since there are good results to be secured by letting sleeping dogs lie. But sometimes one's religion clashes with one's science, or one's hopes with actual affairs, one's affections with one's duties. In such situations both claims have some standing or authority, but one can't make out their relation, unity, integrity" (*DP*, 126). Nor can one ignore the sense of division generated by such clashes.

For such clashes are imperatively disconcerting. In response to them, we seek, often quite desperately, composure.[27] We seek to compose ourselves but, in order to achieve this, we need also to preserve the environment in which the composure of the self is in and of itself an actual achievement and not a private fantasy. Here we see an illustration of what Miller means when he asserts that totality and presence stand or fall together (see, e.g., *MS,* 13): to compose oneself apart from preserving one's world is impossible. It is likewise futile to maintain the actual world apart from revising it. The exigency to revise our world is rooted not in the whims or needs of an isolated consciousness but in the inescapable implosions of the most authoritative forms of human agency (Blumenberg 1985).

We are driven to the past by the inherent confusions in our present circumstances. "The forces once operating and now forgotten or underestimated establish their authority only when the present requires them for the understanding of its own constitutional conflicts and for the composure of its resolves" (AW, 243). Along these same lines, it is necessary to recognize that

> [h]istory is the implication of any self-conscious present. It is the mark of the realization that the present is not eternal but has been derived, and that its derivative status allows it to be identified as present [indeed, as this present]. Without the past the present lacks distinction and peculiarity, suggesting no genesis and no further career. We do not study history because the past is a problem, but rather because the present is a problem. History identifies the present that, without history, is nothing but an arbitrary immediacy, without reason and without will. (JWM, 17:5)

While this is in general true of any present, what genealogical account of our actual present will enable us to comprehend its defining conflicts and, thereby, take a step toward regaining a composed resolve in the face of these conflicts?[28] More simply, what story will illuminate the confusions constitutive of modernity (Baeten 1996)? This question is, in effect, being asked of Miller. It is his answer to this question we now seek.

Conflicts of Modernity

One of the deepest conflicts, perhaps the deepest conflict, at the present time is the struggle between dogmatists and skeptics. Both are responding to the upheavals and transitions noted in the opening paragraphs of this chapter. Formally, the conflict between dogmatism and skepticism was present in all previous ages and most evident at the moments of transition from one age to another. For it is part and parcel of the structure of constitutional conflicts. That is, such constitutional conflicts, by their very nature, mark the arrest of some absolutely basic form of human functioning; and, moreover, any such arrest is attended by the insistence on the part of some—the traditionalist, the conservative, the "dogmatist," and other variants of this position—simply to continue doing the done thing.

The form of skepticism confronting us today is best termed "nihilism." The contemporary nihilist is the militant skeptic who, perhaps out of resentment more than anything else, attempts to arrest the functioning of all others, especially authoritative others. They are, for example, those critics who "are hot on the trail of any pretension to authority. They allow no presence" (*DP,* 105). They desire to debunk any and all authority, to undermine all bases for reverence and all claims to power.

In our own day, skepticism assumes a far more radical and dangerous form than in previous periods. This is one of the distinguishing features of the present time: the threat of nihilism, in one form or another, is omnipresent. As Charles Taylor (1989) notes, the threat of meaninglessness confronting human beings today is essentially different from the threat of damnation felt by Luther or the possibility of ignobility faced by Achilles.

"Of course our current nihilism is itself a historical emergence. It was not original" (*PH,* 192). It was derived from our unwitting continuation and exacerbation of past confusions and conflicts. Accordingly, Miller proposes "a test for the historian," that of identifying "some fatality in the present, a present confusion and conflict brought on by the articulate past" (ibid.). His own attempt to identify the fatality inherent in and, indeed, definitive of the present is perhaps nowhere better formulated than in the following passage.[29]

> To be in history is to see the present as a historical fate, not as above or outside the momentum of the actual. So I say that the current hostility

to the generative power of the act is not without basis. But I assert that this basis is . . . the struggle of the act to discover its own constituents [and its own conditions]. Truth proposed as a fixity has come under attack, and this because it nullifies the process by which fixity has itself been generated. But as rebels from fixity we then fly to its antithesis and embrace Calibanism. (*PH*, 192)

This means, in part, that an ahistoric conception of reason and an anarchical conception of freedom war with each other, each claiming an equally strong authority and entailing equally repugnant consequences. It also means being whipsawed from authoritarian cries for "order" to anarchical demands for "freedom."

In this connection, Miller's differences with Ortega's project are especially relevant. In an unpublished manuscript, Miller is at pains to point out the most basic divergences between himself and his contemporary (JWM, 17:15). There are deep affinities between these two thinkers: Miller possessed deep sympathy for Ortega's general outlook, and he was also fond of quoting Ortega's pronouncement that humans have no nature—only a history. Even so, he confessed that, regarding Ortega: "I have never been quite comfortable with him, although he says brilliant things and moves in a direction away from what is so [i.e., away from discourse about essences and toward discourse as a self- and world-declarative affair]. But if you do [move away from discourse about immutable essences and toward a discourse disclosing historical mutabilities] there are two ways to move, into ideas or into actualities. Now I find Ortega doing the former" (ibid.). Like Miller, Ortega proposes that the business of philosophy is not to say "what is so"—what is true apart from telling—but to exhibit the processes by which the world and the self are constituted. But unlike him, Ortega defines these processes in terms of ideas and of the imagination, rather than in terms of actualities and the forms of functioning: "Ortega, having rejected the view that philosophy tells you 'what is so,' concludes it is a work of the imagination, a fabrication, like centaurs and chimeras. It is a made World, but made by thought and imagination" (ibid.). Miller is not averse to making, to identifying the process by which self and world, presence and totality, are declared as a form of *poiesis* in its original, inclusive sense; indeed, the actual world he so strenuously champions is a made world. The actual world is not, however, a merely imagined world, though the distinctively human forms of actions almost always involve an imaginative dimension. While this is obviously true of such enterprises as art and science, it is equally true of the most basic modes of embodied functioning such as the perception of present objects and the orientation toward the spatial environment. The work of imagination is ubiquitous, but it by itself is not sufficient to explain the fateful shape of either my historical identity or my historical environment.

The explanation of either identity or environment requires the recognition of actuality. Thus, Ortega's flight to the imaginary is, from Miller's perspective, a flight from the actual. It is a flight whose significance extends far beyond Ortega's own failure to come to explicit and uncompromising terms with the actual and fateful course of our history; for his failure can be viewed as symptomatic of one of the deepest tendencies in contemporary thought—the evasion of the actual through a celebration of the imaginary.

It is no accident, then, that Miller in his critique of Ortega observes: "Action has never been a category. . . . Present active participles do not occur in traditional metaphysics. They do in mine. I start with speaking, counting, measuring, trying, failing, singing, etc. But I do not say that [the] Act is a Reality, rather than an Appearance or an Illusion. I say that it is apropos of [the] Act that these [and, in fact, all other] distinctions occur" (ibid.). So, in opposition to Ortega, Miller declares: "I do not live in a world of the imagination, nor yet in the 'real' world of cognition. I live in the actual [world], in the projection of functioning objects" (ibid.). Just because the actual world is the *fateful* projection of a complex array of functioning objects, including one's own body as an incarnate psyche, it is primarily neither a world of imagination nor one of knowledge; imagination and knowledge are explicable, if at all, only in terms of actuality. Actuality must be linked to action; and, in turn, action must be conceived in terms of the self-defining endeavors of human agents and the self-undermining crises—what Miller would call *fatalities*—of human history (Johnstone 1990).

In this critique of Ortega, Miller not only discusses nihilism but also takes this skeptical dissolution of any authoritative outlook to be the fatality of our time. Miller most acutely felt the crises of modernity at the close of that tumultuous decade, the 1960s. They were crises rooted in an evasion of the actual, an evasion undertaken in the name of cognition or of imagination—or both.[30] "One can draw the portrait of our time in terms of the demoralization consequent on a cognitive premise" (JWM, 17:15). This premise is that knowledge is attainable apart from actuality, from actual participation in some historical form of human discourse. It is, in essence, what Miller often calls the Iron Law of Knowledge: this law commands speakers to "Keep Out" of their utterances. Our utterances embody our unique, personal presence or they do not; if they do, then our utterances are thereby disqualified; if they do not, then we as speakers are thereby nullified. How can the speaker be preserved in the act of speaking without undermining the truth or, at least, the possibility of truth inhering in our utterances? In reference to utterance as in reference to so much else, we witness "a shiftless anarchy on the one side, or a dogmatic arbitrariness on the other" (*PC*, 178). In particular, we witness, on one side, speakers who refuse to be bound by the laws of logic and, on the other, speakers who refuse to take responsibility for the laws of logic, making these laws into dicta wholly foreign to the exigencies of speakers as speakers. The traditional ideal of impersonal knowledge ("An ancient and persistent belief holds that to speak truly is to speak anonymously and that otherwise a saying exhibits only the oddities of the speaker" [JWM, 25:2]) and the imperative drive for personal presence in all of our endeavors, including inquiry ("We wish above all to be effective, to count for something" [JWM, 6:13]), are at war with one another. They tend to exclude one another, forcing us to eradicate all traces of personal presence in any utterance pretending to proclaim the truth and, in addition, to remove the restrictions of formal procedure on any gesture pretending to declare our uniqueness. On one hand, we have the nullified self whose utterances entail obliteration of presence; on the other, the anarchical self whose irresponsibility undermines the possibility, or at least the likelihood, of speaking properly. Speaking truly is only one form of speaking properly, for there are occasions in which the function of discourse is not to say "what is so" but to define the conditions in which saying "what is so" or, for that matter, some other form of saying, is possible.

It is one thing to speak truly about a domain of objects and events securely established, quite another to speak insightfully about the constitution of such a domain. The enactment of laws within a constitutional framework is one thing, the radical revision of such a framework quite another. Miller's very language (above all, "constitutional conflict" as a designation for one of his most important conceptions) suggests that he is drawing an analogy between our relationship to the actual (or historical) world and our relationship to our political inheritance. A constitutional government defines the appropriate measures for resolving conflicts but also embodies unresolved conflicts of vast significance. In the history of the United States, for example, the question of slavery might have been provisionally evaded, but the adoption of the Constitution itself ensured that the issue could not be circumvented forever. What is true of our political frameworks turns out also to be true of our philosophical frameworks: definitive crises ("constitutional conflicts") are inscribed in their defining commitments.

One such crisis concerns the modern conception of human knowers (or cognitive subjects). If we conceive cognition apart from actuality, the enterprises of knowing apart from the forms of acting, there is no way of escaping the dilemma in which one horn is the nullified self and the other is the anarchical self. We will have either a total eclipse of personal presence or a total triumph of the vagrant individual. "The present sought its validity in an order which extinguished it" (*MS*, 121), for example, a mechanistic world. Or it asserted its uniqueness in a manner that undermined responsibility. In either case, the result is the same: demoralization. The progressive demoralization consequent upon the "Iron Law" is "a fatality in the true sense of inherent confusion, of a collapse of function, of local control, of the sacred and the revelatory" (JWM, 17:15). What are we to do in the face of such confusion? Miller proposes to "give a cheer to the poet and even the scientist, to utterance which shows person and world" (ibid.). For the utterances of the scientist no less than of the poet, when properly understood, are truly revelations. In these revelations, the utterer, the utterance, and the uttered (the world) are inseparable (*MS*, 70). Neither are we articulate beings in a Silent Universe nor are we passive mirrors of the cosmic spectacle.[31] Our capacity to give voice to the totality reveals something essential about the nature of that totality: it itself is not absolutely mute. But that we have a voice in the telling of truth and a hand in the making of our world does not reduce the truth to anything arbitrary or the world to anything imaginary.

The scope of our confusion, the extent of our collapse, should not be underestimated. "We are not like Hamlets with a world out of joint. We have no world to get incoherent, and no self which is the locus of disarray" (JWM, 17:15). In other words, the assault on the forms of functioning, the means by which presence is declared and totality projected, has been so pervasive and profound that our actual world has been reduced, as far as this is possible, to nowhere. Our personal identities have likewise been severed, again as far as this is possible, from the universal alliances by which these identities can alone win shape and solidity. A world without form is no world at all; a self apart from some fateful, entangling alliances with universals is no self at all.

The celebration of the loss of world and self, the collapse of totality and presence, might well be called "nihilism." It is demoralizing except to the extent that it derives exhilaration from the toppling of the authorities, however humane and indispensable. This exhilaration is rooted in resentment. It takes delight in effectively undermining those who exhibit what it so desperately craves: command of self and circumstance. "If not command, then destruction!" So proclaims the nihilist.

"How do you oppose Nihilism? Not by reason." Then how? Miller makes this suggestion: "I do it by treating a person as there [as present]" (ibid.). One takes the absolute demand for personal presence, however vagrantly asserted, with a degree of seriousness, often with greater seriousness than the person making the demand. "So I have some sympathy," Miller confesses in a letter to Alburey Castell, "with the disreputable forces in this uncouth country. By the same token I like and prefer the disciplined mind when, as people vaguely say, it is 'creative.' There is a lot of 'creation' which is undisciplined, but even so it manifests a dark authority" (JWM, 21:1). However "dark" these attempts to establish an authoritative presence, the need propelling them is, more often than not, authentic and, thus, worthy of respect. For, if "any World is the shape of our doing" (JWM, 22:1), any instance of doing—any assertion of presence, no matter how dark or vagrant—has "cosmic consequences." "Why so? Because the order of finitude [the order entailed by action] is infinite and such order is on the make. The other end of the infinite is the actual present" (JWM, 17:15). But, if this is so, then the other end of any asserted presence is the infinite, a world projected by, yet inclusive of, our deeds and their revisions. Any act by which we assert our presence inevitably projects a totality.

I define myself in reference to others, now in contrast to then, and here in contrast to there. But the others to whom I ineluctably, even only implicitly, refer in an actual assertion of personal presence, radiate from the familiar foreground of recognizable others to an unbounded background of mostly unknown and, indeed, unknowable agents, who are denizens of my universe whether or not I acknowledge their actuality or pertinence to my identity. The finite actuality of personal presence, like that of temporal occurrence or spatial location, carries within itself the formal infinity of not only an interpersonal world of unbounded dimensions but also an impersonal world of cosmic scope. Actuality entails ideality, just as finitude implies infinity and singularity implies universality (see, e.g., PH 7, 18).

To repeat, any act by which we declare our presence and singularity projects a world. And we are bound to assert, in some fashion, our presence. "We do not begin with a theory, or even with a truth, but with the imposing need of establishing our personal reality through our answerability to such men as we may meet" (*PH*, 173). We might, however, try to establish this reality without regard for others who are also actually present; that is, we might treat as negligible our answerability to such persons as we inevitably meet in the execution of our actions. Such is the very definition of "vagrancy." The response to individuals who assert their presence in this way is to take seriously their act of assertion. This does not mean excusing or justifying their neglect of others. Quite the contrary. So, while nihilism is a pervasive cultural tendency to be opposed, nihilists are actual human agents whose self-defeating negations need to be exhibited to the nihilists themselves for what these negations are: genuine but misguided attempts to secure an effective presence in an order deeply hostile to any declaration of such presence. In this sense, the project of the nihilist destroys what it seeks to attain: the drive to be someone, though someone not answerable to others, negates the self. No one is in command, in short, no one at all, is left. Given this project, such obliteration of the self is unavoidable; and given this obliteration, demoralization is equally inescapable.

To draw the portrait of our times in terms of the demoralization and nihilism resulting from our inherited commitment to a cognitive premise (the "Iron Law") exhibits a fatality, a fateful shape of human freedom, but it should not be taken to justify fatalism. For a historical comprehension of the fateful confusion inherent in the contemporary "world" is the first step beyond the demoralizing nihilism so pervasive in our times. A confusion comprehended is a step toward a confusion transcended. The only way out is through (Frost 1995, 66): the historical transcendence of constitutional confusion requires acknowledging the extent to which we are defined by our conflicts.

In practical terms, this comprehension must guide our approach to the crisis of authority, a crisis at or, at least, near the heart of the crisis of modernity. Miller was keenly aware of what today is called the question of legitimation (Habermas 1990; Jardine 1985) and the need to address this question. While he tended to speak of "authorization," what he had in mind was just this question. It would not be an exaggeration to say that this question was one of his deepest concerns. In one place, he announced: "What I propose is that we consider the price to be paid for enfranchising discourse. Discourse needs authority. It is that concern that lies at the core of the philosophy of history" (*PC*, 106, 118).

If we are to appreciate the significance of this text, we must understand "discourse" in the inclusive sense intended by Miller. All of our *acts* are instances of utterance and, thus, of discourse. For example, when I go to the post office to mail a letter, the act not only bespeaks a purpose but also relies on a formal procedure and an institutional framework. Hence, when Miller notes that discourse needs to be authorized or, in our parlance, legitimated, what is at stake is nothing less than exhibiting the bases of authority by which finite, fallible agents in their actual, hazardous circumstances are entitled to speak, count, measure, vote, promise, and so on. What entitles us to the verbs (in particular, the present active participles) by which we declare our unique personal presence and project a comprehensive formal order? More simply, what authorizes our actions, with all their fateful consequences for our personal integrity and our historical environment? This is the question of legitimation as it is encountered in Miller's writings.

Philosophy must not be indifferent to this question. "In a time of decision, philosophy cannot allow itself to become an adventure of enervation. Nor, in a time when arbitrariness has taken new and dangerous forms can philosophy avoid seeking a humanistic solution to problems of authority" (*PC*, 113). Philosophy must speak to persons "who wish to be *both* resolved and critical" (ibid.; emphasis added). My resolution to act can be purchased at the price of my critical sensibility; so, too, my commitment to criticism can be attained at the cost of a resolute will. In the former case, we witness a step toward fanaticism and, in the latter, one toward a disengaged and ultimately irresponsible aloofness from the actual demands of the historical moment. A truly humanistic solution to the legitimation crisis will reveal how it is possible for human agents to attain both critical consciousness and practical resolve. In Chapter 4, I examine in detail Miller's attempt to provide just such a solution to the crisis of legitimation. Here what needs to be stressed is his awareness of the question of legitimation as part of the crisis of modernity and, in general, the way he proposes to address this question.

Miller knew that, especially in our times,

> it is risky and perhaps obscure to be affirmative. On the other hand, the affirmation shows the basis of any remarks one might make about event, cause, presupposition, purpose. So, I keep reverting to my controlling affirmations. No basic affirmation is cognitive. . . . What is basic is functioning. The evidence of functioning is not some reality, something 'known' [or some appearance, something 'perceived']. The evidence is the functioning object. (*MS*, 112–13)

Miller's controlling affirmations concern the midworld, the comprehensive yet constitutionally incomplete realm of those formal procedures (e.g., measuring, speaking) made possible by a distinctive kind of human artifact—functioning objects (e.g., yardsticks, words). This realm is not only constitutionally incomplete; it is also inherently divided (think here of any community of inquirers or interpreters). These divisions within the midworld are what he calls "constitutional conflicts." They are the principal means by which historical epochs no less than personal identities are defined. It is, as it were, by their conflicts that periods and persons are known (see, e.g., *MS*, 187). In this section, I have identified an interrelated set of constitutional conflicts that Miller took to be definitive of our historical moment. We are, at this unique moment no less than at previous times, only "reluctantly driven to the actual" (ibid.). Miller wanted, above all, to show how this drive toward recognition of the authority and sufficiency of the actual world, no matter how strenuously resisted, is not propelled by anything foreign to the human spirit; indeed, it is itself a fatality inherent in the most authoritative forms of human functioning.

The actual world is an articulate world. In one sense, this means that it is a spoken, uttered world: "there is no escaping an account of the sort of world that can include utterances, the affirmations, and denials that permit any world to be intelligible" (*MS*, 129). In another sense, it means that the actual world is necessarily inclusive of articulate beings, of beings who can give voice to the totality while recognizing that it is by virtue of their voice, their capacity to command any variety of media, that the totality is revealed.

The Way Beyond Modernity

For Miller, the movement beyond modernity requires a revision of philosophy, not in the sense of leaving behind what has been moved beyond, but in the paradoxical sense of carrying forward what in its debilitating form has been cast off. At the heart of this revision, there is a movement away from the critique of abstract arguments to the cultivation of a distinctive form of historical consciousness.[32] For the cultivation of such consciousness, what we need is, above all else, an imaginative reconstruction of the dialectical drama in which the constitutional conflicts constitutive of human history can be seen for what they are—violent disorganizations of an outlook (*DP*, 116) and, therefore, themselves occasions for violent undertakings (*PC*, 191). Human history has been a slaughter bench because human outlooks have been vulnerable to violent disorganization and the violence resulting from such disorganization.[33] Confronted with the carnage so prominent in our past, the desire to locate us or at least our ideals outside of history is certainly understandable. It is just as certainly doomed. There is no course but to follow the advice given by Stein to Jim in Joseph Conrad's *Lord Jim*—"In the destructive element immerse" (quoted in *PC*, 136–37). But this immersion in the destructive element—in the finite actualities of human history—need not be a mindless submersion in the chaotic flux of contemporary events. Indeed, it can, and must, be as mindful as it is resolute. We can no more escape reflecting on history than we can escape history itself. Indeed, our historical situatedness is precisely what demands the painstaking cultivation of historical consciousness; it is what demands reflecting on those revisions of outlooks at the innermost core of history and of the utmost concern to philosophy.

For Miller, the cultivation of such consciousness involves nothing less than a pilgrimage, a journey to the shrines of the sacred. History "is made by those who have not shrunk from the conflicts which challenge a present outlook, who have seen those conflicts through in [, for example,] physics or in politics" (*PC*, 73). Philosophy must join those who have the courage to make history, that is, the courage to confront the constitutional conflicts of their own historical time. "Those conflicts are the phenomenology of the spirit, the stations of its career, the secular stations of the cross. It is this story which is both history and philosophy" (ibid.; slightly modified). The phenomenology of spirit—the story of the dialectic generated by these conflicts—is, in effect, a pilgrimage. "Goethe observes that what has been inherited must be reacquired if it is to be appropriated: *Was du ererbt von deinen Vätern hast, Erwirbt es um es zu besitzen.* If we possess the present we must make the pilgrimage that has so far advanced to this station" (*PH*, 84). Apart from this pilgrimage, the present is an indistinguishable now and our identity an amorphous affair. In the light of this pilgrimage, the present acquires distinction and the self acquires form.

"Any actual moment is also a momentum" (*MS*, 14). A moment *is* a momentum, a dimension of time implicated in a particular past and hurling toward a decisive future. More often than not, we desire the moment but not the momentum inherent in it. This, however, is fantasy (*MS*, 14). And all such fantasy is a flight from actuality. "One cannot call one's soul one's own if one cannot call the moment one's own" (*PH*, 173). But to call the moment one's own, one must grasp the moment in its momentum. Hence, to take possession of myself, I must take possession of my present historical moment. But, to take possession of any such moment, I must make a pilgrimage to the actual moments of some comprehensive yet particular career. For the present is essentially part of "a continuum reaching into the past" (*PH*, 61). "In history we cannot disavow what we have done or said" (*PH*, 59). Nor can I disavow my indebtedness to what we have done or said, my involvement with predecessors, without posing a serious threat to my personal identity; for my very status as a self depends on my participation in some actual community, on my continuation of what others before me did and said.

Until somewhat recently, neither the general importance of history nor the particular conception of historicity, our being in history, has been a philosophical commonplace. "It took time to discover history as no less philosophical than the static categories of Aristotle and Kant" (*PH*, 181). The "tardiness" of this discovery is no historical anomaly.[34] Indeed, "[t]he disparagement of time is no fitful impulse" (*PH*, 63). It draws its strength from the dominant orthodoxy in Western thought. The continuing hold of this orthodoxy is a principal cause of our confusion; for the most pressing intellectual need of our time is to come to terms with time, not the clock-time of physics, but the dated-time of history. We need to recognize that our relations with this form of time "are total and constitutive" (*PH*, 54). We also need to recognize that historical time at least "requires its appropriate medium, the distinctive objects that reveal it, objectify it, and are its substance" (*PH*, 109). The distinctive objects comprising these appropriate media, mentioned above, are what Miller calls "functioning objects." But our own most influential intellectual traditions constitute, more than anything else, an obstacle to the satisfaction of these needs.[35] Given the assumptions and ideals of these traditions, neither the character and comprehensiveness of our relations with historical time nor the categoreal status of merely human artifacts could be acknowledged.[36] Accordingly, a philosophy adequate to the present must be not only a philosophy of history but also a history of why philosophy took so long to grant the historical process and its distinctive medium an irreducible status and an authoritative role.

To show this, philosophy must be a pilgrimage, a journey to the loci where humanity tried to stake out a realm of the sacred and a recollection of how these various essays collapsed because of their own inherent flaws, their own constitutional conflicts. The secular course of human history is nothing less than a struggle to secure a realm of the sacred, of what is absolutely precious and intrinsically inviolable. "History is," according to Miller, "a *secular* destiny, and that is a hard idea to present" (*DP*, 149; emphasis added). Yet, history so conceived is not exclusive of the sacred; it, rather than the eternal, becomes the sole possible locus for the inescapable human demand that something be inviolable. Accordingly, Miller states: "If we want reverence, anything sacred and so imperative, we must advance now to history—and I cannot avoid it!—to pure history, which is philosophy. There is the common world, the actual one" (*DP*, 151). He goes so far as to assert that "[i]n any past there is something sacred. It is the barbarian who lays his hands on monuments" (*DP,* 150). It is a person who is animated by a sense of the sacred who refuses, absolutely refuses, to desecrate the shrines, temples, and monuments of others, for such a person recognizes these objects for what they are, the vehicles by which the human spirit has moved, or could have moved, through its secular course.

In a letter dated August 22, 1971, Miller asserts: "So, when I say a word for the 'sacred,' it is *not* in the interest of getting rid of the secular. It is in the interest of the position which enforces the distinction." In this same letter, he characterizes philosophy as "the story of enforced distinctions." In other words, it is the discourse that aims to exhibit not only what distinctions are requisite to discourse as such but also the conditions upon which these distinctions can alone be drawn. Here and in numerous other places, Miller enjoins his students or correspondents to be resolutely attentive to the conditions of their own discourse. Philosophy is nothing less than the systematic alertness to the actual conditions of human discourse, especially on those occasions when speakers are, in effect, destroying the very conditions of their own discourse, undermining the very authority of their own utterances, for example, B. F. Skinner's account of human language in terms of operant conditioning.

In another lecture from this same course, Miller makes a comment especially pertinent to the topic of the sacred. He informs his students: "The only reason for studying history is to fit you to make it. In the past men sought peace, quiescence; now we must seek history. Quiescence is the end [or abolition] of will; the end of self-definement or [self-definition]" (PH 7, 38). Then he notes: "The purpose of this study is to make the secular sacred. If you don't do that, you will be will-less men" (ibid.).[37] But our awareness of the failure of all such struggles makes us deeply skeptical of our own ability to secure and maintain such a realm.[38] What has been proclaimed absolute by any actual human community has proven to be relative to human history. "As we change absolutes we change ourselves and our world. These changes constitute history. History is the story of the transformation of absolutes" (*PC,* 144). But the ever-deepening consciousness of changing absolutes is part and parcel of the crisis explored in this chapter. How is it possible to deepen our consciousness of history, precisely in the sense of "the story of the transformation of absolutes" and still have an absolute warrant for our most basic declarations? How is it possible for us, at this time, to immerse ourselves in the destructive element, to accept the entangling alliances of human history and yet avoid being either authoritarians or nihilists? The crisis of modernity is, in part, a crisis of authority; as such, it concerns what, if anything, would provide an adequate basis for our absolute commitments (Arendt 1968a, chap. 3). Thus, the authoritarian takes nothing in history to be sacred, whereas the nihilist takes nothing at all to be such. Consequently, the authoritarian persists in championing a historically discredited appeal (the appeal to an ahistoric warrant for our absolute commitments), while the nihilist despairs of satisfying an existentially imperative need (the need for a sense of what must not, under any circumstances, be desecrated or defiled in any way).[39]

Miller's midworld of symbols points to a middle way between the historically discredited appeals of authoritarians and the existentially demoralizing despair of nihilists. The persistent force of the Eleatic temper and the growing acknowledgment of human history as the sole locus of human existence bespeak a divided commitment of the deepest order and, thus, generate a constitutional conflict.[40] What revision in our Constitution will resolve this and the other conflicts so forcibly present in our lives? What conception of philosophy will equip us with the rhetorical, discursive, and conceptual resources to deal effectively with the constitutional conflicts thrust upon us by our historically fateful allegiances?

2

Revision of Philosophy

Philosophy is the story of enforced distinctions.
—John William Miller

Just as the movement beyond modernity requires a revision of history, so the turn toward history requires a revision of philosophy. The revision of philosophy John William Miller advocates demands a conceptualization of the midworld, a domain of both experience and the actualities to which experience attests that is not reducible to appearance or reality, mind or world, subjectivity or objectivity (see, e.g., *PC,* 106), or any other characteristic dualism of the modern epoch (cf. Cahoone 1988, 19–23). The midworld is the most primordial world conceivable, from which all other "worlds" are abstracted and in which the actuality of these "worlds" (insofar as they are actual) is rooted.[1] Miller's revision of philosophy is one with his affirmation of the midworld. It is impossible to discuss one without at least touching on the other. Thus, in this chapter, I present how Miller revises philosophy and in the following, how he conceptualizes the midworld, highlighting where appropriate the connections between Miller's reconceptualization of philosophy and his conceptualization of the midworld, which is itself a radical revision of dominant tendencies in Western ontology.

Miller self-consciously revised his understanding of philosophy in explicit reference to his most important predecessors. Indeed, the two greatest influences on Miller's conception of philosophy appear to have been Immanuel Kant and Georg W. F. Hegel.[2] The originality of this conception is beyond question and is best appreciated by attending to the specific ways Miller transformed Kantian and Hegelian approaches to philosophy. Then, and only then, is it possible to comprehend fully Miller's most basic characterizations of philosophical discourse. Then, and only then, are we in the position to appreciate fully the insights to be won from revising philosophy in the way Miller proposes.

At the center of his revision, we find Miller's stress on philosophy as a unique form of human discourse. He often says, "Philosophy is just talk" (*MS*, 58). That is, it is not talk about objects given independent of discourse but a form of talk in which the status and authority of "talk" itself, of utterance in all of its modes, are exhibited. For Miller, the only way to exhibit the status and authority of discourse is historically; in general, "what appears in philosophy is to be viewed historically" (*PC*, 152–53). This means that we need to grasp, as best we can, the genesis and transformations of the criteria and resources—what Miller often calls the "controls"—that we, in our ongoing struggle to maintain a critical sensibility and articulate presence, have secured and must conserve if we are to maintain our capacity to tell the difference between, say, right and wrong, truth and falsity, reality and appearance. For Miller, what prompts reflection on these criteria and resources is not wonder but conflict (JWM, 7:5).

Apart from a historical account of this struggle, we in our present are driven to embrace either some dogmatic position alleged to posses an ahistoric warrant or a radical skepticism in which we do not know how to tell the differences we so desperately feel need to be told. In their most basic senses, dogmatism means an appeal to the arbitrary and skepticism an arrest of activity. On Miller's interpretation, dogmatists cannot really conflict. "Would that they might! They merely negate each other. . . . Dogmas have no common ground except their exclusiveness; but no dogma can [even] recognize any other, since each system has no vocabulary for its alternatives any more than it has significance in itself" (FI, 262). It follows, then, that insofar as parties do have a common ground and a mutually acceptable vocabulary, they do not merit being called "dogmatists" in Miller's sense. Just as dogmatists are unable to engage in a genuinely rational conflict, so skeptics are unable to be guided by any heuristic circumspection. Miller makes this point quite forcibly:

We are not skeptics . . . because we make mistakes, but because we can no longer trust the means of deciding. Nobody is less skeptical than the canny person who knows wooden nickels when he sees them. Skepticism is no grubby caution. It is a point of arrest where we are thrown back on our own resources. And those we have no reason to trust. (*PC,* 108)

Both dogmatism and skepticism represent a failure in our efforts to maintain an adequate basis for effective criticism (FI, 265). Dogmatism makes our criticisms ultimately arbitrary, while skepticism makes them essentially impossible.

As Miller was fond of noting, idealism "occurred historically as the outcome of the attempt to mediate between skepticism and dogmatism" (*PC,* 64; FI, 260); and, as he was quick to point out, this attempt begins with Kant. But the way in which Miller himself undertook this mediation was influenced more by Hegel's *Phenomenology* than by any of Kant's writings; for the way beyond the Scylla of dogmatism and the Charybdis of skepticism is through a historical reconstruction of the dialectic drama of human history.[3]

In this reconstruction, not only do we witness the collapse of discourse in the loss of ability on the part of agents, with whom we cannot help identifying,[4] to tell the differences they so passionately desire to tell, but also we see agents regaining their composure. "Composure is not found or permitted" (*PH,* 164). It is won through coming into possession of the sense that one is able to compose oneself. But, as we have seen in Chapter 1, the capacity to compose oneself is inseparable from the capacity to compose one's world: "Presence and totality stand or fall together" (*MS,* 13). Hence, in seeing agents regaining their composure, we are seeing them reclaiming their ability to forge an identity and to project a world (JWM, 25:21).

So, even in relation to Miller's contention that philosophy is "just talk," it is helpful to bear in mind Kant and Hegel, in particular, Kant's characterization of philosophy as a *transcendental* investigation and Hegel's efforts to exhibit the *dialectic* of consciousness. For Miller arrived at his conception of philosophy as an irreducible form of human discourse through an immanent critique of the idealistic tradition. Accordingly, it should prove illuminating to introduce Miller's revision of philosophy through Kant's notion of transcendental inquiry and Hegel's narrative of the dialectical drama of Absolute Spirit coming to absolute knowledge of Itself.

Kant's Transcendental Idealism

Miller, like Kant, considers philosophy to be a transcendental form of inquiry: it is not about objects but about the conditions for the possibility of there being objects or, for that matter, there being subjects. But whereas Kant takes physics to be the authoritative discourse requiring a philosophical defense against the skeptical implications of Humean empiricism, for Miller, physics is not so much threatened as it is itself the source of a threat to any conception of the universe in which the unique individual can gain a secure foothold. Accordingly, his concern is to defend a hitherto slighted domain of human discourse against the skeptical implications of mathematical physics. Whereas Kant wanted to defend the authority of physics against Hume's critique of causality, Miller wants to defend the authority of history against the demoralizing implications of universal causation (i.e., of the most basic assumption of classical physics). That is, Kant was concerned with the threat to physics; Miller was concerned with the threat of physics.[5] "It is because we are rational that our worlds lack coherence" (*PC*, 190): incoherence could no more befall an irrational creature than death an inanimate being. There is, however, one form of rationality exhibited by theoretical physics and quite another by historical awareness, and how the two are compatible is not at all clear (ibid.).

Miller's untiring defense of historical reason does more than defang the destructive implications of scientistic discourse. It also checks the reductionistic implications of psychology and theology. Physics, psychology, and theology are, from Miller's perspective, "the big three": historically, they have been the three most influential discourses and, in addition, the three most hostile to the recognition of history as an irreducible and authoritative form of human discourse.

To aid history in gaining such recognition, however, something analogous to Kant's transcendental investigation is necessary. In the *Critique of Pure Reason*, Kant (1965, 59) explains that, in his usage, an inquiry is "transcendental" insofar as it is concerned with the mode of our knowledge of objects. Some investigations are devoted to discovering what is the case; others are concerned with illuminating what are the conditions for the possibility of discovering what, in some demarcated field of human inquiry, is the case. Only the latter sort of investigation deserves to be called "transcendental."

"Kant," Miller points out, "addressed himself to nature, not to history" (*PH*, 79). Nor until recently have his successors addressed history in the manner needed to establish the authority of history. But the scope and force of this authority are rarely given their due. "History has," Miller proposes, "no Kant to disclose the organization in terms of which all reports of action get told" (*PH*, 161). This is perhaps somewhat unfair; for Wilhelm Dilthey, Benedetto Croce, and R. G. Collingwood (to name but three) are all candidates for this position: what Kant tried to do for Newtonian physics (secure its status as an authoritative discourse), they tried to accomplish for historical knowledge. Even so, given Miller's differences with these three philosophers of history, it is understandable why he would contend history has had no Kant.

While Miller was interested "primarily not in science but in history" (*MS*, 16), his reflections on the conditions for the possibility of historical agency and on the form of consciousness required by such agency have direct and even profound implications for our understanding of science. That science itself has a history—indeed, that science is the sort of undertaking that must have a history—needs to be incorporated into our account of science.[6] History is, according to Miller, essentially the story of the revision of outlooks, an account of the changes wrought in the very forms of action. The historical record is, as he notes, "studded with proper names" (*JWM*, 25:1); but they are overwhelmingly the initiators of changes having broad and lasting reverberations. Those who have made history are precisely those who have wrought such changes. In the story of these revisions, "we see the awful, but responsible, spectacle of man's reinterpretations of himself and nature, and reassessment of our heritage" (*PC*, 104). Science has been, especially in the most recent centuries, a prominent part of this spectacle.

But, if this is so, a philosophy of history provides indispensable resources for a philosophy of science. For the former illuminates the conditions for the possibility of autonomous agency and the latter is an attempt to account for a distinctive form of autonomous action. "The great world of science results," as Miller astutely stresses, "from action, not from the disengaged spectator of a spectacle" (*MS*, 42). In this way, the philosophy of science presupposes the philosophy of history. In this way, too, the principal concerns of Kant's first two *Critiques*—the concern of the *Critique of Pure Reason* to show how scientific knowledge is possible and that of the *Critique of Practical Reason* to show what is required for moral and, in effect, autonomous or self-legislative action (cf. *PC*, 89)—are much closer together in Miller's account of agents and their acts and artifacts than in Kant's "system."

Hence, while Miller himself assumed the role of Kant with regard to our knowledge of the past, his assumption of this role led him to a radical revision of the Kantian account of our knowledge of nature. In other words, Miller's transcendental inquiry into the conditions underlying autonomous agency and historical consciousness forced him to transform Kant's transcendental inquiry into the conditions underlying our empirical knowledge of the natural world. At the heart of this transformation was Miller's insistence—one might say his dogged insistence—that science is inexplicable apart from action and, in turn, that the distinctively human forms of action are inexplicable apart from a unique type of artifact known as "functioning objects." In the simplest possible terms, there is no science apart from measuring (note the present active participle) and there is no measuring apart from the use of a yardstick or some other instrument. These instruments are not something we use to accomplish purposes framed independently of these instruments; rather, these instruments are themselves the sole conditions for framing the purposes that allow us to proclaim either a world or an identity of our own. Apart from some instrument, there is, for example, neither space nor time. Armed with such instruments, we define or project a spatiotemporal environment, in which movement, memory, and anticipation are not only possible but necessary. "It is action that establishes the environment in which purposes become possible. And this action occurs through the artifact" (*DP*, 156). This statement is but a variation on the theme, "The world is actual in so far as it is maintained by action" (*MS*, 174). An important and necessary addition included in this variation, however, is the insistence that action is artifactual, it always occurs by means of some artifact, if only the disciplined body.

"Science has exorcised doing. . . . [It] has been viewed as having nothing to do with any doing whatsoever. It has even been disturbed by considerations suggesting that the scientist himself is in the picture, that the observer [as Werner Heisenberg's principle suggests] qualifies or changes what is observed. That was precisely what earlier science hoped to avoid" (*DP*, 56). In this, we have been arrested by a threat generated by the career of science itself—the threat of subjectivism. On one hand, "science itself has rejoiced in showing forth a world beyond our tamperings. The word 'subjective' took on the force of disqualification" (ibid.). On the other, the world revealed by science is due to our probings and, in a sense, our tamperings.

This realization does not compromise the "objectivity" of science. It does, however, force us to redefine what "objectivity" actually means in this context and what it alone could possibly mean in any context. That which admits of interpretation cannot be disqualified as merely "subjective" (as ultimately expressing nothing more than the biases of the interpreter), just as that which is established by experimentation cannot be seen as "objective" (as perfectly reflecting what is there apart from our probings and perspectives). One irony here is that the authority or "persuasion of realities disjoined from man and his deeds has grown apace with the enlargement of his own articulate powers" (*PC*, 118). What needs to be seen is that the authority of realities apparently disjoined from agents and their acts is derived from nothing other than the authority, established in the face of much opposition, of self-critical and self-controlled agency itself. What also needs to be seen here is that the impersonal discourse characteristic of scientific inquirers is a personal achievement of purposive agents—the impersonal is one of the most important and powerful forms assumed by the personal (cf. *DP*, 117).

The result of science having exorcised both purposive doing and personal presence in the name of universal mechanism is that one must go beyond science to secure the authority of science. For, "science is a story told by man himself" (*MS*, 122), though it itself offers a picture of the universe from which the storyteller has been exiled (see, e.g., *MS*, 36). For instance, an account of either the utterances put forth by Galileo or Copernicus or Kepler or those put forth by Wilhelm Wundt or Sigmund Freud or B. F. Skinner cannot be given in the terms accredited by those utterances. The irony here (and history is, to be sure, full of ironies) is that this account must be given in the terms discredited by their utterances. "The broad demands of a philosophy of history require the authentication of discourse and a construction placed upon *functioning objects*" (*PC,* 118). In particular, the philosophy of history must accredit or authenticate precisely those forms of utterance that, say, physics or psychology has discredited in order to render intelligible the utterances of either physicists or psychologists.

Although Miller confesses it is hard for him to "keep the story-telling mood" (*PH,* 10), he is an inveterate storyteller. One of the stories he is deeply concerned to tell, indeed one to which he regularly returns is the story of how storytelling, or narration, as a mode of comprehension and explanation has fallen into disrepute. According to him, we encounter in Freud, Skinner, and other apparent opponents of narrative discourse, stories or discourses the effect of which is to discredit and even preclude the possibility of both the act of storytelling and the actuality of the storyteller. These stories involve a collapse of discourse in which the collapse is hardly, if ever, noted. In his own consciously recognized stories, Miller shows the respects in which these collapses were fated to occur and the ways that are now open to discourse. More concretely, he describes the paths that are open to agents-in-history who perforce need to maintain their capacity to tell the differences essential for the exercise of their agency (e.g., appearance and reality, falsity and truth, other and self).

In this connection, Miller stresses the need to acknowledge the legislative status of functioning objects. Apart from what Miller calls the "local control" achieved by means of these objects, my experience is amorphous and anarchical; thus, my consciousness is too fragmented and overwhelmed to contribute toward a distinctive personal presence and the arena of my "actions" is too undefined and haphazard to constitute a world. When I am, by contrast, in command of my immediate circumstances, I am so because consciousness has undergone a discipline and because the environment has been defined in terms of the controls of action—the means by which action is able to be controlled, and thus, the means by which exertions are transformed into actions in the proper sense of that term. By virtue of these objects, then, "one is in control of a functioning and embodied identity" (*MS,* 11); in addition, one is implicated in a fateful and hazardous environment. In other words, these objects define the conditions for the possibility of both presence and totality. In so doing, they are legislative: they define the conditions in which mistakes are possible, indeed inevitable, and provide the means for deciding what is requisite, what is illicit, and what is permissible.

Unorder is distinct from disorder: the former designates a lack or absence of order, the latter a breach or violation of order (*MS*, 125). Hence, disorder presupposes order: there cannot possibly be a breach of order unless there is order. For Miller, however, order is impossible apart from action and, in turn, action is impossible apart from artifacts (at least, the body as artifact). Thus, when he speaks of functioning objects as "*finite* actualities," he is stressing the fact that such objects define limits or set boundaries: While the eye does not create the horizon, for example, it does, by its own act of seeing, define the horizon; and, without the definition of limits, there is no possibility of action. "'Doing what comes naturally' [exerting oneself without setting limits of any sort] is no doing" (*DP*, 102). Only doing what comes artificially, what occurs through the mastery and control of artifacts, deserves the name of action. Think here of dance.

This discussion of functioning objects, unavoidably, has taken us rather far into the main concern of the next chapter, "The Midworld." Now we must turn to the contrast with Hegelian idealism. But first let us recall Miller's main debt to and principal difference from Kant's approach to philosophy. In one place, Miller asserts: "Reflection tells what one starts with. Experiment tells what one ends with" (*DP*, 189). Both he and Kant conceive of philosophy as a form of reflection that enables us to take stock of the conceptual resources making possible in the first place our cognitive undertakings, such as our empirical investigation of the natural world. In Kant's transcendental inquiry, however, the conditions underlying the possibility of a scientific knowledge of the phenomenal world are the immutable forms of sensibility (space and time) and the equally immutable categories of the understanding (such as substance and accident, cause and effect).

In contrast, Miller's transcendental inquiry points to the alterable forms of human action, not the inalterable forms of human understanding. In other words, it points to history, understood here as "the revision of outlooks at the point of conflict between them" (*PC*, 123). But such revisions take place neither in an isolated, disembodied consciousness nor in a mindless, purposeless world—neither in an other-worldly spectator nor in a mind-exorcised spectacle. They take place in the midworld, the comprehensive yet constitutionally incomplete and confusion-prone world of our own doing and making. The midworld is a world of artifacts. It is, above all else, the world of those unique artifacts Miller calls functioning objects. It is also the revelations made possible through the local control, the direct command of immediate circumstances, endowed by the disciplined use of functioning objects. Precisely because he conceives the midworld as "the vehicle of all order and of the revision of order" (*MS*, 110), and because he defines history as the revision of order, Miller contends, "History rides on the midworld" (*MS*, 18).

Hegel's Absolute Idealism

The career of history, however, is no smooth and uneventful ride. It is a difficult and hazardous journey. As Hegel (1988) notes in the introduction to his lectures on the philosophy of history, "Spirit [*Geist*] is only what it makes of itself, and it makes itself into what it already is implicitly" (58). In other words, Spirit is the result of its own activity, an activity of transcending what is immediately present and utterly foreign (82). There is, for Hegel, a crucial difference between the self-realization of Spirit and the growth of organisms. Indeed,

> in the realm of Spirit, things are entirely different [from things in nature]. The transition that is involved in the actualization of Spirit is mediated by consciousness and will. To begin with, human consciousness and will are immersed in their unmediated natural life; their aim and object, at first, is the natural determination as such [i.e., they reflect the immersion of Spirit in nature]. But this natural determination comes to be infinitely demanding, strong and rich, because it is animated by Spirit. Thus Spirit, within its own self, stands in opposition to itself. It must overcome itself as its own truly hostile hindrance. The process of development, so quiescent in the world of nature, is for Spirit a hard and endless struggle against itself. (58–59)

Hegel's phenomenology of Spirit and philosophy of history are attempts to depict the series of struggles in which Spirit wars with itself. In the course of this series, Spirit comes into fuller possession—indeed, full possession and complete knowledge—of itself.

At a more mundane level, Miller notes that we, human beings in historical circumstances, come to a consciousness of ourselves as distinct and unique beings only through our conflicts.[7] He maintains, "In the confusion of conflict one is no non-entity. Rather one cherishes the difficulty, as if one's self-consciousness required it and was found only there" (*MS*, 187). And, indeed, our difficulties and conflicts are, more than any other factor, responsible for our actual self-consciousness: in them, we win an awareness of ourselves. Hence, conflict "does not operate to scatter the self but to establish it, even to organize it" (ibid.).

When we come to a consciousness of ourselves, it is as beings always already on the way—beings whose being here-and-now both depends on and covers over a there-and-then. We find ourselves lost. But we can at least tell that the way we are treading is not the way we were intending. As Hegel puts it in the Preface to his *Phenomenology of Spirit* (1977, 39), "We learn by experience that we meant something other than we meant to mean; and this correction of our meaning compels our knowing to go back to the proposition, and understand it in some other way." This compulsion is just that—a compulsion, for we are driven to a consciousness of history by the confusions in the present to go back, again and again, to the antecedents of the forms of acting. It eventually brings to light connections and patterns among these antecedents themselves, on one hand, and between them and our forms of functioning, on the other. These connections and patterns are, above all else, the forms of struggle and the interrelations among these forms.

We come to see in history an ongoing, fateful *agon* or contest in which defeat can be ultimate—the loss of one's world no less than one's self— though victory can never be more than provisional. History so conceived "is a region of ultimate risk. It is this property of history which gives it both fascination and terror" (*PC*, 186). Radical defeat, being crushed to the very root of our being, presupposes a thoroughgoing commitment to some comprehensive purpose demanding actual embodiment. "But a radical frustration presumes," in Miller's judgment, "a radical aim" (*PC*, 82). In turn, a radical aim involves the most comprehensive responsibility imaginable, this responsibility being identifiable with freedom in its most authentic sense. As Quentin Lauer (1987, 115) notes in connection with Hegel, genuine freedom is extremely difficult to take, for it involves nothing less than "self-reliance and responsibility—for a world!" Or, as Miller puts it, the "environment must be capable of being lost, not just inexpertly met" (*DP,* 125). It is not a question of expertise or technique but one of integrity and composure.

That the environment can be lost and that philosophy is concerned with threats to our ability to compose simultaneously ourselves and our world suggest an important connection between philosophy and madness: philosophy is the struggle to hold oneself and one's world together, while madness is the loss of just this ability (*DP,* 120). In a world gone mad, we seek to maintain or regain our composure. And our world is always a world not too far from madness (*DP,* 138). Philosophy is, from Miller's perspective, the struggle to hold ourselves and our world together at those moments when both self and world are threatened by collapse, a threat posed not by factors external to the self but by the very forces the self uses to define itself (*DP,* 10; cf. 112).

But it is just this sort of struggle we see displayed in the exertions of our predecessors and, willy-nilly, prolonged in our own undertakings. For we are always doing, to some degree, the bidding of our ancestors. Aye, there's the rub: "We are in league with meanings in ourselves that our own experience has not produced. We do not, therefore, know what our words mean unless we search out those experiences of others by which they have come to mean what they now mean to us" (*PH,* 187). Even more pointedly, "Our heritage is a mess and full of confusion. We inherit a confusion of symbols and a confusion of tongues" (ibid.). "We are the heirs not only of past wealth, but also of past debits" (*PH,* 188).

A critical appropriation of this complex inheritance is, accordingly, unavoidable. It is, to repeat, thrust upon us by the confusions inherent in our heritage. These confusions do not bolt from out of the blue but derive from words, monuments, rituals, and institutions (JWM, 23:27). For this reason, Miller insists that philosophers do not invent their problems: the problems of philosophers are the problems of persons in history, as these problems are ineluctably resident in common habits, institutions, and speech on which philosophers depend, as do countless others (ibid.). Our confusions can only be disentangled, to the extent they can, by telling how they came to be and, indeed, continue to exert an influence on the present. A story of the conflicts generative of our confusions is the sole means we have for regaining our composure, our capacity for composing our selves and our world. If we are to take possession of the present, then we must make (as we note in Chapter 1) "the pilgrimage that has so far advanced to this station" (*PH,* 84). But such a pilgrimage is, Miller contends, precisely what we find in Hegel's *Phenomenology.*

> It was Hegel who undertook a systematic study of conflicts. They are the phenomenology of the spirit, the modes of thought's reality and self-consciousness. The solution of any conflict, or rather its resolution, lies in realizing the necessity of the conflict. Each factor is highlighted by its antagonist, disclosing the imperative role only to the degree that it meets frustration. Consequently, each factor has a stake in its antagonist. (*PC,* 71)

The conflicts identified in Hegel's phenomenology are the stations of Spirit's career, "the secular stations of the cross. It is this story which is both history and philosophy" (*PC,* 73). These words make clear that Miller is in deep sympathy with Hegel's conception of philosophy as a narration of a dialectical drama.

He does not, however, take Absolute Spirit to be the central character in this drama; instead, he takes the dramatis personae to be composed exclusively of finite, fallible agents in their concrete historical circumstances. Miller maintains that Hegel "discounted the actual. The owl of Minerva was a spectator, not an actor. That bird did not fly through the air nor seek its prey" (*MS,* 151; cf. OM). The flight of Absolute Spirit toward absolute knowledge, a knowledge in which philosophy ceases to be a love of wisdom and becomes the possession of it, is transformed by Miller into the struggle of human agents for historical consciousness. Of course, Hegel himself conceived the flight of Spirit as such a struggle; but he apparently thought that human consciousness could, through a philosophical comprehension of its essential implication in the life of Spirit, come to a complete and final knowledge of itself. For Miller, we must shift attention from Absolute Spirit to finite actualities; and, as part of this transition, we must trade our devotion to the ideal of attaining total, infallible knowledge for an acceptance of the demands of limited, improvised deeds (cf. *PC*, 132; Tyman 1993, 102–3).

From Miller's viewpoint, the history of philosophy is certainly not one long record of silly mistakes to be corrected in the light of our newest acquisitions in logical technique or rhetorical skill. It is a series of documents giving eloquent expression to the often noble, and equally often desperate, struggles of thinkers to hold themselves and their worlds together. Surely such a view neither belittles nor patronizes Plato's response to the crisis confronting his polis, for example, or Augustine's to the crisis faced by his church. Indeed, how else are we to read with any hope of comprehension Plato's *Republic* or Augustine's *The City of God*? In Hegel's *Phenomenology*, we encounter not only yet another thinker struggling to hold self and world together but also a thinker who tries to accomplish this task in reference to previous such struggles. In other words, here we have a document in which the task of the philosopher reaches a higher level of self-consciousness than previously realized; and Hegel reaches this level of self-consciousness precisely because he attains a fuller measure of historical consciousness than his predecessors. He comprehends them and, thus, himself in a way they did not comprehend their predecessors and, thus, themselves.

But, like Marx and so many other "disciples" of Hegel, Miller tries to beat the master at his own game.[8] That is, Miller endeavors to arrive at even higher self-consciousness, through fuller historical awareness. But this endeavor requires following the dialectic of consciousness in a direction seemingly ruled out by Hegel's own account of this process. For Hegel, the dialectic of consciousness terminates in the absolute knowledge of Absolute Spirit; for Miller it drives us toward a total commitment to and involvement in the actual world, a world constitutionally unfinished and precarious.

For Hegel, Infinite Spirit alone is absolute; for Miller, finite actualities in the systematic interconnectedness that includes their disarray are the only beings having the status of absolutes. There is no equivocation here on the term "absolute," for, in Miller's lexicon no less than in Hegel's, it means the self-conditioned or self-authorized. Human history is not the career of

Absolute Spirit but that of finite actualities, human agents and their actual worlds. These agents and their worlds, as finite actualities, are self-limiting: their finitude consists, at least in part, in their being constitutionally bounded or defined and, thus, exclusive of but allied to an other or an antagonist.

While finite actualities—more concretely, human agents and the artifacts and revelations thereupon constitutive of their world—embody limits, they bespeak infinity or, at least, some order of infinity: a numerical order, for example. When one gets down to counting one's fingers, one gets beyond the immediate and, in a sense, even beyond the finite. Herein we see the dialectical relationship between finitude and infinity. The actual acquires authority only on the condition that "infinity, i.e., order, becomes the form of finitude, and finitude the actuality of the infinite" (*PC*, 137). After noting this, Miller sardonically adds, "But this is difficult" (ibid.).

The career of any actuality as absolute, that is, as self-defining and thus self-revising and self-transcending, involves that absolute in the struggle to maintain itself in its tenacious commitment to some formal order, forever incomplete and problematic (*MS*, 146). The differences between Miller's account of the dialectic of finite actualities and Hegel's narration of the dialectic of Infinite Spirit are at least as fundamental as are the similarities. (Miller does claim that Hegel "more than anyone else, avoided disparagement of the incomplete as the frustration and failure of reason" [JWM, 23:21]) Even so, Miller's debt to Hegel's conception of philosophy is deep, perhaps even enormous. If John Dewey could say that "acquaintance with Hegel left a permanent deposit in my thinking" ([1930] 1984, 154), Miller might say that his encounter with Hegel provided him with a vital resource for his philosophy. As the word "resource" implies, Miller went back to Hegel—in particular, the Hegel of the *Phenomenology*—again and again, to find the means to give adequate expression to the *agon* of human history.

Just as Miller's growing preoccupation with history led him to transform his interpretation of how a transcendental reflection on the conditions for the possibility of knowledge is to be undertaken, so, too, this same preoccupation led him to revise his interpretation of how the dialectic of consciousness and the very conception of the absolute are to be understood. The former marks a fundamental departure from Kant, the latter an equally fundamental departure from Hegel.

Miller's Historical Idealism

One further significant difference between Miller and Hegel concerns how we are to understand the dialectic. A consideration of this difference can sharpen our sense of Miller's divergence from Hegel's outlook as well as introduce Miller's innovative transformation of the idealistic tradition. "Historical idealism," his name—on occasion—for his transformation of this tradition, concerns not so much the process in which dualisms are overcome or opposites reconciled as how to maintain the conditions for telling differences or drawing distinctions. Miller notes: "Hegel, of course, had triads, but I think that the difficulty occurs as a pair. And while such a pair needs a third for its resolution, I prefer to see the third as the state of affairs that enforces the distinction" (*MS*, 186). The best example is the distinction between appearance and reality, a distinction with a long history in philosophical discourse and, in addition, a secure place in common sense: "You can't tell a book by its cover."

Miller provides another example:

> A divorce of knowledge and the individual has long been an ideal and also a defeat. A Proper Name and anonymous truth have seemed incompatible. [But] the very distinction has lacked a basis. Each factor has seemed to exclude the other. A common ground permitting and enforcing the distinction has rarely been proposed but on the premises of the distinction [i.e., the pair of opposites itself] is both essential and impossible; essential if the distinction is to be maintained, and impossible in terms of either fact [taken separately or even side by side]. (JWM, 25:2)

In Miller's hands, the dialectic is designed not to overcome the distinction between impersonal knowledge and personal agency but to secure this distinction, to show on what basis we are entitled to draw and also to maintain the distinctions. To exhibit this basis resolves the difficulty in principle, though not in detail; that is, such an exhibition tells us how in general to draw the distinction, but it is one we are called upon to establish, again and again, in any number of circumstances.

As articulated by Miller, historical idealism explicitly recognizes the need for a systematic investigation of the conditions of our own discourse. Here "discourse" means, above all else, the capacity to tell the differences needing to be told if we are to count ourselves as adequately articulate. For him, again, such idealism also involves a challenge to assume absolute responsibility for the conditions of our discourse. Hence, it issues at once a theoretical and a personal challenge. His abiding concern is to press the questions, *Where does one stand when one draws a particular distinction? Indeed, where could one possibly stand in order to be in a position to articulate this difference?* Two different formulations of his own answer to these questions are the midworld and the actual.

One must have made mistakes in order to be in a position to tell the difference between truth and error. It is helpful to stress that we make mistakes through our reliance on some medium or artifact. "It has been notoriously difficult to tell how error is possible in terms of mind or else of body" (*MS*, 189), especially when mind has been conceived as a disembodied consciousness and the body as a mindless mechanism! But there is "no difficulty in locating error apropos of the artifactual, in the yardstick in use, or in words. If one cannot find error in the pure object, neither can one find it in the pure subject. You have to make a mistake. It needs a vehicle" (ibid.). The totality of vehicles by which we can make mistakes is one way of defining the midworld.

"Idealism occurred historically as the outcome of the attempt to mediate between skepticism and dogmatism" (*PC*, 64; cf. FI). But, in order to move beyond the impasse of skepticism and dogmatism, it is now evident that neither Kant's transcendental idealism nor Hegel's absolute idealism is adequate: neither a Kantian deduction of the a priori forms of sensibility and categories of understanding (a deduction allegedly securing unshakable foundations for our cognitive constructions) nor a Hegelian phenomenology of Spirit allegedly culminating in absolute knowledge truly offers a way beyond this impasse. Only an uncompromising acknowledgment of the actual, a systematic recognition of the midworld, will effectively "mediate between skepticism and dogmatism."

"Idealism lacked an embodied order; realism lacked an apparent presence" (*MS*, 43). The traditional forms of realism have made the distinction between knower and known, mind and reality, into an unbridgeable gulf. In their interest in securing an "objective" basis for our knowledge, realists have made knowing a self-defeating process: like Tantalus, we as knowers reach for objects that forever elude our grasp. Here the influence of Josiah Royce's characterization of "realism" is clear. For, in such "realism," reality is that which, by definition, is other than consciousness and, thus, incapable of being present to our minds. Yet the traditional forms of idealism have attempted to explain human knowledge without paying adequate attention to either the human organism or human artifacts. Descartes, the father of this tradition, did not think it was necessary to begin with embodied action: he took his hands and feet to be incidental to his status as a thinker (cf. *MS*, 85). Idealism, like skepticism "had no yardsticks" (*MS*, 161). Here we might also take Kant as representative of this movement or type of philosophy: He "had space, but no yardstick; time, but no clock; logic, but no language" (ibid.; cf. *DP*, 156). "Where, in the history of philosophy, does one find a claim for the embodied thought?" (*MS*, 151). Where, in this same history, do we find finite actuality being granted categoreal status? But, apart from embodied thought, is it possible to tell the differences we need to tell in order to be articulate?

For reasons stated or implied above, then, Miller appears to have eventually become not entirely comfortable with the label of idealist, however qualified (Fell 1990a, 26). As a designation of his own position, he seems to have moved toward the position that even "historical idealism" gives too much authority to a philosophical tradition offering only halting recognition of our absolute or self-conditioned historicity. In 1943, he could say, "The idealism of the future will be a philosophy of history, of action, of self-generating, lawful finitude" (*PC*, 74). As he became more deeply involved in the philosophy of history, precisely as a reflection upon the conditions of finite actuality—of self-limiting and thus self-accountable action—the results of his reflections seemed to reveal an ever-growing gulf between his own mature position and his youthful espousal of a more orthodox form of Hegelian idealism.[9]

The position to which Miller devoted his life articulating and defending does not seem to have a label with which he was completely satisfied. More fundamentally, the very form of his reflections—the manner of philosophy itself—was a topic about which he had questions and even doubts.

What Manner of Philosopher Is This?

Miller contends: "You damn a man when you classify him as a mere sort of thing. No sort of thing is unique" (*DP,* 144). We all wish to be unique and thus we associate with those with whom our uniqueness is recognized and even cherished (JWM, 3:4). This includes philosophers, especially Miller. But we face a dilemma. On one hand, if we approach Miller as a type of idealist, we thereby might render his writings intelligible, but we also obscure or even effectively deny his uniqueness as a philosopher. On the other hand, if we take him simply and solely on his own terms, we thereby make a gesture toward the acknowledgment of his uniqueness. But this gesture must necessarily be inarticulate; for it cannot say wherein Miller's uniqueness resides. The reason, of course, is that all such assertions depend on the use of terms with general significance.

The dilemma is, however, only apparent. We need not purchase the recognition of uniqueness at the cost of intelligibility. But the dilemma is not so easily resolvable as this remark suggests. What is needed is a conception of discourse or utterance in which the utterer can responsibly appear— can be authoritatively present without undermining in any way, let alone destroying, either the objective validity of the utterance or the authoritative presence of the auditor. This is as difficult as it is important. Its importance, in fact, cannot be exaggerated. For the conception of utterance meeting this threefold requirement is at the heart of Miller's approach to philosophy (the authoritative presence of the speaker becomes tyrannical when it negates either the authoritative presence of the addressee or the objective status of what is disclosed in our intersubjective exchanges). This conception of utterance is also at the base of his metaphysics: his vision of presence and totality and, even more fundamentally, his confidence in his capacity to articulate a vision able to do justice to both the world and the individual. In the following passage he tries to identify this conception of discourse.

> I cannot get a hold on a person *except* as I take him at his word. But does he speak? Has he spoken? Can he appear in utterance? If his voice is not his own, why should he—or [even] could he—listen to mine? If his voice is not legislative, why would mine be? A man must hear his

own voice before he can credit another's. If he speaks, in what way, then, is he, the individual, present in his word? What sort of word would that be? (*MS*, 110)

These are, no doubt, dark words, oracular utterances. But exactly what manner of philosopher Miller is, can only be appreciated by comprehending what manner of utterances these are.

In a letter written in 1975, late in his life, Miller remarks: "G. P. B. [George P. Brockway] wants me to 'write.' I have said that I could not say my say in any of the four modes of prose discourse—narration, description, exposition, argumentation. How was I to speak?" Miller puts "write" in quotation marks because there was, in Brockway's plea, a very specific sense of this activity intended: Miller was being encouraged to write for publication. Independent of publication, he wrote a great deal, to clarify his own thoughts and also to try coming to terms with conflicts he and some friend shared. These conflicts were not between the persons involved (see Strout 1990b). Quite the contrary. They were the basis for community, not a source of division.

Regarding shared conflicts in this sense, it is helpful to recall here that, for Miller, "[i]nsofar as I have another man's problems of form, I am not analogous [to that man] but actually identical. It is this identity of actuality that is also our only community" (*PH*, 129). The arresting character and high quality of what Miller wrote in his private correspondence—in his attempts at clarification and in his personal response to the constitutional conflicts he shared with some other actual person—were, of course, what prompted his student Brockway to encourage him to "write," to issue more public utterances, and to address a wider audience. Miller's own reluctance to do so, however, was deeply rooted in an uncertainty about the very nature of the discourse in which he was engaged for most of his intellectual life. This uncertainty bears directly on his conception of philosophy; for it concerns essentially the nature of philosophy as a unique form of human discourse.

Here it is instructive to juxtapose some further remarks from the letter just quoted as well as from the opening chapter, "The Scope of Philosophy," of Miller's published dissertation, *The Definition of the Thing*. What such a juxtaposition should help establish is that the roots of Miller's late uncertainty about the mode of discourse most appropriate to philosophy can be traced to his early and abiding certainty about the scope of philosophy, especially about what this scope does not encompass.

Throughout its history, philosophical reflection has been assimilated to either scientific theorizing or artistic creation. The philosopher has been portrayed as a kind of scientist or as a kind of artist. Miller took both portraits to involve caricature or, at least, distortion. The various attempts to assimilate philosophical thought to either of these other two undertakings conceal what is most distinctive and important about the philosophical enterprise. In 1975, however, Miller notes in the letter quoted above: "For me it has been a question of manner. What is the manner of utterance which could secure attention merely because of the utterance? Is such attention a seduction? Was Homer a seducer? Plato thought so. What, then[,] is the manner of utterance which commands without seduction of some sort?" In response to his own questions, he goes on to sketch the beginning of an answer, one deserving to be presented here in its entirety:

> Well, perhaps the true Faith is to launch a Word merely believing that someone, perhaps unknown, will find it authoritative but not seductive, and therefore not to be viewed guardedly.
>
> I have said that my calls [i.e., correspondence and conversations] were "person-to-person," not addressed to the Universe but to the universal in the Individual. So far so good. Socrates talked to Meno or to Protagoras. That was a manner.
>
> But, besides, I listened. I was audience to Aristotle or to Kant. I heard voices. Their voices were also mine. Why else listen? As I say, madmen hear voices. Again, so far so good. Who would listen to me who had not listened to Aristotle or to Lincoln? One could not expect it. I even listen to those who do not listen, won't listen, to Homer or St. Paul.
>
> But I have come to feel that person-to-person calls, characteristic of the teacher at a place, time, occasion, are not enough. Nor is listening, essential as it is for any present authority. A third [possibility] now looms as the final faith—to launch the Word into the World which the Word articulates and manifests. That is the ultimate risk. But as for the

manner of it I have not been clear and there is no use in trying to argue anyone into the Word which commands but does not seduce.

This "final faith" is, in essence, Miller's response to Brockway's plea to assume the responsibility of authorship. Private conversation and correspondence are not enough. Public discourse is required. He came to feel the need to launch the Word into the World, in the hope that someone, perhaps unknown, will encounter the Word as an authoritative presence rather than a seductive lure. That is, he felt the need to address others in a manner revelatory of his own personal presence and respectful of their irreducible otherness—and also in a manner befitting the medium of discourse. The author as *I* addresses the reader as *you* by means of utterances not intended to seduce the reader to admire the author or to espouse some cause to which the author is devoted but intended to empower the reader to come into deeper possession of the inheritance of his own discourse.

All speakers are, in a sense, oracles; all utterances are accordingly oracular. This ineliminable dimension of human discourse poses a threat to the speaker and the hearer, the author and the audience. All persons are "mad": they hear voices and, in addition, give voice to forces of which they have little or no consciousness and, thus, over which they have little or no control.

What is at stake here is the avoidance of nullification. There are manners of speaking and writing in which utterers nullify themselves as utterers. There are manners of utterance in which the listener or reader is nullified; and there are manners in which the medium of discourse itself is negated. "By action we undertake to make a world of our own. We become egoists and encounter the egos of others" (*PH*, 148). It is only in the encounter of utterer as *I* and auditor as *I*—as egoists, as agents unafraid to demand recognition and even to assume authority—that nullification can be avoided. But this is not enough; both parties must acknowledge the resources of some shared medium as the form of their own actuality.

Here is it helpful to recall that, for Miller, "[e]goism is the assertion of the moment in the actuality of time" (*PH*, 69) and also that all history displays the equation between selfhood and actuality. I am, to paraphrase Ortega, I and the environment I maintain by my actions. I, in the very act of speaking or listening, identify myself with the words I speak or hear and, in addition, with the medium in which the words are uttered: I accept the present moment as a decisive locus of my actual identity and (what amounts to the same thing) the equation between myself and these circumstances. I do not evade the responsibility to speak carefully, specifically, with care, for self, other, and medium.

Thus, in Miller's philosophical lexicon, "egoism" does not mean any narrow self-absorption or irresponsible self-concern; it means essentially the courage to step forth as an "I," to declare one's personal presence without apology and, indeed, with authority. Even the recognition of oneself as a locus of error requires that one can command the resources to tell the difference between error and truth; it requires, in other words, one to be a center of authority. One should be willing to acknowledge fully and explicitly the authority one perforce wields. Such acknowledgment of one's authority is what Miller calls "egoism." One can argue with the aptness of this term; it would be difficult, however, to deny the point it is being used to make.

One of the best examples of evading such responsibility can be seen in the way both teachers and students often engage one another, half-heartedly and absent-mindedly. There are, to be sure, countless other examples. But all of them point to an evasion of the actual, a shiftiness and even absence in the face of some personal encounter. When we suspect such shiftiness or absence on the part of those with whom we are "engaged," we are often inclined to ask, "Are you there?" The "there" (in truth, the here) to which we are calling a person is, in the most basic sense, what Miller means by "presence"—passionate absorption in the actual moment. But the moment is, to repeat, a momentum; moreover, the here-and-now is a locus in history, but we as inhabitants of this locus need to be brought to a consciousness of its general historical status and its particular shape. "One should not assume that one *does* live in a present. This is to be learned" (JWM, 17:12). Where we actually do stand in history is neither immediately evident nor effortlessly learned. But, apart from such consciousness, presence is impossible; indeed, such consciousness is, at least, partly definitive of presence in Miller's sense. Thus, it is easy to see how his concern for presence and his preoccupation with history are of a piece.

Miller makes several references to Alcibiades to conjure up the image of a "vagrant," one whose shiftiness precludes his presence. Miller suggests: "The problem of the *Symposium* was, 'Are you there[,] Alcibiades?' The brilliant vagrant wept" (JWM, 25:1). He wept presumably because he appreciated the force of the question. In another manuscript, Miller sheds light on how Alcibiades's "vagrancy" contrasts with Socrates's "presence."

> And yet on the record—if one may invoke any record—it was alliance with the universal which was intended to give presence to the individual, to Socrates the regulated talker, but not to Alcibiades the vanishing vagrant, identified neither in actual loyalties to Athens or Sparta nor in the self-criticism of some universal alliance. The conflict between Individual and Universal was early and it was inherent [in the actual engagements of historical actors]. No person dares declare a World as the continuum of his own presence, while the personally neutral universal . . . has exorcised the Local Control in which the Individual ventures to manifest his presence. (JWM, 25:25)

To be sure, this text requires elucidation; by itself, it is unlikely to lead us very far in the direction of clarifying Miller's notion of presence. But, for such clarification, the notions identified here need only to be unpacked. One is vagrant insofar as one refuses to become allied with the universal, whereas one attains presence only through such an alliance. In this context, "universal" does not mean an abstract, disembodied form by which we know a multiplicity of particulars; rather it is an embodied form by which we regulate our conduct and define our world.

Time is an example of a universal. But time is something we tell by means of clocks or some other form of measurement. What Miller stresses, above all else, is the act of telling. But the act by which we are empowered to tell the differences between, say, now and later or past, present, and future is not a self-contained particular; it is an other-defining actuality. Of course, the self in undertaking an other-defining activity is, thereby, engaging in a self-defining project: the self attains consciousness of itself only as an other to some others with whom it is, nonetheless, allied. In any case, the act of telling time is not a brute exertion of energy, but a general form of acting (*DP*, 25).

On one side, there is the refusal to be allied with some universal, with some general, embodied form of acting. There is, in short, vagrancy. In this context, the polis is a universal for it is the embodiment of a form of acting. This is why reference to Alcibiades's "shiftiness" (above all, his switching allegiance from Athens to Sparta in the midst of a war) is relevant here. It is perhaps true that Miller's notion of the vagrant includes the traitorous. Here we need to keep in mind simply that the vagrant is the "individual" who refuses to form an "entangling alliance" with any embodied universal.[10]

On the other side, there is the alliance with universals. But, historically, this alliance has been problematic, for it has taken away with one hand what it has given with the other. For the universals to which ancients, medievals, and moderns have pledged allegiance have undermined the very thing they were supposed to authorize—the unique presence of the individual agent. Hence, universals have posed a threat to the very individuals who have identified and maintained themselves through their alliance to some universal. Almost always, the result of such alliance has been the nullification of the individual as such.

This nullification is even truer of the universe as depicted by modern science than of either creation as depicted by medieval theologians or the cosmos as conceived by ancient Greek philosophers. On the basis of its universals, natural science, the most authoritative discourse for at least the later phases of the modern period, projects what Miller calls "a silent world." This world is still a cosmos, but the order by which it is defined nullifies the presence of scientists and other agents. That is, this world is "silent" because it is one in which utterance as an autonomous or self-legislative activity is, in principle, ruled out. Heteronomy rules the events of nature and these events make up the whole of reality. But who is present to establish any rules? And if no one is present, how can anything be ruled out? In exiling the divine author of creation from what was formerly thought to be his own domain, we have replaced the flimsy and fantastic myths of our unenlightened ancestors with secure and solid knowledge. So the story goes. But who is present, who could possibly be present, to tell such a story? Surely, the utterances of scientists are not themselves natural events governed by external laws? That is, relying only on the terms authorized by the discursive practices of experimental scientists, is not the only valid or meaningful account of the natural world the account of it as an essentially impersonal order? Is not an impersonal world one in which, by definition, personal presence is precluded?

These are the sorts of question Miller persistently posed in his letters and conversations. In one form or other, another question he frequently asked was, Where, in the history of thought, is the universe in which individuals in all their irreducible uniqueness and authoritative presence are allowed to put in an appearance? That he could not find in the views of his predecessors a conception of the universe not obliterative of presence did not cause him to scorn their efforts. Quite the contrary. In his Afterword to Ortega's *History as a System* (1962), Miller makes it clear that not scorn but piety is what our ancestors deserve.

> If thought has taken flight into very remote regions it has done so in order to illuminate the closer immediacies which, unenvironed, present neither a world nor any coherent finitude [neither totality nor presence]. Then we have conjured up visions more vast than dreams and much more persistent. For now as in the past we call that our world which gives status and authority to the immediate. The record of these endeavors is history. There the modes of self-definition become explicit and serve as the vehicles for an understanding of what we have become. (AW, 240–41)

The various manners in which human agents have defined themselves and their worlds also are vehicles for deepening our grasp of what we must do here and now. For we do "have a rendezvous with our time and place, and that is as much of destiny as is generally possible" (AW, 267). Anyone whose life has form and force, a distinctive shape, and an undeniable effectiveness owes these features to having "joined articulate forces" (ibid.). Such an individual has not stood aloof but rather has become immersed in the "destructive element."

An articulate presence, actually being present in one's utterances, is unattainable apart from piety toward the sources of one's own articulate presence. To speak with authority requires speaking with piety. In this context, "piety" means reverence for the sources of one's being and, in particular, of one's being articulate, and thus distinctively and uniquely human. With his characteristic magnanimity, Miller argues that piety is something we owe even to the impious, at least to those among the impious who have in their often eloquent defense of skepticism helped us come into fuller possession of the "articulate forces," the actual institutions, underlying the very possibility of our articulate presence. For example, while he notes that Hume "became, in a manner of speaking, a book-burner" (AW, 263), he nonetheless contends: "From the point of view of the history of philosophy one cannot escape David Hume, nor would one dream of committing him to the flames of purification. To see the point of that inevitability is to stand in history. There one is hospitable, never censorious" (AW, 264). While it is barbarous to destroy monuments (*DP,* 101), and while it is necessary to contest the barbarous implications of the pronouncements of some eloquent nullifier, the pronouncements themselves may be so eloquent and arresting—they may express so forcefully, as it were, the fateful collapse of discourse at some significant juncture—that they constitute a monument of utterance. In such instances, it would be barbarous to call for the destruction or the systematic disregard of this monument.

We turn to history not to judge others but to identify ourselves (*PH,* 85; also 186). For this reason alone we need to open our minds to what might be barbaric in its implications, though eloquent in its articulation. Beyond being hospitable, one must be pious. Reverence is a condition for comprehending the efforts of our ancestors for what these efforts are: endeavors giving status and authority to the immediate by composing, through their distinctive forms of utterance—their buildings and laws no less than their books and speeches—a world of their own. Hence, while the vagrant or fugitive mind evades the conditions and demands of the lucid moment (AW, 265), the responsible mind seeks these conditions and confronts these demands. But where are we to look for the conditions underlying our own utterances? Miller's answer is, of course, history. And how are we most effectively to discover these conditions and to meet these demands? By a pious pilgrimage to the ruined monuments of human utterance. Only then can we "solve" the problem of how "to find an attachment which breeds criticism" (JWM, 17:23) or, more fully, an alliance that generates, authorizes, and sustains the possibility of criticism and, thus, of self-revision. Since history is, in its most basic sense, self-revision, such attachments or alliances are what, above all else, underlie history itself; better, they constitute the core of history.

What manner of philosopher is this thinker who desired, above all else, to be present in his own utterances and, thereby, to be open to the fateful revisions resulting from any actual utterance? He is one who insists that "[p]hilosophy has to be universal, not seek the universal. It has to be individual, yet must show also that in this the human universal occurs" (*PH*, 10). To be universal here means to be consciously and deliberately allied to some embodied forms of human utterance, some actual historical traditions; to be individual means to be allied with these forms in such a way that they establish and sustain, rather than undermine and even preclude, one's unique personal presence. The assertion of this presence is no act of vagrancy, for in this act of assertion I exhibit not only my unique humanity but also my shared humanity.

Despite the difficulties inherent in doing philosophy in this manner, especially beyond the circle of friends and students, Miller came to feel the need to seek a wider audience, that is, to assume a public authorship, albeit with great reluctance and only after much encouragement.

Defining the Scope of Philosophy

If we turn from these late expressions of a felt need to assume the responsibility of authorship to Miller's most significant accomplishment as a young author—his Harvard dissertation—we can see how his continuing uncertainty about the character of philosophical discourse is rooted in his early certainty about the scope of philosophical reflection. That is, he was uncertain about the manner in which philosophy is articulated precisely because he was certain that philosophy is neither a type of scientific theory nor a kind of artistic creation; because he was sure that the scope of philosophy cannot be defined in terms of discovering facts and laws, on one hand, or of an imaginative presentation of a personal vision, on the other.

Already in the opening chapter of *The Definition of the Thing*, we encounter this certainty. Here we are informed that philosophy is decidedly not a branch of science differentiated only by its subject matter from other more recognizable and successful branches of empirical investigation. Nor is it merely, as George Santayana proposes, "a personal work of art which gives a specious unity to some chance vista of the cosmic labyrinth" (quoted in *DT*, 23). It is a form of reflection whose task concerns defining the conditions for the possibility of experience, not attending to the particular disclosures of our actual experience, be these the disclosures of our haphazard, macroscopic experience or those of our contrived, "artificial" probings.

To repeat, "[r]eflection tells what one starts with. Experiment tells what one ends with" (*DP*, 189). By means of defining the "thing," the most basic identifiable unit of any possible human discourse, Miller in *Definition* shows what is presupposed in any form of discourse or at any level of reflection. What philosophical reflection cannot assume is what all other forms of reflection must assume. Apart from our ability to identify, without limit, things in their specificity (*DT*, 27), we are inarticulate. What we confront is an undifferentiated and, indeed, indistinct plenum; and what we utter is an inarticulate gasp. Apart from this ability, reality would be without any joints and our thought would be without any footholds.

The definition of the thing is, accordingly, not a hypothesis about what is but a reflection on what must be in order for there to be either articulate beings or an intelligible world. In opposition to the realists of his day, Miller suggests that the thing cannot be defined in terms of absolute independence of other things or of mindful beings (*DT*, 44). Nor can the thing be defined in terms of absolute fixity. Both what a thing is and our knowledge of what it is are essentially related to other things: a thing is always one thing among others. This pluralism is not simply a fact of our experience but a condition of our discourse, of our being articulate at all. What a thing is must be taken as relatively fixed. Otherwise we could not ever step into the same river twice, for the minimal basis for any possible identification would have been dissolved in flux. What a thing is, however, must not be taken as absolutely immutable. For this leads to nonsense as assuredly as the denial of any fixity or permanence begins with nonsense. Just as a plurality of distinguishable thing is implied in the definition of the thing, so, too, is mutability or revisability implied in this definition. To preserve our ability to distinguish things from one another, we need to accept the necessity of revisions (*DT*, 53). We cannot fully and finally identify anything whatsoever, especially at the outset. Our ability to identify anything is not instantaneous but developmental; it is only operative in a process of identifying that which threatens to become indistinct from what a moment ago was taken to be its opposite. In the course of this process, our ability is fated to be frustrated. By virtue of our very successes in introducing refinements and nuances into our definitions of things, we generate a host of possibilities. Some of these possibilities are simultaneously so persuasive yet so disruptive that we can no longer identify what we previously identified with unstuttering confidence and authority. For example, our ability to identify a virus calls into question the boundary between the animate and the inanimate and, thus, our definition of life.

One way to make this discussion more concrete—a way Miller himself adopts in *Definition*—is to focus on facts and on what is presupposed by the identification of facts. The task of philosophy is not to discover specific facts or general facts. Rather it is to define the notions presupposed by an investigation of facts. Prominent among these is that of fact itself. The physicist and the historian ordinarily presuppose that there are facts, while the philosopher asks what, in its most general sense, must we mean by a fact.

A person thoroughly committed to common sense or one deeply engaged in a scientific investigation is not likely to see any point in expending time and effort on defining the notion of fact as such. One reason is that for neither of these persons is the notion of fact, much less that of thing, troubling. Why, then, does the philosopher take this notion to be problematic? Why do philosophers painstakingly inquire into what others safely assume? And why do philosophers make trouble for themselves and others, especially when troubles are so abundantly found in everyday life or in scientific laboratories?

But troubles are encountered only by agents, by persons in the process of doing something. More generally, nothing is found apart from the activity of looking. Such "looking" can be a casual, virtually aimless process or a controlled, finely directed one; or it can be a process falling somewhere between the most causal looking around and the most concerted looking for. This implies that there are no facts apart from acts: I "find no rock until I pitch it, or bite it, or scratch it, or try to burn it, and so on" (*DP*, 119). And there are no acts apart from agents. Thus, any definition of fact must bring into focus the connection between facts and agents and their activities. This is precisely what Miller attempts to do in *Definition* and countless other writings.

The suggestion that facts are not simply "there," apart from agents and their acts, will inevitably be resisted by "realists." For such thinkers, anything deserving the name "fact" must be absolutely independent of any agent and also absolutely fixed for all times. To suggest that "facts" are either relative to agency or revisable would for these thinkers be analogous to virgins who have engaged in sex.

The essence of "realism" in this sense is an attempt to permit and, beyond this, to enforce the distinction between appearance and reality, between the way things happen to appear to us and the way they are in themselves. According to the realist (John Searle in our own day, Ralph Barton Perry in the earliest years of Miller's philosophical development), the maintenance of this distinction explains the possibility of error, while the dissolution of this distinction renders us unable to distinguish between truth and error, between fact and fiction. What realism makes clear is the necessity to maintain the distinction between appearance and reality. What realism, on its own premises, is condemned to leave inexplicable is how this distinction is to be drawn, let alone maintained. In the terms proposed by realism, the distinction is left a brute opposition, an absolute difference. It is, in yet other words, an unmediated distinction. The real is that which is absolutely other than the apparent, while the apparent is that which is, in principle, debarred from manifesting the real. Thus, realism, understood here as the attempt to preserve the distinction between truth and error by appealing to a reality incapable of either manifestation or revision, ends by defining reality (the object of knowledge) as always and necessarily other than appearance (the object of consciousness). Thereby reality and consciousness, known and knower, are forever sundered. This in effect makes knowledge impossible and the reality so precious to the "realist" powerless to check errors or to guide inquiry. In trying to account for the possibility of error, realism has "established" the impossibility of knowledge!

A dialectic, whatever else it is, is a process full of ironies. For example, efforts to establish law and order often generate chaos and a spirit of antinomianism. We have just seen that the possibility of error cannot be established in terms of realism, that is, in terms of a brute or unmediated distinction between appearance and reality. On what terms, then, can this possibility be established?

The self-regulation animated by our experience of error and sustained by our will to avoid such experience cannot be attained through subjectivism, the position to which realism is principally responding. But the reason why is worth considering here. While realism attempts to define facts apart from acts, subjectivism tries to define acts apart from constraints or limits. For the former, facts are externally constraining factors; they constrain thought *ab extra*, being entirely foreign to mind as such. For the latter, our consciousness is a wholly unconstrained power; it creates its world. Hence, the realist in effect, at least, makes facts absolute: they are what they are, in themselves, apart from all else. In contrast, the subjectivist grants consciousness this same status. The realist makes the other in its absolute otherness the "fact" most deserving of recognition; the subjectivist makes consciousness in its unlimited freedom the pivot of philosophy, the point around which all else turns.

A dialectical approach, however, rules out severing either the other from the self (as the realist does) or the self from the other (as the subjectivist does). The very intelligibility of self, the possibility of identifying myself as an "I," entails others against which the self differentiates itself in order to define itself. These others are not forced on the self *ab extra*, for there is no selfhood without otherness. Others are constitutive of my identity. In turn, the very intelligibility of fact, beginning with our ability to identify the "this" that insists on recognition, entails a self for whom the fact is the terminus of some activity, no matter how provisional. Just as there is no selfhood without otherness, there are no facts without acts.

Realism and subjectivism both assume that constraints are by their very nature external to the self who is the subject of constraint. The imposition of such constraints is violent, since it is an assault on the integrity of the self. So, despite their opposition to one another, the realist and the subjectivist are, at bottom, in agreement. For both, constraints are external and their imposition alien to the nature of consciousness. The differences, of course, remain, most notably that the subjectivist refuses to admit the legitimacy of any such limitations on the freedom of the self, whereas the realist insists on the need for such restrictions.[11]

In opposition to both, Miller denies that constraints are necessarily external. Some are internal, self-imposed. They are demands made by thought itself. Some constraints are limits imposed on the self by the self in its attempt to define itself and its world. Self-definition always entails self-limitation: the self projects for itself an other, the ego a non-ego. Herein thought becomes responsible to itself and for itself (Johnstone 1990, 11).

Miller desires to do justice to discourse and, more specifically, to criticism, here defined as that form of discourse in which the immanent telos of discourse is most manifest. In order to do so, we cannot worship facts or deify consciousness. We need to see discourse and criticism for what they are: an open-ended series of self-limiting acts. "The finite is characterized not by hermetically sealed boundary walls, and by lack of reciprocity, but by the remorseless demand for specification. To still that hunger gives not an absolute, but nothing. The simple entity is not a fiction; it is an unintelligible nonentity" (*DT,* 92). Any intelligible entity, that is, any thing identifiable by us, is relatively stable, inherently revisable.

Acts and the artifacts on which acts depend are the presuppositions of there being any facts at all and fact is the consequence of there being any acts.[12] Given this view, it is clear why history, "the story of acts," needs to be allied with philosophy, the systematic reflection upon the ultimate warrants for the most basic distinctions in human discourse: reality and appearance, fact and fiction, objectivity or subjectivity. These are the distinctions by which we can legitimately claim to be articulate. Without the capacity to tell the differences that need to be told, we are mute and impotent; moreover, our discourse cannot avoid collapse and incoherence. We seek to maintain these differences; they are inherent in discourse and also constitutive of human consciousness in any recognizable form. They are forced upon us by the ongoing, fateful struggle to tell what we feel it is necessary to be able to tell, for example, the difference between right and wrong, reality and appearance, self and other. But this means they are not forced upon us *ab extra*; rather, they are enforced by the very career of discourse itself, the tangled history of human telling. Language is not essentially an instrument in the struggle for survival, on the part of either the species or the individual. Rather individuals and, indeed, the species in its entirety are vehicles by which the career of discourse moves from one generation to the next. But their say has ultimately to do with satisfying the exigencies of an articulate agency, not securing the survival of a biological organism. Human existence is, at bottom, a desperate struggle to give adequate expression to one's absolute or self-defining commitments. The philosopher either speaks to this struggle or speaks without effect or force (*DP,* 124).

The need to speak to this struggle is the reason philosophy is not a science but one of the humanities, one of the disciplines in which human beings decisively and inescapably speak for themselves and to others who are willing to speak in this manner. These disciplines provide the fora in which human beings can encounter one another as such. Apart from training in the humanities, that is, apart from having been disciplined in the distinctively and ineliminably human modes of utterance, we are unable to encounter one another in our capacity as persons; even more fundamentally, our capacity as a person is dubious. For "communication is necessary to a self. To be a self is to communicate. . . . Our aversion to solitude is not merely a queer psychological fact" (*DP,* 170); it is truly an ineradicable metaphysical anxiety, since any loss in our capacity to communicate is essentially an impoverishment of the self, and a total loss of this capacity could only mean the total annihilation of the self.

The humanities are, accordingly, aptly named: they are the disciplines by which we are empowered to take possession of our inheritance and, then, to use that inheritance as a resource to give expression to our self-defining commitments. They are, in short, the disciplines by which we realize our humanity.[13] In this sense, the most basic of the humanities is our native tongue. In another, the most basic is philosophy; for the inevitability of skepticism, the arrest of action, is inherent in any prolonged effort at articulate existence. Quite simply, it is intrinsic to life as it must be lived by humans. Such arrests are disconcerting, often so deeply disconcerting that they force a radical redefinition of the self and a consequent reorientation—"I am no longer a believer"—toward the environment. Because such arrests are inevitable, "[t]here is just one quality in every man which he must change at least once; he must change his philosophy. Only in the discovery of some fatal threat to himself in the framework of his inheritance can he discover freedom" (*PC,* 73). But also, only by acknowledging this threat and resisting the collapse threatening the self and its world—only by engaging in philosophy in Miller's sense—can the self regain its composure, its sense of its own capacity to compose itself and its world.

Engaging in philosophy in Miller's sense does not reduce philosophy to psychology, though it does suggest why there are deep and enduring affinities between these two disciplines, especially when psychologists see their own discipline as one of the humanities. Philosophers are in a peculiar predicament with respect to psychology: they need to find a way of acknowledging a discipline that from the perspective of many of its practitioners, in particular, Freud and B. F. Skinner, rules out philosophy. Given philosophy's status as "just talk," as the discourse in which the collapses of discourse and the recovery from these collapses are absolutely crucial, philosophy cannot afford to be indifferent to disciplines that are hostile to or dismissive of it. One might interject that turnabout is fair play, that philosophy historically has tried to establish a hegemony and, indeed, in doing so blocked the path of science. But this interjection grossly exaggerates the negative influence of traditional philosophy on experimental science. It also does not justify the belittlement, much less the rejection, of that discourse concerned, above all else, with the collapses of discourse.

What is the upshot of these considerations? At the very least, philosophy must abandon its pretensions of being or having the ability to become a science. It must accept its status as one of the humanities, one especially close to history. Indeed, while the topic of philosophy and history needs to be explored more fully.

Philosophy and History

"Philosophy" and "history" are the names for two disciplines that have tried to don the mantle of science. Their status as disciplines, however, derives from something more basic—the actual world as an arena of constitutional revisions. Hence, while "philosophy" and "history" properly name distinct, though inseparable, disciplines or discourses, this is not what they primarily designate.

The authority of science contrasts markedly with the disrepute of the humanities, a source of distress among historians and traditional philosophers. But though neither history nor philosophy gains prestige by pretending to be something it is not and could never be, historians and philosophers are reluctant to abandon the project of transforming their disciplines into sciences and to content themselves with their status as humanities. One reason for their reluctance is that, in our culture, the "humanities lack authority" (*PC*, 160). But the supposition that they do so may have more to do with a mistaken conception of authority than an inherent deficiency in the humanities themselves. So a re-evaluation of the humanities may both depend upon and contribute to a reconceptualization of authority. If the humanities are, as Miller suggests, "the authority of the moment, of the here-and-now, of the actual" (*DP*, 161), the recognition of their authority does seem to demand nothing less. But, for Miller, the two humanities in which the authority of the actual is most manifest are history and philosophy. Thus, our discussion of history and philosophy must encompass, at some point, a consideration of why Miller contends that "the very authority of those who tell us what is so is historical and philosophical" (*DP*, 151). But, first, more basic and less disputable points need to be considered.

Of all the humanities, history is, in a certain respect, the discipline in which the nature of the humanities is most clearly revealed. For it is the discipline in which human beings most manifestly speak for themselves and of themselves. Given the history of philosophy, in particular, given its preoccupation with the eternal or timeless and its drive to be, in Plato's famous phrase, a "spectator of all time and existence," it is understandable why the philosophy of history is only a relatively recent concern. Moreover, the philosophy of history itself has not been immune to the influence of the ahistoric. This influence can be seen in the attempts to explain the substance of history, acts and "the symbols which acts leave as their residue," in terms of some fixed framework or invariant laws (*PC*, 76). Here the philosopher of history must take seriously the practice of historians. "Historians deal in the transitory and corruptible" (*PC*, 74). Not only are they interested solely in events falling within the order of dated time but their interpretations of these events are themselves subject to the vicissitudes of time. "Of this strange involution of his work the historian is often subtly or even explicitly aware" (*PC*, 76).

In Miller's sense, the philosophy of history is an attempt not to formulate the laws of history but to consider whether "the idea of history" is categoreal or not. Thus, questions about the authority of the "idea of history" need to be raised in an explicit and systematic manner. But these questions themselves cannot be posed ahistorically. For, in philosophy, "every controlling term [e.g., God, nature, cause, consciousness] means what it has come to mean in the controversies which alone give it authority" (*PC*, 92) or contest its authority. There is no platform outside of the historically evolved and evolving discourse of our traditions on which we can stand to gain a perspective on the flood of history. We are immersed in this flood. But this immersion does not mean imprisonment; for through a consciousness of the course of history, we can lift our heads far enough above the sustaining and compulsive waters to gain a perspective, even a vast and comprehensive perspective. Our locus in history rules out ever truly being "spectator[s] of all time and existence"; it does not necessitate being a prisoner in this time and this life.

Our terms have meaning and our ideas authority, then, only in the ongoing controversies of human discourse. But the past does not decide the future, it simply conditions what will happen. Hence, that an idea has been denied authority does not mean that it necessarily will never be authoritative. But, because the past does condition the present as well as the future, authority needs in some instances to be won: "An idea must make good, it must make its way. No problem in philosophy is innocent, none is timeless, none is launched from a point of view without environment" (ibid.). For an idea to make its way, however, it needs champions who will fight to establish the legitimacy of a ruler, for example, not hitherto recognized. These champions can be effective only if they comprehend adequately the environment both desperately needing and strenuously resisting the idea to which they have devoted themselves, only if they comprehend the constitutional confusions definitive of their historical moment.

Miller championed the idea of history with a deep historical awareness of the Western philosophical tradition. As a philosopher fully conscious of the history of his own "discipline," he could hardly help becoming focally concerned with the "idea of history" and, in some sense, with the philosophy of history. Moreover, as a thinker interested in action and the revision of the forms of action, he could hardly avoid such concern. For history "poses a problem about the centrality of action, and draws into the orbit of strict philosophy all the terminology which gives form to finitude" (*PC*, 95), which provides us with the conceptual resources to explain, rather than to explain away, the improvised and self-limiting deeds of historically situated actors. "There has always been a great temptation to reduce history to something else" (*PH*, 44). As a champion of the "idea of history,"

Miller opposed all such reductive attempts to explain away human history. Accordingly, the philosophy of history is, in his view, an attempt to deal with history on its own terms; it "is an essay in the rationality that does not exclude the unique—that is, the act—and the moment" (*PH*, 73). Given its historical preoccupation with defining the nature and scope of reason, philosophy in general cannot be indifferent to this "essay."

Four Senses of "History"

What needs to be underscored is that Miller's principal concern was not with history as a narration of events but with history as the fateful process of self-revisory acts. His focus was not on historians but on the makers of history and, less loftily, agents-in-history (*AW*, 267). As Cushing Strout points out in a letter to the author (December 16, 1988), Miller's "interest was primarily in the revisory activity of the historical actor, whom the historian studies."

Thus, to avoid confusion, we need to sort out here some of the most important and relevant senses of "history." This term can mean, in the most straightforward sense, the "story" or "narration" of past acts and events; it is what historians make of the past. And their stories or narratives are, from Miller's viewpoint, just this: attempts to make something of the past. To make something of the past, of course, is quite different from making up the past. Here, as elsewhere, that we have a voice in the telling of the truth, a hand in the construction of a discourse, does not necessarily preclude "objectivity." It does, however, force us to come to terms with what "objectivity" means, the emergent ideal of a self-critical inquiry or the self-imposed ideal of self-critical inquirers.

What Miller says about being "disinterested" is directly relevant to the issue of being "objective."

> The disinterested is not the uninterested, where nothing satisfies and nothing offends, so that one could turn away without loss and entertain one's unconcern with other matters equally irrelevant to egoistic requirements [or self-defining engagements]. The disinterested occurs as a systematic finitude, tenacious of its conditions. It does not occur in abdication. (*PC*, 155)

It occurs only in the passionate commitment to self-critical discourse, a discourse in which limits or boundaries are systematically drawn. In reference to the task of the historian, one such boundary is that between the historian's own time and some past period. The past as a portion of dated time is always relatively discontinuous with the present; and it is the task of historians to render this discontinuity intelligible without, in effect, transforming the past into merely an earlier version of the present. In other words, their task involves respecting the difference between past and present. "The besetting sin of history is anachronism, the description of any past in terms of an abstract present" (*PH*, 186). This sin involves a loss of objectivity, a failure to maintain the conditions of self-criticism. More fully, it involves a failure to maintain the conditions of self-criticism required to tell the differences the historians needs to tell in order to give an account of the past as past, the past as different from the present.

History, then, might mean what historians, in their narrations, make of the past as past: the past as a segment of time relatively discontinuous with the present. But it obviously can also mean the events of the past themselves, not, for example, Herodotus's "Histories" but the events themselves as actual occurrences. Unquestionably, it is imperative to draw this distinction. But it is equally important to understand the vital, living connection between the events being narrated and the narratives being proposed. Historians stand in an essentially different relation to the subjects they portray and the acts they narrate than do scientists to the objects they describe and the facts they explain. The difference is not that historians are necessarily biased and subjective in their interpretations, whereas scientists can transcend bias and attain objectivity. Rather, it is that the relationship between historians and their subject is necessarily personal, whereas that between scientists and their subject is impersonal. "Science eventuates in formulae, and while such universalities bring release from a broken and disorderly privacy where the self is blurred in confusion and impotence, they omit all reference to things done" (*PH*, 107). The universal formulae of scientific discourse are themselves historical achievements of momentous consequence for establishing the Promethean self of the modern epoch, for freeing the self from a fragmentary and chaotic isolation by allying the self with the universal order of an impersonal nature whose ways were predictable and even controllable (*PH*, 147). But these formulae established an order that extinguished the very individual it promised to recognize; for they made of all apparently unique and autonomous exertions only events conformable to uniform and heteronomous laws. "History, in contrast [to science], needs acts, agents, dates, places, desires, and passions" (*PH*, 107). It needs, in a word, persons. It concerns the historical conditions and fateful consequences of personal agency.

In one sense, then, history is a sequence of acts by which revisions in the very forms of acting have been wrought by persons in their struggles to maintain themselves and their worlds; in another, it is a story of these acts, constructed on the basis of evidence and in accord with canons of self-criticism. But acts emanate from agents. The historical record is, consequently, studded with proper names. As a historical actor, a participant in the ongoing sequence of self-revisory acts, I need to come to terms with my ancestors—with, for example, Lincoln in one context and Luther in another. Person-to-person encounters are fated. So, too, the historical narrator needs to come to terms with actors, with persons who presume to be able to tell and, beyond this, to enact the differences definitive of their unique identity and their actual world.

In addition to the two senses just distinguished (history as a sequence of self-revisory acts and history as a self-critical story of such revisions), it is helpful for our purposes to note yet another meaning of "history." Miller is quite fond of writing that "[w]e cannot escape history, and we cannot escape the study of history" (*PC*, 92). But who is the we to whom this utterance is addressed? And in what sense is the study of history inescapable? The term "we" refers to human beings as historical agents: "We cannot escape history if we wish to avoid the paralysis of inaction. Action thereupon looms as the essential moral fatality" (*PH*, 150). Here "study" means essentially reflection, though reflection very often requires study in the formal and strict sense. We as agents-in-history cannot escape reflecting on the medium in which our utterances are expressed, or the forces by which our agency itself has been launched and is sustained. In this third sense, history is the explicitly historical consciousness of the historically situated agent. My suggestion in a previous discussion that Miller's principal concern is with the fateful process of our self-revisory acts should not be taken to mean the bare course of events apart from agents' understanding of the deeds they are undertaking. The process of self-revision is always in some measure the career of self-consciousness; so the actors' own sense of what is taking place is an ingredient in what is taking place. Several qualifications need to be made here, but the necessity to do so should not obscure the basic point: the historical awareness of the agents themselves and, in our case, our explicitly historical consciousness are not epiphenomena, incidental by-products of an "objective" process. Such awareness is not negligible; it is essential to our status as agents and, indeed, as humans. History does not occur primarily behind the backs of agents. These agents are hardly ever mere playthings of forces totally beyond the consciousness and control of these agents.

While the awareness of agents as agents needs to be taken seriously, it clearly cannot be granted an unquestionable authority. We as agents often, perhaps always, do not know fully or even adequately what we are doing. Only in the course of our actions do we clarify our purposes and acquire the powers needed for the attainment of these purposes. But these and other qualifications should not be allowed to lead us to overlook the importance of what historical agents were consciously trying to accomplish.

The fourth and final sense of "history" to be distinguished here is the one most prominent in Miller's writings. One succinct formulation—and there are countless such formulations to be found in his work—is the following: History "is the revision of outlooks at the point of conflict between them. It is the process of putting us in rapport with each other, and with those monuments of expression which are the substance of civilization" (*PC*, 123). This sense comprehends, in a way, the other three meanings. It encompasses the more or less conscious undertakings of agents and the fateful consequences befalling historical actors while engaged in these self-defining undertakings. It encompasses not only what actually took place but also what the participants themselves believed to be taking place. It encompasses, in short, the second two senses of "history" we noted. Finally, the conflicts and confusions inherent in any revision of outlook call forth a process of reflection that is ordained to overcome our present divisions and also our alienation from our own past. It is a process that enables us to speak to one another and the past to speak to us. That the past is able to speak to us, to this cluster of disparate individuals as the bearer of a single identity, is what empowers us to speak to one another. It is what most decisively makes this cluster into a "we."

The reflection generated by the revisions of our outlooks has ultimately given rise to the disciplines of philosophy and history, two ways of coming to terms with these revisions. Philosophy and history have, for good and ill, taken on a life often quite far removed from the disconcerting conflicts ingredient in any actual historical moment. In addition, the relationship of these two disciplines to each other has not always been cordial, most particularly because their overlapping concern, the revision of outlooks, has hardly ever been seen by either historians or philosophers as the central concern of their respective disciplines.

The Historian

We must now address the question, What is the relationship between a historian as a practitioner of a scholarly craft and that same person as a historically situated being? Agents, to repeat, cannot avoid the "study" of history. But can students of history avoid the often severe limitations imposed by committed action? If our historical situatedness demands of us historical reflection, does not that same situatedness demand of historians the honesty to own their commitments and, on occasion, the courage to act on those commitments? Are historians entitled to be aloof or disengaged surveyors of the human struggle?

The single text most relevant to the above questions is the following: "A test of the historian occurs in the task laid upon him when he encounters a monument. What must he then do? If nothing, then I say he has not encountered an act, but only another object or appearance" (*PH*, 159). The historian as historian must do something. It appears that act can be encountered only by act, and one agent only by another. Hence, if historians are passive in the presence of a monument or document, they are not truly in the presence of either a monument or document. It is not simply that the historian must act in some fashion; the historian must be animated by a definite spirit. While "the past seems to lie about us," chronologically distant but immediately accessible, the "case is rather that where nothing is cherished nothing is found" (*PH*, 111). That the past needs to be cherished in order to be discovered is "a matter of some weight, but [one] likely to be passed over, or denied, in our factually oriented idiom. For to cherish requires emotion and will. If there are to be memorials, they have to be treated as memorials" (ibid.).

Is the cherishing of the past, however, truly necessary to the work of the historian? Is it not possible to reconstruct the past without revering it? A scientist is a person animated by the spirit of inquiry, by the desire to discover what is not yet known. Individuals not so animated may contribute, perhaps even significantly, to the cause of science. But they hardly deserve the title "scientist." So, too, historians are persons animated by the spirit of piety toward the origins of their own being, in particular, of their own articulate being. Many may contribute to the comprehension of these origins, but only those who stand to the vestiges of these origins as mediators between a confused present and a potentially illuminating and energizing past merit the name "historian."

For Miller, then, only a cherished past stands a chance of being a recovered past; and any recovery of the past is an encounter with persons whose ways of acting and forms of discourse are not ours but are genetically related to ours. If historians are successful in their reconstruction of some phase of the past, they are able to tell the differences between us-here-now and them-then-there, in such a way that the relatively discontinuous is preserved as just that: the relatively discontinuous.

Human Experience as the Career of Our Critical Engagements

The historical past, the past as relatively discontinuous with the present, underlies the possibility of distinctively human experience. It also raises questions about history as a continuum of self-revising forms of human functioning. Let us take up both of these issues, beginning with human experience acquiring its distinctive form because of its historical past.

To Miller, it appeared that our understanding of experience has been disfigured by an assumption inherited from the "empiricists." In their attempts to do justice to the brute insistence ingredient in our actual experience, the "empiricists" assumed that the mind is essentially passive and acritical. Impressions are forced upon the mind *ab extra*, apart from any activity or any judgment. But such impressions do not and cannot ever add up to experience, if we take "experience" to mean a more or less coherent order of impressions, memories, and anticipations. Such an order is inherently critical: it is the ongoing endeavor to tell the differences between, for example, the pleasant and the unpleasant, the beneficial and the harmful. Apart from such distinctions, the contents of experience lack any coherence and the possibility of control lacks any basis.

"Our yesterdays have no power in the present where experience has no career. Experience has a career only because it is not passive, but critical" (*PH*, 101). Our experience, however, is the career of our doings and it is a career because our doings are inherently critical. At any moment of our experience we are trying to tell some difference or other, be it only that something is one way or is not that way. "Experience breaks out into order as soon as it entails identification and negations" (ibid.). But, apart from the drive to tell the difference between, say, the harmful and the beneficial or the illusory and the veridical, the course of our lives so lacks order that it does not deserve to be called experience.

Experience is not whatever happens to befall a passive spectator. It is the fateful career of critical agents in which the very criteria of criticism are destined to undergo revision. This does not mean that there are no accidents or contingencies in the course of such careers. There are, in fact, countless accidents and contingencies. The realists err simply by trying "to explain the accidental as if it were itself an accident" (*PC*, 54). The accidental is not itself a contingent disclosure or our haphazard experience; it is, instead, one of the necessary conditions of anything meriting the name of human experience (ibid.).

In some places, Miller characterizes history as "absolute empiricism" and, in others, as "radical empiricism."[14] In yet other contexts, however, he identifies "radical empiricism" with pure passivity in the face of data alleged to be wholly external to, or absolutely unconnected with, the concerns and commitments of the subject (*PH*, 101). When he characterizes history as "radical empiricism," this is not the sense he intends. For example, he asserts: "The status of the categories must be nonaccidental if they are not to relinquish legislative authority; but it must also be derivative if they are not to remain arbitrary. History is the absolute empiricism which generates the categories of truth" (AW, 255–56). If the categories are to be authoritatively legislative, they must be necessary. If they are not legislative, then we are in Hume's "universe" where "[a]ll rules are off, and anything is possible—if, indeed, the idea of possibility can be established on such premises" (*PH*, 101).

Although necessary, the categories must also be derivative. Otherwise they are arbitrary and we are dogmatists. "Dogma is always an essay in order" (*DP*, 122); more fully, any appeal to dogma in Miller's sense is an attempt to secure the means to tell the differences that dogmatists desperately, and, often, rightly, feel need to be told. But because they appeal to what is ahistoric and, hence, underived, they cannot avoid being arbitrary. So we must turn to history as the story of the genesis of the categories of truth, of the very forms of telling, to avoid the anarchy of skepticism and the arbitrariness of dogmatism. For only in terms of history can the categories be exhibited in their true character—the necessary but derived forms underlying the possibility of experience, at least of distinctively human experience. The story of the genesis of the categories is, in part, the story of how we have acquired the capacity to tell the difference between now and then, even in those instances where "then" is dramatically different from "now." Here, again, we see a bootstrap ascent. For apart from this capacity, no story of the genesis of the categories would itself be possible. So here we have a narration in which the possibility of this form of narration, a story of genesis, of what went before us but nonetheless resides within us (*PH*, 109–10) is explained in the very course of the narrative.

In the context of noting the way history is a dimension of experience, Miller asserts: "It is only intensity passing into action which regenerates itself in the continuum of productive novelty. Action is certified [or validated] in this continuum" (*PC*, 159). The career of human experience is nothing other than the career of our critical engagements, one "enlisting original intensities in the sustainment of their destined revisions" (ibid.). To enlist original intensities requires recovering originating deeds and utterances, for example, the telling significance of Luther's "Here I stand; I cannot do otherwise" or of Lincoln's "I believe this government cannot endure permanently half slave and half free." But the presumption that these deeds and utterances are recoverable poses the question of the accessibility of the past and, thereby, the question of the continuity of history.

The Continuity and Discontinuities of History

This brings us to the second point about the past as relatively discontinuous with the present. "History, which vanishes if the discontinuous be made absolute, confronts us with problems of continuity" (*PC,* 91). If the past seamlessly flowed into the present, not presenting itself to us as a puzzle here and now, "all transactions in time would appear transparent to a single perspective, or to any perspective" (ibid.). But the past decidedly does not flow seamlessly into the present. Therefore, insofar as the past is discontinuous with the present, it is not at all clear how we can know such a past, especially given the assumptions that have controlled our accounts of knowledge.

In view of these excessively limiting assumptions, Miller argues that we need a new epistemology (see, e.g., AW, 261–62; *PH,* 121). "The pure continuum of history is philosophy, where one never says what is so, but where one develops the ways of telling what is so" (*DP,* 150). In history, Miller explains,

> One deals with things done, *res gestae,* with acts rather than facts, with yesterday rather than with an invariant present, with rise and fall and not with quantitative changes of objects in time and space. The ideal of natural knowledge is the disinterested, the understanding of the ways of things in despite of our hopes and fears. But action, with which history is concerned, is the expression of hopes and fears and is not to be understood by us apart from our personal appropriation of their occasions. If we do not do this, we are not fitted to understand. History can show us only ourselves, for it is our deed. But it is also a deed that continues into the present and so cannot be forsaken or interrupted. It is not a romantic tale or a tale by an idiot, for it is the story which contains the genesis of all such distinctions. We cannot escape it, because it is ourselves. (*PH,* 81–82)

The self-conscious present is, however, attained by an at least felt, if not articulated, sense of relative discontinuity (*PH,* 188): "The past is historical because it is always relatively discontinuous with the present" (*PC,* 91). Absolute rupture with the past is an absolute impossibility for any present; relative discontinuity and the consequent confusion is a necessary feature of any self-conscious present.

Miller did not shy away from metaphysics, at least in a certain sense. He supposed that: "[t]he aversion to 'metaphysics' is the sign of the inability to identify the basis both of the distinctions and of their rejection" (*PH*, 128). The ability to articulate the telling differences demands owning up to one's actual locus in a constitutive history and to the demands inherent in this situation; in turn, owning up to these requires that one re-envision oneself as an integral part of a self-fragmenting history. The sense of rootedness in an actual past is given along with a sense of otherness from one's actual ancestors. We are akin to these others in a way that makes clear both our kinship to and our otherness from them. The continuities of history are omnipresent occasions for critical ruptures; the discontinuities of history are critical opportunities for radical revisions of the authoritative discourses in and through which we define our selves and our world. But there are no authoritative discourses without historical authorities. "Except as a career and a continuum there is no past to write 'about' "; there is thus no history in Miller's sense. But if there is a career and hence a continuum, "then the present has joined and embraced *its* past" (*PH*, 178–79; emphasis added).

One context in which this dynamic conjunction of past and present might be illustrated is that of the classroom, especially when it is used as a stage for the reenactment of those cultural dramas so bound up with contemporary actuality. Miller notes: "If Plato did not come alive in me [as a teacher], then he was no living force [no authoritative presence] at all. That was a troublesome, if vague, realization at the time. But it was a factor in my eventual claim that philosophy was its own history, and that the evasion of the present was a reduction of history to what was itself never a presence" (*DP*, 87). In time this realization became less vague.

It remained troublesome, however, for many of Miller's students and readers. For the rhetoric of piety and reverence seemed to them, at best, outdated. For they revered only irreverence. But in their acts of unacknowledged reverence for annihilative critiques and dismissive ridicule, the bases and character of their own drives toward negation are left unnoticed and hence uncriticized. Even worse, such critics reveal themselves to be barbarians. "It is as barbarous to chip away at Plato as to knock a bit of marble off the Parthenon" (*PH,* 83), Miller points out, referring to the discussion of piety understood as reverence for the sources of one's being. Some will object that this attitude makes a fetish of Plato's dialogues. Well, let us take those who might pose this objection at their word. The power of this word to discredit, often without argument, derives from the authority of the discourse from which it comes, for example, Freudian psychology.

For Miller, the historical shape of human authority demands explicit recognition and, beyond that, formal explication. "So, I grasp the nettle and say that the very authority of those who tell us what is so is historical and philosophical" (*DP,* 151). Accordingly, the question of authority is inseparable from the question of piety. But, at this point in our history, the only place to which we can turn in our quest for a basis for respect and reverence is history itself. "If we want reverence, anything sacred and so imperative, we must advance now to history—and I cannot avoid it!—to pure history, which is philosophy. There is the common world, the actual one" (ibid.). Pure history is the career of self-consciousness. Philosophy insofar as it is identifiable with history so defined is the explicitly self-conscious narration of this career. Narrated history and technical philosophy are both derivative: they derive from the sequence of self-revisory acts itself. In their most authentic form, they are both self-conscious and self-critical forms of discourse in which the career of self-consciousness is exhibited in the terms most appropriate to this career and the historian, as well as the philosopher. Even in their inauthentic forms, history and philosophy often provide resources for and insights into the career of self-consciousness, though these resources and insights are available as such only to philosophers and historians willing to assert the identity between philosophy and history.

The Telling Difference of Miller's Concern with Told Differences

Philosophy is, again, just talk: it is a species of discourse aiming not to tell what is so but to exhibit the status and authority of discourse itself. It involves drawing the truly profound implications from an apparently simple truth: "'[D]ifferences get told.' One 'tells' the difference" (JWM, 25:22). Truth is in the telling; more fully and accurately, the difference between truth and falsity is in the telling and the retelling. "Error occurs in the course of a way of telling that tells the truth" (*PH,* 151; cf. 175).

Philosophy is the form of talk in which the act of telling is granted the status of a category, for by virtue of our acts all differences are told. These acts render the facts and all else intelligible but are not themselves illuminated by any appeal to facts. So, while "space, time, and quantity derive from verbs, from measuring, telling time, calculating in numbers" (*PH,* 175), and while any identifiable reality derives from some form of acting, the forms of action themselves are not derived from either nature or divinity. They are derived from history. But this means they are derived from prior acts, any act being necessarily a continuation of prior acts. Acts as such can be derived only from acts; hence, they are, in a sense, absolute, for they are self-conditioned and self-conditioning. They are nullified as acts insofar as they are treated as facts, as phenomena to be explained in terms of something hidden or as data to be simply accepted in their insistent arbitrariness or contingency.

Three aspects of acts in Miller's sense need to be highlighted here. First, to say acts are self-conditioning is, in effect, to say they are self-maintaining. Since revision is not the opposite of but a phase in any process of maintenance, this means also that acts are self-revising. Self-revision is of their essence: to deny the capacity of revision inheres in a form of acting is, at least for Miller, analogous to denying that three-sidedness is essential to a triangle. An important text bearing on this topic is the following: "If the rule of the intellect is the maintenance of the conditions of error, so too the rule of the will is the maintenance of its own capacity for guilt. The actual is the locus of the assertion and maintenance of these distinctions. It is the individual, the other absolute, of which all articulate infinity is the form" (*PH,* 69). We come into possession of our own intellects only insofar as we use them to define for ourselves the conditions of error; so, too, we come into possession of our wills only insofar as we define for ourselves the conditions of guilt. Since we use our intellects and wills to define for ourselves the conditions of our own emergence, operation, and modification, this is a bootstrap ascent. Insofar as we refuse to define what counts as an error, we cannot learn from our mistakes: intelligence is undermined by its own refusal. The same holds for the will. Insofar as we refuse to define what counts as an infraction—trespass, sin, call it what you will—we cannot enhance our effectiveness in action: will is weakened by its own resistance to the impositions of self-limitation. In this connection, it is relevant to note that "guilt," originally a term drawn from moral and religious discourses, has been debunked to a large extent by the enormous prestige of psychological discourse (JWM, 25:1).

Second, Miller's concern with our capacity to tell the differences we at this stage in our history feel entitled to declare does not imprison us in language (Jameson 1972). Language or, more broadly, utterances in all of their modes (in a word, the midworld) are the only means we have, or could have, for telling the difference between self and other, between us and them, our ways and theirs, and even our language and theirs. Our locus within discourse is no confinement; it is the very source of transcendence because it is the basis of criticism. In one of his most eloquent passages, Miller observes:

> If today the sense of dated [or historical] time fits our temper and nourishes our energies it is for the reason that the enterprises which take time, those which entail a dated past [and demand a pious attitude toward the articulate forces within this past], seem rather to promote than to corrupt the sense of responsible selfhood [and of effective criticism]. What is more it is these enterprises and no other which have also generated the articulate world of nature. We are dependent on Newton and Darwin, on their predecessors and their successors. We do not stand outside the discourse, which they constituted, judging their words from some point of view to which articulate physics and biology are irrelevant. The alleged disabilities of finitude [of limiting ourselves to a particular historical tradition or viewpoint] have become implausible and appear rather as the refuge of obscurantism, the arrest, not the launching, of criticism and of responsibilities. (JWM, 23:12)

We do not stand outside the discourse inaugurated and sustained through revision by Heraclitus and Parmenides, Plato and Aristotle, Augustine and Thomas, and countless others. But to stand inside this discourse is to be always already beyond the limitations of their utterances. For in our alliance with this discourse, which for us can be only the career of discourse as such, we come into possession of the resources and warrants for our capacity for articulation and criticism. Indeed, apart from this alliance, there would be no possibility of being either articulate or critical. Anyone who stands inside the career of this discourse can only be haunted by a sense of the other (*PH*, 72), one persistent form of which is the abiding sense that the way things are is possibly other than what I say. Telling does not make anything so, but it does define the conditions in which what is so might be articulated.

"Only what is itself absolute can discover an absolute antagonist. This is the dialectical process of history, and this mode of our being is itself a discovery of time" (*PC*, 94). Discourse itself as an absolute or self-authorizing continuum historically has defined itself in opposition to what is other than, but allied to, itself (e.g., God or nature). Apart from this allied antagonist—this other with which discourse struggles continuously and necessarily in the course of its career—discourse collapses. Abandon the distinction between what is so and what is said and we are rendered inarticulate.

But make this distinction absolute, make what is other absolutely so, and likewise discourse collapses: for any reality defined in absolute independence of all utterance, even though it is supposed to provide a foundation for our knowledge, actually sows the seeds of skepticism. An other about which we can know or say nothing ceases to guide inquiry or to offer checks to our assertions. This other, then, is real only so in a Pickwickian sense; for it cannot, in principle, exert an influence, or affect the career of discourse, falling forever outside. But we who stand in the complex tradition responsible for critical discourse can truly count as real only that which corrects errors or can exert the force to do so. In addition, we also count as real that which gives action an opportunity. No absolute other can either exert this force or provide this opportunity; only an allied antagonist can do either.

This brings us to our third point about acts in Miller's sense, which can be discussed much more briefly than the previous one. In fact, it is already more or less stated. It concerns the recognition and acknowledgment of heroes. Any act of utterance is a phase in a continuum. As such, it draws its authority from the criteria of self-criticism it has appropriated from the past, while it possesses its vulnerability by virtue of the possibilities for conflict inherent in any act of utterance. If any "utterance" in principle could not conflict with anything whatsoever, nothing has really been uttered. Miller notes, "Homer's heroes may not be mine. Ptolemy's truths may not be mine. But insofar as I have heroes and truths I have ways of telling that are also theirs. Heroes change, and truths; but those changes are consequences of greater control in the act of telling" (*PH,* 153). Insofar as all heroes are debunked, ordinarily through ridicule and scorn, we lose control over our own ability to tell the differences we feel need to be told. We often hear that these differences no longer matter; they have ceased to be relevant. For example, Richard Rorty (1982, chaps. 4 and 6, 1999, chap. 9) would like to blur the difference between philosophy and literary criticism. He insists nothing is lost, indeed much is gained, by erasing this line of demarcation.

Miller writes: "Name your community; it will be an illusion supported by Myth, by Athena, Jehovah, by Nature and Nature's God or by the alleged Reason of man" (JWM, 25:25). Neither "illusion" nor "myth" should be taken in a pejorative sense, for the passage is highly ironic: "From the know-it-all perspective of our contemporary intelligentsia, communities are founded on illusions." What we are still witnessing today to some extent and what Miller witnessed all his life is the emancipation from myth. Today, however, we are seeing an attempt to revive just this notion in the wake of an extended period of demythologizing that took place in a variety of fields, not just theology, and had an impact on culture at large. The ubiquity of the antihero in even popular forms of art is a symptom of this process. But, for Miller, the contemporary dispelling of myths and the correlative debunking of heroes is, in effect, an attack on "any warrant of an articulate and authoritative immediacy. All tales are told by an idiot" (ibid.). And all heroes are, if not idiots, groundless idealizations made necessary by some pathetic deficiency in the character of those who crave heroes. So, at least, the story goes. But, it is told by one whose only claim to authority is the capacity to undermine the authority of others. So, in our time, the "nullifier becomes the authority" (*DP,* 89), indeed, the only authority, all the more effective as such because the nullifier does not claim to speak with authority nor is he or she consciously recognized as an authority. It is, of course, possible to deny consciously what one acknowledges existentially, in one's actions and commitments or, in the case at hand, in one's inability to find a motive for acting or a basis for commitment.

This point clearly relates to the crisis of modernity. Our age is nihilistic because the only authorities we are able to recognize are the nullifiers, though we are not often willing to acknowledge the fact of this recognition. So, the protagonist in Umberto Eco's *The Name of the Rose* (1983), William of Baskerville, helps us see the way beyond tyranny and tragedy by suggesting: "Perhaps the mission of those who love mankind is to make people laugh at the truth, to make truth laugh, because the only truth lies in learning to free ourselves from insane passion for the truth" (491). Our heroes have become those who tell us that no difference between truth and error can, or need, be told. But now, as in our past, the "role of communication is disclosed in its collapse. The disclosure of its function and properties [no less than its status and authority] occurs in those conflicts which threaten it in principle" (*PC*, 122).

We can now return to the crucial notion of "constitutional conflicts" and frame this notion in a different manner than our previous discussions. These conflicts turn out to be threats, ones posed by equally authoritative factors within human discourse, to our very capacity to tell the differences between, say, truth and falsity or right and wrong. In the face of such conflicts, we no longer know what to say or, even, how to tell the difference between responsible and irresponsible utterances. Since our capacity to tell these differences is constitutive of discourse itself, these conflicts are threats to discourse as such: their terror resides in part in the violence they so frequently generate and, in part, in the muteness and, indeed, impotence, they necessarily threaten. In constitutional conflicts, human agents are confronted with the terrifying possibility of being rendered inarticulate and powerless.

The actual world, again, is always in some measure a confused world. Its confusions extend to the very roots of its constitution; they concern the various forms of embodied action by which we establish, maintain, and revise the actual world. This is why philosophy "is not esoteric; it is indigenous" (*MS*, 190). But, in this context, philosophy must be understood as the actuality of those conflicts having the capacity to tear apart one's world no less than one's identity (*PC*, 74). And if it is, then philosophy is also the career of self-consciousness, in particular, the awareness of the revisions wrought by the self in its struggle to maintain its identity and its environment, revision being, in the end, a phase of maintenance or conservation of functioning (*PH*, 21; *MS*, 85). In this sense, philosophy has no audience, only participants (JWM, 14:9).

Miller insists that either the most basic distinctions—truth and falsity, reality and appearance, self and other—get told or they do not occur. The most fundamental distinctions in human discourse are told, not found (*MS*, 38). Philosophy is the discourse in which the status and authority of discourse is exhibited in its fateful struggle to come to historical terms with itself. It does not try to tell "what is so" but rather undertakes to tell a story in which the very self-revisions of telling themselves are revealed as moments in a dialectic. Most authentically, it is the story of enforced distinctions told by an agent at the very moment that agent is experiencing the threat of constitutional confusion: it is an effort to maintain the most basic distinctions in the face of the most radical failure. That philosophy is such a discourse—that it is an essentially historical narration of the most basic, the truly enforced, distinctions—constitutes a telling difference between Miller's approach to philosophy and virtually all other approaches. His approach is based on the recognition that "there is no escaping an account of the world that can include the utterances, the affirmations and denials that permit any world to be intelligible" (*MS*, 129; slightly modified). His achievement resides, at least in part, in articulating and defending just such an account of our world.

Conclusion

"Philosophy is the story of *enforced* distinctions." It is one with history insofar as history itself is the story of the genesis of the distinctions by which we define our selves and our world. Philosophy is, then, a form of discourse exhibiting the conditions by which the basic distinctions of human discourse are established, maintained, and revised. These are the distinctions by which articulation and thus discourse itself are possible; these are the differences that make the ultimate difference: the difference between meaning and nonsense. They are not immutably fixed but rather historically secured and thus essentially precarious. For example, to acknowledge that "truth is in the telling" is to imply that truth is part and parcel of a career, a fateful process of human discourse. The capacity to tell the truth has been won in the course of a long and painful history. Our consciousness of this means truth is knocked from its eternal throne and thrust into the historical domain. But history is, while certainly no unalterable order, no amorphous flux either. Historically secured distinctions are, more often than not, currently reliable resources to which we can go, again and again, to realize our purposes and, even more fundamentally, frame the very purposes by which we define ourselves.

"Philosophy is just talk." That is, it is the discourse in which the status and authority of discourse are exhibited in one's very acts of utterance. It is the discourse in which the fatalities of discourse themselves are recollected as part of a pilgrimage. Finally, it is the form of discourse most attentive to the conditions of discourse as such: it is the form in which the most systematic attention is paid to the historically secured modes of utterance in all of their actual variety and also the form in which the most radical responsibility is assumed for these modes in their inevitable disarray, their constitutional confusion.

No doubt, this sounds highly abstract, and in a sense it surely is. But this revision of philosophy is the result of something as concrete and immediate as using a yardstick or counting on one's fingers. Rather than losing the name of action, let us affirm it. Rather than leaving out the verbs, let us include them; beyond this, let us make them absolutely basic. What, then, follows? The historical forms of human functioning and, thereby, the history of humanity itself acquire categoreal status: they provide us the means in terms of which all else is to be rendered intelligible. In addition, the dialectical drama in which the actual forms of human action contest one another becomes a self-portrait of present agents. For example, philosophy in the person of Plato challenges the authority of myth, or science in the person of Comte challenges the validity of theology. Our agency is due, in large measure, to a complex and disorderly inheritance; thus, the maintenance of our own agency requires a revision of this inheritance. For our present confusion, and the impotence or at least ineffectiveness resulting from this confusion, can be comprehended and thus overcome only by a consciousness of our past. This means grasping our forms of functioning and modes of discourse as continua, processes prolonging the exertions and utterances of our predecessors. It also means the relative discontinuity between our selves and our predecessors. The upshot of these considerations is to grant discourse nothing less than absolute status and to grasp the distinctive forms of human discourse as the fateful results of an essentially historical process. It is, in short, to do philosophy in the manner proposed by Miller.

"One word leads to another word" (*MS*, 63). So, too, one number leads to another and, ultimately, to infinity. But, for a long time, one word led to another with little or no systematic or even explicit awareness of this process and, thus, of the fatalities inherent in the career of discourse. There was "a good deal of telling before the status of telling [or discourse] came to notice" (*MS*, 37). Philosophy is, as we see in this chapter, the discourse in which the status of discourse progressively emerges into fuller and deeper comprehension. "The Greeks had a word for it." It was precisely their capacity to name *physis*, *polis*, and *psyche*—to define the principal domains of philosophical discourse, to launch the logos—that entitles them to the authoritative status they possess in Western history. In their discourse, a decisive step toward the explicit recognition of discourse or logos as such was taken. "'The Greeks had a name for it'; that is why they were so far-ranging, the principal authors of the Mid-World" (JWM, 25:22).

In Miller's conception of the midworld, the formal conditions for the finite actualities of human functioning are brought down to earth. These conditions, characteristically defined in the most abstract terms in philosophical discussions, are here revealed in their true character as concrete immediacies, embodied actualities.

We now must turn to Miller's depiction of the actual world in its concrete immediacy. The actual world is a made world; even more simply, it is an artifact. What enables us to make our actual, common world? Does not the insistence that the actual world is a made world reduce it to an arbitrary fabrication? Does not this insistence entail the most irresponsible egoism? That the actual world is, for Miller, a human artifact (a collective human artifact) is beyond question; that it is also the fateful and awesome revelations made possible by human symbols should be clear at this point in our discussion. These revelations are part and parcel of the midworld, as are the powers they both invoke and sustain. We do not have, from Miller's perspective (as have from Kant's), a ghostly world of noumena or realities forever lurking behind the orderly world of phenomena or appearances. While Kant's forms of sensibility and categories of the understanding provide us with the principles by which we can organize our sensory experience into a coherent world, Miller's functioning objects as the embodied forms of human functioning put us in league with a confused heritage and, through the resources of this heritage, with a chaotic environment. These objects project a world no less constitutionally incomplete than inherently disorganized; indeed, the impossibility of the actual world's being complete is an inescapable consequence of this world's being intrinsically chaotic (*MS*, chap. 12). The actual world is always, in some measure, a confused world: it is never a total mess (it is always to some degree a *cosmos*, the Greek word for "order"), but it is never a fait accompli, a finished order. This feature of our world is, as our discussion in this chapter reveals, why philosophy is not esoteric but indigenous.

The actual world is for Miller both an artifact and the revelation made possible by artifacts. It both depends on us and is disclosive of what is other than us. This characterization of actuality is at least plausible and, in my judgment, compelling. Neither philosophy nor history can rest here, however, while two profound questions hang in the air: Does not the insistence that the actual world is a made world reduce it to an arbitrary fabrication? Does not this insistence entail the most irresponsible egoism, perhaps even a cosmic megalomania? That Miller is able to avoid the theoretically damaging, perhaps even fatal, implications these questions suggest is, at this stage of our inquiry, highly problematic.

3

The Midworld

The actual, that is, the midworld, carries us down to the present as functioning. It makes any composition historical. It is the immediacy that projects infinity.

My affirmation is the midworld.

—John William Miller,
In Defense of the Psychological

John William Miller, like Theodor Adorno, a contemporary philosopher also engaged in thinking through German idealism, affirmed the actuality of philosophy but affirmed it provisionally (Adorno 1977, 120). The actuality of philosophy today depends on its renewed actualization in altered circumstances. This actuality is, however, provisional, since it is a question of not so much whether philosophy is taken up anew as whether the actualization of philosophy drives toward a confrontation with actuality, the historical actuality of our present situation. Philosophy can regain its actuality but only provided that it confronts the actualities of its time and place.[1] Negatively, this means rejecting the illusion with which "earlier philosophical enterprises began"—the illusion that "the power of thought is sufficient to grasp the totality of the real" (ibid.). Rejecting this illusion entails acknowledging the contemporary inadequacy of philosophical thought to recollect the fragmentation of the actual, that is, our world in its fissures and contradictions, its disconcerting upheavals and constitutional conflicts. For philosophy to render itself more adequate to this task, a revision is required wherein the finite actuality of human experience and the other actualities disclosed through the medium of such experience are fully accredited and fundamentally reconceived. In Chapter 2, I focus on the revision of philosophy; here I look mainly at the reconceptualization of actuality. In order to accredit fully the actualities of both our lives and all that is implicated in these lives, an affirmation of the midworld is required—the acknowledgment of a domain of experience and thus involvement more primordial than any yet conceived. The acknowledgment of the actual in the sense intended here is, at the same time, an acknowledgment of the artifactual. Artifacts in general and, among these, symbols in all of their variety attest to finite actualities of the farthest reaching significance (some of these finite actualities having nothing less than cosmic significance). Thus, Miller's affirmation of this domain is the center of our concern here.[2]

The domain in question is not one of sheer fabrication or groundless fictions, for it discloses a region of objects exerting "a stubborn tenacity" and resisting various attempts at reductionistic interpretation (*PC,* 116). "This stubbornness of the objects of nature and of the perceptions associated with nature derives its force from the union of subject and object embodied in the artifact and its implications" (ibid.). Far from robbing us of nature in its otherness, the midworld is the region in which humans encounter nature in its actuality. If we suppose nature, at most, only suffers the imposition of our technological interventions and symbolic representations, then nature fades into an unknowable order beyond the reach of human knowing. But such a supposition must be rejected. Symbols are rather "objects through which nature secures articulation and the mind its exercise" (ibid.). The same must be said for history: only through symbols does it become intelligible.

Just as Miller's stress on human artifacts can mislead some readers, so too can his emphasis on finite actuality. Artifacts are actualities attesting in their use to the traits and, hence, the character of other actualities, at the most rudimentary level (e.g., axes tell us something about stones). Even simple tools are not mere tools: they are proto-symbols, since they reveal the properties and constitution of things other than themselves.[3] Thus, the emphasis on artifacts should not be read as an endorsement of fictionalism, the view that all of our theories and representations are the imaginative projections of our unconstrained minds. For a person who handles a yardstick or even a hammer, "thought is not unrestrained"; the use of such artifacts imposes a discipline and launches a destiny (JWM, 23:36). This is even truer of the person who has recourse to linguistic, mathematical, or other kinds of symbols.

Especially in reference to such symbols, a crucial feature of functioning objects comes into focus. "The yardstick, the monument, the word, in contrast, are the *functioning symbolism of finitude* and propose both the infinity of nature and of the resources of soul" (*PC*, 116). Finite actualities provide more than intimations of limitless expanses (e.g., a region of space too vast for us to measure, a stretch of time too extensive for us to imagine, a ramification of meanings too subtle, multiple, and tangled for us to trace). Finite actualities acquaint us with formal ideality (or ideal infinity). Just as Miller's stress on artifacts does not rob us of objectivity, his emphasis on finitude does not preclude an acknowledgment of infinity.[4] Miller is emphatic on this point: an ideality is immanent in even the simplest functioning objects (i.e., in the form of functioning made possible by such objects). For example, through our various means of spatial measurement, "nature, in respect of its simultaneous diversity, gets established" (*PC*, 115).[5] But the natural world as a spatial field "occurs as the actual operation of measurement" (*PC*, 115–16), if only the implicit, inexact forms of measurement embodied in our ordinary perceptual experience. This operation can be extended indefinitely. It is, in principle, infinite. In texts pertaining to the midworld, Miller uses space to illustrate the dialectic of finite actuality and infinite ideality. In its infinity, nature as a region of space

> indicates the endless extension of an actual and finite object in its use and function. One cannot ask of a unit of measure whether it has application. It is such a unit precisely in that application and for no other reason. Spatial infinity is the order of finitude. But finitude has no order at all unless some *object*, something here and now, is invested with an ideal meaning. Nor has infinity any order until the artifact or symbol becomes its vehicle and present reality [or, more accurately, actuality]. (*PC*, 116)

Miller's conception of actuality is designed to undercut not only the dualism of appearance and reality, the finite and the infinite, the actual and the ideal, but also that of subjectivity and objectivity. "Naturalism finds no *subject* among the objects" of nature (*PC*, 120).

But historicism does. It finds subjects fatefully entangled with objects and, indeed, one another only by means of the tools, artifacts, and symbols in which mind comes to be actually embodied. That is, it finds subjectivity in the midworld, though this discovery is made possible only because subjectivity is always already an actuality, an incorporate agent implicated in an order not of its own making. But human subjects discover an objective order ("an order not of their own making") only through their artifacts—that is, the processes and products of their making.

The midworld is nothing other than the actual world viewed from a distinctive perspective, or turned to reveal several of its most basic aspects (see, e.g., *MS*, 43). The actual world is, to repeat, the world insofar as it is defined in terms of action. The actions responsible for this world can themselves be defined only in terms of action and its conditions.

Thus, history is ideally suited to explain these actions, whereas virtually all other traditional disciplines or discourses (in particular, theology, physics, and psychology) are systematically blind to agents and their acts. These other disciplines go beyond finite, autonomous agents and posit unconditioned, ahistoric factors—an immutable deity, invariant laws, or structural necessities—in order to explain the presence and careers of such agents, while history rigorously limits itself to explaining agency in terms of action, that is, the dramatic engagement of human actors with one another. As Goethe remarks, in the beginning was the deed. And from the deed, other deeds flow. Behind deeds and doers there are only antecedent deeds and doers. These antecedents of our actions, "mother history" (cf. *PH*, 33), provide us with the only authentic means of illuminating human agency as such. The attempts to throw light on our agency by recourse to our Heavenly Father, Mother Nature, or the subterranean forces of the human psyche end up only shrouding this agency in mystery or, worse, effectively effacing the capacity for self-determination. In all three cases, the very order invoked to secure a status for the individual as such has precluded the possibility of presence, of individuals appearing in their acts and utterances. The orders of divine creation, natural mechanisms, and psychological economy are, in principle, incapable of recognizing the individual as such.

"The acknowledgment of the actual is also the recognition of the individual" (*DP*, 160). That is, only by granting primacy to the actual world are we in the position to recognize individuality in its most authentic form.

Granting primacy to the actual world involves elevating human action to the absolute status traditionally claimed for the God of Abraham, Isaac, and Jacob, or for the Nature of Galileo, Newton, and Einstein, or for the psyche of James, Freud, and Skinner. Accordingly, we must turn to history, to the story of our acts, of their conditions and consequences. We must reconcile ourselves to the conditions of our own endeavors (*PH*, 149). Such reconciliation requires undertaking "the quest for the energies which found expression in [, for example,] Chartres or the Magna Carta" (*PC*, 128). For only in such a quest do we "exhibit and discover our energies and thereby ourselves" (ibid.). Hence, human agents become intelligible to themselves by reflecting primarily upon their human ancestors, rather than a personal deity or an impersonal nature or the subpersonal components of their own psyches (e.g., id, ego, and superego). Of course, to the extent that their ancestors appealed to a personal deity, and so on, reflection must include a consideration of the historical influence of ahistoric ideals (see, e.g., *PH*, xxvii, 186).

In addition, the actions responsible for our world cannot be reduced either to realities existing independently of action or to appearances given separately from our exertions. They are neither absolutely pristine facts nor passively received data. They are actualities: they are sustained and fated to undergo revision by the very world they themselves project. "Energies flow from one's world, as any world projects the active self" (*ME*, 90). While I have stressed that such a self projects a world, it is crucial also to see that the world so projected provides a sustaining medium for the active self in any and all of its self-defining activities.

The Actions by Which Our World Is Defined

Because the midworld is the actual world, and also because the actual world is the fateful order defined through human action, it would be helpful to clarify Miller's conception of action. For the purposes of this section, four features of and two conditions underlying action are especially worthy of consideration. While Miller's notion of action is similar to what one might encounter in the writings of Martin Heidegger, Jean-Paul Sartre, Maurice Merleau-Ponty, or even Gabriel Marcel, Miller himself tended to stress the differences. In particular, he sensed in the writings of the existentialists (especially Kierkegaard and perhaps also the early Sartre) morbidity and a withdrawal of the self from entanglements with others (see, e.g., *PC*, 155). Miller insisted that "while loneliness is not to be avoided, it becomes destructive of selfhood when it fails to join those others whose solitude has fitted them for society" (*ME*, 7). Solitude, that is, the ability and willingness of the self to withdraw within itself (see, e.g., Ortega 1957, chap. 1), is a condition for solidarity, not a substitute for it. The only community worth joining is a community of individuals. But only individuals willing to accept the entangling alliances of their historical situations—only individuals who are locally engaged in their everyday world rather than morbidly withdrawn into an inner sanctum—are worthy of our highest celebration and praise. Despite his own efforts to distance himself from the "existentialists," Miller was perhaps far closer to, say, the later Sartre than he realized. Nonetheless, Miller's conception of action deserves examination in its own right.

From Miller's perspective, one important feature of human action is continuity: "The continuum of action is the same as the action" (*MS*, 102; cf. *PC*, 125). Any identifiable action is a distinguishable but inseparable moment in an ongoing series of other such moments. It emerges from a matrix of prior commitments (*PH*, 33); it regenerates itself by trying to produce fruitful novelties, that is, novelties themselves capable of contributing to yet further novelties (*PC*, 159). This matrix is "mother history" (cf. *PC*, 88); these novelties are the progeny of our deeds.

The second feature is the unenvironed character of human action: "The act *declares* the environment and articulates it. The act [itself] is *unenvironed*. Functioning [or action] does not appear where something called 'environment' has been *assumed*" (*MS*, 14). Another way of making this point is to say that any environment in which we act is not simply given prior to and independent of our actions and the actions of our predecessors. Indeed, any environment in which we are entitled to or even capable of acting is one we have a hand in constructing and a voice in articulating, if only by our inheritance, that is, by our appropriation of a bequest (for example, our ability to speak this language or our commitment to the ideals embodied in these institutions). But a cultural inheritance can never be passively claimed; it must be actively appropriated. Think here of how we have won possession of our native tongue. Any single act of mine or any other agent is obviously not solely responsible for declaring the environment. But any single act is not absolutely discrete: it is, to repeat, part of a continuum. In addition, the environment one meets can be met only "in the powers with which one is already in league" (*MS,* 86; cf. *PC,* 182). Hence, when Miller asserts that the "act is *unenvironed,*" he does not mean that it is self-contained. As part of a continuum, any act is essentially related to both antecedent and subsequent acts. As an invocation of an antagonist (the third feature to be noted below), the act is also essentially related to what transcends itself, to what can challenge its authority and even frustrate its momentum.

To say that the act is unenvironed is simply to insist that the only appropriate "environment" in which to situate human actions is human history, the ongoing career of the various forms of human functioning. What is prior to and independent of any act, when the irreducible status and autonomous authority of the act are recognized, can only be prior acts. These acts do not constitute a fixed, external framework; they are themselves historical and also constitutive of our agency. Hence, though Miller frequently uses the term "environment" in reference to his own position, he does so somewhat hesitantly and always qualifiedly (see, e.g., *MS,* 85–86). The most important qualification he insists on is that the environment is not external to the powers of the agents it encompasses: the environment does not confront agents as a fixed and alien arena to which they must adjust (see, e.g., *DP,* 112). Although we are alone in the world (*PC,* 93; cf. 168), the world is not alien to our being (*DT,* 155). For it is a projection of our action (see, e.g., *MS,* 86–87). This world or environment is, in several respects, finite (it is constitutionally incomplete and also is the domain in which the most fundamental boundaries, the most basic differences, are drawn) and infinite (ideally unlimited and also self-conditioning) (*MS,* 87). As infinite no less than as finite, it is akin to our agency.

The insistence on this kinship is no fantastic, much less an infantile, flight from the imperative demands of our actual circumstances. On one hand, Miller insists: "To be human is to be playful. To be human is, thus, to live in a world of one's own creation, for one's own sake" (*DP,* 132). This is the heart of Miller's humanism and, accordingly, is fully explored in the following chapter. What needs to be stressed here is that the world in which we live is a world of our own making and the purpose of our composition is immanent—it is for our sake and the sake of this composition itself. On the other hand, this vision of our world "leads to depravity when the self-contained playfulness yields only fantasy" (ibid.). Perhaps it is better to replace "self-contained" with "self-defined"; for the most basic point can then be more forcefully made. Our self-defined playfulness degenerates into fantasy when this playfulness becomes self-contained rather than other-directed. "The worlds of fantasy are always invoked to give reality to the self when nature and circumstances seem to deny that reality" (ibid.). But such reality is precisely what fantasy is unable to yield, for "it is lawless and aimless." It refuses to set any limits to the exercise of the will. But because willing is accepting the responsibility of self-definition (*PH*, 29), fantasy is will-less. It is not an exercise of, but rather an assault on, the will. Hence, "[a]ction, denied by nature and by circumstance, is not secured in fantasy. Fantasy dissipates the reality of self [and destroys the conditions for agency] because it offers no control over a recalcitrant medium" (*DP*, 132). Only by the passionate immersion in some recalcitrant medium is our agency or our environment (presence or totality) secured. "The mission of all passionate pursuits is to escape from privacy and to establish objective and public reality" (*PC*, 154), that is, to transcend fantasy by confronting what resists and challenges and possibly even frustrates our pursuits.

Thus, the third characteristic is the entanglement of agents through their actions with an antagonist. The claims of action as constitutional or categoreal cannot not be satisfied unless action generates its own antagonist, an other with whom the authors of action are essentially allied but also by whom they are essentially contested (see, e.g., *MS*, 45). "Every essay at control [in a word, every action] invokes a nemesis. When we shrink from these involvements and hazards, as well we may, we can spare ourselves disappointments only at the price of an annihilative inaction" (*PH*, 81). For example, nature can and, indeed, should be seen as such an antagonist. Nature, as revealed by scientific inquiry and even less sophisticated investigations, is not an absolute despot to which human inquirers must blindly submit; she (the personification here being less misleading than its denial) is an allied antagonist with whom we rationally quarrel, wresting from this taciturn nemesis in the course of our rational disputes significant admissions about her secret strategies. "If nature is not *our* world, evolved from inquiry, it is another dogma" (*MS*, 177; emphasis added) or, worse, a despot far more tyrannical than the most capricious god conceived by the human mind.

Human action calls forth an allied antagonist. One way of conceiving this other or nemesis is as the environment declared and articulated by the self (*MS*, 14). About the environment, Miller notes: "The self [or source of action] does not assert itself, know itself, or maintain itself apart from it" (*DP*, 21). What is crucial to bear in mind here is that "[o]ne does not 'adjust' to environment as if it were come upon—external, a finding, an accident, the occasion of a specific and terminating response. The environment ([in the] singular) is met in the powers with which one is already in league—in having spoken, or read a book by someone else who lived long ago" (*MS*, 86). In this sense, the environment is not only "our rude antagonist"; it is also our indispensable ally (*PC*, 187).

The fourth feature is the status of action as utterance. All action gives voice to an order upon which action depends for its possibility no less than its revision. Because action is utterance, the actual world is an articulated world. It is, in other words, a world in which utterance or discourse is inherent or constitutional. On this view, the "person, the utterance, and the world become inseparable" (*MS*, 70). It is also a world in which "myth" and "revelation" cannot be eradicated without undermining morale and assaulting intelligibility. For myths have always been and must continue to be the great springs of action (*PH*, 159); and all utterances have the quality of revelation (*MS*, 153), of disclosing what otherwise would be hidden or invisible. These implications of conceiving action as utterance clearly suggest why the actual world is identifiable with the midworld. These implications are discussed more fully below; here it is sufficient to note that equating action with utterance implies the need for a reconceptualization of "myth" and "revelation," one divesting these terms of their association with the ahistoric.

In sum, any action is part and parcel of a continuum, a series of actions declarative of an environment, allied to an antagonist, and expressive of some order. On one hand, "[a]ny continuum appears as the momentum of an immediacy" (*MS*, 119), that is, of some immediate engagement in some distinctive form of human functioning. On the other, any identifiable action—any specifiable phase in such an engagement—must appeal to the authority of prior commitments and accept the rebukes as well as the rewards of unforeseen consequences.

At this point in our exposition, the two most important conditions underlying actions are artifacts and the formal orders made possible above all by functioning objects, those human artifacts on which every distinctive form of human functioning depends. These conditions are inseparable and, in a sense, perhaps even identical. Some objects do not throw themselves in the way of our exertions (e.g., the objects in my field of vision), but rather are themselves the resources on which some form of functioning (my eyes) relies.

Let me develop this illustration in further detail. My eyes are ordinarily perceiving objects other than themselves and only rarely are they perceived by themselves. Seeing is a form of functioning undeniably dependent on organs of sight. The visible world is a formal order dependent on a unique type of functioning object. It is a formal order because it depends on certain more or less formal procedures on the part of the agent (e.g., blinking) and also because it itself exhibits certain more or less formal properties (e.g., the omnipresent pattern of figure and ground). The visible world is, however, far less evidently a formal order than the quantifiable world, in part, because the formal procedures requisite for visual perception are more deeply embedded in our organic habits than are the procedures necessary for quantification, at least in any complex and sophisticated way. In the perception of depth, virtually all of us manifest an expertise in trigonometry; but when we turn from our tacit ability to triangulate the distance of bodies from one another and from ourselves to the formal calculations of trigonometry, the number of experts dramatically dwindles.

Seen and, more generally, perceived objects are foci of attention; in contrast, functioning objects are loci of control.: "Local control appears in the functioning object" (*MS*, 109; cf. McGandy 1998, 238–54). The former are that to which we attend, whereas the latter are that by which we are empowered to attend objects other than themselves. Perceived objects are more purely objects, beings that willy-nilly throw themselves in our way and insistently demand recognition. Functioning objects are either our bodies insofar as they have been disciplined to execute some form of functioning (e.g., perceiving or speaking) or extensions of our bodies. While "the basic functioning object is the body" (*MS*, 43), the discipline necessary for the transformation of the human organism into a functioning object depends on functioning objects other than the body itself (see McGandy 1998, 246–50). But nonetheless, however, functioning objects in their actual functioning are ordinarily felt to be constitutive of, not other than, the human agent who has mastered their use. If the hammer is felt to be an extension of my hand, how much more so is language felt to be an extension of my innermost self. "To be a self is to communicate" (*DP*, 170) through language and artifacts.

The embodied and communicative character of human agency is, to some extent, even evident in a simple tool such as a hammer, thought strictly speaking such a tool is not a functioning object. Hence, this character is more manifest in functioning objects, ranging from the simplest ones (e.g., yardsticks and clocks) to the most complex ones (natural languages and national literatures, mathematical physics and impressionistic painting). The hand as a unit of measurement is distinct from the hand as a means of grasping, pulling, or pounding. As a unit of measurement, the hand is a functioning object, the formal function of which is, in principle, dissociable from the human body. We can more accurately measure with rulers or yardsticks than with hands or feet. The function of measurement is served by becoming embodied in an artifact other than the body itself. As a part of the living, skillful body of a human agent, it is a means of counting, measuring, gesturing (thus communicating), and other disclosive activities.

The body and its organs are, consequently, the "original symbol" or originary symbolization in which all other modes of symbolization are rooted.[6] So, too, is the body of the originary tool. As a tool or instrument, the body is a functional object; but, as a mode of symbolization making other such modes possible, it is a functioning object. If we start with verbs, in particular, with present active participles such as hammering, sawing, and sewing, as well as counting, measuring, and portraying, then we are in the presence of functioning immediacies. Among some of these immediacies, we discern functions in which universality is, for the most part, implicit and limited, such as with hammers, saws, and needles. Learning how to use a tool skillfully entails learning how particular things are actually related to one another. Such learning is the result of mastering how particular acts are related to particular objects, when animated by definable or determinate purposes. Indeed, a tool of any sort is the medium of the relationship between particular acts and particular objects: "Any reality not a brain storm passes through a medium. Short of a tool any purpose lacks specificity" (*MS*, 138).

But, in the case of other functioning immediacies, the universality is neither implicit nor limited. In contrast to functional objects, functioning objects are manifestly formal modes of utterance and disclosure. "The distinction of tool [or functional object] from functioning object is *made*. It is made in utterance and nowhere else" (*MS*, 140). Indeed, it "developed" and hence is historical. Today we suppose that there was, at a dramatic moment in this historical development, a transition from bodily gesture or vocalized sound serving as an indexical sign (e.g., a shriek signaling the presence or proximity of a predator) to such a gesture or sound serving an evocative function (calling to mind the hunt of the previous day or the hope of a fruitful union).

As a name for the primordial region of finite actualities, the expression "midworld *of symbols*" is not altogether satisfactory. One reason is that symbols are not the only artifacts constitutive of this region.[7] Another is that symbols are ordinarily used in conjunction with other artifacts, so that their power to attest to actualities other than themselves is bound up with these other artifacts. Our minds are, as Suzanne Langer (1957, 51) notes, symbolific. But our capacity to craft symbols is of a piece with our ability to fashion other artifacts. So, rather than isolating symbols from other artifacts, it is better to think conjunctively. In my judgment, then, it is better to designate the primordial region of finite actualities simply as a midworld than as the midworld of symbols. This briefer designation conveys more accurately the scope and character of the field with which we are dealing.

To repeat, all action depends on artifacts (only some of which are functioning objects in the strict sense). Apart from artifacts, nothing worthy of the name of action is possible. But, then, apart from the forms of action made possible by the disciplined body, the sundial, the yardstick, and other such affairs, no order is possible (see, e.g., *MS*, 101). Conversely, apart from a commitment to the formalities requisite for telling time or measuring space or even using one's organs as organs (i.e., as instruments or tools), no locus of control—in a word, no agent—is possible. "A world without action is a world without form" (*MS*, 45). In other words, a world without action is no world at all, a chaos rather than a cosmos. But a world inclusive of action can only be a world defined through action. Negatively, this means that it is erroneous to suppose that action could be found among either the data of consciousness (what is inexplicably given to the mind in its alleged status as a passive spectator) or realities completely severed from our deeds and projects. Action is encountered by agents in the exercise of their agency, or it is not encountered anywhere in any fashion. It is neither a phenomenon nor a reality; it is an actuality. Positively, the claim that the world is defined in terms of action means, in part, that this world is one inclusive of agents, of personal loci of local control. But agency itself is possible only because individuals ally themselves with the formalities or procedures that tell the difference, for example, between noon and midnight or that between three and two feet.

The recognition of agency so conceived should not be confused with a justification of vagrancy. Granting agents responsibility for their world does not mean granting individuals license to say or do anything they happen to desire at some moment. For agency by definition involves an alliance with universals, with the incorporate forms of human functioning. Apart from such an alliance, control is impossible; and apart from control, agency is absent. The agent is, hence, no one less than "the person who has made an alliance with the imperative and actual foreground, accepting its discipline and giving expression to its implications" (*PC*, 181).

In its dependency on artifacts, human action reveals itself to be essentially artifactual; in giving voice to such an order, human action reveals its status as utterance, as an essay in articulation. When these facets of action are highlighted, the actual world—the world defined in terms of action— merits a designation that helps brings these facets into focus. For this purpose, Miller proposes the term "midworld," though it was a term with which he was never completely satisfied. One of the ways he defines it is as "the region of artifacts" (*PC*, 106). Another is as "utterance in all its many modes, the locus and embodiment of control and all constitutional distinctions and conflicts" (*MS*, 7). The region of artifacts, the actual world in its artifactual character, has been unduly neglected. As a consequence, the status and authority of the various modes of human utterance—especially, the "utterances" of artists, historians, and philosophers—have been, at best, insecure and, at worst, denied, for example, in being disqualified by positivists as "meaningless."

Thus, Miller suggests: "We need a new epistemology, one that does not shrink from giving ontological status to artifacts. The past rides on them, and they are symbols and voices" (AW, 261–62). He further suggests: "The discrimination of [the] modes of utterance and their relation is the philosophical task: What is the structure required by any distinctive utterance, a number, a poem?" (*DP,* 158). What is the status and authority we must grant to the irreducibly distinct forms of human discourse, if we are to maintain our own critical capacities to tell the differences we ourselves take as definitive of ourselves and our world? Before turning to either Miller's formulation of this "new epistemology" or his discrimination and validation of the modes of utterance, however, we need to discuss the actual world as actual. Our discussion of the actual world as articulated (in other words, the midworld) needs to wait for a discussion of one more aspect of the actual world as actual. This is, in truth, only a continuation of our efforts to clarify Miller's conception of actuality. For the actuality of our world and the primacy of the actual are fully intelligible only in reference to Miller's refusal to grant primacy to either the phenomenal world or the real world. In turn, his formulation of a new epistemology and his execution of the philosophical task of the validation and discrimination of the irreducible forms of human utterance are themselves best appreciated in the light of this refusal.

The Real, the Apparent, and the Actual

The actual world is, as we have seen, the world insofar as it is established, maintained, and revised by our actions. Granting primacy to this world, as Miller does, discounts neither the real world nor the apparent world. However, if we grant primacy to either the phenomenal world or the real world—the world as it appears to a disengaged consciousness or the world as it exists apart from human action, respectively—not only do we lose the name of action; we also lose any basis for the distinction between appearance and reality. Thus, in granting primacy to actuality, Miller strives to capture the insight of the phenomenologist no less than that of the realist.

For he strives to respect the motives underlying both the phenomenologist's painstaking attention to the way things appear and the realist's efforts to secure the basis for the distinction between appearance and reality. Since neither realists nor phenomenologists can achieve their objectives on their own premises, and since the objectives of both are valid and important, it is necessary to go beyond realism to secure for reality the status and authority realism desires to grant to it; so too it is necessary to go beyond phenomenology to secure for phenomena the status and authority phenomenology desires to grant to them. Appearances as such are not to be discounted; nor is reality as that which is always possibly other than appearance. Appearances are revelatory of reality and, nonetheless, reality is irreducible to appearances, even the totality of appearances.

On the premises of phenomenology, what is other than appearance is ultimately lost and, with this loss, the significance of the term "appearance" is effectively destroyed. Insofar as consciousness is transformed from a disembodied spectator into an embodied agent, a transformation involving a shift from viewing the world as pure spectacle to a *Lebenswelt*, a significant step has been taken in the direction of recognizing actuality. On the premises of realism, reality is, by definition, that which is forever out of our reach. Whatever bears the fingerprints of our hands or the echoes of our voices is, thereby, discounted as "unreal" by the realist. But this insistence as effectively denies efficacy to the real as the insistence of the phenomenologist on the self-sufficiency of phenomena empties the terms "appearance" or "phenomenon" of their meaning. For how could reality, so defined, make a difference? And apart from the efficacy or power to make a difference, does "anything" deserve the name "reality" (see, e.g., *PH*, 98)? On one hand, "[m]any have tried in vain to distill reality out of appearance. The philosopher's stone is supposed to transmute base metal into gold" (*MS*, 88). On the other hand, many have endeavored—equally in vain—to define reality as absolutely other than what is cognitively immediate or experientially encountered. But what is so thoroughly other is also thoroughly unknowable and, thus, of no value to inquirers.

The distinction between appearance and reality can be maintained on the basis of neither what appears to consciousness nor what falls outside consciousness. Where can one stand in order to draw this distinction (cf. *MS*, 186)? It would be difficult to exaggerate the importance of this question. One reason is that "knowledge is not the search for the real, but the maintenance of the distinction between appearance and reality" (*MS,* 162). Thus, if the basis of this distinction is uncertain, the nature of knowledge itself is unclear. At this point in our inquiry, it should not come as a surprise that Miller's answer is: "The actual is the watershed that permits the distinction of appearance and reality and generates both" (*MS,* 89). But the actual world in Miller's sense is not an impersonal order. It is, quite the contrary, the world insofar as agents are responsible for themselves and their world. Without persons, there is no environment, that is, no world, for the environment or world is, as we saw above, "the organization of their acts and utterances" (*MS,* 88). The immediate environment is the foreground of an infinite domain. This domain is infinite in at least a twofold sense, for it is in principle unbounded (or interminable) and it transcends finitude also by virtue of being inherently open to having not only its boundaries redrawn but also the means of demarcating its regions continuously (or regularly) revised.

This domain is, despite its infinity, constitutionally incomplete and, despite its incompleteness, totally inclusive. But, since "there is no escaping an account of the sort of world that can include the utterances, the affirmations, and denials that permit any world to be intelligible" (*MS,* 129), this domain needs to be conceived as inclusive of utterances and utterers. Alternatively put, the actual world is not a silent world but the spoken world. There can be no such world, however, apart from speakers, apart from persons who in their utterances provide the resources for defining our world. "In the end, authority is in the person who *reveals* an environment [or projects a totality]. Few do. But where there is grace and genuineness, one is under arrest [i.e., one is arrested by the commanding presence of such persons]. Persons stir no emotion except as they are revelations, and this is the immediacy of the actual, of functioning, and of its manifestations" (*MS,* 89). If we are truly gracious and genuine, we can only be stirred and, indeed, arrested by the vision of the cosmos articulated and defended by, say, Newton or Einstein.

To develop this alternate epistemology, we must clarify the term "immediacy" and its cognates. The "immediate" to which Miller appeals is to be contrasted with "the impersonal, anonymous, inexorable, predicable, uniform, universal" (*DP,* 3). It is the locus of the personal (ibid.). Most often, Miller means by "immediacy" an immediate or direct engagement in some mediated or symbolic activity (*DP,* 84).[8] Only persons are capable of such engagements; only by virtue of such engagements are persons capable of forging an identity or declaring their presence. For instance, in measuring the base of a wall, one in the act of measuring is immediately engaged in a mediated activity, for the yardstick or some instrument of measurement (be it only one's own feet) mediate between the measuring hand and the measured space.

In addition to becoming clear about "immediacy" in general, it is helpful to note that, for Miller, there are at least two forms of immediacy, cognitive and functioning (see, e.g., *MS,* 85). The former he considers spurious, the latter legitimate.[9] In one context, Miller notes that the empiricists "have rejected a cognitive immediacy and properly so; but they have been blind to a functioning immediacy, to an actuality, which requires and absorbs data on functioning terms" (ibid.). Although he does not unpack the meaning of this claim, it seems safe to suggest that empiricists, precisely in their insistence on the appeal to experience, require that any claim to know reality immediately is fraudulent. Our knowledge of anything whatsoever is mediated by our experience. Apart from such mediation, knowledge is unattainable. But, having rejected cognitive immediacy in favor of experiential mediation, "empiricists" have elevated passively received data to the most epistemically authoritative position. These data are both alleged to provide an unshakable foundation for human knowledge and supposed to possess their authority by virtue of their coerciveness over consciousness. But, as Miller so astutely observes, such data are not any part of our actual experience; they are rather the fabrications of so-called empiricist philosophers. Nor do we, as knowers, require such a foundation for our claims to know.

"The experience that I am bidden to consult sends me back to simplicities and to immediacies" (*MS,* 55), though not absolute simplicities or cognitive immediacies. Are these simplicities and immediacies, in any case, discrete or disorganized data, simply thrust upon our consciousness with no connection to our purposes or projects? Not if they are the result of looking, listening, or functioning in some other manner (ibid.). But, apart from some form of functioning, there are no data.

Apart from immediate involvement in some actual function (e.g., perceiving, measuring, hammering), empiricism lapses into a form of vagrancy (ibid.). Stated positively, only by virtue of its alliance to a formal order, to a criticizable and thus controllable procedure for discriminating objects or qualities, can empiricism secure the conditions by which the appeal to experience avoids being a blind acceptance of "miraculous data" (*MS,* 120). Such data have become, in effect, the secular equivalent of religious revelation (JWM, 25:9): they are to be accepted even though they do violence to our reason. Their authority derives not from their contribution to rendering our world intelligible but from their brute compulsion or coercive force. However, such completely brute data or facts, in truth, command no assent and possess no authority. For data and facts derive their prestige and authority from the discourse or practice that accredits them (*DP,* 181). It "is only as a consequence of a problem that the very region of fact can be defined. Fact, or thing, or object is not an original datum or idea" (*DT,* 184). And the definition of any problem presupposes some form of discourse, some mode of utterance. Hence, facts or objects are derived from discourse. To be sure, the "facts do not reflect our wishes; [but] they do reflect our acts" (*PH,* 26) and the discourses and practices to which these acts attest.

"The environment is the extension of an articulate and controlled immediacy never fully conscious of itself and of the modes of its maintenance" (*MS,* 86). The only meaningful appeal to experience is, in essence, one made by agents always already engaged in such articulate and controlled immediacies as speaking, counting, measuring, and other forms of analogous activity. In Miller's own words, "I cannot be sent to the facts [I cannot be confronted by any data] unless I have *never left* the scene of action with all its furniture and functioning" (*MS,* 55).

There are no facts without acts, no data without some form of functioning. But action is no self-enclosed event; it is a world-declarative utterance. While the actual world is an articulate world, an order in which utterance and thus utterers have a constitutional or categoreal status, the real world is an essentially silent world (see, e.g., JWM, 25:22). In a silent world, in an order conceived in such a way that speakers as speakers (as agents in potential control of their own fateful utterances) are nullified, presence is lost and, along with it, totality (*MS,* 16). The apparent world is a private world.[10] Here totality is lost and, along with it, presence.

As a means of establishing a basis for presence and totality, Miller proposes that our world is essentially actual. By virtue of the forms of action (of the present active participles), appearances can effectively be interpreted as revelations of reality and, in addition, realities can effectively be distinguished from phenomena. The way the dimensions of the wall manifest themselves to the eyes and hands of one who wields a yardstick can, for instance, be taken as revelations of what those dimensions really are. Although the stick immersed in water appears to me to be bent, there are ways of acting that allow me to distinguish this optical illusion from the stick's real shape. To grant appearances their function as revelations of reality or to grant reality its status as something other than phenomena, there is no need either to try distilling reality from some set of appearances or to posit a reality beyond the possibility of appearance. Indeed, there is every reason to resist these temptations. As agents, we are driven by impasses in the continuum of our own activity to consider, "What really exists?" or "What really happened?" So, too, it is precisely in our capacity as agents and, more specifically, as a result of a frustration to ourselves as agents that we learn the importance of considering whether what is manifest can reliably be taken as a sign of what is hidden.

As we have had occasion to note previously, history is full of ironies. For example, theists who have worshipped a tyrant, a "God" who commands devotion through threats and punishments, have disfigured the face of the divine; they have thereby rendered implausible and contemptible precisely what they sought to make most authoritative and holy (Whitehead [1925] 1967, chap. 11). In so doing, they have failed essentially; for herein we see the defeat of theists by their own hands; for precisely the ones who would speak of their God in such a way as to manifest the authority and blessedness of that God are responsible for depicting an unlawful and unlovable being. Something analogous can be seen in both the phenomenologist and the realist. The phenomenologist loses the name of phenomenon no less than the realist loses the name of reality—for both have lost the name of action. If one regains that name, if one grants categoreal status to the actual world, then it is easy to show either how appearances can function as revelations of what is not apparent or how realities can possess a status quite different from the way they manifest themselves to us in this or that context. However, if one loses the name of action, one also loses phenomena and realities in any authentic or even minimally meaningful sense; for one thereby loses any possibility of showing how phenomena could be revelatory of reality or how reality could be other than its manifestations.

"In a rejection one needs to provide for the occurrence of the belief that one rejects. Otherwise one could allow no force to a rejection. What is rejected must be a miscarriage of a *valid* procedure [or a legitimate concern]" (*MS,* 177). The relevance of this principle of criticism to our discussion should be clear. Neither phenomenology nor realism is simply to be dismissed. Their occurrence and, indeed, persuasiveness needs to be explained. They need to be seen for what they are—persuasive yet self-defeating attempts to satisfy a legitimate claim. Hence, it is especially important for Miller to show how both "reality" and "appearance" are effectively distinguished and thereby meaningfully defined only in reference to actuality. The legitimate but contrasting concerns of the phenomenologist and the realist are fulfilled only on the condition that one grants primacy to actuality.

The actual world is neither the apparent world nor the real world as these terms have traditionally been understood or defined. But it is what alone allows us to tell the difference between the apparent and the real. The actual world is the articulated world, in a word, the midworld. It is now time to consider the question: What are the most important traits of the actual world insofar as it is an articulated world, insofar as it is the midworld?

The Midworld: The Totality of Our Discourses and Their Revelations

The midworld is the actual world viewed in the light of at least three essential connections. These are the connection between act and artifact, between artifact and articulation, and between articulation and revelation ("Out of the silence a voice, out of the darkness a light"). The actual world is a world of our own making; and every effort at composition bespeaks the presence of an artist or, as it was, the composer. But every composition also reveals what is other than the composer. What is other than me may, nevertheless, be akin to me; but my kinship with any ancestors establishes my identity with them only in a qualified sense, a sense presupposing my difference from them.

This important point concerns how the individual as such stands to the universe. Miller's conception of the individual with respect to the universe took form partially in reaction to Josiah Royce's idealism, and Royce's own position took form partly in reaction to William James's pragmatism. In both James and Royce, moreover, we encounter rival ways of dealing with the competing claims of being with and being against. Accordingly, it would be profitable to examine the context in which Miller's position is rooted.

Philosophical idealism in the United States, the tradition in which Miller was reared and to which he allied himself for most, if not all, of his life, was deeply colored by James's lifelong opposition to what he called "the block universe" of absolute idealism. At Harvard, James engaged his colleague and friend Josiah Royce in the battle of the Absolute (Perry 1935, chap. 50). Although Royce persisted in his defense of idealism, the form of this idealism came to resemble the opposition in some significant ways. In particular, Royce took the emphatically empiricist and voluntarist elements of James's outlook seriously. Indeed, Royce more fully saw the need for idealism to take seriously finite experience and individual will than James saw the need for pragmatism to consider carefully anything more than contingent, provisional needs or a finite, pluralistic universe. While James convinced Royce of the need to attend to the individual as such, Royce does not appear to have been successful in persuading James of the need to depict our world as a *uni*verse. For Royce no less than for James, truth can be defined in terms of the satisfaction of a need; but for the former, truth is the satisfaction of an absolute and unconditional need, whereas for the latter the postulation of such needs is always provisional, perhaps even suspect. James's pluralistic pragmatism "is not fond of anything that appears too absolute" (Royce 1908, 247), while Royce's "absolute pragmatism" (Royce [1913] 1968, 2:123) is unsatisfied with any view that does not respect the absolute need for a genuine *uni*verse. Because of James's imperative desire to do justice to finitude, he rejected, in effect, the absolute (or constitutional) need for unity; because of Royce's imperative desire to do justice to the ideal unity underlying any finite undertaking, he posited "a city out of sight," a superhuman and eternal unity of the world-life (Royce 1908, 246).

One way to view Miller's project is this: he (unlike James) accepts Royce's constitutional need for unity but denies that this acceptance compels us to posit "a city out of sight," an eternal and comprehensive order of which any finite act, agent, or enterprise is a partial and incomplete manifestation. While this order is largely invisible to finite agents, it is ultimately authoritative: it, and it alone, provides the basis for not only coherence or unity but also values and ideals. For Miller, the need for unity can be satisfied without any recourse to eternity. While the imaginative transcendence of any actual moment is an omnipresent possibility, the transcendence of temporality as such is impossible. The acceptance of finite actuality does not involve an imprisonment in a particular time; it does, however, demand recognition of our historical situatedness. This situatedness is the pad from which we launch all of our endeavors, the source of the resources empowering us to draw the distinctions essential to our form of consciousness, including that between "now" and "then." The capacity to maintain this distinction guarantees the possibility of transcending, in some fashion and to some degree, any "now" in which we happen to be situated. The more refined and penetrating is our ability to tell the difference between "now" and "then," the less the present is a confinement and the more it is a resource for transcending itself. We must turn our gaze from the city out of sight to our habitation in the here and now, but we must do so without abandoning the need to see this habitation as the foreground of a universe. This universe is nothing more or less than what gives status and authority to this foreground (AW, 241). Any local habitation is propelled by an inherent dynamic beyond itself (for example, the citizens of Athens appeal to the gods on Olympus). Any such habitation is propelled by the inherent energies to envision itself in some totality. But, for Miller, this envisioned totality is not an eternal city. It is a projection of the foreground, of this time and place.

Another way to view Miller's project is in reference to one of James's characterizations of materialism and idealism. James suggests that the difference between materialism and idealism, as doctrines about our relationship to the cosmos, is at bottom a conflict between rival intellectual temperaments. For the idealistic temper, it is unacceptable to depict the nature of things as radically alien to our own being (James [1897] 1958, 89). The universe is our home and everything encountered in this dwelling is, to some degree and in some fashion, our kin. For the materialistic temper, reality is absolutely indifferent to our presence and projects. Our "desire for communion" with whatever confronts us and even combats us should not be allowed to blunt our recognition of "the rough, harsh, sea-wave, north-wind element, the denier of persons, the democratizer" or leveler (ibid.). For the former, intelligibility and the possibility of atonement lies in the heart of things; accordingly, it is always possible for us to act with what is other than us. Indeed, all action is, when properly understood, acting with others—in a word, co-operation. For the latter, the ultimately irreducible opacity of absolutely brute facts is the final word. Such facts hold forth no possibility of kinship or intimacy; they demand resistance or opposition. From this perspective, our relation to the universe should be one of opposition, of standing against a vast and impersonal power destined to overwhelm us in the twinkling of an eye. But there is nobility in this absolute refusal to depict this absolute indifference in ways more comforting but less honest. Such nobility is clearly evident, for example, in Albert Camus's *The Myth of Sisyphus*.

James goes on to suggest that, for the idealistic temper, there "is no radically alien corner, but an all-pervading *intimacy*. Now, in certain sensitively egoistic minds this conception of reality is sure to put on a narrow, close, sick-room air" (ibid.). When confronted with such a view of reality, "every strong man of common-sense" will feel that intimacy with the nature of things has been purchased at too high a price, the denial of that "rough, harsh, sea-wave, north-wind element" mentioned above. But it is illuminating to pay careful attention to the precise way James makes this point: the materialistic temper feels this element is "there," is undeniable, "because it calls forth powers" that persons of this temper confidently feel they possess (ibid., 89–90). Does not this feeling bear witness to a kind of intimacy or kinship? Is there not here a kinship with the other as other, the other as something irreducible to either our momentary desires or even our ongoing projects?

Near the conclusion of his dissertation, Miller contends that his "analysis of the thing paves the way to a theory of value" (*DT,* 155). The reason is: "It makes man at home in the world, makes it his world" (ibid.). But this home exudes no narrow, close, sick-room air, because it is a wide-open and open-air expanse so vast that individuals are dwarfed but so constituted that they are not nullified (*MS,* 16). Evolution is a radical revision of the Western outlook, but it is one that preserves, in its own way, the sense of kinship so central to the story of creation, the outlook it dramatically revised and effectively displaced. All creatures are children of the Creator. Such a vision is truly inspiring. But evolution has its own inspiration; and it does "because it shows the potentialities of slime, and because it makes man of the stuff of nature so that brother fire and sister water are not strange denominations [or meaningless vocables]. But if man's mind is alien, then we live in a cold environment which is alien to our fundamental value" (*DT,* 155). Miller immediately notes that such considerations are, however, no part of his essay. Nor are they any part of any phase of his career.

Even so, he takes very seriously the fact that the world revealed by some of our most authoritative discourses (e.g., natural science and other disciplines insofar as they have been modeled on such science) seems to confront us with an order in which speakers and their utterances are, in principle, precluded. It is an old story, an ancient myth—the child devouring its parent. In this context, nature as the vast, impersonal order revealed by science devours speakers and, thus, scientists. Here we witness a collapse of discourse generated by its success in the efforts to tell more truly how we arrived upon the shores of the present. But how can the success of discourse entail liquidation of speakers, the absolute preclusion of any articulate presence? We have already seen that the collapses of discourse are, in general, fateful occurrences in which the possibility of comprehending the structure, status, and authority of discourse (see, e.g., *PC,* 72) becomes a necessity. We have also seen that one of the most important constitutional conflicts inherent in postmedieval discourse has been generated by the scientific world being a silent world, a world from which speakers have been banished—"the persuasion of realities disjoined from man and his deeds has grown apace with the enlargement of his own articulate powers" (*PC,* 118). On one hand, science is itself a dramatic enhancement of our articulate powers; on the other, it is a story about nature and humankind in which all myth making and myth makers are illusions to be dispelled by an ever more comprehensive application of the experimental method. The "mythic," no less than the "subjective," has become a term of disqualification: if it can be shown that a position depends for its validity on a story, it is thereby disqualified as a "myth." Stories simply do not carry the same authority as experiments, but why this is so is itself a "long story." Moreover, the report of any experiment is essentially narrative. Somebody must tell what was done and what occurred as a result. Hence, the report of an experiment is a story and the experiment itself a deed.

These obvious points have profound implications for the scope and authority of any discourse purporting to provide a comprehensive or even adequate account of our world. One of these implications is the ineliminability of the autonomous deeds; another is the ineliminability of narrative discourse. Autonomous deeds and narrative discourse are inseparable. Agents acquire and maintain their autonomy by virtue of a particular form of historical consciousness: they take account of what they have done and they imagine the consequences of what they might do. "Agency is responsibility—and therefore one's own—only as it becomes the continuum of an articulate utterance" (*PH*, 176). Such consciousness obviously depends on the capacity to tell a story about agents and their acts; it also depends on the ability to differentiate among "I," "you," and "they" in narrative voice. In short, historical consciousness is narrative consciousness. Stories are told; they are themselves deeds flowing from and contributing to the agency of their narrators. Storytelling, like any other exercise of our agency, can be responsible: "We can help what we say. We can correct whatever we may say, and judge whatever we may do" (*PH*, 171).

Even though there needed to be "a good deal of telling before the status of telling came to notice" (*MS*, 37), once this status did become noticed it invited countless stories to explain it. We have not only told the differences between, say, what is objective and what is subjective, but we have caught ourselves in the act of telling such differences. "Until a story has been told [or a distinction articulated], no question of its claim to be an innocent report in which the telling played no part could be raised" (ibid.). But once we catch ourselves in the act of telling, the question of whether the tale is responsible cannot be avoided. As always, we need to attend here to the conditions of our own discourse. It is we who ask this question of ourselves. Where do we stand when we pose this question? Do we occupy an objective position? a subjective one? While the distinction between objectivity and subjectivity is necessary, neither the one nor the other pole can provide a basis for the distinction itself. "In pure subjectivity one loses the 'subject' itself, just as one loses the 'object.' So, too, in pure objectivity, the distinction is lost. To cry up either subject or object as absolute is to lose the base for asserting *either* and, equally, for maintaining the *distinction* between them" (*DP*, 32). One can, however, only offer a responsible critique if one is able to draw this basic distinction; but since the distinction can either not be drawn at all or be drawn only arbitrarily, the possibility of such a critique appears to be ruled out.

On what conditions, then, can one tell a story of humans as the loci of responsibility (*PC*, 102)? In particular, on what conditions are we entitled to draw the distinction between objectivity and subjectivity? Miller's answer is: "No idea can be articulated until peace has been made with actuality. There is no pure subjectivity; no pure objectivity" (*PC*, 63). Only an alliance with actuality provides a way for telling the differences essential to criticism. "The assumption of criticism is that we shall have a world of our own. . . . But what we must have is then to be not only our own, but also a world" (*PC*, 118). Such a world is both essentially akin to our powers as autonomous agents and irreducibly other than and resistant to the exercise of these powers. Our world is a "recalcitrant medium": our being is one with our articulations, our expressions in and through this medium, while this medium stands ever resistant to our essays at expression. Our relationship to our world is analogous to our relationship to our language. In some respects, language is resident in my habits and abilities; in other respects, my language encompasses me. We have an instance of what Whitehead ([1933] 1967, 201) calls "mutual immanence." My language both defines me and allows me to define myself; it also transcends me. It makes possible a self-defined identity and inevitably an other-contested self.

The claim that our relation to our world is analogous to our language is perhaps too tentative; it might be more accurate to affirm that, for Miller, our world is a language in the sense he himself assigned to this term. "Language of all sorts is not the *means* of communication, but the actuality of communion" (*DT*, 189). It is the actuality of communion that allows for the possibility of communication. This actuality also generates conflicts of the deepest and even most violent kind. Meaningful disagreement (as distinct from a brute conflict) presupposes, as Richard J. Bernstein has noted, a common universe of discourse in which people can disagree (Bernstein 1971, 1; cf. Hocking 1926, chap. 1).

Presence requires a totality, the individual demands a world: the self is with others, but this dimension propels the self into conflict. The actuality of communion is the fatality of conflict. Thus, there is no need to purchase our sense of kinship with the universe at the expense of our recognition of its otherness. That any antagonist we are fated to confront is akin to our powers provides us with a basis for hope; it also reveals the omnipresence of possible tragedy, for it shows us what is ultimately at stake in our failures.

The midworld is, accordingly, the *Mitwelt*, the realm in which it is possible to be *with* one another, with those long absent as well as those now present.[11] It is the table at which humanity has sat and still sits, but not without first having constructed it and continuously needing to refurbish it. As Hannah Arendt has noted, a table both holds apart and brings together those who sit around it (Arendt 1958, 52). So, too, the midworld provides the basis for distinguishing self and other and, in doing so, the opportunity for self and other to encounter and even conflict. "Signs as language are always the marks of broken worlds. There is not one language, but many, and each person and society has to some extent his own. This is one of the true bases of pluralism, of the actuality of finitude. Communication is not the mark of complete agreement, but of partial agreement." (*PC*, 122). It is also the basis of inevitable disagreement.

Just as presence requires a totality, any totality revealed by any of our discourses presupposes the presence of persons. The efforts of psychology to explain actions without formally recognizing—and, in some cases, explicitly denying—human beings as essentially rational agents are doomed to failure. Miller contends, for example, "learning and reason are necessary conditions for discerning instinct. I would like to see either Watson or Freud define an act. Neither does. Neither can. . . . The reason is that both want to begin with the facts, but with the facts not already colored by reason" (*DP*, 8). In general, he confesses to a sense of disbelief and helplessness over any theory of the person that refuses to give critical capacities or rational agency the primary authority (*DP*, 9). He insists that rationality "is essential or constitutional: no rationality, then no man" (*DP*, 177). The efforts of physics to explain mechanistically all natural events and, thus, all human actions are equally doomed to fail. No discourse that precludes "the actuality of reason," an actuality appearing only in "self-generated and self-policing utterance," can provide an adequate account of our being-in-the-world. For the acknowledgment of this actuality is a necessary condition for telling a convincing story of persons as centers of responsibility. Newton, Einstein, Freud, and even Skinner obviously have much to teach us; yet what they have to teach us, we who assume radical responsibility for our own affirmations and denials, need not—indeed, should not—be allowed to demoralize us by persuading us to reject our rational agency as illusory.

The actuality of such agency is inseparable from the midworld. "Rationality and the mode and vehicle of its exhibition must be the same. And they must be immediate to man and identical with him" (ibid.). While rational agency resides in our ability to criticize and, by means of self-criticism, control more effectively what we do, say, and make, such agency depends upon utterance, the articulations made possible through language, art, science, and other media of disclosure. It depends upon, in short, the midworld. What is required for rationality is, above all else, that "vehicle which is neither ego nor environment but the very condition of that distinction, and of all formal and organizational distinctions" (*DP*, 179). Miller identifies this vehicle as "utterance." The midworld is the totality of all utterances and the revelations made possible by utterance.

What needs to be highlighted, perhaps even more than Miller himself did, is that utterance has the quality of revelation. If this point is not stressed, then his position is easily misunderstood and seriously weakened. For example, Miller's conception of the midworld is, apart from this emphasis, vulnerable to the criticism Hannah Arendt voiced when she wrote: "The modern age, with its growing world-alienation, has led to a situation where man, wherever he goes, encounters only himself. All the processes of the earth and the universe have revealed themselves either as man-made or as potentially man-made. . . . In this situation of radical world-alienation, neither history nor nature is at all conceivable" (Arendt 1968a, 89). There are, unquestionably, many passages in Miller's writings that might appear to express such an alienation from the world. For example, he asserts: "We now live a long way from nature in the raw. We work with tools and machines that science and technology have produced. We earn a living in the marketplace. . . . Our stimuli to thought and action occur apropos of objects which have, for the most part, been made by man. . . . We actually do, or think, very little except under the stimulus and control of what has already been done and thought" by us and other human beings (*PH*, 80).

"Our world is our own. It is what we have made it to be" (ibid.). And it has, in a way, made us; or, more accurately, it has provided us with the conditions by which we have carried on the task of securing a unique presence in a fateful environment. But, it is precisely this world that provides us with the means of revealing nature in its vast impersonal otherness and history in its relative discontinuity and identifying fatalities. It would be ironic if the midworld rendered history, of all things, inconceivable. For Miller formulates this conception primarily as a way of making sense out of history. Even so, his one-sided emphasis on the tasks we must undertake to reveal either nature or history makes it difficult to see how he could sufficiently appreciate the extent to which both are gifts (cf. Corrington 1990). Nature and history are inherently dynamic and, in some measure, self-disclosing. Insisting that neither one imposes itself *ab extra* on a passive or inert subjectivity is correct; but this does not imply that neither fails to be imposing in a quite forceful way.

While Miller takes piety to be essential for acquiring historical consciousness, this attitude is conspicuously absent from most of his discussion of the natural world. What John Dewey says about "aggressive atheism" appears to apply to Miller's "stubborn humanism": it seems "to have something in common with traditional supernaturalism.... What I have in mind especially is the exclusive preoccupation of both militant atheism and supernaturalism with man in isolation [from nature]" (Dewey [1934] 1986, 52–53). Both lack "natural piety. The ties binding man to nature that poets have always celebrated are passed over lightly" (ibid., 53).[12]

Miller had little sympathy with the romantic celebration of nature and the more or less wholesale condemnation of technology. He would have taken the deliberate retreat of his famous German contemporary into the Black Forest as an evasion of the actual. His opposition to such romanticism inclines him to stress—in my judgment, to overemphasize—our role in the revelation of nature. He believed that our alternatives are not exhausted by the options of either accepting uncritically or rejecting entirely contemporary technology. Here as elsewhere, there is no promontory overlooking our actual circumstances on which we can stand, judging what is occurring beneath us without we ourselves being involved in these circumstances (cf. *PH*, 83). Aloof critics who presume to occupy such an innocent position are neither reliable nor honest.

Especially during the last two decades of Miller's life, advocates of a movement back to nature were prominent among such critics. He asserted, "in so far as we live in an artifactual order we are under attack" (*MS*, 136). We are under attack by, among others, those who espouse a return to nature.

> The current cult is nakedness, back to nature. Let us shuck off these artificialities. Back to impotence. Power corrupts. The word uttered meets a jeer in its very pretension to name or express any reality. The hammer, like the word, perpetuates illusion. A pity that these heralded artifacts were ever devised. One sees only too plainly what they have led to. Back to Paradise, where Adam needed no spade and nakedness was no shame, indeed, was not even perceived. (Ibid.)

"Back to nature" is, in truth, a call "to shunt back to consciousness; and there everything becomes a chaotic mess or a mad fixation" (*DP*, 34). Such shunting is a flight into fantasy. While any actual moment is also a momentum, one of the dominant forms of fantasy is the dream of seizing the moment while avoiding its momentum (*MS*, 14). This dream entails "the loss of the actual. It is the cultus of feeling that has no consequences. The drug-culture is only incidentally chemical. It is not plausible to suppose that its chemical mode would have assumed present proportions were the temper of evasion not already widespread" (ibid.).

We are invited by this culture to go back to nature not in order to discipline our souls but to unlearn the indoctrination of the disciplinarians. We need to unlearn the artificialities imposed on us by a decadent and destructive "civilization." Put positively, we need to cultivate the spontaneities of a benevolent and liberating nature. We need to expand the limits of consciousness to the point where we transcend all limits and restrictions, and to expose all restrictions on conduct as despotic. Further, we need to see all declarations of power as fascistic and all desire for control over self and circumstances as pathological. Those who assume authority in their own person need to be confronted and contested; those who desire control need therapy or counseling.

Miller saw all of this as patent and dangerous nonsense. He also associated it with a romantic celebration of nature over civilization, of spontaneity over discipline, of boundless imagination over tempered rationality. There is a spontaneity born of discipline. So, too, are there imaginative flights demanded by all rational undertakings. And the vision of nature as a school for the discipline of the soul is a noble and ennobling vision; but it is encountered primarily in poets and other writers. Miller opposes freeing imagination from all rationally imposed constraints, though he endorses wedding rationality to imaginatively projected possibilities. A spontaneity able to sustain itself is the fruit of discipline, just as an imagination able to generate productive novelties is a capacity developed in conjunction with reason. To see, for example, the woods through the eyes of poets and other artists is to have our perceptions finely attuned to what would otherwise be indistinct or perhaps even invisible. From the romantic perspective, the untutored eye and illiterate mind are, however, supposed to be better adapted to the perception of nature. Unfettered spontaneity and boundless imagination are likewise thought by the romantic to require nothing beyond themselves for their continuous development.

Miller's view of nature needs to be appreciated in the light of his opposition to this form of romantic naturalism. He insists that the midworld is a condition for nature: the natural world is revealed to us by means of a complex array of functioning objects.[13] But the midworld "robs nobody of nature" (*PC*, 118). Our measuring instruments and other probes enable us to say what is really there in nature, quite apart from our wishes and even ordinary modes of perceptual experience. Hence, Miller's insistence that the midworld is a condition of nature does not reduce nature to a figment or illusion. But nature is no more an arbitrary tyrant to which we must blindly submit than she is an arbitrary fiction over which we exercise unconstrained power. Any form of despotism destroys the possibility of our rational agency. Little or nothing is gained by dethroning a divine despot, only to replace it with tyrannical nature. Miller seems to have rejected the possibility that God could be conceived in a way compatible with our freedom; but he is confident that nature not only can but also must be defended in the name of our freedom (see, e.g., *MS*, 177).

I return later in this chapter to the topic of nature and, then, in a later chapter, to a fuller consideration of whether Miller lacks what John Dewey and George Santayana called "natural piety." At this point, it would be helpful to consider how Miller conceives his own investigation of the midworld. An inquiry into this domain "lies between epistemology and metaphysics and is the bridge between them" (*PC,* 107). In other words, such an investigation bears upon both questions of knowledge and questions of being and, in addition, it tries to display how epistemological and metaphysical questions bear upon each other. From an epistemological perspective, the midworld is primarily a realm of possible mistakes. From a metaphysical viewpoint, it is principally the domain of fateful revisions and the revelations, actual and possible, resulting from these revisions.

The question of subjectivity needs to be addressed from these two perspectives. In one place, Miller notes, "metaphysics in its search for the real must escape the subjective; but this cannot mean it must escape the subject" (*PC,* 53). So, too, epistemology in its quest for the means whereby we can effectively distinguish the veridical from the illusory, the objective from the subjective, cannot avoid questions regarding the status and authority of our own subjectivity. All attempts to make another object of the subject have failed, as they were doomed to fail (*DP,* 154). But so, too, have all attempts to secure the status and authority of subjectivity by turning inward—by turning away from shared media and the essentially public arena established by mastery of these media. If human subjectivity is neither another object nor an unobjectifiable inwardness, what is it? "The subjective element keeps coming back. It may be as skepticism, as pragmatism, or as mystical intuition" (*MS,* 24). But, regardless of what form it assumes, two features of this element are especially noteworthy. First, "the concept of the subjective is not a subjective concept" (*PC,* 53). Second, the ineliminability of the subjective—its persistence in coming back, virtually at every turn in some form—points to the irreducibility, though not the centrality, of the subject. The resurfacing of this element reaffirms "the experiences of the subject" (*MS,* 24), and these experiences themselves imply the omnipresence of our subjectivity. In the history of philosophical reflection on this tangled experience, as well as in our actual experience, there arises the need to come to terms with our own subjectivity. But, to repeat, how can we account for subjectivity as such without either reducing it simply to an object of some sort or imprisoning the subject within the walls of its own consciousness (*PH,* 121)? The subject is neither reducible to an object nor separable from objects; it is neither just another public fact nor an inaccessible inwardness. Human subjectivity is primarily embodied agency.

Human Subjectivity

Any adequate account of human subjectivity must do justice to both presence and totality—the unique, autonomous individual and the incomplete, yet comprehensive universe. On one hand, many accounts nullify subjectivity. They depict the universe in such a way that autonomous agency is, in principle, impossible. Any of the many variations on universal mechanism, including structuralism and perhaps even certain forms of deconstruction, would be an example of such nullification. On the other hand, many theories of the subject secure the unique and autonomous status of the self by effectively or, in some rare cases, explicitly denying nothing less than the universe. Such cosmic egoism is no more persuasive than personal nullification. A self for whom the "other" is nothing but a figment is as comical as a universe in which "I" could not have any standing is absurd.

Descartes famously argued for the separability of the "I" and the body. There is a spiritual presence capable of operating and, hence, existing apart from one's physical presence. In more traditional terms, one's soul or mind is ontologically separable from one's body. But the presumption of this separability has generated intractable problems for subsequent thought. Our use of symbols forcefully exhibits the presence of persons who reveal themselves in and through these symbols (*DT,* 71). Yet, there has been a pervasive and persistent tendency to explain these persons as essentially inner agents only contingently related to other such agents, language, and even their own bodies. "It is not clear, however, that *inner* and *outer* are well-defined terms; their use presumes a metaphysics and a theory of knowledge. . . . It is exactly here that is laid 'the great Serbonian bog where armies whole have sunk'" (*DT,* 72). Or, to have recourse to an alternative metaphor, "Once the split between the inner agent and the outer fact is made not all the king's horses and all the king's men can patch together the pieces" (ibid.). While Descartes proposed the "inner self" as the only possible starting point, "the history of philosophy subsequent to him has positively discredited this beginning as futile and fallacious" (ibid.).

What Descartes presumed to be merely contingent—the self's relationship to others, language, and its own body—must be seen as inherent features of any possible human agent. Miller was one among many contemporary philosophers who sought to replace the Cartesian cogito with an embodied subjectivity. What is most distinctive about his rejection of the cogito is his identification of the human organism itself as a functioning object and, in addition, his recognition of the various artifacts on which human agency is dependent. "The primary and ultimate functioning object is the organism" (*MS*, 170). This organism "is, like a symbol, both an object and the condition of objects" (*MS*, 155). For example, it can itself be perceived and it is that by which other objects can be perceived; as perceived, it is an object and, as perceiving, it is the condition for objects other than itself. But from the human hand as a functioning object flow countless artifacts, not only ones serving an immediate purpose, but also ones defining a formal aspect of our actual world. Among the artifacts crafted by humans, some do not serve a specific and realizable objective; they define a region in which the pursuit of such goals is possible (see, e.g., *PC*, 128). Even though these regions are concretely and specifically instantiated at any moment of function (e.g., this wall measures eight feet high), they are inherently formal and universal. Space is a form by which the conditions for the pursuit of purposes are defined; as such, it is "predicable of many"; it is illimitably utterable, though there are perhaps purposes (e.g., the drawing of a valid inference) to whose pursuit the conditions defined by space are irrelevant.

Miller's position differs from pragmatism because his concern is not with the satisfaction of conditional purposes but the definition of the necessary conditions underlying the pursuit of any possible purpose. Spatially and temporally defining the world of our agency does not serve any purpose; it projects an arena in which purposes might be sought.

His position differs from another dominant current in contemporary philosophy because he does not narrowly focus on language, as has been a tendency of many philosophers and other thinkers in this century. His concern is to underscore the various modes of human utterance and, thus, to resist the temptation of privileging one mode. This stance does not deny the importance of language in the narrow sense; rather it contextualizes this importance. Any natural language is a complex system of functioning objects supportive of and supported by other functioning objects.

But, here as elsewhere, the circumstance of being with generates the fatality of being against. Not only does one word or, more generally, one symbol lead to another; in any process of utterance there arise moments of contestation, of one symbol contesting another—the utterances of the scientist challenging those of the theologian. In these moments, what is challenged might turn out to be not this or that utterance but the entire form of discourse from which the challenged utterance derives its intelligibility and authority. We no longer utter incantations and many of us no longer say prayers. These forms of utterance have not survived the challenge issued by other forms. Ordinary language itself can be and, in fact, has been subjected to the most radical challenge—to be treated as merely a useful tool, indispensable in everyday life but bereft of any revelatory function. The language of our daily exchanges enables us to cope with our circumstances but does not empower us to reveal what underlies these circumstances. For such revelations, we must turn to some other form of discourse, such as the language of scientific experimentation. In effect, by treating ordinary language as a mere tool, one effectively denies its status as a form of discourse at all. Utterance is the enactment of a form of discourse, and revelation is a feature of any utterance. Hence, to deny any revelatory function of a "discourse" amounts to nothing less than denying its status as a genuine discourse.

In general, the fatality of contestation and even of collapse are inherent in discourse. No form of discourse, no mode of utterance, is absolutely secure: every form is fated, not by any external force external, but by the dynamic inherent in discourse to undergo revision and, thus, transformation. In time, these transformations can profoundly alter the forms of discourse, so much so that the originators of these forms seem to have little or nothing to say to the inheritors of these transformations. Even as brilliant and educated a person as Thomas Jefferson could say, in response to a query about a new translation of Aristotle's *Politics:* "The introduction of this new principle of representative democracy has rendered useless almost everything written before on the structure of government; and, in a great measure, relieves our regret, if the political writings of Aristotle, or of any other ancient, have been lost, or are unfaithfully rendered or explained to us" (Jefferson 1963).

This is, however, a position with which Miller would strenuously disagree. For the writings of the agents are monuments and, in turn, monuments are "what keep us in mind" (*PH*, 121; cf. *MS*, 19). Our mindfulness and agency are dependent on our pious appropriation of our actual past. If the writings of the ancients are lost, so is in some measure the possibility of comprehending ourselves in the present. Miller notes that Americans interest themselves in the decline of Athens or Rome "because our political identity came through Athens and Rome. The very word 'politics' is Greek. . . . Their career is also ours" (*PH*, 135; cf. McGandy 1998, 241). "We join them in self-definition, not in a technical problem. By knowing them better we know ourselves better. We profit not from a technical skill or failure but from the common political purpose that is self-disclosing" (ibid.). History is the process of this self-disclosure. Monuments—writings should be included under this rubric—are the only means we have for interpreting this process. Through this ongoing and self-critical process of interpretation and reinterpretation, we acquire and maintain our rational agency. The technical innovation of representative government does not relieve citizens of democracies of the responsibility to take into account what, for example, Plato and Aristotle said; indeed, our political identity demands a political literacy encompassing acquaintance with the ancients no less than attention to the news of the day. Citizens of a democracy are no more "free" to ignore the news than are the members of a religion "free" to abstain from the rituals and practices of their *cultus*, or are parents "free" to ignore the needs of their children. To claim such "freedom" is to shirk the responsibilities of membership and, thereby, to undermine the possibility of identity. To the extent these are shirked, their membership is nominal rather than actual; in addition, identity is likely to evaporate into a mist of momentary desires, unable to sustain itself as the center of an abiding purposiveness. So, too, to be citizens of a democracy is to be the inheritors of institutions and practices whose value lies not in their ability to serve our private purposes but in their contribution to our identity and effectiveness. Membership requires recognition of our status as inheritors and a gratitude for our inheritance. For these institutions and practices are nothing less than sources of empowerment: by virtue of them, we are mindful agents. By virtue of them, we establish a unique identity as well as an effective presence in the precarious world of the historical present.

Human subjectivity is, accordingly, an embedded agency. It is embedded in a history, that is, a career in which there is a more or less self-conscious struggle to attain a fuller grasp of the meaning and the resources of the career itself (cf. *PC,* 167). It is also, as we have seen, an embodied agency. "The phrase *'the* body' is nonsense where *the* body is *a* body. Nobody finds *his* [or *her*] body as a body" (*MS,* 142). "Science has no way of authorizing the phrase 'the body' or *'my* body'" (ibid.). We are entitled to these expressions only by virtue of our embodied agency itself; "my body" is not found but declared, and no one other than me declares it. Scientific inquirers are authorized to use this expression only insofar as these inquirers are themselves instances of such agency.

The human body "is the absolute *artifact,* that is, it is the artifact that in its functioning creates all other artifacts and symbols" (*MS,* 46). In addition, it "is the absolute actuality, that is, the union of form and content in functioning" (ibid.). This body "is neither abstract form nor abstract content"; this and, indeed, all other distinctions occur only apropos of its functioning or activity (ibid.).

To treat any functioning object as merely a means for one's purposes is to mistreat it. Actually to mistreat such objects is the secular equivalent of a desecrative act, especially with regard to one's own and another person's body. "Just as the care of the body is the most elementary love, so its disregard is [the] most elementary barbarity. The moral defect of mistreating the body of another derives from the place of the body as the actuality of the person, so long as the body can *function* as actuality" (ibid.). Miller goes so far as to say: "The injury of the body is the denial of actuality *in principle"* (*MS,* 46–47; emphasis added). If we recognize this, then the care for and the defense of the body can be properly conceived. That is, recognizing what is at stake in injuring the body makes it clear why the maintenance of health is absolutely basic and, in defense of one's body, the recourse to violence is morally justified. While it "is thought proper than an attack on an idea be treated with forbearance," it is thought not improper that an attack on the body be met, at least in some circumstances, with such violence. It is perhaps more accurate to say that, in the defense of the body, we have a right to use such force as will insure its protection, even that degree of force for which there is no guarantee that the attacker will not be seriously injured or even destroyed. "He who attacks an idea is already on the side of ideas. But violence to the body brooks no delay and courts a reply in its own terms" (*MS,* 47).

The possibility of violence implies the inviolability of subjectivity. Just above, we note that human subjectivity is a historically embedded and organically embodied form of agency. But, in a way, even more fundamental than either of these features is the dimension of agency itself. The subject "is the doer and speaker, the maker of a historical career" (*MS*, 100). The subject is essentially active, is always and everywhere an agent in one way or another (*MS*, 156).

The subject as the self-conscious locus of error is nothing other than the agent who, in the course of some mode of functioning (e.g., measuring or counting), is compelled to confront what this agent has done previously. The epistemological subject—the subject as knower, as one capable of telling the difference between, say, truth and falsity—is the agent who has come to discover its own mistakes. The subject as self-defining purpose is the agent in its fateful struggle of coming to effective terms with its confused inheritance. The metaphysical subject—the subject as a being capable of making a difference in any context whatsoever, of self-consciously establishing its presence among others—is the agent who has come to revise its own outlook.

"The mistake is the revelation of the subjective" (*MS*, 174). The revelation of this element reaffirms "the experiences of the subject" (*MS*, 24). It reaffirms, to repeat, our status as subjects, even if we experience our subjectivity in this context primarily as locus of error or ignorance. But, in ordinary circumstances, this experience does not lead to skepticism, the loss of any confidence in our ability to tell the difference between truth and falsity. It is, on the contrary, a manifestation of this ability. To know now that we were then mistaken, to be able to identify the point at which we went wrong, implies that our subjectivity is more than a locus of error and ignorance; it is also a source of power. But it is a power we acquire and maintain only through our participation in the midworld, a participation involving subjection to the discipline demanded in mastery any form of discourse. Just as surely as the mastering of any discourse demands discipline, any engagement in a form of discourse entails a destiny (JWM, 23:26). We learn by doing and being undone by our doings. "Learning by doing is incorporate [or incarnate]. It does not show us an aloof, disembodied, and ghostlike agent directing alien hands and other tools" (*MS*, 79). It shows us an engaged, embedded, and embodied agent. The scene of engagement is the midworld.

The Realm of Possible Mistakes

At one level, we inherit the resources to tell the difference between truth and error. Most of us live most of our lives at this level of discourse. At a deeper level, we are fated to revise the ways differences are told and even the way in which the forms of telling, or modes of utterance, are justified. These fateful revisions are the "constitutional conflicts" discussed earlier. It falls to epistemology to provide an account of the most important resources by which such differences as truth and error, fact and fiction, reality and illusion, are told. It falls to the history of philosophy to consider what revisions have actually been made in the course of human or, at least, Western history; and it falls to the philosophy of history to provide an account of human action and utterance capable of rendering intelligible the constitutional conflicts that human discourse is fated to generate. Insofar as the philosophy of history is, in Miller's sense, devoted to establishing not only the categoreal status of human action but also the functional character of all our ultimate categories (*DP*, 59), it is in effect assuming the central task of traditional metaphysics.

Miller takes it to be remarkable how confidently the most basic distinctions have been made and, yet, how infrequently the process of their derivation has been undertaken (ibid.). These distinctions, that is, the categories, have been either loudly but dogmatically defended or cleverly but ineffectively denied. What is needed is a derivation of the categories in which their actual genesis is made part of their essential meaning, rather than a derivation in which their alleged immutability is secured by an appeal to pure reason—a reason so pure as to be in possession of its most essential resources apart not only from its own lived experience but also from its historical inheritance.

In this section, we confine our attention to the so-called problem of knowledge. In the next section, we turn to the categoreal revisions at the core of human history. In other words, in this section we consider, in a very general way, how we are able to tell the difference between truth and error or reality and appearance; in the next, we examine why our categories are fated to undergo revision. Both this and the following section are brief, for the key points have already been either explicitly made or clearly implied at various points in this and the previous chapters. Even so, these points need to be remade in reference to the midworld. Herein we are following the pattern of Miller's own thought, which continuously circled back to his most basic affirmations. Just as, say, Husserl would return time and again to the intentionality of consciousness or Ortega to his claim "I am I and my circumstances," both trying to show how traditional problems are transformed in light of their most basic affirmation, so, too, Miller would return time and again to his most fundamental assertions.

In reference to epistemology, this means explaining knowledge in terms of actuality. To begin with, we need to accept the insolubility of "the problem of knowledge," as this problem has been traditionally formulated. "Cognition needed a basis, which it could not supply from its own resources" (*MS*, 11). "Cognition requires at least the possibility of a mistake, yet on its own terms can produce none" (*MS*, 9–10). Thus, we need to go beyond cognition in order to explain cognition. The basis of cognition is found neither in what appears to consciousness nor in what exists apart from consciousness; it is found in the forms of functioning or, in a word, in the act (*MS*, 11; cf. Tyman 1993, chap. 2). But, since action is essentially continuous—since the forms of action are continua in which the repercussions of deeds can call into question the validity of these deeds—the characterization of the act as the basis of cognition is not an instance of foundationalism. In this context, the act serves as a basis not in the sense of an absolutely secure foundation upon which one builds, once and for all, the edifice of knowledge but in the sense of a self-maintaining and, thus, self-revising process in which the authority of the process itself is fated to be challenged by other modes of utterance.

As we have seen, the body functions as a symbol does. It is an object, itself discernible in some way (though not necessarily at the level of consciousness), and it is a source by which objects other than itself are revealed. So do all other functioning objects. All knowledge of any objects whatsoever moves through and relies upon this sort of object. "No object is otherwise known. All objects are denoted through symbols; all hypotheses expressed and tested through them" (*MS*, 155). This makes it clear that all of our knowledge of either self or nature is mediated (*MS*, 154). It is in and through institutions and artifacts that we learn about ourselves and our world (ibid.). "Nature and self are both utter blanks apart from the media [the words, instruments, and hypotheses (ibid.)] that in their function—not in logical implication [but in actual functioning]—lead to them" (*MS,* 189).

"To know is possibly to be mistaken. But the avoidance of a mistake is the preservation of a present" (*MS,* 9). The ultimate consideration is, thus, what would be avoided if a mistake were actually avoided, mistake being here yet another organizational (rather than denotative) term (ibid.). Apart from the possibility of making mistakes, cognition is impossible; limited to cognitive terms alone, however, mistakes are impossible. We make mistakes. This is the simple but profound point that needs to be stressed; otherwise actuality is reduced to the purely cognitive. "The problem of knowledge occurs because of a distinction between appearance and reality, or thought and reality, or the psychological and the non-psychological. The problem takes the form of joining these two factors somehow" (*PC,* 56). "The philosophy of knowledge is the problem of how to tell that one *has* made a mistake, or not made one. But one must be able to tell the difference" (*MS,* 176).

Miller notes that "[I]t has been notoriously difficult to say how an error is possible in terms of either mind or else of body" (*MS,* 189), the terms in which the problem of knowledge has been addressed and, even more fundamentally, framed. "But I find no difficulty," he announces, "in locating error apropos of the artifactual, in the yardstick in use, or in words. If one cannot find error in the pure object, neither can one in the pure subject. You have to make a mistake" (ibid.). But, in order to be in the position to make a mistake, you need a vehicle. Any such vehicle is an artifact, if only the body transformed by the discipline imposed gaining mastery of its own organs and limbs. For this reason: "We need a new epistemology, one that does not shrink from giving ontological status to artifacts. The past rides on them, and they are symbols and voices" (AW, 261–62). Since "[t]here is no saying of words, as against the making of noises, apart from what has been said" (AW, 262), words contain within themselves echoes of the past. They are, in essence, echoes of voices no longer among us. So, too, are all of the symbols by which we are empowered to make sense of whatever we feel or encounter, of whatever springs from or impinges on our embodied subjectivity.

These voices and symbols are momentous. They carry within themselves the energies of the past. But these energies, sustained by their appropriation from one generation to the next, also contain within themselves the sources of our confusions and conflicts and, thus, the necessity for their revision.

The Realm of Actual Revisions

"The aversion to 'metaphysics' is," Miller notes, "the sign of the inability to identify the basis both of the distinctions and of their rejection" (*PH*, 128). Just as the midworld is a realm of possible mistakes because it is one of past mistakes, so the midworld is a realm of revisable outlooks because it has been one of fateful revisions. Our critical capacities and the disconcerting arrests which all of our self-critical discourses are fated to suffer are rooted in an inheritance at once empowering and confusing. This inheritance is, in our appropriation of the articulate forces embodied in our historical institutions, the source of our power and, in the conflicts inherent in these institutions, the cause of our confusion.

These fateful revisions have been the new and startling ways to tell difference hitherto unknown—indeed, unknowable because ineffable. Their importance lies, however, neither in their novelty nor in their startlingness but in their capacity to enlarge the scope of our power.

The midworld is what the makers of history, the initiators of revisions, have said or uttered: to keep a tally, to use a yardstick, to read a clock, and perhaps most momentous of all to fabricate aural and graphic signs of increasing complexity and sophistication. These revisions concern, above all else, the telling differences by which self and world are more sharply defined and tightly intertwined. Since these points are discussed in detail above, there is no need to treat them more fully here.

Discoursing about Discourse:
Semiotics, Deconstruction, and Rortyean Neo-Pragmatism

Much contemporary discourse is not only about discourse but also insistent that there is nothing else it could possibly be about. Signs can refer only to other signs; any signified or object of signification dissolves in the process of signification into another signifier. There is no "transcendental signified," nothing that is an object of signification but not itself also a signifier. There are only signifying practices, in which objects come and go as a result of the play of signifiers: "There are only texts." This, moreover, is said to be not an ontological claim. But, given the current stress on performativity, it is a claim typically made by assuming a position in the actual world, that is, by allying oneself with some form of action, most often the action of resistance or transgression.

There is an interesting coincidence in the emphasis on difference found in both Miller and Derrida. The distinction between them is, however, dramatic. For Derrida, difference emerges out of the play of signifiers; for Miller, it is established by the fateful momentum inherent in the finite actualities of functioning objects, precisely in the ongoing course of their actual functioning.

"There can be no absolutely general *theory* of signs" (*MS*, 156; emphasis added). "The reason for this derives from the impossibility of treating signs as objects. No sign can be studied as an object.... To treat a sign as an object is to lose it as a sign" (*MS*, 156–57).

Common sense presumes that speakers make sense only if they are talking about something; our utterances are worthy of attention only if they are something to which we can unambiguously point, thereby identifying an object not itself defined by discourse (*MS*, 59). But pointing is itself not another object; as a meaningful gesture, the *act* of pointing "implies an artifactual context" (*MS*, 156). "Object is a status within a discourse" (*MS*, 64).

"You can't talk 'about' talk; you can't see your eye as object, where no seeing eye does the seeing" (*MS*, 71). You cannot see your utterances (including your acts of pointing out objects), where no articulate voice issues the utterances. The identification of an act is essentially different from that of any object. While an act cannot be reduced to an object, an object—in order to be identified, in order to be an object—is related to a series of acts. "Our names are our deeds. Objects acquire names as part of our control over them" (*PC*, 121). "The object, which already embodies act, is the vehicle of further action" (*MS*, 71). Hence, we are led back to Miller's affirmation of the actual: "Action and a world [indeed, our world] are inseparable. The word, symbol, artifact focus [or define] the actual world. The expansion of the immediate occurs *via* what has been done" (ibid.). Any immediate circumstance expands, by virtue of our immediate engagements, beyond itself to embrace all other circumstances, to link itself to a totality. The immediate is always the insistent foreground of some totality, just as the totality is the fated background of any present immediacy, never adequately articulated but always at least vaguely felt.

On one hand, then, there is a deep affinity between Miller and certain contemporary tendencies evident in both semiotics and deconstruction. At the heart of this affinity is the refusal to separate us and our world from the discipline and disclosures of discourse. Our discourses do not supervene on an intrinsically silent world devoid of discourse; rather, our world evolves from our essentially articulate presence. Our universe is inseparable from our utterances. Hence, Miller states: "What I am unwilling to say is 'There is the world, and here are the signs.' That seems to me impossible" (*MS*, 75). "It is often supposed that everyone clearly knows what objects are, while ignorant of what subjects or signs may be. But the status of being an object is no more clear than the status of being a sign or a subject" (*DT*, 183).

On the other hand, there is a shiftiness, an evasiveness, in contemporary discourse—especially in the more fashionable discourses of the deconstructionists—completely lacking in Miller's affirmations of the midworld. The question we need to ask of those preoccupied with illuminating the force and forms of discourse is not, What are you talking about? It is rather, Where do you stand? Miller contends, "talk is not to be found. I join it" (*MS*, 63). On what conditions am I entitled and empowered to join a community of discourse? What attitudes are required for sustained and effective membership in such a community? Are Miller's avowed humanism and liberalism passé or, rather have the totalizing critiques of poststructuralist authors become themselves outmoded?

The current stress on performativity (see, e.g., Butler 1990, 1997) seems in some respects close to Miller's understanding of discourse as a process of enactment that is ineluctably also (to some extent) a process of *re*-enactment. So too is the continuing or, in some cases, resuscitated affirmation of emancipation. In "Force of Law," Derrida asserts: "Nothing seems to me less outdated than the classical emancipatory ideal. We cannot attempt to disqualify it today, whether crudely or with sophistication, at least not without treating it too lightly and forming the worst complicities" (Derrida 1992, 28). Of course, the acts whereby freedom is secured and maintained, extended and enhanced need to be understood performatively.

But what authorizes emancipatory discourse? What is actually implied when one invokes the name of freedom? Has the invocation of this name ever been anything more than an instrument of oppression, securing the advantage of one part at the expense of another? How can the searing lucidity demanded by a genuine commitment to critical consciousness result in anything other than disillusionment and thus demoralization? Is not humanism but the dying gasp of a tenacious theism trying continuously to reinscribe the still point of a transcendental subjectivity invulnerable to the vicissitudes of its own history? Do not the negations—the negations of traditional authority, inherited pieties, and cognitive certainties—so commonplace today leave us nowhere and, thus, make of us nobody (no-*body*)? While the midworld of symbols is identifiable with the domain of actuality, and the actual world is defined in terms of human action, for Miller action itself is linked to affirmation, accreditation, authentication, authorization, and similar words. He realized, of course, that the "local efficacy that would proclaim the general order, and would stand as its own evidence and warrant, is not [now] permitted" (*DP,* 69). Such efficacy is systematically undermined and, hence, such order is effectively eliminated. As a consequence, we "are nihilists" (ibid.). Humanism is (as we see in the next chapter) considered to be not a way around but an accomplice of nihilism. Is Miller's insistence that discourse needs authority (see, e.g., *MS,* 106) simply the futile gesture of an impotent authoritarian or is it rather the sole corrective to the fateful crisis of contemporary nihilism? If the midworld is Miller's affirmation, does it itself have the power and authority to break the impasse of the two mutually sustaining positions of arbitrary dogmatism and paralyzing skepticism?

Conclusion

There is perhaps no better summary of this chapter, or transition to the next, than Miller's own words. Two passages seem especially pertinent here, the first as a means of summarizing the present chapter and the second as a transition to the following chapter. "The *ground* of the distinction between the skeptical absolutes is the artifact, or the symbol, because it is the local and actual embodiment of ideality and of criticism. It generates infinity, but only as the form of an actual finitude and an ideal finitude. It is the reason for the stake we have in nature and institutions. In its extension [along with the extension of all other artifacts] it is the midworld, the basis of a responsible humanism" (*MS*, 119; emphasis added).

We must now turn from this basis to the form of humanism it makes possible. As an aid to this transition, let us recall that "[w]hile the actual, the midworld, the functioning object, the utterance, the accidental as constitutional, the world as incomplete, the world as philosophically defined—while all that may seem very esoteric, it derives from counting my fingers and going to the post office" (*MS*, 191). Let us, in addition, recall that intellectuals traditionally have not had any verbs; they, perhaps more than other group, have been responsible for losing the name of action. In contrast, common persons possess a steady confidence in their mastery of at least the most basic verbs, the most fundamental forms of human functioning. For this reason, Miller does not hesitate to confess his solidarity with these persons: "I am joining that common man. And if this is a free country, we'd better get ourselves a metaphysic that has respect for the man [and woman] on Elm Street. As it is, he is treated with patronage and disdain. Nor does he quite know how to stand in his authority because he is there and therefore projects a world in his doing" (ibid.). That is, common persons confidently assume in their everyday actions an awesome authority but only darkly grasp either the source or the scope of their power and authority. A truly responsible humanism—a metaphysics and ethics that has the deepest respect for common persons in their everyday pursuits—must bring into the sharpest focus nothing less than the source and scope of their power.

Although Miller often stresses that the most commonplace verbs carry, within their own fateful unctioning, ontological import—that a metaphysics is implicit in the quotidian comportment of human agents—he also emphasizes that his philosophy requires the person on Elm Street. The celebration of the commonplace is clearly implied in Miller's affirmation of the midworld; but, given his insistence on the inherent pressures toward constitutional revision, it is a celebration of the commonplace continuously in process of transfiguration. The overcoming of nihilism demands nothing less than a transfiguration of the commonplace (see Fell 1997). But an uncommon understanding of the commonplace might begin by taking the suffix of this word in its straightforward meaning. Such is my proposal. So questions concerning place will become focal concerns in the upcoming chapters. We ordinarily use such expressions as "a man of his time" or "a person bound to a particular place" to signal limitation and even myopia. Is it, however, possible and perhaps even necessary to revise this "commonplace" understanding of historical place? One trajectory inherent in Miller's texts is a radical revision of our inherited conceptions of the finite actuality of historical place. Since tracing out this trajectory allows me to put Miller in dialogue with a variety of influential authors, mostly contemporary, the prospects of doing so are in accord with his own vision of philosophy as a confrontation with the actualities of one's time and place.[14]

Miller opens one of his most compelling essays, "The Scholar as a Man of the World," by announcing, "Education makes us men of the world" (*PC*, 174). Of course, education is not to be confused with schooling. All humans "possess some perspective, all live in some world, more or less orderly or confused, more or less dark and incoherent, but never wholly formless or inarticulate" (ibid.). Education is inherent in living, such that we are driven willy-nilly toward framing some vision of the totality in which we are present. But, for the scholar, "the articulate world has become a deliberate quest and an acknowledged need" (ibid.). As we have seen, "what we must have is . . . to be not only our own, but also a *world*" (*PC*, 118). This demand is satisfied only by acknowledging the midworld, accrediting finite actuality with the actual authority it exerts in our lives. But the midworld is not an order of groundless symbols, much less a region of ethereal abstractions. It is our human world, humanly reimagined. It is, ironically, the world from which we moderns have been exiled. The dominant tendencies of modern thought tend to displace and, thus, to annihilate us. Resistance to the annihilative tendencies of modern thought, then, requires reclamation of our historical actuality in its full significance. This reclamation is at the center of Miller's affirmation of the midworld. But its force and meaning are discernible only when we trace out the trajectory of this affirmation in the direction of such *topoi* as place itself, dwelling, displacement, and estrangement.

4

Historical Displacements and Situated Narratives: Locating Responsibility

> History is of all subjects the most earth-bound.
> —John William Miller,
> *The Paradox of Cause and Other Essays*, 74.

Miller was a man of his time. His being so signals not so much a limitation as an exemplary confrontation with the finite actuality of a particular phase of late modernity. Paradoxically, his relevance to our time is largely a function of his confrontation with the actuality of his time.

There are, however, obstacles to appreciating his relevance, not the least of which are rhetorical or terminological. In particular, the terms by which Miller identified his outlook and approach—idealism and humanism—are unlikely to dispose contemporary readers to a favorable reception of either his distinctive orientation or rigorous procedure.[1] If anything, these terms are likely to make him seem outdated and even quaint. But he himself was far more interested in articulating his position than in naming it. He even appeared to shun labels for his own outlook for just the reason that they all too often convey the illusion of familiarity by suggesting a line of descent or, worse, a set of theses straightforwardly expressible and directly demonstrable. His orientation and approach are, hence, best identified in terms of the problems with which he was preoccupied, the *topoi* to which he was so anxious to return, again and again, in conversations, lectures, letters, and essays—above all, the problem of thinking historically about history and, less obviously, the *topos* of place itself. When Miller identifies himself as an idealist or humanist little interest is stirred. When he asserts that the "philosopher, like the artist or statesman, must settle with some actual and self-defining difficulty and speak to its demands" (*PC*, 87) and, further, when he identifies himself as a philosopher with the *problematique* of history, however, there is an immediate, vivid sense of an arresting, eloquent presence: here is someone we ignore only at the risk of impoverishing ourselves. Even so, I cannot simply ignore the terms by which Miller philosophically identified himself. In fact, I have not done so. Most of these terms are discussed in previous chapters; however, Miller's use of "humanism" as the name for a movement with which he identified remains to be considered (cf. Said 1999, 2000). But my approach is somewhat circuitous; for Miller used this term to designate something quite different not only from the better known versions of humanism in his day—the stoic humanism of Bertrand Russell or the naturalistic humanism of John Dewey—but also from that which is identified and then attacked as humanism in our day, for example, the target of Heidegger's critique in his "Letter on Humanism" (1977) or of Michel Foucault's critique in his *The Order of Things* (1970).

In one of the most (in)famous texts in contemporary philosophy, Foucault announces "the death of man."

> Rather than the death of God—or, rather, in the wake of that death and in a profound correlation with it—what Nietzsche's thought heralds is the end of his murderer; it is the explosion of man's face in laughter, and the return of masks; it is the scattering of the profound stream of time by which he felt himself carried along and whose pressure he suspected in the very being of things; it is the identity of the Return of the Same with the absolute dispersion of man. (Foucault 1970, 385; cf. *PC*)

So, Foucault concludes this work, subtitled in one English translation "An Archaeology of the Human Sciences," by asserting: "As the archaeology of our thought easily shows, man is an invention of recent date. And one perhaps nearing its end" (ibid., 387). If the fundamental arrangements of human knowledge disappear just as they have appeared, if they are displaced in the same manner that they themselves displaced earlier modes of conceptualization, then "one can certainly wager that man would be erased, like a face drawn in sand at the edge of the sea" (ibid.).

There is today a powerful, pervasive "tradition" of philosophical antihumanism that draws its inspiration and insights from Foucault, as well as from Friedrich Nietzsche, Martin Heidegger, Jacques Lacan, and numerous others.[2] Hence, any discussion of Miller's humanism that would be of contemporary philosophical interest cannot avoid the delicate task of squaring Miller's affirmations and advocacy with these critiques and denunciations. Part of what I hope to show in this chapter is that, in the name of a humanism allied with historicism, Miller attacked many of the positions that Nietzsche, Heidegger, Foucault, and the many thinkers whom they have influenced identify with humanism itself. The equivocity of this term is thus likely to mask in this instance deep affinities, overlapping sympathies, and also overlapping antipathies. So pains must be taken to bring into clear focus the principal meanings of this protean term "humanism."[3]

Nihilism: The Masked, Inhuman Face of Humanism Itself?

As a first step toward clarifying humanism, taken here more as a historical phenomenon than as a philosophical doctrine, and even more precisely as a pivotal development in late modernity, it is instructive to juxtapose two essays, written eight decades apart. In juxtaposing William James's "The Essence of Humanism" ([1905] 1975, chap. 5) and Gianni Vattimo's "The Crisis of Humanism" (1991, chap. 2), we can observe how at the outset of the twentieth century James puts the affirmation of finitude at the center of humanism, whereas near the close of the century Vattimo sees humanism itself as one of the roots of nihilism. Miller was of course familiar with James but not with Vattimo, nor was Miller acquainted in any intimate or detailed way with those thinkers with whom Vattimo is in dialogue here (Ernst Bloch, Edmund Husserl, and, above all, Martin Heidegger).[4] Even so, he would have seen himself in most crucial respects closer to the Heideggerian Vattimo than to the pragmatist James, a point to be developed below.

In *The Meaning of Truth*, William James describes humanism as "a ferment that has 'come to stay,'" also noting that "it is not a single hypothesis or theorem, and it dwells on no new facts" (James [1905] 1975, 236).

Humanism "is rather a slow shifting in the philosophic perspective, making things appear as from a new centre of interest or point of view" (ibid.) In *Pragmatism*, he suggests that, since the really vital questions for all of us are "What is this world going to be?" and "What is life making of itself?" the "centre of gravity of philosophy must . . . alter its place. The earth of things, long thrown into shadow by the glories of the upper ether, must resume its rights" (James [1907] 1975, 62). And elsewhere he argues that if "we have no transphenomenal absolute ready, to *derealize* the whole experienced world by, at a stroke" (James [1905] 1975, 230), then that experienced world is "absolutely" real. As defended in *The Meaning of Truth*, Jamesian humanism is in fact a resolute refusal "to entertain the hypothesis of trans-empirical reality at all" an uncompromising rejection of a "transphenomenal absolute" (ibid., 238). James declares that its "essential service" is to assist us in seeing that "tho one part of our experience may lean upon another part to make it what it is in any one of its several aspects in which it may be considered, experience as a whole is self-containing and leans on nothing" (ibid.; emphasis omitted). He forcefully makes this point in another text (one from *Pragmatism*), asserting there that: "All 'homes' are in finite experience; *finite* experience as such is homeless. Nothing outside of the flux secures the issue of it. It can hope salvation only from its own *intrinsic* promises and potencies" (James [1907] 1975; emphases omitted). That the emphasis is on finitude and historicity as much as on experience (that it is on experience as finite and historical) is made explicit in *A Pluralistic Universe*, where James confesses: "I am finite once for all, and all the categories of my sympathy are knit up with the finite world *as such*, and with things that have a history" (James [1909] 1977, 144). For him, "nothing in the universe [not even God] is great or static or eternal enough not to have some history. But the world that each of us feels most intimately at home with is that of beings with histories that play into our history, whom we can help in their vicissitudes even as they help us in ours" (ibid., 145).

Thus, the world of finite human experience is no ontological beggar, the planetary place of human dwelling no mere vestibule to an unseen temple.[5] Our planetary place is not only a cosmic speck but also a historical actuality wherein human agents conspire with divine forces to improvise an unauthored drama (cf. *PH*, 167). But "the earth of things" is no more a mere stage than it is a mere vestibule: it is a conspiring force, a systematic antagonist, and a sustaining presence.

In "The Crisis of Humanism" Gianni Vattimo (1991) reflects upon Husserl's "Philosophy and the Crisis of European Man" and Heidegger's "Letter on Humanism." In fact, the title of Vattimo's essay is a fragmentary echo of these other two titles. Whereas Husserl traces the crisis of humanism to the eclipse of subjectivity, Heidegger traces it to the triumph of subjectivity. For Husserl, the enemy is naturalism, a view of reality in which subjectivity is an epiphenomenon. For Heidegger, in contrast, humanism itself is one of the names of what must be opposed—in the name of humanity but also in that of the Earth. He sees the degradation of humanity being bound up with the hegemony of humanism and, as part of this hegemony, the primacy and transparency claimed for subjectivity. "For Husserl the crisis of humanism is," as Vattimo observes, "linked to the loss of human subjectivity in the mechanisms of scientific objectivity and, subsequently, technological objectivity" (ibid., 35). The only way out of this crisis is "through a recovery of the central function of the subject," one Husserl explicitly links to the traditional name of *ratio:* "The *ratio* now in question is none other than spirit understanding itself in a really universal, really radical manner, in the form of a science whose scope is universal" (Husserl 1965, 190). But the form of subjectivity to be recovered here "continues to harbour no doubts about its own true nature, which is only externally threatened by an ensemble of mechanisms created by this same subject, but still capable of being reappropriated by it" (Vattimo 1991, 35). This self-understanding Spirit born of self-interrogating subjectivity fails to take seriously its own opacity and its inherent entanglements: "There is not the shadow of a doubt that, although these dehumanizing [scientific and technological] mechanisms have been set in motion by the subject, there might be something wrong with the very structure of the latter" (ibid.). In other words, the crisis into which European cultures are thrown might be one in which they are implicated more deeply than even Husserl allows. The decentering of the subject, not the recovery of subjectivity, provides a way out that does not wind back into the innermost regions of our cultural labyrinth. It suggests a response to our crisis that does not make this crisis even more intractable than it now is. Thus, for Heidegger, "the subject that supposedly has to be defended from [scientistic and] technological dehumanization is the very root of this dehumanization, since the kind of subjectivity which is defined strictly as the subject of the object is a pure function of the world of objectivity [thus, no escape from 'naturalism' in Husserl's sense], and inevitably tends to become itself an object of manipulation" (ibid., 46). Of course, "subjectivity is not something that can be simply shed like an old, worn-out garment" (ibid.).

For James, the essence of humanism is the recognition of human experience in its true character. It at least appears to be a doctrine of immanence. Everything whatsoever has its home in finite experience, but such experience itself is homeless. For Vattimo, the crisis of humanism forces upon us the need to recognize that human subjectivity is not so much an indubitable reality as a dubious heritage. Since "humanism is the doctrine that assigns to humanity the role of subject, that is, of self-consciousness as the locus of evidence" (Vattimo 1991, 43–44) and responsibility, and since in turn the notion of *Erde* (Earth) "derives its importance precisely in connection with the Heideggerian critique of the self-conscious subject" (ibid., 43), the decentering of the subject and the reappropriation of the Earth as matrix and habitat are intimately linked.

While James would no doubt agree with Vattimo in holding that "'humanity' can be fulfilled in history only through a profound revision and transformation of the very notion of humanism" (ibid., 179), his understanding of how this revision and transformation are to be effected would not (in Miller's judgment at least) cut deeply enough. To alter the metaphor, it would (again, from Miller's perspective) stay too much within the narrow orbit of our intellectual traditions. James's own mature doctrine of radical empiricism was intended to rout solipsism and nihilism (see, e.g., "The Place of Affectional Facts in a World of Pure Experience" in James [1912] 1976) by deconstructing the ontological duality of knowing subject and known object. According to this doctrine, the distinction we at this juncture insist upon drawing between our own subjective experiences and an objective order is functional and fluid, not primordial and ontological. Our inherited modes of self-portrayal destine us not only to misdescribe but also actually to disfigure the disclosures of our experience in the very process of our experiencing. This point is not simply that any actual disclosure within human experience is a complex interplay of revelation and concealment; it is rather than the very status and authority of our experience as a medium of disclosure have been so thoroughly questioned and effectively undermined that we ourselves can only feel that "distortion" and "disfigurement" are more apt terms than "disclosure" to use in reference to experience. Insofar as we are still committed to objective knowledge (not to the utterly fantastic ideal of absolutely objective knowledge but to the more modest one of a reliable account of, say, the way things happened or the way things work), the inescapable feeling that human experience is a process of distancing and distortion, not one of intercourse and disclosure, can only be disconcerting. Insofar as we are animated by a Dionysian sense of reverie or an aesthetic vision of our own existence, this feeling will be, at least at first, not disconcerting but liberating. A sense of exhilaration will attend our belief that we have thrown off the narcissistic tyrant of objective reality whose minions never tire of insisting that our highest task is the selfless reflection of this other being. The history of philosophy might even be described as the mythic scene of a watery tomb and disembodied voices: Narcissus destroys himself out of love of the self-same, while Echo lives as disembodiment, becoming at once ethereal and beyond the possibility of being addressed by others because of her very fixation on the absolutely other. To be confined within the limits of self-reflection or to be fixated on the reality of the other as well as on the otherness of reality defines a vast terrain of Western philosophy.

James's doctrine of experience as inherently neither objective nor subjective is an attempt to find a path out of a labyrinth in which roads promising to be ways out so often are actually ways back into the most interior regions of the labyrinth. But the phenomenological appeal to primordial experience (i.e., experience prior to being dirempted functionally into an inner state of consciousness and an outer state of affairs) is only the first step in an effective deconstruction of the ontological duality of, for example, *psyche* and *soma*, inner and outer, or subjective and objective,

Much more needs to be done to decolonize common sense. Regarding a closely allied model, Charles Taylor suggests: "Powerful philosophical arguments have to be marshaled to convince people to think differently about these matters, to shake them out of what seems obvious" (Taylor 1993, 325). At the very least, compelling phenomenological considerations need to be brought to bear on the issue at hand and, moreover, careful philosophical argumentation needs to assist in showing why and how these phenomenological considerations carry within themselves a revisionary force. But, following Miller, who is himself following Hegel, phenomenology is less a matter of observing than one of undergoing: it is a subjection to a course of history in which we own up to a sequence of fatalities by living through this sequence. Thus, the observations of the phenomenologist are those not of a detached observer but of an implicated participant, an observer implicated in the very processes to which he or she is bearing witness. Religious language seems especially apt here, for what is at stake is as much the character of the witness as the contours of the witnessed. Do we have the courage and humility to bear the weight of being witnesses to the shapes of our own consciousness, precisely as these have taken shape in a history in which we as witnesses are rooted? For Miller, the task of phenomenology so understood requires a thicker sense of historicity and hence a deeper sense of fatality than is found in James. Whether Miller is fair to James is not addressed here. James surely felt the lure of stoicism and experienced the arrest of functioning—existential no less than intellectual—for which Miller reserved the word "skepticism" (e.g., *PC,* 150, 152). Moreover, he conceived of these to some extent as fatalities: given his own intellectual history and the cultural development in which this was rooted, it would be impossible to find stoicism unattractive or skepticism congenial. Even so, the lure of worldly engagement worked against that of stoic detachment, just as the attractions of a restless skepticism, the value of an abiding doubt about our most secure criteria and effective procedures, informed his defense of religious belief. But the terms for articulating the *situs,* the placements and displacements, of his own thought were not ones to which he devoted much systematic nor even careful attention. They were, however, focal objects of Miller's philosophical attention.

Although Miller does not explicate humanism in the manner I do below, he provides us with a warrant for our procedure. Although he does not focus on stoicism (the "first" moment in Hegel's account of the struggle to realize the freedom of self-consciousness), he does focus on skepticism, going so far as to assert that no one can be a philosopher who has failed to experience the force of skepticism (*PC,* 71).[6] Note that he does not reduce experiencing the force of skepticism to entertaining a hypothesis or suspending judgment. In this context, then, skepticism is not a composed, glib posture but a severe, disconcerting trial. Skepticism in

Miller's sense is far more than a doctrine to be propounded and defended; it is truly a travail to be undertaken and experienced. The force of skepticism is an immanent force, one launched by the self-defining commitments of self-conscious agents. It derives its strength and authority from commitments constitutive of self-consciousness, though at a stage where these commitments are inadequately comprehended and fatally exaggerated.

More generally, Miller was deeply appreciative of Hegel's achievement. What he prized above all was the suggestive manner in which Hegel carried out a systematic study of the constitutional conflicts in and through which human self-consciousness has attained its actual shape, a shape discernible in instituted practices and discourses as much as in personal sensibilities and outlooks (ibid.). It was perhaps to the author of *The Phenomenology of Spirit* more than that of any other Hegelian text to whom Miller was drawn; for in this work constitutional conflicts in both their broad cultural and intense personal significance are exhibited.[7] These conflicts are threats to thought that erupt within thought (*PC*, 70). Strictly, they concern not consciousness but self-consciousness, for consciousness as something alleged to exist apart from our expressive and symbolic capacities remains completely hidden (ibid.). One might even find the most basal form of human consciousness in effect reduced to unconscious nature (ibid.). "It is," nonetheless, "only in self-consciousness that thought draws its own portrait" (*PC*, 70–71). And its self-portraits are integral to the history of its self-conflicts.

Self-consciousness is not achieved in a single step or a small number of fluid movements (*PC*, 35). The disconcerting conflicts, the arresting crises, by which self-consciousness struggles to attain a secure foothold in a crumbling wall are analogous to the fall in the Garden of Eden. "For only as man was tempted and fell, could he realize the meaning of his values and begin the desperate struggle to recapture them" (ibid.). For example, the meaning of the stoic value of being able to gather oneself within oneself is adequately realized only when the fatal flaw within the stoic stance is exhibited, just as the meaning of the skeptical power of negating appearances and suspending judgment is sufficiently comprehended only on the transcendence of skepticism. What is manifest in the cases of stoicism and skepticism is also true of all philosophical ideas and positions—they "emerge from the pressures of commitment" (*PC*, 86). Apart from the commitment to controlling what is within one's power to control, stoicism could not exist; it emerges as a self-reflexive stance from this self-defining commitment. Apart from the commitment to exercising the power of negation as a power refusing to confine itself within any bounds, skepticism could not exist; it emerges as a self-reflexive stance from a self-defining declaration: *I identify myself with the power of negation and, in turn, this power with a limitless power of absolute negation.* Miller was certainly aware that the systematic study of constitutional conflicts would require a prolonged exhibition of the distinguishable forms of determinate self-consciousness, those forms dramatically exhibited in a single life (e.g., that of Sextus Empiricus, David Hume, or Thomas More) often acquiring the authority of cultural exemplars. But, in his study of these conflicts, his objective was to be not encyclopedic but incisive. He insisted that, in this study, "it is at last a matter of [dramatic] exhibition, rather than of abstract argument" (ibid., 86). The force of skepticism needs to be dramatically exhibited in its most disconcerting shapes so that this force might be felt, so that we might undergo the experience of skepticism. We are not thinking through these constitutional conflicts unless we are living through them, and experience is at bottom not just what the English word suggests (a trying out) but also what the German word *Erlebnis* highlights (a living through).

For Miller, the only possible resolution of any constitutional conflict "lies in realizing the *necessity* of the conflict" (*PC,* 71). In other contexts he speaks of fatalities of thought. By whatever name we might use to designate the urgency and indeed compulsion inherent in the conflicts and crises any actual shape of finite self-consciousness is fated to undergo, it is imperative to own up to the consequences of our own commitments as these consequences assume their fateful shapes in our actual lives (for example, as they make of our religious selves a person unable to pray or of our intellectual selves a person utterly uncertain of not only our judgments but the validity of all of our criteria).

Especially in the last half of the nineteenth century and for the full expanse of the twentieth, we can observe in diverse contexts and with contrasting emphases a commitment to the survival and flourishing of humanity, apart from any divine decree, natural sanction, or historical guarantee. During this same time, and extending into the twenty-first century, we also witnessed mass destruction and human degradation on a scale and of a character unique to our times.[8] What are we to make of our humanism in the light of our inhumanity? How can we narrate the story of this commitment or, more modestly, one thread within this narrative?

The Crisis of Humanism: Contemporary Shapes in Hegelian (Dis)Guise

Supplementing Miller's terms with those of Hegel, I want now to cast the crisis of humanism as an instance of the dialectic of self-consciousness, precisely as this dialectic is exhibited in the section of Hegel's *Phenomenology* entitled "Freedom of Self-Consciousness: Stoicism, Skepticism, and Unhappy Consciousness." In a very general sense, the humanistic subject is a dramatic instance of stoic self-consciousness: it is a self-conscious self-gathering such that an inaccessible interiority becomes the sole locus of authentic humanity, that is to say, an interiority accessible to the self and the self alone. But the inherent instability of the stoic stance is made manifest to stoic self-consciousness itself when the insistence on maintaining the distinction between what is within and what is without its own control is radically undermined by the realization that its own imperative to live in accord with nature makes no sense, on its own terms. But from the perspective of stoicism itself the status of the other and thus of Nature is effectively denied, for whatever appears to stoic consciousness is stripped of its authority to speak for itself, of its power to disclose its inherent character. The scope of stoic freedom is so expansive that virtually everything whatsoever falls within it, such that the distinction between what falls inside and what exists outside of the stoic self's power is not only blurred but thoroughly erased. If the pain of a broken leg or the sting of a deliberate insult resides not in the physical injury or the personal assault, respectively, but in how the self chooses to respond to these; if more generally appearances are assigned their meaning and value by the self in its isolation from its world; if the freedom of the self is located exclusively in the capacity of the self to recede ever more deeply into its own interiority and, from the depths of that interiority, to treat appearances as naught or as wholly other than and thus wholly indifferent to the self for whom they are nonetheless appearances; then the unbounded scope of stoic freedom destroys the distinction upon which such freedom is predicated. That is, the dualistic ontology implicit in stoic self-consciousness—the ontological duality of inner, controllable states and outer, uncontrollable affairs—dissolves itself into a self-enclosed sphere of appearances having the same standing. To lose one's world in this fashion, to be forced to acknowledge that one's own commitments destroy the framework in which those commitments can be expressed and enacted is of course to be driven into skepticism. Skepticism is akin to madness because it means that the skeptic loses nothing less than the world itself, at least the world in a recognizable shape. The term here refers not to the comfortable, often self-congratulatory cynicism of those aloof individuals who ironically detach themselves from virtually every one of their engagements and institutions, including those by which they are sustained; it refers rather to the absolutely disconcerting realization that one's self-defining commitments are self-destroying. The enactment of these commitments is anything but the realization of the form of agency structured and indeed defined by these commitments: the enactment of these commitments entails the dissolution of this form of agency. For the stoic to lose the ability to draw the distinction between what is within and without his control is to lose the ontological dualism by which stoic consciousness defines itself; it means he loses not only his ontology but his world; not only his view of reality but also his lived sense of practical involvement, of existential placement. The inability to maintain this distinction means essential defeat for the stoic stance; it means the inability to maintain oneself as a stoic, if this stance is taken to be adequate on its own terms. Stoicism thus needs to be radically modified to the point of being essentially altered, of becoming something other than it was. Of course, the "truth" of stoicism cannot be gainsaid: whatever else freedom encompasses, it encompasses the capacity of the self to distance itself not only from its own world but also from itself, from its commitments and ideals as well as its perceptions and passions; it encompasses the capacity of the self to gather itself within itself—to recollect who he or she has been. The extent to which the self can actually accomplish this and, moreover, the conditions enabling such distancing are, however, open to question. The link of self-determination and self-differentiation and, in turn, that of self-maintenance and self-revision cannot be severed without denying ourselves the resources for articulating an intelligible account of human freedom. Miller never tires of stressing that self-revision is the price we must pay for self-maintenance.

We see that the collapse of stoicism spells the inauguration of skepticism. But is skepticism itself a stance that can acquit itself in terms of its own aspirations, judging itself by its own criteria and commitments? With skepticism, the ontological duality of an inner, controllable sphere and an outer, uncontrollable domain is transposed within consciousness itself. But here, again, the very distinctions by which this shape of consciousness defines itself, by which this stance constitutes itself as the placement of a self, are ones that cannot be maintained by the skeptics themselves, for skeptics are ones who trade the world for their stance. To maintain one's skeptical stance one must acknowledge what one cannot acknowledge in terms drawn solely from one's own position; the maintenance of skepticism entails the transcendence of skepticism as an allegedly self-sufficient stance.

And we see that the power of negation by which the stoic can deny that pain is pain, that this painful experience is an authoritative disclosure of an actual occurrence, expands to the point that the stoic transforms himself into the skeptic. One thread of continuity between the two stances is thus the centrality of negation for both stances. But it is in reference to the power of negation not only that is skepticism linked to stoicism but also that skepticism is divided within itself in such a way that it calls forth a radically different stance, that of unhappy consciousness, that form of alienated awareness resulting in being cut off from the sustaining conditions of one's actual existence.

What unhappy consciousness reveals in the end is its own imperative drive toward recognition and reconciliation with the actual. Such consciousness demands that the immanent ideals by which finite human consciousness is compelled to assume the shape of unhappy consciousness are fully acknowledged and accredited in their actual immanence. Consequently, the immanent *telos* of unhappy consciousness is ultimately a steady and steadying recognition that the actual locus of operative ideals cannot be the self in isolation from the world: unhappy consciousness is skeptical consciousness transcended and transformed. There is no self without a world, no subject completely gathered within itself, for to maintain consistently one's skepticism means calling into question the scope and source of one's own power of negation, a power characteristically exercised by the skeptic in voicing doubts and suspending judgment. Who authorizes these doubts? What compels these suspensions? The self cannot be without a world for it cannot be without other selves, a truth revealed within the self-imposed limits of the most resolutely skeptical positions. Hence, to call the scope and source of one's own power of negation into question in a thoroughgoing and rigorous manner compels one to confront the dialogical character of all articulate consciousness, even if articulation contents itself with negation. In turn, this character reveals within the constitution of consciousness itself an Other to whom the finite, erstwhile skeptical self is beholden. This Other has the status of an authoritative self to whom the finite self cannot help but appeal.

Skeptical consciousness is nothing if not critical consciousness, that form of awareness insistent upon defining itself in terms of critique. But it is consciousness that has turned within itself as well as upon itself. Its own impressions and tendencies—above all, its tendencies toward affirmation—are the sole objects of its critical attention, for it has suspended judgment regarding what is other than itself. Critical consciousness is, however, divided consciousness: just as stoicism deliberately distances itself from an outward, uncontrollable domain, so skepticism deliberately distances itself from its own tendencies toward affirmation, its own bias toward judgment, thereby distancing itself from itself. But this judicative consciousness can maintain itself only by owning up to its divided and thus dialogical character as judge and judged, critic and criticized. The Other to whom the finite self appeals and by whom this self is haunted is at first merely a shadowy other, a fleeting image within skeptical consciousness itself. But is this sufficient for the maintenance of skepticism? The power and authority of its negations at least seem to explode the bounds of a merely finite consciousness. The infinite is not so much born of the longings inherent in finite consciousness, as it is borne by finite consciousness in its unquestionable capacity for infinite negation. In brief, the infinite is resident within the finite. Here as in countless other cases, it has taken time to realize this truth about actuality and it will require much more time and much greater labor than have been expended thus far to draw out the implications of this truth.

Unhappy consciousness is rent asunder by its unreconciled and, from within its own outlook, unreconcilable commitments. If the history of humanity is the story of the fatalities of human commitments in the actual circumstance of their absolute affirmation, then it is the story of humanity constitutionally beside itself, inevitably at war with itself. In *Phenomenol-*

ogy, Hegel exhibits some of the most crucial moments in the fateful struggle of human consciousness to overcome its estrangement from itself and its status as an exile in the world. In the dialectic of consciousness presupposed by the dialectic of self-consciousness, he displays a series of self-inverting positions, all of which illustrate the opposition between a certain epistemic norm and what we are actually able to know in attempting to satisfy this norm (Taylor 1975, 148). What drives the dialectic of consciousness are the inevitable, inherent frustrations of finite consciousness to satisfy its own epistemic demands. In contrast, what drives the dialectic of self-consciousness is the longing for recognition, the demand to be acknowledged as a self by other selves. This dialectic is thus aptly described as human longing and its fateful vicissitudes (ibid.). It is a process in which the annihilative tendencies knit into the very fabric of finite consciousness are shown to be ones involving an inescapable reciprocity: the self cannot annihilate the other without in some respect also annihilating itself. The most immediate forms of human satisfaction—eating and drinking—being also the most limited forms, are unsatisfying. So, too, the most characteristic forms of human relationship, being among those forms most hostile to the principle of reciprocity, are in truth modes of estrangement. What Hegel's dialectic of self-consciousness shows, in detail, are historically determinate and recurrent shapes of finite actuality wherein what we claim to be and what we actually are stand not just in uneasy tension but in fatal opposition to one another (ibid.).

In this section, we are focusing on three such shapes of finite consciousness. The career launched by the struggle between master and slave (the struggle most immediately presupposed by the sequence of stoic, skeptical, and unhappy self-consciousness and most clearly revealed in frustrated longings of unhappy consciousness) shows nothing less than this: human consciousness is an incessant longing for absolute recognition. This longing might be dismissed as infantile, but such dismissals seem to do nothing, or even less than nothing, to eradicate such longing. For in dismissing or denying this longing there is a failure to own up to it as a constitutive feature of human consciousness; and this failure can only mean that the longing operates in a subterranean way. The absolute affirmation of human freedom definitive of stoic consciousness is destined to destroy that form of consciousness, for it is destined to destroy the world in which such consciousness can alone be at home: the ontological dualism of an outer, uncontrollable, and senseless order and an inner, self-controlled, and meaning-conferring order. Note that not only do outer and inner split apart into two utterly separate domains but also that actuality and meaning split apart, such that external actuality is inherently meaningless and internal significance is ontologically rootless. The strategy of retreat from the entangling alliances and thus from the fateful entanglements of external actuality is greatly intensified in skeptical consciousness, to the point where the externality of the actual can no longer be granted. Finite consciousness by virtue of an absolute commitment to infinite negation withdraws so deeply within itself that, in terms of the world it has defined for itself by this withdrawal, there is no principled way any longer of distinguishing within and without. But, even so, within itself there still operates an incessant longing for absolute recognition. This longing launches a struggle by a form of consciousness acutely aware of its own mutability to secure an immutable ground for its own actual existence, by a shape of awareness painfully conscious of its own limitations to attain the orienting vision of infinite scope.

Finite consciousness is bound in a life and death struggle with an absolute other, to which it is allied as a systematic antagonist: it can establish neither its finitude nor the level of self-consciousness with which it identifies itself without allying itself to an infinite other. But this other is not in its possession; indeed, the very attempt to construe in possessive terms this constitutive relationship to the absolute other cannot but destroy the status of this other as other. At the level of unhappy consciousness, the absolute other is at once an integral aspect of finite consciousness and an irreducible actuality to which such consciousness is yet unreconciled. The gradual and painful process of reconciliation will either revert to one of the stages by which this level of self-consciousness has been obtained or move toward an actual reconciliation with the actual conditions of that finite actuality known as human consciousness. Since Miller tends to suspect that most other forms of humanism are insufficiently self-conscious, especially in reference to their own historicity, he also tends to suspect that they are but moments in a dialectic about which they were largely unconscious. He himself tends to focus on the movement from dogmatism to skepticism and, then, the movement either back to a disguised form of dogmatism or forward to a position beyond both dogmatism and skepticism (a position he often calls "idealism").

As we have seen, the essence of humanism has historically meant, among other things, the centrality of subjectivity. Humans are above all subjects in the sense of agents who are apparently able to dissociate themselves from any and every attachment and association, and who are thereby able to withdraw from the world and to gather themselves within themselves. So envisioned, subjectivity seems to be the space in which a human being can gather a self as such. It is where the individual authentically resides. In celebrating the space of this subjectivity, however, philosophy has in effect effaced the actuality of "space," not only the immediate, palpable locus of the lived body but also the equally immediate, sustaining sites of the body's living engagements. Because interiority is presumed to be the essence of subjectivity, and in turn, because subjectivity is presumed to be the sole site of authentic existence, the essence of humanism—not as an abstract philosophical doctrine but as a concrete historical development—is inextricably linked with the site of interiority. And it is difficult, if not impossible, to see how advocacy of humanism can avoid reinscribing the ontological duality of inner and outer; it is equally difficult to see how such a reinscription can avoid the nihilism that humanism supposes itself to be combating.

This section exhibits the integral moments of contemporary humanism in terms of the Hegelian dialectic of the freedom of self-consciousness, the fateful shapes of self-consciousness in its struggle to win for itself an adequate form of self-determination. What the discussion discloses is, in the first instance, humanism as a more or less disguised form of stoicism in Hegel's sense; in the second, humanism as a form of skepticism emerging directly out of the collapse of stoicism; and, in the third, the humanistic stance as a telling instance of unhappy consciousness fated either to regress to less adequate visions of self-determination or to reconcile itself with the actual world, including its planetary home, as an appropriate habitat for human dwelling. In reconciling itself with the world as it actually is, here and now, unhappy consciousness ceases to be unhappy: alienated consciousness overcomes its alienation by identifying itself with, and thereby reconciling itself to, that more or less integrated array of finite actualities making up its actual world. Reconciled consciousness—awareness attuned to actuality as the condition of its own emergence and flourishing as well as an ensemble of practices and institutions for which this awareness assumes the responsibility to maintain—is by definition no longer unhappy consciousness. Such reconciliation means that the actual places of this earth, not the imagined sites of our own psyches, provide the loci in which humans dwell. By crawling out of the cave of skeptical consciousness we can once again crawl into the caves of human history and travel to other memorialized scenes of human involvement. We can discern the protean shapes of our contemporary existence (e.g., of humanism in our century) not so much by plumbing the depths of our inwardness but by tracing the configurations and transfigurations assumed by self-conscious agents in their actual struggles to secure abiding forms of a self-defined existence.

One of these historical shapes is, somewhat ironically, the recurrent tendency to ground oneself within oneself, to seek for oneself within the depths of one's own inwardness. Others, at other times and in other places, have attempted to do just what we at some moments in our own lives feel compelled to do. In general, history is the psyche writ large. To an uncanny degree, the forms assumed in the course of this struggle are at least akin to, possibly identical with, those assumed by the lives of my readers and myself. To reconcile oneself to actuality is to make peace with the ephemerality of one's own achievements. But making such peace with ephemerality does not mean disowning the need to give determinate and even lasting form to one's freedom. For the midworld enforces a discipline as much as it unleashes a destiny; and in enforcing a discipline upon us it prompts and goads and guides the formation of a resolute will and the maintenance of a civil habitat. In short, it forces us to give articulate, arresting, and enduring shape to our lives and our world. But our lives are in the first instance an inchoate series of bodily engagements and our world is in its most immediate aspect the unintegrated scenes of human striving. But, as we pregnantly say, in time this series of movements becomes less inchoate and the scenes of our striving more integrated.

The overcoming of unhappy consciousness entails reconciliation with the actual world. In turn, this reconciliation encompasses a reappropriation of our earthly existence. At the very least, to appropriate anew our earthly existence is to celebrate, perhaps for the first time, our earthly habitat. It means reconciling ourselves to the Earth as our home.

Miller's Humanism: Owning Up to the Demands of Self-Authorization

Why have our philosophical outlooks tended to discredit our earthly habitat along with our historical actuality? Is this discrediting of the human abode connected to the derealization of human historicity? How might we accredit this abode and the stories of our dwelling here in such a way that both humanity and its habitat are fully given their due? To use Thomas Nagel's phrase, "the view from nowhere" is as much a denunciation of the historically defined places as of the geographically situated histories by which our actual identities are formed, maintained, and revised. These identities are—and not simply in a psychological or anthropological sense but in an ontological one—topologically as well as historically inflected; apart from such inflections, we are inarticulate. Apart from determinate places as the memorial sites of determinative histories, we can neither name nor define ourselves. Why then have these places along with these histories been accorded so little attention and, not infrequently, so much contempt by traditional philosophy?

Miller's humanism is an attempt to answer such questions. It is implied in his revision of philosophy; hence, it is of a piece with his historicism. This historicism does not bid humans to comprehend their age upon its alleged fulfillment (Hegel 1973, 12–13) or to evacuate the actuality of one's present locale for the hope of a utopian future. For it philosophy comes neither too late, spreading its wings only at dusk, nor too soon, laboring for a morning it will not see. The actual present as a gathering place of the distinct dimensions of human temporality, the present site where the full weight of the past presses on the coalescing shapes of the future, is not (contra Hegel) an actuality effectively cut off from the future or (contra Marx) one dramatically severable from the past. Human history precludes absolute ruptures: no epoch attains the sort of closure that would make of it either a self-contained actuality or a self-generated possibility. The finite actualities of human history are, by virtue of their finitude, self-transcending; likewise, the concrete possibilities of human action are, by virtue of their concreteness, seized only in the interstices of our inheritances.[9] Instead, Miller's humanism bids humans to live unreservedly in the here and now, to accredit fully their particular place at just this historical moment.

Miller's central notion of "local control" is the other side of what is largely left implicit in his voluminous manuscripts. Correlative to local control are those appropriated locales, those personal places, serving as the defining regions, thus the limiting conditions, of human comportment. Just as functioning objects such as yardsticks give us local control over some actual scene of human involvement, so the human body as the paradigm of a functioning object gives us, at least potentially, local control over any earthly scene. A disorienting scene presupposes a motile being capable of orienting and thus of reorienting itself; disorientation might be described as a provocation to such a being. The struggle of such a being "to regain its feet" indicates the extent to which the actual capacities of such agents make immediate, imperative demands on unfamiliar, even inhospitable circumstances. But the inhospitality of such circumstances itself bears witness to the abiding sense we have that the Earth is hospitable, soliciting and sustaining our strivings and even our struggles. Most primordially, the ground as that on which I stand and walk is, in reference to my own body as a functioning object, what I mean by an appropriated locale of human comportment. To use James J. Gibson's apt term, the ground is an affordance: it affords me opportunities for placement and motility. Note that in saying the ground affords me an opportunity, I am implying a temporal aspect of lived "space." But the ground does so because I have mastered the movements of my own limbs and the control of my own muscles. The ground affords me this opportunity in a way quite different from the more remote affordance it offers to a very young child just learning to crawl. In gaining control over my own body as a functioning object, in the actual maturation of my body itself into a (more or less) integrated array of complex capacities, I am in effect appropriating a vast spectrum of physical locales. I walk into a room for the first time without thinking about the delicate bodily negotiations by which this physical transposition is accomplished; I converse with a stranger without in the least attending to the various semiotic processes by which this miraculous exchange is made possible. But I appropriate this spectrum of locales as an agent always already enveloped by and implicated in them. It is not as an alien but as an earthling that I learn to inhabit more fully and finely the Earth that gives me name as well as being.

Other examples of what I am calling the appropriated locales of human comportment are the street on which one lives that is one's own, the place one works that is one's own, and perhaps most intimately the place one lives that is most fully one's own. For the vagrant soul, human places are essentially vacant spaces to be defined solely in terms of contemporary whim; vagrants define any place in any way they desire. Their declarations of where they happen to be are not animated and controlled by the declarations of those who have gone before them. For them there are no sacred places or essential loci: they can only happen to be somewhere. Their placements are never more than merely contingent. The vagrant is a *flâneur* (Benjamin 1968). For civil persons, in contrast, determinate places are almost always partly the essence of their actual lives. They do not just happen to live here rather than there. Precisely because the history in and through which they identify themselves is a series of fatalities, their placements and dwellings also bear the marks of fatality. This is as true in our historical time as it was in previous times, though we pride ourselves on our mobility and adaptability. For example, Virginia Woolf's identity was bound up with London no less than Socrates's was bound up with Athens. While it is clear that civility has to do with self-imposed constraint, it is far less clear that civility also has to do with self-maintained enclosures. These enclosures are heterogeneous: they include deliberately sustained spheres of privacy that might serve as sites of intimacy (private dwellings, private gardens), formally consecrated places that might serve as occasions for human commemoration and celebration (churches, temples, cemeteries, battlefields, libraries, national parks, public gardens), culturally authorized places reserved for the defining activities of that particular culture (laboratories, markets, universities, libraries serving a function different from simple commemoration), civically instituted places designed to embody the public will of a people to live justly (as this public will is embodied in such public institutions as assemblies, courts, and other fora).

Of course, one might be estranged from one's own place and all of its particularities. One might even disclaim responsibility for one's workplace or even one's own habitat. Those who are characteristically disposed to disclaim responsibility for the locales of their lives are what Miller calls "vagrants": in the name of freedom, they refuse to be attached to any particular locale and often to any particular persons. They see all laws as the external imposition of arbitrary forces, all agencies of enforcing law as enemies.

In Miller's moral lexicon, the antonym of vagrancy is civility. Moreover, civility is the flower of piety. When one knows where one is, one knows how to act. And one knows where one is only when one knows who it was who bequeathed these places to one. Does our outlook have the resources to identify the ground of our outrage at the incivility entailed by littering? by defacing public buildings or private dwellings? By mocking an elderly person or eroticizing very young children? If we are to have a metaphysics for persons on Elm Street, for ordinary persons engaged in the quotidian tasks of ordinary life, then it is crucial that this metaphysics exhibit the ground of what is still felt by most of us as outrage at the incivilities abounding in our time. Could it be that "ground" here is no mere metaphor? Cultivating an ethos of civility is of a piece with cultivating a sense of place; in turn, cultivating a sense of place is of a piece with attaining the loyalty and gratitude traditionally associated with the classical virtue of *pietas* (so eloquently defended by, among others, Socrates, Cicero, Thomas Aquinas, and George Santayana).[10] For Miller, nothing short of a self-consciously situated ethos of civility will suffice. To be self-consciously situated is to be historically self-conscious. More basically, "to be in History is to be an heir, but an heir to defect as well as to achievement. They go together. The doctrine of 'original sin' reappears as a constitutional feature of heritage" (PL, 452). But one can enjoy the benefits of an inheritance without being conscious of being a beneficiary. The appropriation and maintenance of a self-consciously situated ethos are enactments of our responsibility for nothing less than our world: we, the inheritors of these traditions and practices, living here and now, assume responsibility for our inheritance, for its confusions, exclusions, and occlusions as well as its illuminations, enfranchisements, and affordances (*PH*, 188). As has become passionately felt by many people today, our world includes our planet. To be indifferent to the Earth manifests a degree of ingratitude and infidelity for which we have only a thoroughly discredited word, impiety.

When in Plato's "Crito" the character of Socrates imagines the Laws of Athens rising up to confront him as he is about to play the role of vagrant, he is stayed by the sting of their charge. His own ethos, as internalized, forces him to confront the impiety—the infidelity and ingratitude—entailed by refusing to submit to the penalty imposed upon him. He condemns Athens itself for its condemnation of him by proving himself to be, even in the face of injustice, its most exemplary citizen. Although his own interrogation cannot stay the steps of the presumptuous youth Euthyphro, Socrates's self-interrogations in the "Crito" enable him, despite the urgings of his friends, to stay put. That is, while Euthyphro runs away from his interlocutor, the result of Socrates's self-enacted drama is to remain where he has virtually always been. He cannot leave Athens for Athens cannot be excised from his soul, without destroying that soul. We have here a dramatic instance of what A. N. Whitehead in another connection calls "mutual immanence": the polis inhabits the citizen no less than the citizen inhabits the polis.

Terms of opprobrium might be construed largely as reminders of locale. For example, to call an act "indecent" might mean not that the act itself is inherently evil but rather that it is simply out of place. Insofar as any densely historical place is reduced, however, to purely physical space wherein contemporary wills enact their spontaneous contemporaneity, the force of such terms evaporates. What force does it have to remind students at a university, slouched in their seats with baseball hats worn backwards, that the place they currently occupy is a place carved out by Plato and countless others for whom learning defines a way of life, not an instrument or ornament. It is not that we are just now living amid ruins. Instead, there has for many centuries for vast numbers of humans hardly been a time when humans have not lived in the presence of the remnants of temples to unforgotten gods and of edifices of vanquished cultures. Our civility is measured by how we live amid such ruins, beginning with our recognition of their significance. Do we feel any compulsion to grant our ancestors or the ancestors of others the respect they themselves tended to accord to their ancestors? The earliest cultures treated their own dead respectfully. They took pains to bury them and to memorialize their loss. To return to the Earth one's own, on one side, and the refusal to allow either natural forces or human cupidity or indifference to destroy cultural monuments, on the other, are curiously connected. While the one act returns to nature the irrevocably lost person, the other fights against the natural decay and human destruction of what is also irrevocably lost. Just as it would be a desecration to leave a human or even animal body unburied, so it would be a desecration to allow the Parthenon or Pyramids to be lost. "Barbarism leaves no monuments.... The theogony of a free people is its history. The Greeks invented the historical temper. Their sense of freedom and history are linked" (PL, 432).

How are we to live amid the ruins of our histories? The humanities properly understood should provide us with resources for answering this question and, even more basically, for experiencing the compulsion to address this question in its full sweep and significance. Once we have acknowledged the "necessity of history," we are in the position to experience the necessities within our own history, the fatalities inherent in our inheritances. The humanities assist us in this task. They should remind us of who we are by reminding us of where we are. Note that in this context "where" designates a densely sedimented historical place. Of course, we live amid the ruins of our own civilization as historical actors committed to building new edifices, new places of, for example, habitation and congregation, of education and business. We are not destined to dwell in ruins the way cave dwellers contented themselves with the enclosures provided by the Earth. The ruins are themselves responsible for stirring a deep and recurrent disquietude, for engendering wild and even fanatical hopes. They prompt our rebellion against dissipating our lives, against the immense pressures to move in a desultory fashion or to fixate on insignificant matters. They both call us to ourselves and call us beyond ourselves. In sum, theirs is a disquieting presence insinuating that the absent ones are not those whose hands piled these stones or those who assembled in this forum or worshipped in this temple: these ruins insinuate the terrifying possibility that it is we who are actually absent from the Earth on which we apparently dwell.

Colleges and universities are places allied with the ruins of human civilizations and, at the same time, devoted to technological innovation and scientific discovery. In response to the question "Well, then, doesn't a college have to stand for something?" Miller asserts: "Yes . . . but only for the opposition to a man's being a dunce" (PL, 673). At bottom, then, Miller was proposing that our terms of opprobrium have the force of asserting: "*We* do not act that way *here*." In this assertion *we* and *here* are bound together. Just as *we* are place-bound, here is a self-consciously inherited place such that it implicates us in the history of a community, of a nation, of the whole array of living beings, or even of the cosmos itself. While locales may only invite habitation and often even bar it, communities demand implacement. Of course, community and locale can be sundered in various ways. One way is when the members of a community because of the fateful consequences of their own intellectual commitments and technological innovations abstract themselves from the particularities of the places that they inhabit. As our attachments to actual locales become ever more attenuated, our identities become ever more abstract and often amorphous. Moreover, our morally charged reminders of who and where we are become ever more ineffective in evoking a telling sense of the particular historical place we are trying to defend against barbarians and vagrants. This is perhaps nowhere more apparent than in the case of impiety. We live irreverently, whereas Socrates died piously. Piety means for most of us today something either quite remote from its earliest meanings or something completely antiquated or even ridiculous. But this lexical loss might signal a spiritual deprivation. For it is beyond question that we live by the graciousness of forces other than ourselves. These forces are both natural and historical. The presumption of self-generation is the depth of self-deception.

Along with Josiah Royce, Miller advocated a form of provincialism. Just as Hans-Georg Gadamer (see, e.g., 1975, 239–53, and 1976, 64) has tried to expose an untenable prejudice against prejudice as a defining element of the Enlightenment sensibility, so Miller tried to expose the untenability of an abstracted universalism. Such universalism is itself the prejudice, in the pejorative sense, of a group of provincials who are systematically blind to their own status as provincials. Just as forejudgment needs to be rescued from the unacknowledged prejudices of most Enlightenment thinkers, so the integrity and, arguably at least, the sanctity of local shrines and sites must be rescued from the continuous onslaughts of an abstracted intellectualism that presumes a universal authority because it disowns particular attachments.

Miller's relationship to Williamstown was not unlike Emily Dickinson's relationship to Amherst—or, for that matter, not unlike Heidegger's to his village in the Black Forest—though because he was not so reclusive it was also markedly different. He diligently read the local paper and attended town meetings. He even made newspapers a focus of his philosophical attention. In an intriguing letter, he announced to his son Eugene, who worked as a reporter and editor: "Let me warn you that the *status* of news is a metaphysical problem of the Actual" (PL, 547).

It is instructive to contrast Miller's attitude toward news with Henry David Thoreau's disparagement of the news as a distraction from what is essential in life. In *Walden,* Thoreau ([1854] 1980) confesses, after announcing that he could easily do without the post office, that he could as easily do without newspapers. The public agency instituted to facilitate private correspondence and those private enterprises designed to facilitate public debate are disparaged in the same breath; Thoreau moves from the one to other in a single sentence, condemning in a single breath, as it were, two institutions taken by Miller to be requisite for civility.

> And I am sure [just as I have almost never received a letter worth the postage] that I never read any memorable news in a newspaper. If we read of one man robbed, or murdered, or killed by accident, or one house burned, or one vessel wrecked, or one steamboat blown up, or one cow run over on the Western Railroad, or one mad dog killed, or one lot of grasshoppers in winter, —we never need read of another. One is enough. If you are acquainted with the principle, what do you care for a myriad instances and applications? To a philosopher all *news,* as it is called, is gossip, and they who edit and read it are old women over their tea. Yet not a few are greedy after this gossip. (Thoreau [1854] 1980, 68)

In contrast, Miller contends: "News is an element of personal maturity. It supposes a local interest and a local responsibility, a personal equation with specific events and their control. News concerns the Individual in his activity, in what he is *now* doing, now and here" (PL, 545; cf. Dewey [1927] 1984, 347-48, on "news"). He goes on to note in this same letter: "Children do not read newspapers. They are not yet involved in the maintenance of their peculiar environment" (ibid.), their unique locale. This observation recoils on the theme of maturity, for he further notes that those not yet involved in maintaining their locale rather well define their status as children, as it well might define the immature relationship to place that is characterized by vagrancy.

It has been said that, once the printing press was invented, democracy was inevitable. The communal deliberations of a truly democratic culture are carried on, more than anywhere else, in newspapers and magazines, on radio and television. The maintenance as well as institution of democracy thus depends on what might be called a daily ritual of democratic civility—reading one's local newspaper as a way of attending to local events, thereby assuming local responsibility. While not a few of us are greedy for gossip, all too few of us demand that the media provide us with something else, those local reports vital to sustaining our actual locales. We get the news we more or less deserve. In more than one place, Miller reflects on the distinction between editorial criticism and local reporting, to suggest that what needs to be distinguished should not be separated. For him, there is perhaps no better example of local control than the local newspaper responsibly read. In any event, locating responsibility must mean, above all, something utterly mundane and quotidian. It must mean those daily or at least regular activities by which we affirm and refine our personal attachment to a particular place. One such activity is reading the local newspaper. Another is conversing with a neighbor. Yet another is writing to a friend about what is going on where one lives. The need for privacy may become so urgent that one quits the company of one's neighbors and goes into the woods in order "to live deliberately," in order "to front only the essential facts of life" (Thoreau [1854] 1980, 66). But to front the actuality of our lives in the places where those lives are ordinarily lived can itself be a way of living deliberately, with a resolute will to attain full consciousness of our actual locale.

With the same passion and commitment with which Thoreau turned to Nature, Miller turned to history. And Miller turned to history for the same reason that Thoreau turned to Nature: to front the essentials of life, to see whether he could learn what it had to teach, and not, when he came to die, to discover that he had never lived (ibid.). With the same intensity and devotion that Dickinson turned to poetry, Miller turned to philosophy. His lecture notes and personal letters contain his finely crafted utterances. They, too, contain a celebration of the quotidian, an affirmation of the mundane. But, as all three testify, this earthly place and this fleeting moment are not without their cosmic radiance.

The connection between Miller's historicism and his humanism is immediately evident in, for example, chapter 6 of *The Paradox of Cause*, entitled "History and Humanism." It is manifest in numerous other texts as well. But humanism is most often defined by its rejection of theism, not by its alliance with historicism. Miller does himself assert that we are today on our own, without "the traditional comforts of supernatural support" or even the attenuated assurances of a rational order exhibited in our natural habitat (*PC*, 93). We can appeal to neither God nor Nature to underwrite the authority by which we condemn the treachery of the traitor or praise the heroism of the patriot, by which we distinguish the erroneous statement from the accurate one, the unjust deed from the just one. Yet, just because we are on our own, "our acts and purposes lack adequate authority. Since they are only identifiable in time, they seem insubstantial and ephemeral" (ibid.). We ourselves feel our acts and purposes, thus our relationships and lives themselves, to lack the status and authority we desperately desire for them. Often our own lives feel to us to lack shape and substantiality. They feel untethered.

What, if anything, is the relationship between the feeling that our lives lack shape and substantiality, on one hand, and the feeling that they are untethered or uprooted, on the other? Can either or both of these feelings be explained by the fact that we acknowledge our acts and purposes to be "only identifiable in time" but refuse to grant absolute authority to such temporal affairs? Is it possible to live the truth of our lives as this has been historically disclosed to us, to live what is by now a glib commonplace—the "truth" of our lives is that there is no truth? If rugged individualism has for quite a while looked a bit ragged (Dewey [1929] 1984, 66–76), Promethean humanism in turn seems not only to lack foresight but above all to lack hindsight, not only to be untrue and inadequately unconcerned with truth but also inhumane and insufficiently attentive to suffering. This should not surprise us, for Promethean humanism is at bottom the compensatory faith of those who will not do without God. Such humanism elevates humanity itself into a deity and thereby reveals its own lunacy. Our ancestors might merit our reverence, but humanity at large can never be an appropriate object of religious adoration (Findlay 1964, 48). Discrediting the Deity, even in the form of humanity, however, does not mean discarding the sacred, as that which we here and now hold to be inviolable. Even so, our sense of the sacred is in no small measure vitiated by our awareness of our own historicity: others at other times and others even now in other places, be it only next door, sacralize what we denounce. So, while discrediting traditional objects of worship does not necessarily preclude an ingenuous commitment to marking as sacral occasions the birth of a child, the death of a parent, the commitment of oneself to another, a recurrent awareness of the discredited fantasies of traditional religion works against sustaining this commitment.

But our sense of our own historicity does not only work against our sense of the sacred. It undermines our confidence to mark virtually all of the differences we are actually committed to marking, including the difference between truth and error as well as that between veracity and deceit. To make this clear, let us recall some of the ways this confidence in our ability to tell the telling differences has been undermined. The very notion that the telling differences (the distinction between justice and injustice, or that between truth and falsity, or that between the sacred and the manipulable) are at bottom humanly told differences is itself enough to discredit them in the eyes of many. But other inferences also serve to undermine this confidence. Here is a sample of them. If everything is merely contingent upon our actual history, then nothing within our moment of that history is necessary. If every object of human worship with which we are familiar has in time become desecrated and discredited, then not only is nothing worthy of our worship but nothing is sacred. Moreover, if the sacred is only what we, as the heirs of history, hold to be inviolable, then the sacred itself is reduced to a pathetic illusion, lacking authoritative status even more than arresting presence. In the words of the traditional spiritual, God does not always come when you want him but he always comes on time. And when the divine does erupt into history, the habitual sequence of everyday tasks is suspended; at least some portion of humanity is stopped in its tracks. If the "sacred" did not have the power to stop and to redirect human energies, it would not truly have the status of the sacred. Whatever else divinity is, it is neither tame nor tamable. If there are only historically accredited standards by which to detect our errors, then there are no absolutely valid criteria by which we judge ourselves; and if there are no such criteria, no responsible judgment is even possible. To repeat, this need not be the case. After stressing that one needs a past, Miller makes clear just what character such a past must have: "A historical past is more than a thing of time; it is always the bearer of infinity, the dynamic of divine forces in time" (*PH*, 167). But the dynamism of the divine in history seems pale and bloodless when compared with what we, looking back, suppose to have been those awful theophanies to which the sacred scriptures of various traditions bear witness. (Think how words like "awful" and "adorable" have been destroyed without being replaced.) Moreover, it "is in history that truth becomes identified with the faiths of men. Truth has stepped down from eternity into time" (ibid.). But in becoming identified with the faiths of men and women truths have ceased to carry the authority of truths and have become *mere* opinions (simply something someone *happens* to believe, something utterly idiosyncratic and contingent). In stepping down from eternity and entering into history,[11] truths have been transformed into beliefs and, in turn, beliefs into opinions and, finally, opinions into the arbitrary assertions of untethered individuals, individuals who refuse to define themselves through their commitments to historically generated and sustained practices and institutions (such purely arbitrary assertions alone being what deserve to be called *mere* opinions). As all formalities tend to be characterized as *empty* formalities and all rituals as *hollow* rituals, all memory as *rote* memory and all traditions as *blind* traditions—just as all appeals to tradition are immediately interpreted as requests to follow blindly what itself is (allegedly) nothing more than blind stumbling, so all requests by teachers for summarizing a text are demeaned by students as demands to regurgitate what someone else has written—so too truth becomes equated with *mere* opinion and the presumption to speak the truth becomes identified with pathological forms of intellectual tyranny.

Accordingly, assured from previous epochs that there is a Truth beyond time, we have devolved to a time without any confidence in our own ability to tell the truth, so much so we are suspicious of, if not hostile to, the very notion of truth. Except in ever more trivial or remote contexts (on one side, those concerned with locating cats on mats and, on the other, those concerned with inquiries in which we are ourselves not participants), the presumption to tell the truth tends to be greeted as an intolerable arrogance or benighted superstition—or both. In its most important personal and cultural form, skepticism is the arrest of functioning: the fluency with which one formerly marked the distinction between, say, truth and falsity is currently and perhaps permanently lost. One is utterly at a loss to know what to say or even to know whether anything at all can still be said. This loss can be experienced at first as liberation; but in time it comes to be felt by at least some as being imprisoned within the circle of their own impotence, of their inability to tell the differences that they feel yet need to be told. Others are (to use Miller's own term here) "vagrants": they tell themselves and others that truth needs to be exposed for what it always has been and still is, a debilitating fixation and, worse, a policing device. In its most tragic shape, skepticism is the arrest of a mode of activity with which agents are yet allied and by which they identify themselves to themselves as well as others. Think here of religious persons unable to pray or worship, experimental inquirers unable to establish the controls by which fruitful investigation can be distinguished from fraudulent speculation, democratic citizens who have completely lost confidence in the actual workings of the deliberative assemblies alleging to represent them. It is inevitable that such self-arrest is felt to be self-laceration.

But is not this time without truth the shadow cast by a Truth outside time? Is not the nihilistic *Stimmung* of our historical moment the self-protective posture of human beings who have once too often been deceived by the false lure of timeless truth and, more generally, of immutable authority? Is not nihilism in its earlier phases the celebratory mood of those who have fled an all too close sick room, dramatically immersing themselves in the destructive element, while nihilism in its later phases is the sullen mood of one who feels betrayed by a parental surrogate but does not have the courage or the honesty to own up to this feeling? The vacillation between irresponsible celebration and unacknowledged sullenness, of annihilation masquerading as celebration and of immaturity cursing yet denying its own dependency, is a manifest feature of our cultural life. It could not be otherwise, for ours is a nihilistic epoch. It can be otherwise, for ours is a historical moment in which the historical moment in its finite actuality and insistent authority can, finally, be accredited. But this suggests that we ourselves are on the verge of telling yet another triumphalist tale in which we can look upon our poor benighted ancestors with "bemused condescension" (Rorty 1982, xxx) for their centuries-long self-deception. Can humanism, even in its most resolutely historicist articulation, avoid the pose of ironists who refuse to confront our current crises of authority or the delusions of triumphalists who fail to appreciate the extent to which they themselves are complicit in carrying forward what they suppose they have moved beyond?

While Miller's humanism clearly avoided the ironic pose so characteristic of the deracinated sensibility of Western intellectuals—self-defined outsiders with arched critical brows distancing themselves from ingenuous involvement in the actual affairs of the historical institutions sustaining their lives—and identified himself with Williams College and Williamstown, it is by no means obvious that his humanism avoided triumphalism. In what might seem paradoxical, making history constitutional means making place primordial. To grant history categoreal status is to grant place absolute significance. In yet other words, the discovery of historical time is above all the recovery of the actual places in which human histories are rooted. For this and other reasons, then, Miller contends: "History, morality, and truth conspire to elevate the particular and the local" (*PC*, 94). But the elevation of the local is, at the same time, the insistence upon locale, the acknowledgment of the actuality of place as the ground of authority. Such at least is the burden of this chapter. To recall once again Hannah Arendt's image of the table, of that which simultaneously unites and divides us (unites us by dividing us, by allowing our differences to be, and divides us by uniting us, by bringing us together), place not only performs these complementary functions but also engenders our articulate presence. Our capacity to tell both the most rudimentary differences (e.g., the difference between here and there, now and then, nose and ear, my own body and that of another) and the more sophisticated ones (e.g., the difference between reliable and misleading utterance, noble and ignoble deed) is rooted in our bodily habits because our bodies themselves have been and are rooted in distinctively human places, such as home and playground, school and marketplace. We inhabit our world not unlike the way we inhabit our own bodies; and just as there is no possibility of prying the self from the body, there is no possibility of prying our own articulate, embodied presence from those environing, sedimented regions in which we live and through which we move. It is, then, to the *topos* of place that I now turn.

At the center of Miller's humanism is the insistence that the ultimate locus of human responsibility is the individual person fatefully entangled in the historical alliances of some actual place. Hence, locating responsibility means without exaggeration locating it in some identifiable here and now.

It means retelling the narrative of one's placements in the light of one's own displacements, not only one's own personal but also one's own cultural displacements. These cultural displacements must be taken in a twofold sense: the displacements of oneself in one's contemporary cultural engagements *and* those of one's own culture over the course of its history.

Martin Heidegger was another contemporary philosopher for whom the discovery of temporality and the recovery of place were seen to be distinct features of a single project. He was also a thinker attuned to the significance and reverberations of displacement. But there is much in Heidegger that seems to push directly against the defining tendencies of Miller's historicist humanism, indeed against the impulse to advocate humanism at all. In his "Letter on Humanism," Heidegger (1977) even suggests that humanism itself is animated by a vengeance against time. While Miller's reflections on history disposed him toward humanism, Heidegger's phenomenology of time pitted him against this doctrine. But Miller himself was sensitive to the ways even the most carefully nuanced appeals to history almost always carry an effectively disguised commitment to transcendence. The ahistoric cleverly reinscribes itself in the very texts of historicists.

The immediate differences between the two contemporaries, Miller (1895–1978) and Heidegger (1889–1976), however, might mask deep affinities. Hence, despite Heidegger's role in calling humanism into question, the very questions by which he accomplished this might serve us in illuminating the distinctive form of the humanistic position defended by Miller. It is especially instructive for us to recall that, in a later work, Heidegger asks: "By what authority, and on what grounds, is the distinction [between what-ness and that-ness, between essentia and existentia] made? How and in what way is thinking called to this distinction?" (quoted in Fell 1979, 173). Miller too asked just this (*PC*, 96) and closely related questions. On countless occasions, the dis-ease (nihilism) of his time with itself took shape in such questions as: By what authority, and on what grounds, can we at this moment distinguish between appearance and reality, between falsity and truth, between the vagrant and the lawful, and other equally imperative distinctions? What permits and indeed enforces the distinctions through which both self and world are more than either amorphous dreams or fixed entities, through which self and world are exhibited in their finite actuality and their immanent ideality or significance? Like Heidegger, he sought the grounds of authority neither in transcendental subjectivity nor arbitrary will; rather, he sought authority in the historically situated practices and narrations of agents who are themselves displaced yet always already situated. Agents can be displaced only if they already inhabit a place from which to be exiled. History is a scene of displacements. In their triumphalist narratives, however, humanists tend to undermine not only the authority but also the weight of the past, supposing it to be completely malleable. In such stories, contemporaneous subjects who are systematically insulated from squarely confronting the imperative need to think through their historical inheritances are, in terms of their own outlook, not historical subjects, for the immediate enjoyment of their inheritance does not entail the ongoing work of appropriation. Moreover, triumphalist humanism supposes the past no less than the future is theirs to shape in accord with what are in effect the whims of the moment. Like the future, the past is taken as a projection of theirs. This perspective relieves such humanists of the responsibility of owning up to the measure and manner in which they are projections of their past, not an abstract, impersonal past but a concrete, determinate one. The contemporaneous will relishing its own disrupted contemporaneity, its own ek-static present, is free to interpret the significance of what has been done and undergone, just as it is free to determine what will be done.

In its triumphalism, humanism has tended to reinscribe an ideal of authority at once anonymous, timeless, and unsituated. So, perhaps the better way to frame the question is this: On what grounds, and thus by what authority; from what place, and hence by what immanent power within the finite actualities of one's historical situation does one try to tell the difference between appearance and reality, error and truth, barbarity and civility, ingratitude and piety, and other telling differences? Yet, to locate the ground of authority in the finite actualities of one's own historical place is effectively to undermine the basis of both one's own authority and all appeals to authority. A nameless, dateless, and placeless authority is still the only one having any chance of commanding recognition. But in actuality, the only loci of authority are persons and their worlds, functioning objects (yardsticks, calendars, numbers) of an apparently humble character, and those arresting monuments of human achievement that are at once themselves functioning objects and haunting silences, at once eloquent and mute.[12] The impersonal authority of the scientific inquirer appears to be a notable exception, but upon closer examination the authority of science itself is ultimately derived from the personal responsibility of fallible agents to cultivate an ethos in which impartiality, disinterestedness, and objectivity are prized. What is here morally compelling is intellectually discredited: while only persons in command of themselves and their circumstances (and only in command through functioning artifacts and the local control consequent upon the mastery of these and other artifacts) actually bear authority, all such persons bear names and are bound by place no less than time. Theirs is not a nameless, dateless, and placeless authority. But just because it is not, it is suspect. Hence, while a nameless, dateless, and placeless authority cannot practically function with anything approximating the actuality of one's own language, practices, and institutions, all personally, temporally, and topologically identified forms of authority are intellectually suspect. So, to repeat, what is morally compelling is intellectually discredited; what is actually operative is theoretically disallowed.

The constitutional conflict implied in this radical incoherence is of course a defining feature of contemporary nihilism. If nihilism is "a radical, thoroughgoing *skepticism*" (Fell 1997, 9), the effect of which is to discredit virtually all of the criteria by which we feel authorized to mark the telling differences, then none of our affirmations or our negations carries any weight or has any authority. Our intellectual conscience deprives us of a moral conscience, as though the first were not simply an extension of the second. In short, what is morally compelling is intellectually negated. In a contradiction often unremarked, the absolute negations of nihilism themselves lack authority, at least the kind of authority necessary for nihilism to carry the sting it supposes it is able to deliver. If nihilists feel authorized to issue absolute negations, we might fairly wonder about the grounds of their own authority. We might justly wonder about where they actually stand when they presume to issue their negations. If they refuse to confront this question, they begin to lose their claim to unblinking intellectual honesty. That is, they reveal themselves in their refusal to confront this issue to be dogmatists. If they, however, confront the question of the grounds of their own negations, they might claim either that their negations are groundless (this seems but another way of enjoying the prestige of skepticism without paying the price; i.e., this seems but a way that dogmatism can mask itself as skepticism) or that their negations are grounded in some contingent, finite actualities such as their own temperament or circumstances. If nihilists admit the possibility that there are grounds for their negations, and further if they identify these grounds in terms of actuality, then assertions of contingency invite questions about fatality, the yet undisclosed necessity perhaps lurking underneath the absolute negations of those who are, after all, historical beings enmeshed in an actual history. Nihilism is a fatality blind to its status as such. Insofar as it refuses to acknowledge its status as a fatality, it is dogmatic. Insofar as it owns up to this status, it propels itself beyond absolute negation, toward nothing less than absolute affirmation of its own grounded authority.

Accordingly, the nihilist can either regress toward dogmatism or progress beyond nihilism. The position being held is untenable on its own terms, those of an unblinking intellectual conscience, one unwilling to dupe itself by relying on the comforts of illusion. To say that truth itself is an illusion may be one of the more comforting illusions in human history. At earlier stages, it may well have been a sign that human agents were willing to assume radical responsibility for their utterances. At later stages, however, it is far more likely to signal the refusal to take seriously the need to authorize the criteria by which nihilists themselves are able to tell the differences they stake themselves upon telling.

When our categoreal distinctions are seen as historical achievements wrested from the mutabilities inherent in our self-defining commitments, and when these self-defining commitments are themselves seen as bound up with our self-frustrating inheritances, the category of humanity and indeed all cognate and associated categories (e.g., action, utterance, authority) need to be approached historically. That is, humanism can only take the form of historicism.

Although, historically, the alliance between humanism and historicism has been largely formal and frequently spurious, Miller's historical idealism was also truly a historicist humanism, a version of humanism in which the actualities of history are fully accepted and indeed explicitly accredited with the actual authority they (more or less) command in our actual lives. Against traditional Western theism, Miller denies humans the name of creature; and against scientific naturalism, he denies them the name of either entity or process when either is conceived as the instantiation of a nature fixed prior to, and thus apart from, the fateful travails of its actual history. We might thus say: "Humanity, thy name is history." Such in effect is the central claim of Miller's historicist humanism. One text in which he himself highlights this point deserves to be recalled here.

> History is the place one goes when one gives up passing judgments and accepts identifications. It is the alternative to seeing all things *sub specie aeternitatis*. They are to be seen *sub specie temporis*. This is the heresy of history. But it is also the condition of all humanistic concerns. (*PH*, 85)

Historicism is heretical because the ahistoric outlook has been for most of Western history the dominant orthodoxy. But when we turn from condemning others—especially our own ancestors—to identifying ourselves, from self-aggrandizing condemnations to self-authorizing avowals, we must turn toward the actual loci of an ongoing process in which we are implicated and, often despite our protestations and denials, by which we are defined. History is the place where we must go in order to know ourselves. Yet even now, perhaps especially now, the lure of the absolute moment deflects attention from the demands of the historical moment. But this is a moment without momentum, "coming from nowhere and going nowhere" (*PH*, 86). It promises to be self-contained. The historical moment, however, comes from a determinate direction and drives toward a circumscribed future. Hence, in contrast to the absolute moment, it is an actually derived and possibly divisive occasion wherein agents perpetually risk being exiled from their homes, from those regions in which fluency of action and forms of authority are firmly in place.

At the heart of Miller's humanism is the affirmation of humanity's responsibility for itself. Not only are humans self-narrating actors; theirs are self-authorizing narratives,[13] so that in these narratives humans speak solely in their own name and appeal ultimately to their own authority. In short, humans are self-authorizing narrators.

In a variety of ways, Miller posed the question: "On what condition, then, can one tell a story of man as the locus of responsible power?" (*PC*, 102). And since it is only on the condition that we grant human history categoreal status, thereby making it irreducible to anything allegedly more fundamental, that we can tell a responsible story of human responsibility I am prompted to assert once again that Miller's historicism is of a piece with his humanism.

In agreement with José Ortega y Gasset, Miller contends that human beings are not defined by an invariant nature but instead define themselves through their fateful alliances with an ongoing history (ibid.). They can no more stand outside of history than they can, at least at this actual historical juncture, avoid reflecting on their peculiar locus within this precarious process. To repeat, such self-definition is inevitably redefinition: the task of redefining oneself is rooted in the self-frustrations and self-distortions inscribed in one's inherited modes of personal identification (e.g., the manner in which one was brought up to assert and defend one's own and others' rights, to launch and sustain investigations, to conceive and approach the sacred). The more or less determinate shape of any human existence, then, cannot be explained in terms of a timeless essence or invariant nature impressing itself on the recalcitrant material of an individual life; it can be explained only historically. Who one is becomes explicable only in reference to who one was, to what one has done and undergone, where one has gone and when one has lived. This does not make us prisoners of a past; it makes us inheritors of a history.

Our complex inheritance is at once limiting and liberating, disfiguring and ennobling. It provokes an argument with itself through the media of our own lives; put differently, we feel compelled (because there is truly a compulsion here) to argue with our inheritances, with the traditional modes of personal identification. How, if at all, can I continue to worship the God whom I was raised to adore? How, if at all, can I maintain my allegiance to the country, my fidelity to my religion, and my relationship to other historical actualities? To assert that our inheritance provokes an argument with itself through the media of our lives, that our constitutional conflicts are cultural crises in personal guise, is to stress that there are in history fatalities as well as contingencies; moreover, it is to stress that the personal is the cultural. In contrast, to assert that we conduct the argument with our inheritance is to emphasize our role as agents and, by implication, to insinuate something about the queer character of historical necessity. The necessity of history, of identifying with and reflecting upon the actual course of human engagement, was historically denied. The history of Western consciousness has been, to a great extent, that of a militant effort either to equate history with sheer contingency or to elevate history to absolute necessity. The fateful alliances of historical actors have consequently been distorted beyond recognition. In particular, they have been either divested of their fateful character (for some there is in history no necessity, only contingency) or invested with a despotic power (for others, in history all power is impersonal and all persons impotent).

The actual shape of human freedom, however, points toward a dialectic of fatality and freedom wherein being historically compelled and being personally autonomous are not mutually exclusive but in truth (better, in act) inseparably linked. We ordinarily suppose that historical compulsion is a species of external compulsion; so conceived, such compulsion renders our agency illusory. It acts upon us in such a way as to preclude our own acting being truly our own. On this supposition, then, there is no possibility of human action. So, too, we customarily suppose that human agency is a transcendent capacity; so envisioned, such agency makes our historicity incidental. On this view, there is no necessity of human history; nor are there any fatalities within our local histories. Part of the difficulty here is that the philosophical imagination is held captive by a spatial metaphor: external forces and internal freedom compete for intellectual allegiance in a manner intolerant of any rival. But the all too simple picture of either outer forces or inner control, of either things acting on humans from the outside *(ab extra)* or humans determining their lives in a vacuum, occludes the extent to which human identity is itself a fabric woven of fateful alliances to historical practices (practices of inquiry no less than those of worship, of citizenship and humane conduct no less than art and aesthetic perception). Descartes' disembodied *cogito* or Kant's transcendental subject is, when interpreted historically, the deracinated self, the self uprooted from the formative and sustaining institutions and practices making possible, in the first place, the soliloquies of linguistic actors or the critiques of reflexive inquirers. "The troubled *experience* of skepticism is not to be understood in calm passivity" (*PC*, 109; emphasis added). It is the disconcerting experience of an agent undermining its agency by is own exercise: it is the arrest of function. It results not in specific doubts but in wholesale despair. "The hand that inflicts the wound is also the hand which heals it" (Hegel 1975, 43).

The way one inhabits one's own body is linked to the way one inhabits those places one calls one's own. Just as it is crucial to distinguish between clock time and dated time—physical time measured by clocks and other instruments, on one hand, and historical time memorialized in monuments and other artifacts, on the other—it is imperative to distinguish between physical space and historical place. But just as we ought not to identify physical time with an objective process and historical time with a subjective sequence, so too we ought not to view physical space as objective and historical place as subjective. This is worse than misleading. The midworld of symbols is a region of actualities that are also formalities: place-bound actualities, yet open-ended formalities. Space not any more than place is a datum: the actuality of space is intertwined with such actions as measuring distance, telling time, and weighing objects, as well as the actuality of place cannot be separated from narrating events, making maps, portraying persons, painting landscapes, and enacting rituals. Truth is in the telling and, even more, in the retelling, especially in those instances in which the narrator self-consciously feels the absolute need to reframe the inherited narrative by which he or she has lived up to this point. One way to mark the difference between space-time and historical place is this: while space-time is an abstract, impersonal mode of actuality, historical place is a concrete, personal mode. But both are modes of actuality; and, as such, both are connected with action, albeit different forms.

Physics provides us with means for knowing our "place" within the cosmos. In contrast, history offers us strategies for knowing the place*s* from which we depart and those to which we journey. In history humanity is always taking its leave and leaving its home. The necessity of history encompasses the inescapability of *Unheimlichkeit*, of being thrust beyond the confines of one's inherited identity, of being exiled from those regions in which fluency of action and forms of authority are firmly in place. For these individuals, to be in place and to know one's place pertain to the same nexus of actualities. Unquestionably, the expression "knowing one's place" is deeply problematic, for it has more often than not served as an instrument of oppression.

Places are characteristically evocative of memory. They often evoke a sense of histories in which we are implicated and yet ones from which we are somehow detached. These histories gather themselves here, at this grave or in these ruins, in such a way that they call upon us to call upon the very names of those with whom we feel we are now dwelling, especially when we do not know the names of those we feel ourselves called upon to invoke. What Virginia Woolf calls "the pressure of dumbness" evoked when she walked through the streets of London is often felt as a pressing toward articulation.

> All these infinitely obscure lives remain to be recorded, I said ... and went on in thought through the streets of London feeling in imagination the pressure of dumbness, the accumulation of unrecorded life, whether from the women at the street corners with their arms akimbo, and the rings embedded in their fat swollen fingers, talking with a gesticulation like the swing of Shakespeare's words; or from the violet-sellers and match-sellers and old crones stationed under doorways; or from drifting girls whose faces, like waves in sun and cloud, signal the coming of men and women and the flickering light of shop windows. (Woolf [1929] 1981, 93)

Although she often spoke of moments in which scenes revealed themselves to her in their entirety and revealed themselves as spectacles, suggesting a detached observer of an essentially synchronic configuration, her fiction and other writings suggest rather an intimacy and even identification with the figures and scenes observed or conjured in imagination. Indeed, the pressure of dumbness felt by her in the streets of London carried for her an inherent momentum toward not only articulation but also self-articulation, where one's struggle to give shape to one's own life is felt to be bound up with the evoked presence of "infinitely obscure lives."

> All that [the women at the street corner with their arms akimbo, etc.] you will have to explore ... holding your torch firm in your hand. Above all, you must illumine your own soul with its profundities and its hallows, and its vanities and generosities, and say what your beauty means to you or your plainness, and what is your relation to the ever changing and turning world of gloves and shoes and stuffs swaying up and down the faint scents that come through chemists' bottles down arcades of dress material over a floor of pseudo-marble. (ibid., 93–94)

But the finite actualities of these infinitely obscure lives, with which our own lives are so mysteriously intertwined, are the unrecorded dramas of an encompassing story. We are somewhat familiar with the more fateful shapes of this encompassing drama. To assert this point does not imply that these obscure lives do not need to be saved. It does not imply that in knowing the encompassing drama there is not need to attend painstakingly to the actual contingencies of common women and men in their unique placements and engagements. Quite the contrary. As Alice Walker (1983) notes in discussing Woolf, the task of the artist is nothing other than the saving of lives: to save the quotidian lives of uncelebrated persons from our own obliviousness may be tied to saving our own lives from the oblivion of nihilism, for the process of trying to do so helps us to realize that the fateful shapes of human consciousness have their actual loci in human beings passionately absorbed in the historical places of their daily lives.[14] These shapes are nothing remote or otherworldly; they are rather near at hand, rooted in the Earth in the only manner in which humans can humanly dwell here—coursing down a city street, or ambling down a country path, or sitting by a river, or climbing along a ridge.

Conclusion: Retracing the Main Steps of an Extended Argument

"We are demoralized today because we proclaim liberty but have no actuality as local control and as [authoritative] revelation. Nothing is to be revered. There is no eloquent presence. Our orthodox world [generated and sustained by our most compelling discourses, above all the most successful natural sciences] is the silent world" (*MS*, 191). In our world, no voice is present and no presence articulate. For us, then, the "midworld is a myth" in the pejorative sense. But to own up to the implications of our own skepticism, in particular to our radical doubts regarding the disclosive power of human deeds, utterances, and narratives, compels us to move beyond skepticism, to reconcile ourselves to the actual conditions of human existence. But the transition from skeptical to unhappy consciousness is neither easy nor immediate. It takes time and demands work; specifically it demands working through our actual history as it is embodied in the monumental texts and other fateful achievements of those humans whose practices, institutions, and discourses we have inherited—in a word, of our ancestors. It means giving our ancestors their due, not in the manner of either an obsequious or an ungrateful child. To an uncanny degree, their struggles are our struggles: the forms of their constitutional conflicts and even radical defeats are parts of our history and thus of our world and ourselves. In our enterprises, in our attempts to govern ourselves and to know nature, to cultivate moral character and to exhibit aesthetic form, to acquire learning but also wealth, we in subtle and obvious ways join them, deriving momentum from their exertions and direction from their achievements. In the silent world of late modernity, nothing is to be revered. But (to use an expression of W. E. Hocking, one of Miller's teachers at Harvard) the "passage beyond modernity" requires the transcendence of subjectivism and the overcoming of skepticism. Put positively, it demands not only recognition of but also reconciliation with the actual; it demands that the immanent ideals by which finite human consciousness is compelled to assume the shape of unhappy consciousness are fully acknowledged and accredited in their actual immanence. Such unhappy consciousness will in time become unhappy with being a merely disconsolate conscience. It will demand its immediate satisfactions. It will assume its secular tasks not as school lessons but as absolute demands of its own actual commitments. It will suck the marrow out of life, this very day; not waiting for either tomorrow or eternity; and tomorrow it will return ravenous. Hence, when we shrink back from the hazards and involvements solicited by the shifting scenes of our quotidian existence, as we often do, "we can spare ourselves disappointments only at the price of an annihilative inaction" (*PH*, 81).

The perpetual perishing of the present moment is, despite a deeply entrenched bias, no telling argument against the absolute worth of the fleeting moment. What A. N. Whitehead called the "vacuous actualities" of scientific materialism are of course at the farthest remove from what Miller intends by finite actualities (see, e.g., Whitehead [1933] 1967, 219). While Whitehead designed an elaborate categoreal scheme to show how actuality, concretely understood, is the actualization of values, an always creative ingression of eternal ideals, Miller—though animated by the same concern with according actual occasions their inherent worth—moved in a different direction. For Miller, philosophy discredits itself when it offers purely speculative answers to essentially experimental questions. A theory of cosmic time is one thing, a philosophy of human history quite another. The former properly falls in the domain of experimental science, the latter in that of philosophical reflection. Nonetheless, finite actualities are not inherently vacuous but rather historically encoded actualities. Of course, the legibility of the past inscribed in the heart of the present depends greatly on the acuity of our vision. Whatever else it is, "the past is a foreign country; there is very little we can say about it [and thus about either ourselves or our present] until we have learned its language and understood its assumptions" (Howard 1991, 13). The illegibility of the past, however, points not to the vacuity of the present but to the present as a vocation, as a place to which we have historically been called.

This point suggests that the more instructive comparison here is with Ralph Waldo Emerson, not with Whitehead.[15] For the transition from skeptical to unhappy consciousness also means tracing more steadily and extending more boldly than Emerson did one of the trajectories of his own thought, a trajectory with which Miller explicitly identifies himself. Miller saw in Emerson "an example of a man whose thought expresses the conflict between present actuality and an ideal somewhat remote and contemplative" (*PC,* 183). For Miller, we must resist the lures of a remote ideal, passionately realizing that "it is *in the actual* that the ideal is immanent" (JWM, 22:7 [Aesthetics]; emphasis added). Although he was seduced by this lure, Emerson offers resources for resisting it as well. In "Character" he announces: "The moment is all, in all noble relations" (Emerson 1951, 342). But he also observes in "Experience," an essay from which Miller might have borrowed the term "mid-world" (ibid., 306): "Our life seems not present, so much as prospective; not for the affairs on which it is wasted [going to the post office or dining with friends], but as a hint of this vast-flowing vigor. Most of life seems to me mere advertisement of faculty: information is given us not to sell ourselves cheap; that we are great. So, in particulars, our greatness is always in a tendency or direction, not in an action" (ibid., 313–14). But in holding ourselves so dear we desecrate the moment and in effect annihilate ourselves (cf. *PC,* 95). To confront the moments of our lives in this fashion means that there will come a moment in which we are confronted with the tragedy of a life not lived (Thoreau [1854] 1980). So Emerson advises that if we are to be strong with Nature's strength, "we must not harbor such disconsolate consciences. . . . We must set up the strong present tense against all the rumors of wrath, past or to come" (Emerson 1951, 306–7). In a passage from "Experience" partly quoted by Miller in his essay "History and Humanism" (*PC*, 95), Emerson instructs us:

> Since our office is with moments, let us husband them. Five minutes of to-day are worth as much to me, as five minutes in the next millennium. Let us be poised, and wise, and on our own, to-day. Let us treat the men and women [whom we encounter here and now] well: treat them as if they were real: perhaps they are real. Men live in their fancy, like drunkards whose hands are too soft and tremulous for successful labor. It is a tempest of fancies, and the only ballast I know, is a respect to the present hour. Without any shadow of doubt, amidst this vertigo of shows and politics, I settle myself ever the firmer in the creed, that we should not postpone and refer and wish, but do broad justice where we are, by whomever we deal with, accepting our actual companions and circumstances, however humble or odious, as the mystic officials to whom the universe has delegated its whole pleasure for us. (Ibid., 304)

It is impossible for me to read Miller's own insistence that "[w]e may not turn aside from the moment or . . . dismiss those we encounter" without hearing echoes of Emerson.[16] The Emersonian tone of so many other passages as well suggests a deep kinship, suggests the capacity to experience exhilaration in the commonplace. Miller's life as well as his writings ring so many changes on one of Emerson's defining affirmations: "every hour and season yields its tribute of delight; for every hour and change corresponds to and authorizes a different state of mind. . . . Nature is a setting that fits equally well a comic or a mourning piece. . . . Crossing a bare common, in snow puddles, at twilight, under a clouded sky, without having in my thoughts any occurrence of special good fortune, I have enjoyed a perfect exhilaration. I am glad to the brink of fear" (Emerson 1982, 38). Like Emerson, Miller realizes: "One cannot call one's soul one's own if one cannot call the moment one's own. . . . The moment is all; the readiness is all. Respect for experience [as a direct yet mediated engagement with finite actualities] has gone too far with us to be recalled. At bottom it is respect for persons" (*PH*, 173).

For Miller, persons are truly real beings because they are actual: "I want the actual to shine and I want to feel the wonder of a yardstick, a poem, a word, a person. The here-and-now appears to me quite dreamlike unless it can declare the world. I am glad that the dream is dispelled for me" (*MS*, 191–92), even if the price be the unleashing of the fates! A world without shape or solidity is, in actuality, no world at all; it is a dream, even if it be a dream of our (supposedly) boundless possibilities. However exhilarating initially in its intimations of infinity, an oneiric world in time becomes a tiresome affair, often even a paralyzing nightmare. In its evasion of actuality and thus its slighting of finitude, its "freedom" signals bondage as well as the loss of vitality. As Wordsworth says, "Me this uncharted freedom tires; / I feel the weight of chance desires" (quoted in Diefenbeck 1990, 51). The weight of our chance desires is a weight that ultimately pins us to the floors of our own souls, whereas the weight of our fateful passions diverts our attention from a morbid introspection and directs our energies toward wholehearted engagement with those ongoing concerns by which we issue nothing less than an ontological declaration: These artifactual acts define our actual world, the world that we will maintain at all costs. It is a world we will maintain, that is, we will *to* maintain, not because it is convenient or comfortable or profitable to do so but because it is the sole locus of human actualization.

The actual world as we have inherited it, accordingly, demands an absolute commitment, though most of us most of the time might struggle to circumvent this demand.[17] To meet this demand is to commit ourselves to maintaining the actual world at all costs, including of course various kinds of threats to us.[18] For some of us at least some of the time, life is not a game; or, if it is a game, it is one we play for keeps. The players who maintain for themselves the option of withdrawing when "fortune" turns against them, that is, when the significance of their "moves" is fatefully revealed to them (since fatality is a form of eventuality, it takes time to disclose itself), are ones who prove themselves unworthy of the game.

The actual world is a fateful world at least for those who will to maintain this world at all cost, for those who play for keeps. So defined, this world is absolute, not despite but because it is radically implicated in the here-and-now. "There is," as the narrator in Virginia Woolf's *Jacob's Room* asserts, "something absolute in us that despises qualification" (quoted in Hussey 1986, 22). To accept any world on any terms is to nullify us; in contrast, to espouse our historical world on the actual terms of our own existential investitures is to establish the conditions of selfhood. That these conditions inevitably confront the self with threats to its own integrity means that the conditions for the emergence and maintenance of selfhood are one with those of its destruction. Just as "the ego finds itself in the superego, the self [finds itself] in the integrity of the dynamic conditions of conflict" (*DP*, 10). The only selves to be found are those who have forged themselves by forging a link with the conditions of conflict. The self is first forged, and only then found. "Conflict does not operate to scatter the self but to establish it, even to organize it" (*MS*, 187). Or, in scattering the self and shattering its world—in destroying a determinate form of human integrity and, allied to this form, the actual arena of human functioning—conflict makes possible the self-revisionary acts at the center of our self-constituting lives. A static self is no self at all. The steadfast self, by virtue of the very commitments enjoining the self to stand fast, to hold its ground against a potentially destructive adversary, may be a composed agent (see, e.g., *PH*, 164; *DP*, 180) but is not an immutable object. What makes steadfastness admirable is precisely the mutability of the self.

If we affirm that the moment is all, then "[t]here are no remote finalities, but there are present ones, hidden in the living reality of any actual deed, and compelling just in the measure that the deed drives onward with persistent power" (*PC*, 37). There are no static absolutes but there are dynamic ones; and in their dynamic thrust toward actualization they disclose the inherent flaws calling for their self-transcendence and self-transformation. The great do not argue or apologize; rather they affirm and celebrate such finalities (*PC*, 36).

So we return to the question so arrestingly stated by Miller himself: "On what conditions, then, can one tell a story of man as the locus of responsible power?" (*PC*, 102).[19] We can either deny the possibility of telling such a story, thereby licensing our own licentiousness, enforcing our own vagrancy, or do what we have historically done, look beyond history for the conditions of responsibility. "Actual men, identified historically through dates [e.g., Plato in ancient Athens], did support their institutions and utter their works of art under the influence of ahistoric ideals" (*PC*, 139). We are still tempted to do so today. As Richard Rorty observes, "[A]t times like that of Auschwitz, when history is in upheaval and traditional institutions and patterns of behavior are collapsing, we want something which stands beyond history and institutions. What can there be except human solidarity, our recognition of one another's common humanity?" (Rorty 1989, 189). In losing our sense of the eternal, we also seem to have lost our sense of reverence and responsibility (*PC*, 160). But the choice between the dogmatism inherent in all ahistoric ideals and the skepticism consequent upon all thoroughgoing self-negating and self-discrediting does not exhaust the possibilities. We might reconcile ourselves with our finitude and align ourselves with our actuality, and in doing so impose on us the infinite task of human revision. We might bear witness to what history reveals: "this equation of selfhood and actuality. This is the stage on which all action occurs" (*PC*, 87). In doing so, we might also unleash unanticipated possibilities for human transformation. At the very least, we can find direction: "If we can find the actuality which is for us self-defining, and hence absolute, we shall know what to do" (ibid.). We may even discover what we must do.

Self-revision is the price we are fated to pay for self-maintenance, desecration of the idols the burden for retaining any sense of the sacred, openness to abuse the price for civility. Rebellion is always the possible price we must be willing to pay for any cause worthy of our loyalty. Not to countenance this possibility is to have purchased identity and security too dearly and also too cheaply, too dearly because it has cost us our autonomy (i.e., our selves in their actuality and singularity) and too cheaply because it allows itself whenever convenient to throw off the ever imperative demands of cultivating a historical identity. In a double paradox, we can become only what we are by owning up to what our ancestors and we have been. At every turn, the self-imposed discipline of owning up to what our ancestors and we have been requires of us direct involvement and uncompromising identification with the finite actualities of, for instance, our own language, government, and neighborhood. In addition to our role as citizens, the work of scholars, scientists, and artists captured Miller's philosophical attention. To make more concrete the meaning of Miller's commitments it is necessary to trace them to his accounts of the scholar, scientist, and artist.

"As the new world of humanism takes shape we may expect art to proclaim its existence, and so to make it a self-conscious force" (*PC,* 168). "The scholar must have the courage and the persistence to repossess [i.e., to reappropriate] his heritage and, if possible, to go beyond it" (*PC,* 174). But this does not make the scholar "a furtive appropriator of superior means" (*PC,* 184). "The function of scholarship is the discovery and maintenance of such modes of the infinite forms of finite actuality" (*PC,* 181). "Like all enterprises, art has a history, i.e., a career in the fuller grasp of its own meaning" (*PC,* 167). So, too, "science itself has a history, a record not only of accumulation, but of basic revisions in controlling concepts and procedures" (*PC,* 186).

In keeping with Miller's ideal of the scholar in his own person, as conveyed through his own texts, is his assertion that "[t]he scholar can deal only in the fateful, but he overcomes fate [to the extent that it can be overcome] by identifying himself with its laws" and, even more important, with the conflicts among those laws. Dealing with the fateful is an adventure, with enough romance in it to satisfy anyone who is both passionate and intelligent. Miller in effect asks: What more could there be for humans than to secure for themselves a presence in that order, simultaneously disciplinary and infinite (thus, constraining and expansive), through which any world can be defined?

As should be clear by now, to stand in the presence of such an order is no secure stasis, no invulnerable refuge. For the only worlds that humans have ever inhabited are ones that they themselves have made. "Our world is our own. It is what we have made it to be," and it has remade us: *our* world has compelled us to revise ourselves and remake it as part of this revision (*PH,* 80). The worlds that are generated and sustained by exertions and suffering are always ones threatened by their own inherent collapse (see, e.g., *PC,* 188). Thus, to stand in such an order is always a balancing act: the formal orders by which our actual world is generated, sustained, and revised are shifting grounds.[20] The scholar helps us see that we are always already standing within an interwoven fabric of formal orders and also helps us to learn to keep our balance within such orders or as we attempt to move from one to another, e.g., from physics to philosophy.

Before turning to three paradigmatic ways human beings today can do deep as well as broad justice to where they are, accepting their actual companions and circumstances, let us answer directly the question regarding the relationship between humanism and nihilism. For it would be difficult to find anything more fateful with which contemporary scholars actually engaged in their historical moment could deal, or to find a more fundamental objection to the humanistic outlook than that it is a masked form of nihilistic metaphysics. "Of course our current nihilism is itself a historical emergence. It was not original. It should [accordingly] be seen as history, not truth" (*PH*, 192). But how is it possible to follow Miller's advice here, to identify oneself with "some fatality in the present, a present confusion and conflict brought on by the articulate past," when that fatality is nihilism itself? How can such identification avoid being annihilation? If the uncanny visitor is truly at the door (as Nietzsche insists), is it possible to imagine that any person is there to greet this visitor? If *nihil*, then *nemo*. The very assumption that "history is always 'impure' in motive [that there must be a timeless fount of absolute purity in which we can bathe] leads to the skepticism of all motive, both as fact and as value. That is nihilism" (*PH*, 21). This is close to, but also markedly different from, what James describes when he writes, "In nightmare we have motives to act, but no power; here we have powers, but no motives. A nameless *Unheimlichkeit* comes over us at the thought of there being nothing eternal in our final purposes, in the objects of these loves and aspirations which are our deepest energies" (James [1897] 1958, 83). Let me present more fully the Jamesian position and, then, suggest a possible divergence between Miller and James.

Many historical religions and much traditional philosophy agree with what James suggests is a defining tenet of religious consciousness: "the best things are the more eternal things, the overlapping things, the things in the universe that throw the last stone . . . and say the final word" (ibid., 25). Like Emerson and also Miller himself, James insists: "The great point is that the possibilities are really here. Whether it be we who solve [or realize] them, or he [the creator] working through us . . . is of small account, so long as we admit that the issue is decided nowhere else than *here* and *now*. *That* is what gives us the palpitating reality to our moral life and makes it tingle . . . with so strange and elaborate an excitement" (ibid., 183). Again like Emerson but unlike Miller, James seems to compromise his celebration of the actual moment by succumbing to the lure of the eternal and thus of the remote ideal. This is true of most of the most famous of Jamesian texts, including: "If this life be not a real fight, in which something is eternally gained for the universe by success, it is no better than a game of private theatre from which one may withdraw at will. But it *feels* like a real fight, as if there were something really wild in the universe which we, with all our idealities and faithfulnesses, are needed to redeem" (ibid., 61). In "What Makes a Life Significant," James simply asserts: "The solid meaning of life is always the same eternal thing, —the marriage, namely, of some unhabitual ideal, however, special, with some fidelity, courage, and endurance; with some man's or woman's pains. —And, whatever or wherever life may be, there will always be the chance for that marriage to take place" (James 1977, 659). But he habitually identified such ideals as not unhabitual but eternal, though it is rarely certain how literal or strong a sense he intends. Moreover, his interest in parapsychology might be interpreted as a flight from the actual, though this suggestion certainly might not be fair. His was, nonetheless, a generation in which some of the most authoritative voices argued for stoic reconciliation with "the notion of a purposeless universe, in which all things and qualities men love, *dulcissima mundi nomina,* are but illusions of our fancy attached to accidental clouds of dust which the eternal cosmic weather will dissipate as ceaselessly as it has formed them" (James [1890] 1981, 1260). His is a heroic humanism, for its stake in eternity is, in a sense, selfless or impersonal. He is acutely aware of the fact that: "Religion . . . for the great majority of our own race *means* immortality, and nothing else. God is the producer of immortality; and whoever has doubts of immortality is written down as an atheist without farther trial" (James [1902] 1985, 412; cf. [1890] 1981, 317). But James is content with a life that is moral and a God who is finite. But the value of such a God is in effect to be the producer of eternity, that is, to be the guarantee that our ideals are eternal and perhaps even that our fidelity to them will be remembered eternally. Hence, James writes, "If our ideals are only cared for in 'eternity,' I do not see why we might not be willing to resign their care to other hands than ours" (James [1902] 1985, 395).

What seems imperative to James is that our ideals have a locus in addition to their actual loci in human history. They may fortuitously have an actual standing that is due to some human espousal, but they must essentially have an eternal status. Thus, while the marriage of human beings and their defining ideals is always consummated in history, one of the parties to this union must apparently be a denizen who has descended here from a region outside of time. These ideals must be in themselves eternal. If they were merely historical, they could not be absolutely authoritative or infinitely precious. But it is just this correlation between the value and the timelessness of our ideals that Miller questions. Does historical consciousness of the uncompromising sort advocated by Miller preclude absolute commitment? If all is relative to the moment as the pivot of revision (the historical present properly understood being "a moment in constitutional revision" [*PC*, 157]), then nothing is absolute.

Miller however rejects—emphatically rejects—this inference. He contends: "As self-maintenance the present is absolute. But it is also structured" (*PH*, 128). And it is inherently revisable. Is this a mere sleight of hand or play on words? "Life itself is a hazard, its prolongation dubious and its effectiveness indemonstrable. . . . Its basic hazard is absolute, and to that absolute risk there must be an absolute answer" (*PC*, 22). "Utopia is inevitable; it inheres in the actuality of any person" (*PC*, 30). "We are incurably utopian, since we must arm ourselves with boundless resolve in so far as we propose to reach and maintain any goal whatsoever" (*PC*, 21). This might seem to some readers an untenable assertion, for bare survival hardly seems to demand boundless resolve. But the progressive enervation of any human life not animated by wild hopes and absolute commitment is the most telling symptom of our nihilism, our spiritual disease that is in its own way not only a sickness unto death but a death-sick life.[21] "It is [in fact] death masquerading as life" (*PC*, 31). "It was Hegel's idea," one Miller endorses, "that a turning point was reached in the history of cultures when death was seen as the sole condition for an absolute affirmation of life, and the sole evidence of a belief in life" (ibid.).[22] Those "who have not hesitated to affirm their ideals in that way" shame us into suspecting that for most of us most of the time there is not life after birth or much beyond infancy. These exemplars "reached out for rich experience [and impossible achievement] with eager hands and were above a niggardly moral economy and the miserly weighing out of personal satisfactions" (ibid.). Miller suggests that Nietzsche saw this point, but in a distorted way. In an uncharacteristically mocking tone he pronounces Nietzsche's

Übermensch to be a monster who lived by a theory; he "had to keep reminding himself not that he was alive, but that God was dead. And so he is a sapless, humorless, and joyless creature. Zarathustra's ten years of meditation on the mountain bore only this sour fruit" (ibid.). The *Übermensch* is himself a dead man who after all appears to be trying to remind himself that he is alive by shouting God is dead. Since he lives so much by the intellect, we "need not worry about him"; because he is so invested in the rhetoric of ridicule and the cleverness of argument, he can be tamed. His self-celebrated cleverness is a self-compensating illusion, for he "is not a genius" (ibid.).

But there is another point that, from Miller's own perspective, Nietzsche not only saw but also saw clearly, though Miller does not note it. "And life itself confided this secret to me: 'Behold,' it said, 'I am *that which must always overcome itself.* Indeed, you call it a will to procreate or a drive to an end, to something higher, farther, more manifold: but all this is one, and one secret" (Nietzsche 1966b, 115). But Miller can only see this self-imposed task of continuous self-overcoming to be too closely connected with what might be called, without exaggeration, Nietzsche's *contemptus mundi:* "The now and the past on earth—alas, my friends, that is what *I* find most unendurable; and I should not know how to live if I were not also a seer of that which must come" (ibid., 138–39). But if we take this and other texts as evidence, the uncanny quest is not only at the door; he is already inhabiting the psyche of he who would presume to diagnose his own time and, in addition, a string of centuries leading up to his own contemptible moment. His antihumanism is, in terms of the dialectic discussed above, an arrested development, a stunted humanism: his is an unhappy consciousness that genuinely feels the lure of finite actuality but is yet unable wholeheartedly to reconcile itself to his actual present. The dream of the future alone redeems the present. In itself, the moment—this history and this Earth—is unendurable. Physician, heal thyself! So I imagine Miller remarking. Miller's version of humanism is not so much a disguised form of nihilism as is Nietzsche's antipathy toward the here and now, humanity and history, a disguised form of Christianity.

James ([1902] 1985, 290) proclaimed that humankind instinctively takes the world to be a theater for heroism. Is it a pathetic illusion or an ennobling insight to suppose that human endeavors such as scholarship, science, and art might provide sufficient fora for the still too seldom celebrated heroism of historical actors in their everyday lives? To address this question, let us now track down scholars as they cluster together in cafés or classrooms, also as they sit alone in libraries or studies; moreover, let us track down scientists in their laboratories and the fields, and the artists in their studios and on their sojourns into the city or the woods. Let us sketch, with Miller's aid, portraits of scholars, scientists, and artists as individuals engaged in maintaining—thus, in revising—their worlds. For here are among the scenes in which the fateful shapes of human freedom are discernible, once we are attuned to the significance of the quotidian.

Attuning ourselves to this significance requires a transfiguration of the commonplace; in turn, such a transfiguration demands a recovery of the sacred.[23] The name of humanity can be something other than the shadow cast by tyranny or monstrosity, only if an authoritative sense of absolute inviolability is recovered. How, if at all, are we to recover this sense of inviolability? It is one thing to say, "If we want reverence, anything sacred and so imperative, we must advance to history. . . . There is the common world, the actual one" (*DP*, 151). It is quite another to show how, in our own time, such an advance is to be made. In the next chapter, I sketch a path for such an advance. It is a long and somewhat circuitous path, but only such a way can show how, at this actual juncture, our alliance with history is to be maintained, thus revised.

5

Critique, Narration, and Revelation

> I cannot get a hold of a man *except* as I take him at his word. But does he speak? Has he spoken? Can *he* appear in utterance?
>
> —John William Miller, *The Midworld of Symbols and Function Objects*, 110

The pivotal point of the previous chapter is one of John William Miller's most basic affirmations: a price is to be paid for critique. In particular, self-critique requires the self-maintenance of those discourses, institutions, and practices on which all forms of criticism depend.[1] The sciences, arts, and humanities reveal in their own ways this feature of the midworld. Moreover, they are discourses in which utterance, critique, and disclosure are interwoven.

The intellectual revolution wrought by Thomas Kuhn's *The Structure of Scientific Revolutions* (1970) was one congenial to, and even anticipated by, Miller's radical revision of philosophical idealism. Miller was keenly appreciative of the fact that "science itself has a history, a record not only of accumulation, but of basic revision in controlling concepts and procedures" (*PC*, 186). In other words, he was clearly aware of what Kuhn later would call "paradigm shifts." What is true of science is also true of the arts and humanities. "Like all enterprises, art has a history, i.e., a career in the fuller grasp of its own meaning" (*PC*, 167). The humanities (e.g., philosophical reflection and narration, literary analysis and criticism, historical narration and analysis) tend to be self-consciously historical disciplines, ones conscious of their own historicity as well as the historicity of their objects. What nature is to the physicist and chemist, the midworld is to the historian and the philosopher. That one might reconstruct the history of, say, the telescope and, furthermore, that one might reflect on the connection between scientific inquiry and such heuristic instruments as the telescope, microscope, and far more complex functioning objects points to the way history and philosophy can contribute to the self-understanding of science. Thus, the scientist may be as much a denizen of the midworld as is the artist, historian, or philosopher. While the task of the philosopher can be described as giving an account of humanity's articulate presence within the total array of its historical discourses—its presence within that totality known as the midworld—the practitioner of any one of these discourses exemplifies some feature of the midworld; beyond this, he or she is likely to grasp in understanding what he or she embodies in actuality. Scientists, artists, and humanists all have a stake in the midworld, for it is the actual locus of their self-defining enterprises. Hence, they have a stake in maintaining this world and, thus, in confronting necessity at critical junctures of constitutional revision.

The willingness to commit oneself without reservation to the maintenance of the midworld—maintaining this world being the same as maintaining one's identity—is a sign of having begun, in principle, to move beyond unhappy consciousness. But such willingness is insecure or misguided if it fails to accept that the inherent drive of self-maintenance imposes the fateful task of self-revision: one can maintain one's identity only through a series of revisions, often radical.

Revelation Unveiled, Stories Untold, and Criticism Unbound

We encounter in Miller's writings a historicist transformation of the transcendental question, What are the conditions for the possibility of critique? The possibilities of critique depend, above all else, on the actuality of discourse, not as anything objectifiable, but as something immediate. But, unlike so many other appeals to immediacy in Western philosophy (e.g., those of Henri Bergson and William James), Miller's was not intended to circumvent the demands of discourse or to transcend the limitations inherent in all the inherited modes of human utterance. His repeated stress on finite actuality was intended rather as an invitation to meet these demands and also to resist the temptation to seek an order above, behind, or beyond that of the midworld itself. His own examples of immediacy (counting, measuring, weighing, speaking, and proclaiming) all make this clear.

"The word must be its own warrant" (*DP*, 161). Any discourse must carry its own authority within itself. On one hand, to locate the authority of discourse outside of discourse is to put that authority beyond reach of critique. But all efforts to establish such an infallible ground of discursive authority are never anything more than the desperate posits of fallible dogmatists. On the other hand, to deny the authority of one's own utterances in the very act of uttering them is to arrest the function of discourse. No matter how fluently these denials and demurrals are made, the act of utterance has turned on itself, becoming an act of self-nullification. In this respect, then, skepticism (the arrest of function) and dogmatism (the positing of an authority beyond discourse) are identical: the effect of both is the nullification of oneself. Just as dogmatic assertions invite skeptical challenges, the negations of the skeptic prompt the search for absolutes, for what would not be susceptible to such negations. The fluency with which skeptics denounce their own authority and even the need for the actuality of authoritative norms should not hide from us that such fluency masks arrests. The articulate denial of discursive authority likewise masks an inevitable lapse into the inarticulate. Think of how the relativistic doubts of people leave them with nothing to say about their own commitments. These doubts stop conversation; far from opening space for disagreement, they undermine its possibility. Their inability to say anything here is a revelation of their breach with the finite actualities of inherited discourse and, consequently, their lapse into the inarticulate.

If words must be their own warrants, if the only forms of authority that allow us to avoid the dilemma of dogmatism and skepticism are ones inherent in discourse, then the articulate immediacies designated by the most commonplace verbs cannot be denied their actual authority. Any denial of this actuality—in particular, the actuality of the authority inherent in discourse—would itself be a denying (one the most dramatic instances of a present active participle). Of course, the act of denying characteristic of the dogmatist would invoke the name of something outside of discourse and thus beyond criticism, whereas that by which one becomes a skeptic is in effect a despairing: one despairs of one's own discourses having inherent in them the resources to tell the telling differences, to authorize the necessary distinctions, without which our world is not merely a mess but no world at all. But to allow that words are their own warrants, that discourse carries within itself its own authority, has proven to be extremely difficult. Such articulate immediacies as Miller stresses seem to be nothing but the most ephemeral acts of manifestly fallible agents. They have seemed and still seem to many to provide an insufficient warrant for our critical dicta (*PC,* 160). One reason is that in granting such acts such authority seems to license vagrancy: anyone can say anything he or she wants, for the words he or she uses are self-warranting, their utterances are self-justifying, their critiques self-certifying. Far from allowing us to get hold of a person, this uncompromising affirmation of discursive authority seems to make it impossible ever to get a hold on anyone, including oneself. But, in actuality, any person *can* say anything that person wants, even if the utterance is sub voce. The point is not to get anyone to stop saying what we do not like to hear but to invite and even insist that each one of us at least start to own up to what we have said and are now saying. This is a far more difficult challenge than most of us are likely to imagine, for the task of owning up to our acts of saying, counting, and so on encompasses the task of maintaining the discourses in which such acts are alone possible. To take responsibility for ourselves means that, in taking responsibility for present active participles of our own articulate immediacy, we must take responsibility for nothing less than the midworld as such, as the matrix of discourse, critique, and revelation.

> [T]o be simple, I emphasize yardsticks and clocks. They are verbal, not substantive. You *handle* a yardstick, you *tell* a tale, you *tell* time. But you do not "react" to a yardstick unless someone uses it as a weapon, and then it has lost its status and functioning authority, as a commanding and momentous present. It is impious in a deep sense to treat any of the items of the midworld as another inconsequential object—the body, or a laboratory instrument, the idol of the heathen. In fact we now put such idols in a museum. (*MS,* 18)

In doing so we exhibit a piety for cultures often far removed, historically as well as chronologically, from our own. The deities honored in these artifacts are frequently no part of the history shaping our identity, but insofar as they are parts of the history of humanity they are worthy of a respect spilling over into reverence: they demand our piety. To repeat, anyone can say anything he or she wants, but has their saying actually been that? Is the person actually speaking? Has he or she actually spoken? Has he or she assumed the authority requisite for utterances to be revelations, acts in which the world no less than the selfhood of this person is disclosed? So, the important issue—in the classroom or the courtroom, the political forum or the scientific debate—is whether the persons assembled actually have spoken and whether they are willing to accept the demands imposed on them by their own utterances, by their actual self-placements in some discursive context. Miller believed that the most authoritative ideas of the twentieth century disqualified or discredited discourse in the sense he thought needed most to be acknowledged and, indeed, celebrated. In his sense, discourse is inherently critique. The historically evolved forms of human utterance reveal, as nothing external to them, constitutionally critical forms of utterance. Critique is inherent in discourse: its forms are one with and constitutive of even the most commonplace of human utterances.

In the light of these considerations, Miller was led to assert: "We have become misologists. No utterance commands, none has ever been heard. Nor, by the same token, can the present speaker submit to the authority of his own utterance" (JWM, 28:12).[2] Implied in this statement are the essential linkages among the evasion of actuality: the evacuation of the present, the refusal to grant human history categoreal status, and the refusal to grant human utterance authoritative actuality. But, in this context, the stress most appropriately falls on utterance and what we ordinarily identify, even if only metaphorically, as the source of utterance.

Looking back over his life, Miller once noted in a letter: "[M]y folly was that I heard Voices, not so much that I spoke. I was audience before I became speaker, indeed in order to become speaker. That was my grave error. These Voices were all illusions in a Voiceless World" (JWM, 25:20). But Miller did insist on speaking in his own person, precisely because he had undergone the tutelage or initiation of having been an auditor. He came to feel that his utterances were often considered oracular, his claims to have heard in a Platonic dialogue a voice quite human but nonetheless authoritative were often considered arrogant or worse, because so many of his colleagues and even so many of his students resisted accrediting any human voice with critical authority, much less with revelatory power. The rule of his day was, as that of ours still is, "[N]ever take a man at his Word and never take the Word as the man" (ibid.).

Only those who have heard the voices of others can have a voice of their own. But those who hear voices are condemned as mad, while those who have never heard anyone one else actually speak are mute. The eloquent defenders of the silent world are, in effect, the guards in an asylum, convinced that those who claim to have heard voices are to be confined. But Miller refused to countenance that our actual world is a silent one; he resisted the efforts of these guards to take his utterances as evidence of the need to establish his philosophical insanity. If the most authoritative voices within contemporary philosophy rendered suspect or worse the insistence to speak with a human voice, to have an authoritative as well as articulate presence in one's actual world, then the authorities were in no position to pronounce others insane. On their own premises, they could in fact not make any pronouncements whatsoever.

Even so, Miller realized that affirmations were risky (to affirm anything is to open oneself not only to criticism but also to ridicule) and, moreover, when affirmations so deeply cut against the grain of the dominant tendencies in one's intellectual milieu they can only appear to be obscure (*MS*, 112).[3] Yet he did not hesitate to stress: "My affirmation is the midworld" (*DP*, 72). He credited the deed and invoked the midworld, not as either appearance or reality but as the source of this and all other distinctions (*MS*, 138). In one of his more modest formulations, Miller states that the midworld is the vehicle of all order and, thus, of all our revisions of order; it is the arena of self-revision (*MS*, 110). In one of his bolder affirmations, he identifies it with revelation as well as revision: it is the totality of those symbols by which whatever can be called real is revealed.

Miller grew "insistent on the ontological status of the articulate immediacy" actually embodied in a vast array of functioning objects (*DP*, 160–61). Where one grants in one's philosophical outlook, the commanding status to human discourse which it actually has in countless contexts of one's everyday life, there one has opened a place for the humanities and the arts to declare for themselves the significance, efficacy, and authority they have historically displayed and, to some extent, still culturally retain. One can feel "the attraction of song for the poet and why Homer is a sort of magician. But so was Plato, as events prove [i.e., as history exhibits], only Plato never gave his own utterance ontological force" (*DP,* 162). In fact, even before "Homer smote his lyre, there had been words and symbols. Every word has some magic in it" (*MS,* 70). The magic inherent in poetic utterance springs from the magic already resident in a language as an inheritance. But, even though every word has magic in it, poetic utterance possesses the most dazzling magic.

Above we noted the rule that we are never to take persons at their word or their words as these persons themselves. Miller explicitly relates the insistence on this rule to an aversion to revelation. He acknowledges that "revelation" is a bad word, because it is most likely to be misleading. All words mean what that have come to mean and, in this instance, the term is likely to suggest something authoritatively laid down in such a way as never to be open to revision or challenge, precisely the opposite of what Miller intends. When confronted with the choice of saying with Kant that the critique of human reason demands that we posit an order of reality, in principle, beyond the possibility of disclosure or with Hegel that the history of our own critical discourses requires that we retain the notion of revelation (that reality refuses to wait forever in the wings, that it insists on putting in an appearance—on appearing in countless guises which, for finite consciousness, cannot but be *dis*guises), Miller sides with Hegel. Any utterance is a revelation. He goes so far as to propose that any utterance has the quality of revelation: "A yardstick or a clock is a metaphysical actuality, an incarnate power. Until the word was made flesh, it had no actuality" (*MS,* 153). But, once the word is made flesh, once symbols become incarnate, revelation has a commanding authority, because it has an immediate actuality. The opponents to utterance did not deny this but were opposed to utterance because they themselves assumed that utterance is revelation. Because they effectively granted this function to utterance, they denied its status as utterance; because they acknowledged that this is what the word conveys, they denied that there was actually any instance of such a process. To grant utterance would be to grant revelation and that would be, on cognitivist premises, obscurantism. Since revelation is "to be granted neither to others nor to oneself" (JWM, 25:20), utterance is to be rejected. We can allow human speech as a case of operant conditioning, as an instance of adaptive behavior, but we cannot allow human utterance as a truly revelatory power.

Realism tends to lapse into dogmatism because it characteristically insists on a reality independent of discourse. But the impossibility of separating reality from discourse is what German idealism, beginning with Kant, established, at least in Miller's judgment. It is worthwhile to recall that Kant identifies his philosophy as critical: the tradition of idealism, born of the conflict between dogmatic metaphysics and skeptical empiricism (*PC*, 64), was one in which the crucial concern was not showing that everything is reducible to mind or even that everything is susceptible to critique; rather this concern was to show how truly radical forms of critique are possible. What price must be paid, what processes posited and presuppositions defended, if such forms are truly possible? Such forms of critique always ultimately assumed the shape of self-critique—of self-conscious agents struggling to assume absolute responsibility for their discursive practices, for their most accredited scientific theories, most defensible moral positions, most innovative artistic achievements. Whereas realists tend to take words foremost as denotative tokens (as names for realities given apart from any acts of naming), Kant insists on the legislative status of such categoreal words as, for example, substance and accident, cause and effect. To take all human words as ultimately reducible to denotative terms is to leave the impasse between dogmatism and skepticism just as we have inherited it. For the words are simply given; as brute data about which all criticism is irrelevant, they are to be accepted without question, without the possibility of any questioning. This amounts to dogmatism. Or words might be questioned in such a way that they lose their authority; that, in acknowledging that names indeed result from acts of naming, and these acts are our own, we undermine our own confidence to name anything at all. It is as though, in coming to name the act of naming as such, we deprive ourselves of our capacity to name the objects and processes seemingly disclosed in human experience. There is an arrest of the function of naming; and the name for such an arrest is skepticism!

But, if words are not taken as denotative tokens but granted their legislative status (and this goes back to Kant), a possibility of moving beyond the impasse between dogmatism and skepticism appears. With Kant, however, our categoreal terms (our constitutional words) are granted a legislative status but denied, as far as reality goes, any revelatory function. On Miller's telling, to conceive of these terms as essentially *historical*—having their origin and function in history—and *revelatory*—having the capacity to disclose reality, not merely to give intelligible form to sensory appearances—was the achievement of Hegel. The moral, political, and intellectual revolutions subsequent to Hegel's death in 1831 did not make his thought less relevant but all the more pertinent to thinking through the crises of authority so manifest in the second half of the nineteenth century and, in with increasing intensity, each decade of the twentieth. To be in a position to think through these crises, Miller believes that it is necessary to acknowledge what he takes history to disclose: "The person, the utterance, the world become inseparable" (*MS,* 70; cf. Davidson 1991). Miller admits, "symbols are objects too. But they are generative and critical" (*PC,* 62). They are, in an important respect, only incidentally perceived objects; they are essentially functioning objects. They generate orders (e.g., space or time) in which other objects, in the immediate guise of perceptible actualities (an object perceptibly locatable in, say, a spatial or temporal continuum), can appear; moreover, they propose criteria by which we might evaluate particular appearances in particular circumstances. They are critical as well as generative, legislative as well as revelatory.

On Miller's view, then, the "symbol is a legislative actuality" (*MS,* 160; emphasis omitted). But its character as legislative needs to be understood as immanent and (in a sense) absolute. For "its legislation is not from above, or outside, but upon the same region in which alone it actually exists" (ibid.). The yardstick can be considered as part of the region it declares, just as a clock might be considered in reference to that region it declares (e.g., the construction of the clock might be measured by the continuum of clock time made possible only by the construction of clock mechanisms). But symbols are, in a sense, absolute as well as immanent. While their immanence means that their ontological status is that of a finite actuality projecting formal infinities. Any symbol is an identifiable actuality amid countless others; any symbol is, indeed, located in the field of actuality. The status of symbols as absolutes (a feature closely related to their immanence) means that they are not derived from anything other than symbols. "There is no reaching objects until one already has an object which is absolute. The symbol is absolute, but not unknown, because it is the condition of further inquiry" (*DT,* 188).

This absolute need not be absolutely so; that is, it may be relative to other symbols. But the symbolic as such has the status of absolute for at least two reasons. First, "it is the vehicle of the relative"; second, it is derived from itself. Nature, culture, and history itself are identifiable only through symbols; but the symbolic can be derived only from the symbolic. That is, the historically constituted and constituting symbol is explicable only in terms of other such actualities. This does not make impossible criticism of the symbols by which our world takes form; instead, it makes their critique necessary. But since these symbols are undeniably ours, this in turn means that the necessary critique of human modes of symbolization can ultimately take only the form of self-critique. But self-critique itself can ultimately take only the form of self-narration, in which our own utterances and the criteria by which we evaluate them are self-consciously acknowledged to be the fateful prolongation of prior utterances. So, just as critique is the destiny inherent in all modes of symbolization, so a genealogy of critique is that irreducible form of historical consciousness that our critiques of these modes are themselves destined to assume. Human symbols drive toward critical self-evaluation; such evaluation in turn drives toward a reconstruction of the journey by which critical consciousness has arrived at its present locus, that is, the steps by which such consciousness has attained its actual authority as a critical outlook. The links among symbolization, critique, self-criticism, narration, and self-narration have been forged in the crucible of the history of symbolization itself. Hence, "we discover other minds and our own via the vehicle of mind [i.e., through the symbols on which our own and other minds rely, and by which they are constituted]. The story of the growth of the mind is the same as the story of the revision of its vehicles" (*DT,* 189). The story of the self-revised symbols on which self-critical consciousness depends is a story in which such consciousness is implicated; it is thus destined to take the form of a genealogy.

Neither the mystic nor the skeptic grants a constitutional place to human symbols. The "mystics are alone with the alone. They want to escape from discourse, which, being finite, is exploratory, and being exploratory, rests on symbols of order" (*DT,* 188). Mysticism resides in the aspiration "to apprehend a reality directly and without intermediary" (ibid.) or, more boldly, in the claim to have apprehended reality in this way. The skeptic too "has no place for the symbol"; for this figure looks for the revelation of a reality not accessible through what takes place in consciousness. But he or she finds no such revelation there. In this the skeptic "is quite right" (ibid.). But, to accord ontological status to the legislative actualities of human symbols would radically transform the issue; for then human consciousness is no longer seen as an inaccessible realm, closed in on itself and cut off from reality, but a privacy correlative to the potential publicity of symbols, a spontaneity correlative to the inherent discipline imposed by mastering some discursive media.

Realists and empiricists have noted the prevalence of symbols but suppose that there are data or realities to which we can lay claim without also laying claim to the symbols through which these data and realities are revealed. This supposition is just what Miller denies: he is unwilling to say, "There is the world, and here are the signs" (*MS,* 75), for that would imply that the order of reality and the orders of discourse can be pried apart. The very word "midworld" voices a protest against any and every attempt to pry reality apart from discourse. This protest was, as we have seen, issued in the name of criticism.

But what Kant observes in his own time is even truer in ours: "Our age is, in especial degree, the age of criticism, and to criticism everything must submit" (1965, 9). The bounds of critique are as quickly transgressed as they are established. Criticism unbound is the inevitable result of this frenzied movement of self-transgressive critique. But can critique survive in any recognizable and effective form this frenzy of self-transgression and self-overcoming?

What Miller says of discourse might here more pointedly be said of critique: We must be alert to the conditions of our own critique. If Miller's self-conscious identification with the philosophical tradition of German idealism (inaugurated by Kant, running through Hegel, and creatively appropriated by Josiah Royce and William Ernest Hocking) means anything, it means critical alertness to the sustaining and authorizing conditions of critical discourse. Critique ever alert to its own inherent regressions to dogmatism and also to its inherent self-stultifications (the skeptical arrest of its critical function) is the only form that would realize the historical task of this philosophical tradition (again, see *PC,* 64). But this historical task is immanent as well as emergent: it not only has actually emerged out of a particular development in our cultural history but also is destined to operate within a historically constituted, and thus, to some extent, constitutionally incoherent, present. The incoherence of this present is in no small measure due to the inherent dynamic of critical consciousness to transgress one boundary after another.

To cast the story of human consciousness in terms of the drama of human transgression is, of course, an old story. It may, nonetheless, be a revelatory story. But to see this story as a story, as a historical utterance having its origin and place within human discourse, is (to use Paul Tillich's expression) to break the myth. The keeping of faith might require the breaking of myth; the recovery of reverence might require facing squarely the fatality that the story is not a divinely authored disclosure but a humanly won articulation. This has proven and still proves to be difficult. For we either break the myth and lose the basis for reverence or we refuse to break the myth (i.e., to deny that our most sacred stories are at bottom human tellings) in our desperation to retain a sense of reverence. But the concluding sentence of Ralph Waldo Emerson's "Montaigne; or, The Skeptic," one of his representative men, suggests a way between the horns of this dilemma, the way Miller in fact articulated and defended: Let a man "learn to bear the disappearance of things he was wont to reverence without losing his reverence" (Emerson 1982, 336).

When criticism historically became unbound, reverence was endangered, and for many, completely lost, because revelation was unveiled to be something other than it pretended to be, something other than what humans said it was. In the monumental texts of sacred scripture one hears a human rather than divine voice. But the effect of discrediting divine speech has been to discredit human speech. We have condemned ourselves to a silent world in which our most authoritative utterances are, as human utterance, illusory and, in turn, a world in which our most accredited objects are absolute data. These objects are, in their status as brute immediacies, "realities" exerting a brutal authority: humanity simply must submit to them, without question and especially without complaint.

Josef Pieper's definition of revelation is a succinct statement of what might plausibly be taken as the one traditional understanding of a highly contested concept. Divine revelation is divine speech: it is the word of God addressed to human beings either at the beginning of time or in the course of their history (Pieper 1962, 128–34; 1964, 161). Out of the darkness light exploded; out of the silence a voice emanated; out of the chaos a cosmos was brought forth by an artist transcending that cosmos. "Out of the silence a voice, out of the darkness a light" (*DP*, 102). Or, according to more ancient stories, a universe was crafted out of shapeless clay by the less than adept hands of a divine potter (Gen. 1:2).

Sacred revelation has been and still is taken to be an inviolable text. It demands certain kinds of questions of its auditors (e.g., Have you been faithful to the words of this text? to the holy names of He who has authored this sacred text?), while precluding other kinds. To ask these other questions is to break the trust, to violate the faith encoded in this scriptural behest. But the full acknowledgment of the untold stories of various religious traditions, often overlapping and even more often contradicting one another, has freed criticism from within the narrow bounds imposed, often quite brutally, by religious authorities. As we have seen, criticism unbound has meant revelation unveiled: divine revelation has in human history been revealed to be a textual monument erected not by a divine architect but by human hands. Criticism unbound has always led to paradise lost; but the loss has been considered a gain, for the world lost has come to be seen as nothing but a fool's paradise.

Hence, the only story we are entitled to tell about divine revelation is, Miller "argues," one in which the ongoing critique of authoritarian pronouncements is the very heart of the drama. The story of revelation is, ineluctably, the story of our critiques of what has within our history claimed the title of revelation.

Although our myths are broken, though our stories come to be seen as stories (Tillich 1936), they do not thereby necessarily lose their revelatory power. For example, a defining part of the sacred scriptures on which Western consciousness has been nourished over centuries is the story of exile and wandering. These texts attest to a history wherein the Jews were forced to wander through the desert and other regions, dwelling where they were seldom welcomed. They lived in exile for centuries but retained a consciousness of their status as homeless. But the status of this people might be taken as itself a revelation concerning the fate not simply of themselves but of humanity. The sense of being exiled in a world utterly hostile to one's presence, to what one deems most high or sacred, thus what is most deserving of realization in the here and now, characteristically takes its most acute form in those who have attained the highest level of critical consciousness.

We can be at home only in a world of exile, one in which any actual location is under foot only as the result of a series of dislocations. We have journeyed to the ground on which we now stand; but, even with respect to this ground, our standing is transitory and indicative of countless transitions. Historical self-consciousness is attained only by the steady refusal to evade the painful consciousness of humanity's actual displacements; it requires accepting our status as self-exiles from homes that once enveloped us as wombs. But, once we have recognized the necessity of accepting this status, the decisive issue becomes what to make of our status as exiles. We might make too little of it, by making too much of it; for we might allow our awareness of this status to make of us an unhappy consciousness, one unreconciled to its own actual conditions. In contrast, we might locate ourselves in the present with a deep, detailed sense of the historical dislocations by which we now stand just here, and nowhere else. Such a sense does not need to abate the intensity or to undermine the authority of our present actuality. If, in the words of Percy Bysshe Shelley, "We look before and after, / And pine for what is not" (quoted in *PH*, 89), this actuality is effectively disqualified; but if we refuse to make of our lives the relentless pining for an imaginary home (cf. Lacan 1981; Rushdie 1992; Rieff 1993), an acute consciousness of our historical displacements can actually intensify and authorize our actual placement. We are then self-conscious exiles committed, nonetheless, to making a home for ourselves where we now actually stand.

Following Hocking's usage, Miller identified "spiritualism" (what we might call "animism" [Fell 1997, 11]) as the type of philosophy from which we are self-exiled, first of all, by the growth of self-consciousness. The animistic outlook was, he told students in Philosophy 1-2, "the original philosophy"; it is thus the one most deserving to be considered "an innocent philosophy" (PH 1–2, 5). While it has itself no derivation, it is the outlook from which all others are ultimately derivative; while it has "no philosophical ancestry," it is itself our oldest identifiable ancestor. The animistic outlook is, in its immediate mythopoieic form (Frankfurt 1970), a truly primeval view; it is even more a practical orientation toward the experienced world than an outlook from which human agents can in the least degree detach themselves. They approached the world from this angle of vision without being, in the beginning at least, aware of their own angle of vision or orientation toward the world. Insofar as this orientation has coherence and thus an identity, it is to be found in the way the stories and practices making up this orientation attest to the controlling belief that human beings are incarnate spirits amidst and subject to other spirits. In the course of its articulation, this orientation provided humanity a means of separating itself from nature; only thereby does humanity become humanity. While still seeing itself as a part of nature, humanity is able to see itself apart from nature, as an imperceptible spirit and thus power transcending the perceptible objects and processes of its immediate environment. Only thus does humanity find itself out (ibid.). Then, quite early in the semester, Miller played his hand: he revealed the main thrust of his historicist approach to philosophical reflection when he announced that:

> The discovery of agency is also the discovery of *criticism*—to judge, to detect a defect, a maladjustment, a wrong, a falsity. Anyone who says he has made a mistake is a Spiritualist to that extent, because he recognizes that he has made a miscarriage of purpose. Once discovered, of course, criticism can be made inappropriately as well as appropriately. If you can call your ancestors names of a nasty sort, you're considered to be getting somewhere; it's considered smart. "Thank God that I am not like other men." What nonsense! But here—in philosophy—man identifies himself with the rest. He who explains these types of philosophy [beginning with spiritualism and culminating in a form of idealism] becomes an attorney; he tries temporarily or provisionally to make a case for what he is studying. But in identifying with the rest, one must] say *"mea culpa!"*; it's my fault, not just the fault of the environment or of circumstance. (Ibid.)

Our sense of spiritual displacement depends on our abiding ability to dwell imaginatively in the spiritual homes from which the fateful growth of critical consciousness has exiled us—that is, from which we have exiled ourselves. It depends on our ability not only to identity these ancestors as ours but also to accept the full force of this personal identification—these ancestors are inseparable from who we now are. Such identification makes of our history a task, and of the errors and confusions inherent in that history something for which we must take responsibility, hence, our ability—perhaps the necessity—to say *mea culpa*.

The first fateful shape of human freedom was, from all available evidence, the spiritualistic (or animistic) orientation. This was the first spiritual home from which human consciousness was exiled. The critical energies and strategies by which this home was defended—by which humans resisted its own inherent collapse—led to a radically different orientation, one in which narratives in terms of doers and deeds was replaced by explanations in terms of causes and effects. In short, naturalism, or mechanism, came to supersede animism. But, whereas animism does not allow for an impersonal region of natural processes that become increasingly impossible to deny, naturalism does not allow for a uniquely personal region of irreducibly historical practices. A world alive with spirits is one in which every sound is likely to be the fragment of an utterance, the sign of a presence at once near and articulate. In contrast, any mechanistic world is one devoid of personal agency and of the historical practices in and through which such agency is initiated, sustained, and altered. It is a world of causes, not one of purposes; it is a world of impersonal laws and mechanisms, not one of personal spontaneity and autonomy. It is a world from which humanity itself is apparently banished. So, while spiritualism is ultimately untenable because it cannot do full justice to the natural world as an encompassing field of impersonal forces, so naturalism is in the end untenable because it fails to take into account the matrix out of, and the arena in which, humanity and indeed the phenomena of life emerge and act. Naturalists are so effective in establishing nature as an impersonal totality that they obliterate themselves as personal presences. No sound, not even that of their own utterances, is to be taken as the sign of such presence; no sign or other perceptible mark can, in principle, ever be taken as indicative of an authoritative voice. For theirs is a silent world; it is also a lifeless one. The "mechanistic doctrine would kill the world and all that move upon it; we are [in the only terms provided by this doctrine] dead men. Some there are who pretend to be alive, even as they admit that life is an illusion and less than a dream" (*PC,* 18). To accept this doctrine is to subject our selves to "lassitude, inertia, viciousness, and triviality"; but to displace this doctrine demands a radical revision of what have proven to be authoritative, thus inescapable, premises. Is there a way of narrating the historical emergence of this fateful doctrine that will allow us both to accept its force and even inevitability and to exhibit its limitations and untenability? For Miller, such a story might be told in terms drawn from resources principally found in the idealist tradition. Of these terms, none is more important than revelation (or disclosure), discourse, critique, narrative, history, and that distinctive form of historical narration known as genealogy.

Whereas our self-critical discourses must ultimately assume the form of historical narrative, they potentially have the function of objective disclosure. In other words, Miller is unwilling to jettison the notion of revelation (see, e.g., *MS,* 152–53). In casting this notion overboard, we needlessly impoverish ourselves. His objective is not to defend the infallible revelations of an absolute authority. It is to affirm the midworld, to defend the authoritative against both the authoritarian and the skeptic; he insists that in the self-revisable modes of human discourse we have what, from our position in history, ought to claim our absolute allegiance. But he identifies the midworld with actuality; and, in turn, actuality with that which "carries us down to the present as functioning" (*DP,* 98). Such actuality "is the immediacy that projects infinity" (ibid.). The hand that made marks of some sort as the most rudimentary form of human counting illustrates one such immediacy. But what Miller calls an "actual immediacy" (*MS,* 19), also an "articulate immediacy" (*DP,* 162), can be "a commanding and momentous present" (*MS,* 18) only because it is an embodied and historical moment. Its locus is neither a disembodied consciousness nor a mindless order of brute data. We are mindful and, in being so, we are on the go. But, just as all human dwelling testifies to prior dwell*ings* (just as behind any known or identifiable day is a yesterday, however obscure or unknown), so every instance of human functioning and every act of human utterance presupposes an embodied history (i.e., a history embodying in finite actualities the functioning authority of those who before us have crafted the means to measure and count, to make words sing in poems and music sing in stone—"Architecture is frozen music"). "The mind in career seeks an objectified career in persons and institutions and is [through these objectifications] more at ease with itself; self-revision is never solitary. It comes to be noted that it is in career, in self-revision, that the not-self is most surely found" (*PH*, 133).[4] This comes to be noted because the human mind in its careering through history is always already an objectified career. This bears directly on that form of critical consciousness known by the name of philosophical reflection.

A Rough Sketch of a Contested Terrain

Philosophers do not fabricate their problems out of their own imaginations, however much philosophical reflection truly depends upon human imagination. The most responsible forms of philosophy might even demand the wildest flights of imagination. These problems are resident in our most commonplace expressions, established habits, and secure institutions (JWM, 23:27). They are part and parcel of our inheritance. The earliest philosophical problems do not seem contrived but quite sensible, "as in the quest for a permanent stuff holding steady in the change of objects" (ibid.), or that for a social order insuring the possibility of justice. While G. E. Moore once confessed that the writings of other philosophers were the sole source of his philosophical puzzlement, Miller was puzzled how anyone could not find disconcerting the constitutional confusions inherent in any human inheritance. The problems he addresses, then, were of the same character as he supposes were those addressed by Thales and Heraclitus, Plato and Aristotle, Descartes and Locke, Kant and Hegel, and countless others. They "were not bolts from the blue but derivative from words, monuments, utterances, and institutions" (ibid.). To some extent, these figures were cognizant of the historical actualities out of which their intellectual concerns grew. But one of the most influential ways of accounting for the origin of philosophical reflection compromised their cognizance. Thus, countering a traditional claim, one met in Plato and Aristotle and repeated countless times in successive centuries, Miller denies that philosophy originates in wonder. As ordinarily understood, wonder suggests too passive, intellectual, and impractical a source of philosophical reflection in its most customary form (JWM, 7:5). Philosophical affirmations are often made with severe stridency, philosophical issues approached with savage ferocity, opponents denounced with deep bitter savagery, and results prized for their "deep serenity" (ibid.). The problems that drive us to philosophy are, hence, deeply disconcerting, so much so that they threaten a twofold dissolution—that of our world and ourselves. To regain our composure (*PH*, 164) upon living through the disconcerting experience of a constitutional conflict—to compose ourselves and our world in a single stroke—understandably brings us a peace deeply savored. Not wonder but disconcertment drives us to philosophy; not the consoling vision of the aloof spectator but the composition of oneself, in some defining domain of one's personal agency, is ideally the outcome.

Taken in their totality, words, monuments, institutions, and other artifacts make up the midworld. This world is a mess but not so completely that inclusive orders cannot be proclaimed or intricate harmonies cannot be discovered. Physical space with regard to material objects or historical place with regard to human actors are illustrations of such conceptual orders, the nervous system and even simply a single cell ones of such dynamic harmonies. The midworld is not a trackless sea but a contested domain of protracted boundary disputes. The task of renegotiating the boundaries is made necessary by (in Emerson's words) the "self-evolving circles" of human discourses; in their self-evolution, they are destined to overlap with one another. In overlapping they are fated to contest each other's authority. The task of renegotiating the boundaries among overlapping, conflicting orders of discourses and, to less an extent, overlapping, conflicting discourses within a single order (e.g., economics and sociology) falls to philosophy. Miller maintains: "The discrimination of modes of utterance and their relation is the philosophical job: What is the structure required by any distinctive utterance, a number, a poem?" (*DP*, 158) What is that form required of a statement about a past occurrence, an interpretation of an ancient text, the formulation of an abstract argument, the prediction of a solar eclipse, the narration of a philosophical story, the self-maintenance of our attempts to be self-critical?

The sciences, the arts, and the humanities are broad categories by which three distinct orders of human utterance can be distinguished. That is, they are traditional names for three vast stretches demarcated within the midworld. The midworld is, like all other human places, contested ground: it is the site of momentous conflicts between, or among, distinct discourses.

For example, some physicists might suppose that the success of their discipline has thoroughly discredited philosophy along with theology; they feel confident that, for their own work, either philosopher or theologian can say nothing arresting. Likewise, some philosophers might suppose that the constitution of their own discourse is such that scientists are not, as scientists, truly members of the commonwealth of philosophy; so scientists can dwell within this discourse only on the terms laid down by philosophers. For the maintenance of this realm, the utterances of science are (allegedly) inconsequential; hence, ignorance of science is justified, even by those who would presume to be epistemologists. Thus, scientists are not among the lawmakers of this terrain: their voices carry no authority, their utterances no weight.

The Disclosive Media of Functioning Objects

The sciences, the arts, and the humanities are, then, distinct orders of human discourse but ones having evolved out of a history in which the discursive and the disclosive have been linked. Historically, some discourses have been accredited with the power to disclose features of our world as well as us. Sacred scripture and human speech have been traditionally accredited with this capacity. Although mysticism has ironically had its eloquent defenders, Western thought has never accepted the thoroughgoing disqualification of articulate speech, in its recurrent insistence to carry within itself a genuinely disclosive authority (*PC*, 185). The question has tended to be not whether discourse could be disclosive but rather which discourses actually are revelatory; and, of those discourses that are disclosive, which ones have the widest scope and farthest reach. The advances of scientific discourses seem to have undermined the credibility of traditional religions, though this claim needs to be qualified and justified if dogmatism is to be avoided.

Even so, the disclosures of scientific instruments speak to us with an authority in some respects comparable to the authority accorded by our ancestors and, indeed, many of our contemporaries, to the revelations of their sacred scriptures. The self-avowed corrigibility of scientific utterances does not undermine but rather secures their authoritative status; somewhat paradoxically, these revelations stand up only because they can, in principle, be knocked down and because, to date, they have actually stood up against severe, systematic tests. In other words, they carry within themselves the highest authority humanists would ever grant to any utterance. That the authority they carry within themselves is open to challenge cannot be challenged, for it is an absolute commitment of any responsible inquirer. Science (though not science alone) offers the only forms of revelation we will countenance, ones offered by those who are willing to acknowledge their fallibility. But without relinquishing a fallibilist outlook, the yardstick *and* the poem, the microscope *and* the novel truly function as means of revelation. We can yet say that the cathedral of Chartres speaks with an eloquence as arresting as the dialogues of Plato. The drawings to be found in the caves of the Pyrenees reveal the presence of humanity; and they reveal this presence with a force no less compelling than the photographs being sent back to Earth by a probe in some remote part of our solar system revealing potentially significant details of a remote region of our natural world.

Nothing is gained; indeed, much is lost by failing to distinguish categoreally the sciences, arts, and humanities from one another. But also much is left inexplicable by failing to relate these orders to one another and, moreover, to trace each one of them to what might be called the actuality of the act (an expression explained below).

The actuality of human acts is dependent on their embodiment in functioning objects: the act of measuring requires a physical organism to do something physical if anything intelligible is to be revealed. The human organism might roughly approximate, simply by observing with unaided sight, or accurately measure, by recourse to precision instruments, the distance between itself and some object on the horizon. "The antithesis of scientism is not humanism but historicism" (*DP,* 158). If science is not our only means of disclosure, it is primarily because history offers an alternative to the discourses of science itself ("science itself has a history" and science is at bottom what this history discloses of the activities of experimentalists and theorists). The philosopher and, more generally, the "humanist must embrace both the scientific and the historic" (ibid.), without trying to transform philosophy or any of the other humanities into either a science or one of the traditional forms of historiographical discourse. Although it strives for a kind of objectivity, philosophy is not a branch of scientific investigation; though it exhibits a fidelity to the past, it is not a form of traditional historiography. The "humanist can exploit what the scientist is doing" (ibid.) but not by aping the methods of the experimentalist or by trying to incorporate the most assured conclusions of experimental investigation into a picture of the universe, inclusive of humanity.

The humanist can exploit what the scientist is doing by attending carefully to this form of doing and, then, drawing out the most important implications for a self-drawn portrait of self-critical agency. If this is done, what becomes apparent is that "every control word in science is an action word and not the name of any object under the broad blue canopy of heaven" (*DP*, 158–59) and, moreover, that these action words (e.g., measuring) require functioning objects (yardsticks) in order to have the fateful status they actually have within a particular tradition of scientific discourse. They allow my statements to come back to haunt me, my claims to come back to claim me as the author of an erroneous prediction or inaccurate account. What embodied mistakes force on us can be also a feature of effective functioning, that any act of utterance is part of a continuum and, as such, can be conjoined with earlier utterances.

We actually make mistakes (*PH*, 175–76) and, of greater significance here, actually identify them as such, because we have mastered the artifactual means by which local control over some determinate aspect of our immediate circumstances might be exerted. I can count and plot the traces left on a photographic plate and, thereby, test a hypothesis regarding the behavior of subatomic particles. My claim that the room is spinning, that space itself is swirling about me can be confronted with testimony from sources other than those of my immediate perceptual experience. These sources are themselves linked to the authoritative disclosures of perceptual experience, though such experience is authoritative only when disciplined through its reliance on functioning objects in immediate control of immediate circumstances. The functioning object of paramount importance is of course the human organism. It is by itself ordinarily able to detect in the course of its own perceptions those that are unreliable or illusory; in countless cases—the disclosures of my experience when I am in control of myself and my immediate environment, when I am able to negotiate movement with fluid effectiveness and to enjoy stasis without disconcerting dizziness—enable me to tell the difference between the room and my head spinning.

The factor common to the scientific and the historic approaches is reliance on the functioning object. The instruments, formula, and theories of scientific investigation reveal the way nature acts; in contrast, however, the documents, monuments, and other pieces of evidence through which the historian sifts reveal how humanity has acted. These documents need to be replicated and preserved, these monuments protected and revisited, if the past is to be disclosed more fully and intricately than is now possible. The discovery of other documents and the omnipresent possibility of deepening our understanding of available ones make it necessary to preserve in some form whatever documents we have already discovered, for only then can future discoveries and deepened understanding contribute most effectively to the ongoing work of historical research.

The factor common to the scientific and the historic is, at the same time, the "locus of action and autonomy" (*DP*, 158). The achievements of science are of historic significance, but so too is the narration of history itself. Scientists and historians are thus among the makers of history. These makers have been scoundrels as well as saints, mean-spirited as well as great-souled; but whatever else they might have been, they were efficacious. They have acted in ways that have made and, indeed, still make a difference; and, in acting, they have shown—even in their most wild moments of reckless abandon—an autonomy for which they rarely apologized. Nothing great has ever been accomplished without great passion, as Hegel stresses in his *Philosophy of History* (1956). But no passion has ever been expressed except through the human body and the symbolic media through which, say, blind rage is translated into anger often as eloquent as it is destructive. So, once again, we are led back to the midworld, the intricately interwoven orders of historically evolving discourses in which our simplest utterances implicate us. "Given the yardstick, what must I then do and say? Vast things, of course. Given the Constitution, what ensues? And so with the Parthenon or Plato or Shakespeare" (*DP*, 158).

Miller moved a distance from yet retained his identification with Kant, Fichte, Hegel, Royce, and Hocking. He never supposed that purely technical expertise in conceptual analysis and formal argumentation makes one a philosopher; but rather insisted that anyone's identity as a philosopher was tied to that person's identification with a long tradition of critical discourse. Of course, he realized that different persons will pick up the story of this tradition at different points, becoming especially absorbed in certain conflicts and being largely unmoved by countless others; but he was suspicious of those who did not appreciate the drama of this story in its full sweep, contenting themselves with several recent episodes taken in isolation from the whole (e.g., G. E. Moore's and Bertrand Russell's attacks on F. H. Bradley and other absolute idealists, showing no sensitivity to the legitimate demand to frame a truly synoptic vision). He often began his introductory course to the philosophical tradition of critical discourse—of logos trying to establish and maintain itself as critique—with a book entitled *Before Philosophy*. So, he himself picked up the story before logos dissociated itself from mythos, when human thought was mythopoieic thought. Only from the perspective of the immediate identity of logos with mythos could the eventual rupture be appreciated. Hence, the pre-Socratics, so significantly named, were not themselves insignificant figures in this intellectual drama. But, partly because of historical accident (we have only fragments of their utterances, whereas the monumental texts of a literary genius have survived), the figure of Socrates, as portrayed in the dialogues of Plato, assumes an even greater significance in this historical development. But the contingencies of this history ought not be allowed to eclipse its necessities, either the necessity *of* history or the necessities *in* history, that is either the need to turn to history or the fatalities revealed in this confrontation. It may not be "a journey every stage of which is necessary" (JWM, 5:15), but it is one in which all of the most crucial steps are fateful acts, including fateful evasions. In the name of Mercy and Justice no less than Truth, we have mercilessly put human beings on the rack, forcing them to confess to crimes they never committed and beliefs they never held (a phenomenon arrestingly depicted in Eco 1983). In declaring religious heresy to be a capital offense and ecclesiastical tribunals to be competent judges in this matter, was not a trajectory defined, one pointed toward (though certainly not necessitating) the Inquisition? In forcing upon the nation of Germany after World War I the humiliating terms of the Treaty of Versailles, was not another trajectory defined?

While the tremendously influential revelations of a transcendent God have been exposed as a human story and while even the revelatory power of human speech has been described as a pathetic illusion, cannot the voice of humanity itself be heard in the disqualification of divine utterance and the doubts regarding its own disclosive power? Is not the critical voice of human beings who desire, above all else, to be accountable to themselves and perhaps also to one another for what they say and do, audible in the most thoroughgoing negations and in the most radical doubts? Even if human speech has no disclosive power, it has a critical function. Whatever can be said can be contested; whatever revelations are alleged can be challenged. No matter how radical our skepticism, then, the skeptical self is defined by an absolute commitment to establish and maintain itself as a relentlessly critical self. This is its true self. So we turn from revelation to critique.

Joining the Historical Career of Critical Reflection

Miller takes his own philosophical identity to be established not by his possession of technical skills but by his identification with the historical career of logos, going back even before the fateful dissociation in ancient Greece of logos from mythos. In general, human identity is the always somewhat precarious identification of a historical actor with the constitutional conflicts generated by an ongoing career. For example, Einstein not only *was* the physicist who formulated the theory of special relativity but also *was* one who both strenuously resisted indeterminism ("God does not play with dice") and with equal determination persisted in searching for a compelling way to conceive nature as a field in which all apparently different forces are reducible to a single force. He was the scientist who solved certain problems, evaded certain implications of discoveries in his own discipline (e.g., the indeterminism implied in quantum theory), and persisted in pursuing what forever eluded him. This is who he *was* intellectually. The photographs of him and Neils Bohr locked in argument, or pausing between parries—Einstein insisting that "God does not play with dice" (chance is a subjective illusion) and Bohr responding that Einstein should stop telling God what he can or cannot do!—poignantly capture a scientist who self-consciously defined himself in terms of the problems inherent in his discipline. Here we have a good illustration of Miller's central claim that "[c]onflict does not operate to scatter the self but to establish it, even to organize it" (*MS*, 187).

Thus, the identity of any person, intellectual or otherwise, is rooted in a process of identification. Here as in every other context, one must grant primacy not to nouns but to verbs: the emphasis must fall, foremost, not on identity, but on identifying oneself with something, where the something with which one identifies is also a process—in one of Miller's favorite words in this connection, a career. Whereas this verb "identifying" suggests a relationship no less than a process—one identifies *with* something other than oneself, something having tenure apart from one's own life though dependent on the intersection of one's life with that career—the noun suggests neither dynamism nor relationship.

Miller's refusal ever to stand aloof from the project of critique, wherein the self-conscious narration of our self-critical discourses emerged with Hegel as integral to this project, was an instance of piety in his sense. Hegel's *Phenomenology of Mind* was "the story of the process by which reflective self-realization is won" (JWM, 5:15).[5] Robert Gahringer has observed that, because Hegel helped Miller so greatly in coming to see how constitutional concepts take their actual shape in the fateful conflicts of our intellectual history, it "is no accident that Miller treated the preface to *The Phenomenology of Mind* with special reverence" (Gahringer 1990, 35). This story allowed him to come into his own philosophically; hence it was one he revered. Part of its achievement was, in Miller's judgment, simply to establish the need to tell a story, the necessity for reflective self-realization to take the form of self-accountable narration—that form of narration in which human narrators hold themselves accountable for their prior utterances and also for the very narratives disclosing their accountability for what they have said and done. Hence, he identifies the tradition of German idealism with the discovery of human history as a series of fateful conflicts. Moreover, Miller identifies it with the task of self-critique in its struggle to avoid a regression to dogmatism or the immobility of skepticism. He views his own efforts to provide a compelling narrative of critical consciousness as rooted in this distinctive, often misunderstood and thus often caricatured tradition of philosophical reflection.

Miller's comments about political history pertain equally to intellectual history. In politics, people want answers and also experts who will supply them, but they tend not to want, even strenuously to resist, what their own questions entail: an identification with the discourse in which their own problems alone can be posed (*PH*, 135). "External interests determine to what use a technique is to be put" (ibid.). In contrast, historical identifications determine to what tasks we have committed ourselves, whether or not we have the will to own up to our commitment. Whereas the self is free to define the uses of any technique, inheritance defines the tasks of any self. Abraham Lincoln (to use one of Miller's favorite figures in this regard) did not offer answers or even presume an expertise; instead, he disclosed what history demanded of him and anyone else having the courage *to identify with* a nation truly dedicated to the proposition that all men are created equal (Strout 1990a, chap. 9). In our intellectual history, the significance of Kant is to be found not so much in the elaborate structure or the specific details of his transcendental critique of theoretical reason but in the sheer fact of owning up to the need to reconcile the presuppositions of scientific explanation with those of moral conduct—as it is often put, to reconcile Newtonian physics with human freedom. His dedication of his first *Kritik* to Francis Bacon was significant, for the author of *Novum Organun* had at the outset of that work explicitly stated the need to steer a course between dogmatism and skepticism. The task so sharply stated by Bacon was not carried by him or anyone else to its completion: what needed to be done was, in crucial respects, left undone. So, just as Lincoln self-consciously took up the unfinished task of the early (though not the later) Thomas Jefferson (Strout 1990a), so Kant self-consciously took up the task so eloquently formulated in the opening paragraphs of the *Novum Organum*. But he intended his own *Kritik* to be that *Organum*, as Lincoln intended the revised form of the American polity to be the more adequate articulation of the founding vision.

This concern with critique immediately translates into an emphasis on discourse. For Miller insisted on conceiving the sciences, arts, and humanities as discourses. But they are obviously discourses in which critique is not anything external. Although external critiques of any historically constituted discourses are of course possible (e.g., the creationist must try to show why biology has gone astray in its account of evolution), these carry little force if they cannot be connected with the central terms on which the discourse being criticized relies. The only way the creationist critic of Darwinian evolution can get a hearing is by joining the brethren of scientists, by couching the critic of evolution in the terms of science itself. Critics will not be heard unless they join the discourses to which their critiques are directed. Have they truly done so? Or are they merely lambs in wolves' clothing? Is this critic one who understands this discourse in the only way it can be actually understood, through passionate, informed participation in its current constitutive conflicts, or is there, underneath what might be commanding cleverness and persuasive glibness, only the show of identification with this discourse? For example: Is a gradualist account of biological evolution an adequate one, or does one need to introduce punctuated equilibrium?

To conceive the sciences, arts, and humanities (including philosophy) as discourses means that they are not sets of objects to be spoken *about* but discourses to be joined (see, e.g., *MS*, 63). In one sense, these discourses need to be joined together, at least to the extent that each is seen as an instance of historical continua dependent on an articulate immediacy for their ongoing continuity. "Any continuum appears as the momentum of an immediacy" (*MS,* 119). "Any continuum resides in the actual, in the verb, in the midworld, never in passivity and its discrete and miraculous data" (*PC,* 125). Apart from the inherent dynamism in some articulate immediacy (e.g., the person now counting), there is no historical continuum, no actual continuity. While any discursive continuity can reveal itself only in the immediate actuality of some finite act, such actuality derives its momentum largely, perhaps exclusively, from the energies resident in its inheritance. But these points should not be allowed to obscure the far more simple claim that the discourses of the sciences, arts, and humanities have to be joined together; they have to be shown to be dramatically different variations of the same theme—human action bound up in the ongoing career of its absolute self-affirmation.

But these discourses need to be joined in another sense as well. We join them as we might any other discursive community. But there is something paradoxical here, for we are required to join actual communities in which we are already, in some deep respects, actual members. In ordinary circumstances, we move from being an outsider to being a member of a community; the act of joining effects this transition. In the historical discourses now being considered, however, our status as outsiders is largely illusory. To paraphrase Groucho Marx's joke, he refused to join any community that would have him for a member. Here it seems that we cannot even "join" any community except one in which we are already a member! The possibility of joining depends on the actuality of membership. This point can be overstated, as I have just done; and when it is, it is all too easy to overlook the quite strenuous demands of initiation ordinarily imposed by the fully accredited members of these discursive communities and the paramount importance of the conscious acts by which one affirms one's actual membership in a historical community. But the deep impiety of contemporary consciousness is that we today do not ordinarily feel the need to disavow membership in the actual communities sponsoring and supporting our actual selves. We are so estranged from them, they are so little a part of our sense of identity, that we do not feel the need to disavow membership in them. From the perspective of such estrangement, language is supposed to be a mere instrument, occasionally handy but not absolutely indispensable. From this viewpoint, the way Miller, Heidegger, and Peirce speak about language can only seem to make a fetish of it. The ability to stand apart from every institution and, yet, to be in possession of an actual identity and articulate presence is never questioned by most people today. But is this a systematic illusion carrying tragic consequences? Is this not itself one of the roots of nihilism?

The determination to face the consequences of our commitments, themselves consequent upon our actual membership in historical communities, depends on acknowledging these commitments as our own, as ones by which we define ourselves. Until persons define themselves in terms of their commitments, we cannot get any hold on them—a serious difficulty confronting anyone who approaches the teaching of philosophy or any one of other humanities not as an attempt to impart technical skills but as an invitation to join the ongoing career of a critical tradition. The evasion of actuality is, at one level, the refusal to confront the consequences of one's own commitments; it is, at a deeper level, the refusal to own up to one's own commitments, as in "I didn't say that" or "I may have said that but I didn't mean it." The refusal to stand by one's own utterances unburdens one of the responsibility of confronting the consequences of these utterances. If nothing has been actually said, then nothing has actually to be accepted, and thus nothing painful needs to be endured. One can deflect the painful and avoid the onerous by opting out of what, after all, falls outside the present and may not fit the whims of the moment. But the price for dissociating oneself from one's own utterances and other deeds could not be higher: a form of suicide inevitably results from this infidelity, from this failure to keep faith with what was, after all, actually said and done.

This evasion of utterance is, thus, nothing less than a nullification of the speaker. In this more radical refusal, the self becomes vaporous—nothing anyone can get a hold of—because it has rendered itself vacuous: the evasive self evacuates the only possible ground from which an articulate career can be launched, thus the only ground on which an articulate presence can be maintained. This ground is the actuality of the act itself, the act as the residue of prior doings but also as a demand on present exertions. The actuality of the act means, first of all, that something has actually been done (some word spoken, some offense given, some consideration omitted); beyond this, it means that whatever has been actually done has not been actually completed. Present action does not close upon itself, rounding itself off in the form of static completion, but opens on a future, thrusting itself forward in the form of a constitutional incompleteness. "Thus to inherit a history is to inherit a task" (JWM, 5:15). The evasion of actuality in its most characteristic form is the rejection of an inheritance that makes an absolute claim on finite agents in the actual circumstances of their immediate undertakings. But the acceptance of actuality has proven difficult, even for those who affirm their commitment to do so.

In "Helen's Exile," Albert Camus recalls Antoine de Saint-Exupéry's rejection of the actual world in which he was doomed to live: "I hate my time" (Camus 1970, 152). Camus's response echoes views being articulated at the same time (1948) across the Atlantic by Miller: "But, however overwhelming his cry may be, we shall not take it as our own. Yet what a temptation, at certain times, to turn our backs on the gaunt and gloomy world. But this is our time and we cannot live hating ourselves" (ibid., 153; cf. Rorty 1998, 34). But how is it possible to live after the bombings of London and Dresden, the death camps of Auschwitz and Buchenwald, the nuclear incineration of Nagasaki and Hiroshima? Camus may seem to offer too little, but that he offers anything at all might mean a great deal: "It is [only] by acknowledging our ignorance, refusing to be fanatics, recognizing the world's limits and man's, through the faces of those we love, in short by means of beauty—this is how we may rejoin the Greeks" (ibid.). And it is only by rejoining them that we can join ourselves to the finite actualities of our historical circumstances.[6] There was a contemporary, and at one time an intimate, of Camus who offers us a more effective means for bringing into sharp focus the distinctive character of Miller's stress on actuality.

Rival Understandings of Critical Consciousness

In *What Is Literature?* Jean-Paul Sartre announces that he stands for an ethics and art of the finite (quoted in Murdoch 1989, 112). In this announcement he appears to be in effect aligning himself with the position hammered out by Miller at roughly the same time. But Miller sees in Sartre's existentialism not so much an allied position as a concealed romanticism fatally disposed toward vagrant gestures, toward wholesale condemnations of the actual world from a perspective not essentially beholden to actuality.[7] The presupposition of such condemnations is not the absolute affirmation of finite actuality but rather the desperate retention of transcendent ideality, even if the sole locus of such ideality were the rebellious consciousness of isolated individuals. Here we see yet another instance of what Miller so pointedly identifies, the tendency to posit a transhistorical perspective in order to judge our time-bound transactions (*PC*, 130).[8] Of course, rebellious individuals can, precisely in reference to their revolt against actuality, feel solidarity with one another. But this solidarity is derivative; indeed, to presume solidarity among human beings prior to a consciousness of their shared denunciations would be, from the Sartrean perspective, a denial of human freedom. "No one can decide to join his actual community" (JWM, 31:3). Our actual communities are those fateful alliances in which personal freedom assumes effective form. "Isolation has no universal. . . . Community is not a derivative of privacy" (ibid.). Human community is rather a primordial actuality. So, like Heidegger, Miller is suspicious of Sartre's identification with actuality: the famous French author might emphatically announce his commitment to an ethics and art of the finite, but other commitments seemed more deeply rooted and, thus, more decisively controlling. In particular, to be fenced in by, or pinned down to, the finite actualities of one's inherited circumstances would require Sartre to choose between capitalism or communism, when he desired above all to denounce utterly both economic regimes (Murdoch 1989,

111–12). He supposes that both regimes are morally bankrupt but does not appear to realize the "bankruptcy of the past offers poor security for the solvency of the present" (AW, 255).

Yet, rather than declare the present insolvent, Sartre declares consciousness sovereign. The self-declared sovereignty of consciousness is, however, a far way from the self-authorized discourses of the midworld; for these discourses are finite actualities from which human agents cannot extricate themselves, not an impregnable domain into which a supposedly finite self sequesters itself so that it might secure a transcendent perspective from which to issue wholesale condemnations of its inherited institutions, of the only possible alternatives offered at its historical time. But, just as Sarte judges capitalism and communism to be absolutely intolerable, he deems any actual alternative to be utterly impossible. While Miller supposes that our actual past makes our personal agency possible, Sartre supposes that this actuality makes agency impossible (JWM, 23:7). Hence, the actual is denounced as completely corrupt, the ideal is abandoned as completely unattainable. As Iris Murdoch notes, "when one is caught between the intolerable and the impossible nothing is justified except a state of rebellion, however vain" (Murdoch 1989, 111). Our task is not to become what we are but to become what we are not and have never been: the only authentic form of human freedom then is the absolute repudiation of those finite attachments, those historical identifications, which would claim our souls if we would but consent. But freedom resides in dissent, dissociation, and denunciation.

Sartre saw no *via media* between capitalism and communism, whereas Heidegger thought through the 1930s and until the end of the war that his own locus in history actually provided him with a way other than those of the two dominant economic regimes of Western technological society—indeed, his condemnation of both capitalism and communism is no less harsh than Sartre's own. Miller assumes that there is more than an incidental historical link between free markets and free institutions (cf. Novak 1965). He also thinks that it is political lunacy to be unable to see any fundamental moral difference between the democratic ethos of the United States and what Albert Camus aptly calls the totalitarian socialism of the Soviet Union.

Sartre's advocacy of an ethics and art of the finite is clearly quite distant from Miller's own repeated affirmations of finite actuality. It is nonetheless illuminating to develop somewhat further this contrast by considering Murdoch's characterization of Sartre's outlook: the Sartrean perspective is at bottom a more or less disguised form of romantic rationalism. Murdoch (1989, 105) contends that Sartre is a rationalist because he takes the supreme virtue, our saving achievement, to be critical self-awareness. For him, sincerity means, more than anything else, "the ability to see through shams, both social shams and the devices of one's own heart" (ibid.). Rational lucidity and self-luminosity are alone what justify human existence, just as nothing degrades it more than our ignoble self-deceptions. The exposure of hypocrisy and, underlying the project of combating sham and especially self-deceit, the task of attaining self-possession are not aimed at the reform of the world. They are the way the self lessens its complicity with the structural evils of its inherited circumstances, the Sartrean equivalent of moral purity. That is, they concern moral rectitude, not the actual reform of one's actual world.[9] Sartre's rationalism is, thus, a celebration of Reason as a critical and, above all, self-critical capacity; the principal focus of this critical capacity is Reason itself. Accordingly, Murdoch judges Sartre's rationalism to be "solipsistic and romantic, isolated from the sphere of real operations" (ibid., 106). Thus, whereas Sartre's despair of ever actualizing the ideal of a kingdom of ends makes of his rationalism a form of romanticism, Miller's own absolute affirmation of human existence, his utopian humanism, make him suspicious of all forms of romanticism.

The concluding paragraph of Murdoch's discussion of Sartre's romance of rationalism is especially pertinent to drawing as sharply as possible the contrast between him and Miller. Here she notes what can be described, using Miller's vocabulary, as a fatality inherent in the development of one of our most self-assured attempts at self-critical utterance—that is, scientific inquiry. Science "has altered our societies and our key concepts with a dreadful speed" (ibid., 113) and thus with disorienting effect. The discoveries and pace of science have so thoroughly disoriented reflective persons as to displace them. Such persons have been banished from any universe that in any degree approximates a home. Human beings are thus cosmic exiles destined to do nothing more than, momentarily, break a silence that will shortly—and everlastingly—swallow all of their utterances without a trace of the struggles and achievements of those discourses by which they define and revise themselves. Humans might either deceive themselves about their status as such exiles and regress to an unreflective life or accept the burdens of disclosures that cannot be gainsaid without critical intelligence being destroyed. But to accept these burdens is to be lost in place, to be so displaced from one's actual world as to be stripped of one's cosmic standing, of one's effective status as an articulate presence. So, just as those of us who are committed to critical consciousness cannot choose an unreflective life, so we cannot "express a view of what [and where] we are in any systematic terms which will satisfy the mind" (ibid., 112). We have crossed the Rubicon of self-critical consciousness: we can no longer go back to an all-encompassing outlook, an all-inclusive vision.

> We can no longer formulate a general truth about ourselves that shall encompass us like a house. The only satisfied rationalists today are blinkered scientists or Marxists. But what we hold in common, whatever our solution, is a sense of a broken totality, a divided being. What we accuse each other of is 'metaphysical dualism'. All modern philosophies are philosophies of the third way. (ibid., 112–13)

But not all philosophies are equally effective in articulating a *via media*, or in conveying a sufficiently nuanced and critically efficacious sense of the broken totality of the human midworld. Our celebration of difference has become monotonous, our strategies of critique all too often authorize uncivil denunciations of others and personal absolutions for ourselves.

"To this day the emancipated intellectual hesitates to say that he lives on Elm Street. He is a man of mind, a universalist of sorts, but not of a formal sort" (*MS*, 145). But there of course have been intellectuals who have defined their task in terms of local struggles and particular histories. Although Jean-Paul Sartre's insistence on actuality might be quite other than what it announces (might be a retreat to Cartesian subjectivity rather than an advance to our actual midworld), Michel Foucault's active alignment with the actual struggles of his own time and place seem, in fundamental respects, quite close to Miller's own ideal of such alignment. As Gary Gutting notes, Foucault's "characterization of *Discipline and Punishment* as 'history of the present' applies to all of his histories" (Gutting 1989, 10). This is precisely the form of historiography in which Miller was most interested. While traditional history in its self-consciously critical form has taken itself to be, potentially at least, a reliable reconstruction of an irrevocable past, the form of historiography that Miller seeks to accredit is that of genealogy, in effect a history of the present. This becomes apparent when we attend carefully to his suggestive identification of history with "genealogical novelty" and his own gloss on this suggestion: "One cannot look for history apart from the urgency of its present interpreter who knows that the past has been its own critic and therefore entails for its understanding a novel, but derived and responsible sequel" (AW, 244). This sequel is what Miller most often means by history. He claims, for example: "The irrevocable past is not the historical past, but only the events and experiences which served as the occasions of a [still] developing clarity [because still insufficiently clear present]. History is the implication of any self-conscious present. It is the mark of the realization that the present is not eternal but has been derived, and that its derivative status [alone] allows it to be identified as present" (JWM, 17:5), as this actual, determinate present imposing quite specific demands and enforcing an inherent discipline.

"Archival" versus "Monumental" Genealogy

But the affinities between Foucault and Miller, above all their commitment to the necessity of reconstructing the history of the present, enable us to appreciate the depth of their disagreement. Whereas Foucault, precisely in his role as genealogist, emphasizes rupture, contingency, and self-overcoming, Miller, in exactly the same role, stresses continuity—albeit an always already broken continuity needing to be re-established—fatality, and the self-maintenance of the discursive and institutional orders securing our never altogether secure possibilities of self-criticism. Although Foucault knows as well as, if not better than, any thinker who has ever lived that humans cannot jump outside of their own histories, that they cannot pry themselves apart from the discourse, practices, and institutions to which they have been subjected and thus by which they have been constituted as subjects, he constructs his genealogies primarily as a way of undermining the authority of certain authoritative discourses. In contrast, Miller appreciates as well as any radical that the most stable structures are mutable, that the fateful course of human history is shot through with contingency, that static forms of community cannot but be inhuman ones, and that self-determination is destined to take the form of self-overcoming. Because of his appreciation of these factors, Miller stresses the necessity to assume responsibility, in a reverential way, for the finite actualities of our historical inheritance.

Foucault's disposition was of course to scoff at what he saw as the desperate attempts to retain such a reverential attitude. If history teaches anything, it is irreverence and contingency. Hence, in one of his most influential essays "Nietzsche, Genealogy, History," Foucault advocates a distinctive understanding of what he calls a historical sense. This sense can be acquired only by means of that "gray, meticulous, and patiently documentary" work known as genealogy (Foucault 1977, 139). Where a man stands becomes clear, as Miller himself notes (though without reference to Foucault), when one takes notice of his opposition. Foucault identifies his opposition as "the three Platonic modalities of history" (ibid., 160). By a strange quirk, however, what he attributes to the dominant metaphysical tradition of Western philosophy, a tradition deriving its authority in no small measure from Plato, might seem attributable to Miller himself (though, of course, Miller was not a Platonist, despite his explicit reverence for the Platonic dialogues). With a succinctness not to be matched, Foucault summarizes this threefold opposition:

> The historical sense gives rise to three uses that oppose and correspond to the three Platonic modalities of history. The first is parodic, directed against reality, and opposes the theme of history as reminiscence or recognition; the second is dissociative, directed against identity, and opposes history given as continuity or representative of a tradition; the third is sacrificial, directed against truth, and opposes history as knowledge. (Ibid.)

This historical sense is effectively "counter-memory," that which disrupts and undermines our tendency to memorialize the past, to sacralize tradition, to stabilize institutions in their current shape; it thus involves "a transformation of history into a totally different form of time" (ibid.). Not only is dated time to be distinguished from clocked time but the traditional use of dated time is to be eclipsed by a self-consciously transgressive reconstruction of some actual dated sequence, wherein ruptures are exhibited (rather than covered over) and contingencies likewise are disclosed (rather than denied their central efficacy in the name of some reputed necessity).

Foucault's engagement with history is, however, only partly parodic. He recognizes himself in the ancient Skeptics and Cynics and, indeed, is assisted by the exemplary execution by these remote ancestors of the discursive practices in and through which he actually forged a historical identity. Although he is the author of "What Is an Author?" (an essay in which authorial self-effacement is alleged to be the historical fate of a rigorously critical approach to those discursive configurations available to us in individuated texts or bodies of such texts), his voice is one of the most distinctive, that is, the most immediately recognizable, voices in our own time; though he speaks of the need for the philosopher to be masked, his own face is, again, one of the most recognizable of any contemporary philosopher. While Foucault insists in some contexts on the need for anonymity, he also makes it plain in other contexts that the pretensions of the universal intellectual—one able to speak in the name of universal values and principles, thus one able to speak for any human being, in any place and at any time—were ones with which he, speaking personally, would have nothing to do. He can speak truthfully only if he owns up to being the man bearing this particular name (Foucault 1984, 105), erotically oriented in this way, standing on this ground, speaking to these particular others.

Foucault's own emphasis on an "esthetics of existence" owes much to his careful reading of classical texts. These texts are in effect monuments to a style or mode of living that was eclipsed by the otherworldly practices of Platonic and, later, Christian schools of thought; these texts are for him monuments even if he characteristically resists acknowledging them as such. It would appear that his parodic history actually operated in the service of a monumental history, for it opened the space for the recovery of those texts in which the force of an aesthetics of existence might still be felt. Transformative energies yet reside in these textual monuments; they still speak eloquently, if only time, care, and skill is taken with the reading of them.

But just as the parodic use of history seems in Foucault's actual authorship to be ultimately subordinated to a monumental use, so too does his use of history as an instrument of dissociation and disruption, whereby the self is rent asunder by its own genealogical critiques, seem to be subservient to the self-constitution of a truly ethical self, the self standing truthfully to itself, though only because it has mastered the self-discipline of *parrésia* or truth-telling (a topic discussed at the conclusion of this section). In some respects, Foucault might seem to be an evasive figure fond of donning disguises and wearing masks; but when one reads his writings chronologically and, moreover, when one takes the decisive emphases of the last years with the utmost seriousness, one is struck by the persistent preoccupation with truth-telling, with the emphasis on telling, on the historically conditioned modes of discourse as what alone makes representation, disclosure, and critique possible. The self divided against itself, the self always already disciplined into the practices of others, is a subject by virtue of its ineluctable, ongoing subjections to the disciplining, and thus normalizing, practices constituting its actual culture. But the self is itself a participant in these subjections, in such a way that the constitution of subjectivity is always in some manner and measure a self-constitution. The divided self exhibits a remarkable capacity to hold itself sufficiently together to able to give and often to keep its word; to speak the truth and to tell when it has not.

It turns out that the third point is not one about which Foucault and Miller disagree, for Miller no less than Foucault thinks that history is concerned far less with truth than with actuality. History is the actuality in which not only particular "truths" are exhibited as untenable views but also entire discourses are exposed as historical contingencies.

Our endeavors to take aim at the heart of the present, to construct narratives of the fateful steps by which the historical present actually took shape would be doomed to miss wildly were we deprived of either the sort of monumental genealogies advocated by Miller or the kind of archival ones practiced by Foucault. If we do not consider Miller and Foucault exclusively in reference to the differences brought so vividly forward by attending to the contrasts articulated in "Nietzsche, Genealogy, History" (an essay that originally appeared in *Hommage à Jean Hyppolite*) but rather consider them in reference to the very last topic on which Foucault focuses his attention—the ethics of truth-telling, as an act of one willing to stake one's being on the telling—then we have a category (that of parrhesiast or truth-teller, *parrésia* being a transliteration of the Greek word for the practice of truth-telling, *le franc parler*) inclusive of both Miller and Foucault. In his last course at the Collège de France, given very shortly before he died, Foucault picked up the topic on which he lectured in the previous year (*parrésia* or the practice of truth-telling) but shifted the focus from *parrésia* examined as a political virtue to it as a moral virtue (Flynn 1994, 102). Foucault distinguishes parrhesiasts from rhetoricians: the former has to run personal risks before the others to whom they speak, whereas the latter do not (ibid., 103). He also distinguishes *parrésia* from other forms of truth-telling, those of the prophet, the sage, and the teacher-technician. The difference between the parrhesiast and the prophet is at least threefold: first, whereas prophets do not speak in their own name but invoke the name of some divinity, parrhesiasts do speak in their own name; second, whereas the utterances of prophets are oracular and thus require interpretation, those of parrhesiasts tend to be direct and clear; third, whereas prophets try to read the signs of the times and thus to mediate between the present and the future, parrhesiast speaks directly about the present, deliberately forsaking the language of apocalypse.

Hence, Foucault and Miller stand in marked contrast in terms of the form of genealogy each advocated, but they are allied in not only being themselves both parrhesiasts but also philosophers interested in highlighting the price to be paid for enfranchising discourse (*PC,* 106), that is, deeply concerned with the practice of truth-telling. Many ways of discoursing about discourse objectify discourse in such a way that the truly crucial questions get systematically deflected: Who is speaking? In what context? For whom? By what authority? Who is permitted to respond to this speaker? Who is not permitted to talk back? (cf. Halperin 1995, 88). And, perhaps the most basic question of all, has anyone actually spoken? The objectification of discourse tends to lose sight of the most important questions concerning objectivity, questions having to do with how actual speakers hold themselves accountable for what they say, entering into dialogic partnership with others so as to enforce real risks and lessen the possibilities of self-deception and self-delusion (Bernstein 1992, 4, 165–66). Is it not telling that both Foucault and Miller so often use the term "discourse" in overlapping senses, ones stressing what Miller would describe in terms of present acting participles?

The Actual Shape of Critical Consciousness: Miller's Socratic Historicism

In an illuminating study and vigorous defense of Michel Foucault entitled "Whence Does the Critic Speak?" J. Carlos Jacques stresses that the only place from which anyone, Foucault or his critics, can speak is some actual locus in an actual history. So a crucial question for the actualization of critical consciousness is always, Where does one stand in one's role as critic? "And where, pray, does one stand in alleging the distinction which is necessarily neither wholly dark nor wholly light? What is that neutrality which permits the distinction?" (JWM, 31:3). What is the actuality underlying this neutrality, not merely permitting but necessitating the distinction between confusion and clarity, or incoherence and consistency? Closely allied to this question is an equally important one, With whom is one standing when engaging in critique? Third, the truly self-critical person must carefully consider the form and effect of the critiques he or she is disposed to make.

Consider Miller's answers to these questions. First, we as critics cannot stand anywhere but the midworld. But to stand in the midworld is to stand in history. It is to immerse oneself in the destructive element, the menacing mutability of finite actualities—points quite familiar by now. But the actual locus of truly critical consciousness is the actual world, an inherited midworld. The midworld alone provides the authorizing ground of critical consciousness.

Second, to stand in history is to ally oneself with others, both those who have gone before and those contemporaries who derive their identity from the ancestors whom one claims as one's own. Moreover, committing ourselves to the present forms of human discourse as the only available means of self-transformation, we are also committing ourselves to the future. For, in so doing, no human discourse is accepted as a *fait accompli*, each only as a discipline driving toward a transformation of itself. It is also to stand by what one has said and done, but also in effect to stand with others and possibly even by oneself. Only persons who are willing to stand by what they have said and done can stand with others; conversely, only persons in their willingness to stand with others are in the position to know the significance of their own utterances and actions. This is partly what Miller means when he in colloquial fashion refers to his own desire to make "person-to-person calls." There must be persons at both ends of the line. Before his ancestors, he felt the necessity to stand in his own personhood; no self-effacing obsequiousness would do here. But neither would any other-denying arrogance be appropriate here. Ancestors in their otherness as well as in their kinship need to be addressed; only thus can a "person-to-person call" be made. The dynamic of historical change is not to be found in any agency outside of the historical process itself; rather the source of this dynamic is "a self-generated inadequacy" (JWM, 12:7), where the inadequacy is both individual—mine, my inability to make good on my commitment to racial equality—and collective. The individual and collective forms of personal agency are distinct but ultimately inseparable facets of the actual shape of the human will: no possibility of asserting myself, assuming responsibility for myself, apart from actual and possible identification with others; likewise, no possibility of enacting our will save through the concerted efforts of individual actors. In whatever form, individual or collective, the dynamic of historical change is actually located in personal agency. Unquestionably, impersonal forces need to be included in any sufficiently nuanced story of human striving. But they can never be the whole story or the most decisive agencies in human history. In the assumption of agency as mine, I truly *make* it so. But, at this juncture, it is no surprise for us to learn that personal agency can never be circumscribed within an insular contemporaneity, a present indifferent or hostile to its inheritances. "The past affects the present as a condition of morale. *It makes agency possible"* (JWM, 23:7; emphasis added). "Agency is responsibility, and therefore one's own, only as it becomes the continuum of an articulate utterance" (ibid.). Only in aligning itself with the historical continua of human utterance (continua punctuated by ruptures) can human agency truly be responsibility and thus avoid vagrancy. So, I cannot merely stand in my own person but also need to stand with those others by whose graciousness, however unwitting, I have been able to establish an articulate presence in my actual circumstances. Moreover, I need, too, to stand with those others who also as inheritors stand today with these same ancestors. So, too, my present links me with a future. The midworld is thus a *Mitwelt:* to dwell here is to be *with* others, contemporary, past, and even future others.

Critics stand in the midworld and, in doing so, both stand by themselves (stand by what they have said and done) and stand with others. Implied in these statements is the answer to the third and last of our questions. The form of critique must be immanent, and its most appropriate effect will be the effective appropriation of the affirmations authorizing critique, negation, and the radical revisions made possible and even necessary by our critical negations. The primary task, both in the sense of being chronologically first and in that of being of the first importance, is to construct those narratives by which situated agents can, to themselves and others, own up to their own actual commitments. The effect of such narratives is to draw individuals into the story of their own lives at a more self-conscious and self-critical level than would be possible otherwise.

Hence, if the form of critique were immanent, then the task of the critic is, foremost, that of the storyteller. Miller saw clearly, long before it became fashionable and in ways that are yet not adequately understood, that one cannot effectively argue persons out of their commitments; one can only exhibit the grounds on which those persons actually stand and, moreover, exhibit the fatalities to which those commitments have already driven those persons, without their awareness, or have driven other persons in other circumstances when animated by the same commitments. Of course, we seldom like to be bound by, much less identified with, what we have said and done (JWM, 17:14). It seems unnecessarily restrictive to bind ourselves to past deed or utterance, to identify ourselves with inherited institutions and practices. Time and again, Miller confesses that all he could do as a philosopher was to tell a story in which the telling of stories becomes itself a leitmotif. In a very personal context, he admits: "I want to be original, but not argumentative, not telling anyone off, not supposing that others were wrong, or stupid. The very manner of doing it is obscure, more like poetry than philosophy" (JWM, 30:3).

Miller once observed that the cogito of Descartes is not itself biographical. In abstracting from its lived body and its historical placement, be it only before a fire in its own study, the cogito abstracts from its history, that is, the story of its life. One can no more narrate the biography of the Cartesian cogito than one can assign a color to a cardinal number: numbers are not physical and thus colorful objects, nor is the cogito the subject of a colorful life or even any humanly recognizable life. The cogito is the result of the cognitive self trying to attain absolute self-possession, the attainment of which involves hyperbolic, methodical doubt—the self-directed abstraction from the allegedly self-determinative involvements of embodied agents. It is in the actual history of Western thought rather one of the most dramatic instances of the thinking subject denying its own biographical actuality: "the 'cogito' is not biographic but draws its authority from an ideal of mathematical order" (JWM, 17:15). But to stop here is to miss the moral of the story, for one has missed the act of narration by which Descartes establishes this order as ideal. What one misses is what Descartes actually accomplished: in establishing the ideal of mathematical order, he has eclipsed the authority of historical narration, but only by offering a biographical sketch of his intellectual life and its fateful resolution to call all things into question. So we should not overlook that "the charm of Descartes lies in the story of his own experience [the story he himself tells of his own difficulties, their source, confrontation, and—to his mind—resolution], much as a Platonic dialogue keeps to the question of what Socrates or Protagoras can make of a word spoken, a belief expressed" (ibid.). Given the self-generated inadequacies of his own intellectual tradition, inadequacies responsible for launching Descartes' own assault on that tradition; and, given the self-generated inadequacies of our own antitraditionalism; the charm of Descartes' story lies largely in the compulsions therein disclosed.

Of course Descartes was not himself a skeptic, though he made systematic use of skeptical arguments. That is, his strategy of radical doubt was enlisted in the service of apodictic certainty; in turn, the alleged attainment of absolute certitude was one with his absolute affirmations: I exist; God exists; and an external world of physical bodies instantiating mathematical form also exists. His radical critique of tradition was intended, self-consciously, to establish a tradition of relentless criticism and systematic doubt. The most impassioned of those who now follow Aristotle "are like ivy that tends to climb no higher than the trees supporting it, and even which often tends downward again after it has reached the top" (Descartes 1968, 37). But, in this context, Descartes is self-consciously addressing what he identifies as "our posterity" more than his contemporaries themselves, bidding those who would come after "never to believe the things people say came from me, unless I myself have revealed them" and bidding them to adopt his own method of doubt rather than the traditional methods of disputatious debate: "while each person in the dispute tries to win, he is more concerned with putting on a good show [and establishing a commanding reputation] than with weighing the arguments on both sides" (ibid.; cf. Bacon 2000). The counsel of Socrates is echoed in Descartes's request of posterity, ironically revealing the extent to which his request is the prolongation of an utterance long antedating his persuasive case for the intellectual necessity of methodical doubt, of tireless questioning. In the case of Socrates no less than of Descartes, the process of questioning is sustained by the capacity of questioners, in the very process of questioning, to regain their composure, because they can by this process make affirmations of which they are assured. The provisional affirmations launching any critical discourse are, in time, replaced by the absolute affirmations of a self-critical consciousness in complete self-possession or, at least, the candid acknowledgment of the actual affirmations underlying our most radical negations. In brief, critique either in its Cartesian or its Socratic form does not preclude affirmation, radical criticism does not rule out absolute assertion; instead, the possibility of critique is rooted in the actuality of affirmations, even if these are systematically occluded or loudly denied.

Such occlusion and denial are, in Miller's judgment, characteristic of the dominant fashions of intellectual criticism in the twentieth century. He thinks that, in our time, criticism is overwhelmingly nihilistic. "It can only disconcert and demoralize" (JWM, 17:15). "[O]ur orthodoxy is obliterative of the articulate" (JWM, 5:3). It is of course hostile toward the affirmative and violently hostile toward any even merely implied presumption to utter *absolute* affirmations.

But Miller is convinced that criticism need not be nihilistic. The nihilist is, however, not simply dead wrong. Still the nihilist might be an accomplice in a wrongful death. The series of displacements by which critical consciousness has uprooted itself from its actual dwellings has resulted in our being neither here nor there, faithful neither to the Earth nor to the other world, neither actually ourselves nor anyone else. Eliot's famous lines still offer an apt description of our spiritual malaise:

We are the hollow men
We are the stuffed men
Leaning together
Headpiece filled with straw. Alas!
Our dried voices, when

> We whisper together
> Are quiet and meaningless
> As wind in dry grass
> Or rats' feet over broken glass
> In our dry cellar. (Eliot 1934, 77)

One response to the hollowness of our own existence would be to turn, as Eliot himself turned, toward a traditional form of religious confession. Another would be to dance in joyful anticipation of the Nietzschean *Übermensch*, denouncing with each step the otherworldly seductions of those ghostly figures who would make of our lives what they have so successfully made of their own—a living death. Yet another response would be to denounce the self-despairing dream of human self-overcoming but not the gods themselves; it would be to accept the bankruptcy of humanism and thus to acknowledge our need simply to wait for the gods to return. All of our efforts to make a heaven here on earth, as Karl Popper notes (1966), have resulted in hell. The Baconian dream of human dominion over the natural world has turned out to be a nightmare in which the human soul has been, if anything, more deeply maimed than the natural environment itself. Hence, the proponents of this position counsel: let us renounce our will to dominate nature, and let us begin to remember simply to let things be themselves, so that the Being of being might reveal itself in a way allowing for the gods to return.

But each one of these responses is, from Miller's perspective, an evacuation of the present and, hence, not a response to nihilism so much as yet another reenactment of this position. But it is not enough to *say* this. It is necessary to *show* the series of steps by which critical consciousness has exiled itself from its actual world, by which the self-understanding in which it most comfortably resides (its stoic vision of itself as a cosmic exile) has attained its authoritative status and pervasive power. This series is a fateful sequence perhaps best revealed in the actual course of Western philosophy. So, at least, Miller supposed. But the success of showing the fatality inherent in these steps and, thereby, the fatality inherent in our own outlook— that is, our current nihilism as "itself a historical emergence" (*PH*, 192)— requires not only affirming the midworld but also attending to the distinct forms of human utterance made possible by the symbols and artifacts making up the midworld.

The Sciences, Arts, and Humanities:
Distinct Modes of Human Utterance

Some modes of discourse can in crucial respects abstract from their own actuality, from the "fact" that they are at bottom modes of telling, and despite doing so fulfill their defining purposes. Ordinarily, these discourses can only fulfill these purposes when they abstract from their own actuality and status as discourse or utterance. The experimental sciences are the most obvious examples of such discourses. In contrast, other discourses must, at least at certain stages in their development, confront squarely and consistently their own status as discourse. These discourses characteristically take an explicitly reflexive form. Part of the task of literature is to pose the question of literature. Part of the function of art is to ask the question of art. So too with philosophy.

Miller is not only willing to link philosophy with poetry. He also is disposed to defend poetry itself against poets, at least those who would make of it a secular surrogate of religious transcendence. Of all those who engage in utterance the poets ought to be in the best position to appreciate the midworld as the actuality with which they identify. This midworld is not in the least hazy, however tangled it might be; the haze emanates from those who allege some other basis for their utterances and, in that allegation, fail to recognize the midworld in its actuality and authority. Nature itself then becomes a haze and (in the words of Shelley) "life, like a dome of many-colored glass, stains the white radiance of eternity" (quoted in *DP*, 103). In response to these lines, Miller asserts that "if Shelley had accounted for glass, domes, colors, from life itself, he would have not written those *despairing* lines" (ibid.; emphasis added). The purity of the eternal is, for this poet, destroyed once it is touched by rays refracted through the prisms of earthly media, of temporal stuff. "A poet, above all men, should avow the power of the word. Without the actual word we would not have that eloquent line any more than $E = mc^2$. There is Shelley. He spoke. But I am not allowing anyone to allege that 'this is a piece of glass' unless he accepts the potency of the utterance" (ibid.). Here we have the philosopher insisting that the poet avow the potency of the poet's own utterance, the philosopher defending poetic utterance against its unwitting desecration by a famous poet. What poetry reveals most of all is the revelatory power of human utterance. To compromise this power is to desecrate discourse, the last act a poet ought ever to commit.

Miller feels that it is time for him and others "to decide whether utterance obscures or reveals the world" (JWM, 6:7). His position is by now clear: the authoritative utterances by which the revelatory power of human utterance has been undermined need themselves to be set in a narrative context, need to be made part of a story in which we ourselves are characters.

"We have become misologists. No utterance commands, none has ever been heard. Nor, by the same token, can the present speaker submit to the authority of his own utterance" (JWM, 28:12). For to submit to the authority of what he is now saying would entail submitting to the authority of what has been said; it would also entail accepting the consequences of what one has said.

Miller's revision of philosophy is, then, linked to the recovery of poetry, of poetic utterance with the full weight of its ontological import. The objectification of Being (that of being here and of the boundless orders launched by the seemingly insignificant acts of speaking, counting, measuring, weighing, and dating) is a distortion of Being, if each of the modes of objectification is not seen to be one nested array of human discourses among other, quite distinct, forms of utterance. To claim that the world is made will automatically be taken by most people to mean that it is fabricated, a fabrication of the imagination. But this completely overturns Miller's meaning. The polar oppositions of appearance and reality, the inner and the outer, the subjective and the objective, the imaginary and the actual, need to be transformed into dialectical pairs, by introducing a third term (for Miller this term was "actuality") that does not resolve these oppositions but permits the possibility and even enforces the necessity of couching such discourses in terms of, say, how things appear to us in particular circumstances and what they are quite apart from this circumscribed apparition, though not necessarily apart from manifestation.

It is one thing to infer that the artifacts and symbols composing the midworld are instruments used to fabricate an imaginary world, quite another to infer, as Miller does, that they are the media indispensable for revealing a real world, one whose realities manifest themselves phenomenally and whose phenomena attest to processes and mechanisms never fully revealed in these phenomena. Poetry gathers language in a way that allows language to gather itself and us in ways of potentially the greatest significance.

"Self-Evolving Circles"

Two images help us to appreciate the sort of dynamism that is inherent in the three distinct orders of human discourses (the arts, sciences, and humanities), as Miller himself saw this dynamism. In "Circles," Emerson suggests "[t]he life of man is a self-evolving circle, which, from a ring imperceptibly small, rushes on all sides outwards to new and larger circles, and that without end" (Emerson 1951, 214). What is true of our life is also true of the discourses, practices, and institutions (in a word, the midworld) in and through which our lives take shape and attain significance. But the inherent thrust of any historically evolving discourse is not simply outward; periodically, the direction of movement is reversed and discourse drives back toward what, in the historical present, can be taken as the center.

A text from Charles S. Peirce captures just this feature of discourse, offering us our second image. But the stage must be carefully set for this image to be adequately appreciated. In a late manuscript, Peirce asserts that while the ultimate purpose of human thought is currently—perhaps forever—beyond human comprehension, we can at least say that thought and autonomy are intrinsically connected. Human thought is the attempt of thought to take control of itself, to police itself, both to lay down the law and to hold it strictly accountable to self-imposed directives and, ultimately, to be faithful to self-espoused ideals. Peirce puts it this way: "it is by the indefinite replication of self-control upon self-control that the *vir* is begotten, and by action, through thought, he grows an esthetic ideal" (Peirce 1931–58, 5:402 n.3). The *vir* is defined above all by the possession of strength and that strength of character known as courage. Although this language is hardly suited to a contemporary audience, the ideal of persons who refuse to be the playthings of others, who insist on asserting themselves and accepting the consequences of their assertions, is not a thoroughly discredited one. It is arguably one of the defining ideals of much feminist thought. Many women have learned that the felt need to apologize for the desire to attain and enhance their personal power, their power over their lives and circumstances, is a need better eradicated than satisfied. In this, then, the Peircean ideal of autonomous agency (what he calls the *vir*), wherein autonomy is as much a communal as an individual achievement, is nothing alien to the movement which would be most put off, and put on guard, by the terms in which Peirce actually couched this ideal.

Peirce observes that the ideal of autonomy (of thought driving to take ever fuller and firmer control of itself) inevitably modifies the rules of self-control; in turn, this modification just as inevitably modifies action and thus experience, most of all by securing for human agency novel arenas for its most spontaneous exertions and also its most deliberate undertakings. The advances of scientific inquiry, for example, can be viewed as so many journeys into unfamiliar regions. In any event, the greater the autonomy, the greater the vulnerability; for human agency by virtue of its newly established power has unleashed utterly unsuspected consequences. The cozy home of quotidian engagements has been traded for some strange world in which our most assured modes of conceptualization and categorization are, in some respects, no longer allies but enemies. In many instances, composure is regained, but only as the result of what initially can be the somewhat desperate strivings and struggles of a precariously placed actor. Novel spheres of action entail surprising shapes of experience; such surprise is always to some extent disconcerting, for it indicates that we do not know our way about. Hence, in modifying the range of our action, we modify the character of our experience.

Having set the stage, we can now appreciate the twirl of the text that complements Emerson's emphasis on the outward movement of self-evolving circles. Peirce describes action in terms of a centrifugal movement: it drives from a center outward, toward engagement with what is other than the self. The modifications engendered by such engagement are among principal features of human experience. So, action and experience are bound together in being bound toward actual engagement with the finite actualities of some immediate circumstance. But the self-evolving spirals of human action and experience are not limited to movement in this direction; for, as Peirce notes, "this centrifugal movement thus rebounds in a new centripetal movement, and so on" (ibid.). The movement in which the self is thrust back upon itself, in the very course of being engaged with things other than itself, is thus an integral moment in human experience. The rhythm resulting from the alteration of centrifugal and centripetal movements, of the self-evolving spiral flying outward and then—often quite dramatically—reversing its direction and driving inward is the characteristic rhythm of human experience. Any human discourse is thus a fateful entanglement of self and other wherein both self and other are inevitably modified, along with the media by which the self is disclosed to the self and, in turn, by which the self is exposed to the other.

To characterize human discourses as self-evolving spirals is to affirm that they develop according to an immanent logic. If we have a voice in the telling of truth, if we have a hand in the shaping of the stories by which the possibilities of truth-telling are secured, then this is a human voice immanent in the truth being told and a human hand inseparable from the stuff being shaped. The human voice apart from its inherited discourses is a contradiction in terms; the human hand as something other than a tool transformed by its use of other tools is also such a contradiction. "Whatever is right or wrong, true or false, good or evil, ensues upon the authority of a self-critical utterance" (*MS*, 123). "Functioning is its own guide and its own energy" (*MS*, 114).

So Miller insists: "It is always destructive of the living word to ask what it is 'about.' It is either magic, or else a poor substitute for journalism and psychology" (*MS*, 69). The "magic" inherent in any utterance resides in its capacity to conjure up realities and a world, a field in which realities occupy a potentially intelligible even if often surprising place. The act to be accredited is the *living* act, the word to be authorized is the *living* word. By them "a world is projected"; hence Miller's claim that utterances make magic (ibid.). But to ask what a discourse is "about" implies that one can step outside of the discourse and evaluate its claims about the realities conjured up by its utterances. But to insist on this is to break the spell. It is also to fail to acknowledge or accept that persons, their utterances, and their world are inseparable (*MS*, 70).

Miller believes that it was worth noting and indeed stressing "we often associate for just talk, enjoying remarks and stories, talk for its own sake. There is something about this in mathematics, where we go on talking in mathematical terms" (*MS*, 60). This can seem irresponsible, even degrading, because it appears to alleviate the responsibility of speakers to anything outside of their discourse; it also appears to trivialize these discourses. Serious, important, responsible talk is, it would appear, talk about what has a status apart from our talk. But, rather than insuring the seriousness of discourse and the responsibility of the speaker, Miller believes that to insist on making all "talking" into "talk *about*" would only degrade discourse and free the speaker from the inherent discipline of responsible utterance.

But he also maintains: "To be human is to be playful. To be human is, thus, to live in a world of one's own creation, for one's own sake. On the one side, this idea (or demand) leads to depravity; on the other, to the discoveries of genius" (*DP,* 132).[10] "Fantasy dissipates the self because it offers no control over a recalcitrant medium" (ibid.). "Enjoyment has become fantastically difficult. For example, parents no longer enjoy children. If 'intelligent' and 'educated,' they must 'train' the child. He becomes a problem and a pest. Nobody but a yokel, it seems can close with life and taste it. Thought has become a malady, instead of a delight. This is due to the current frame of reference of thought, namely the inhuman" (*DP,* 910). Miller would seem in his own way also to be committed to what Foucault calls the aesthetics of existence. A long and complex tale would, however, need to be told regarding the different ways Miller and Foucault meet the difficulties befalling enjoyment. Foucault's almost maniacal preoccupation with limit-experiences, with, for example, the effects of drugs and the sensations unleashed by sadomasochistic erotic practices, stands in sharp contrast with Miller's untiring insistence on self-maintained limits. But each senses the peculiarity and importance of a pervasive cultural phenomenon, having tangled historical roots: enjoyment has become fantastically difficult for countless people, so much so that human physical touch is often little more than the inert juxtaposition of what might as well be inanimate objects, and that the sensuous qualities of food invite no deep savoring.

To understand Miller's desire to join the common woman and man we must keep in mind our discussion about the imperative to join those discourses in which we are already implicated. Miller realizes that to join the common woman and man requires crafting for us a metaphysics that would have respect for such persons. But whereas traditional metaphysics tends to ontologize historically contingent circumstances, thereby elevating a historical contingency into a metaphysical necessity and thereby eliminating the possibility of revising these circumstances (an immutable order being of course an unrevisable one), Miller insisted on historicizing human discourse precisely in its efforts to map the contours of itself and its world. In joining common persons in their quotidian engagements, Miller thus supposes himself to be joining a network of intersecting discourses having a long history but only (for the majority of these discourses) a precarious authority. He joins them not with the hope of answering their questions, solving their problems, establishing his own expertise, or identifying the expertise of another person or institution; instead, he joins them with the hope their conjoining inheritance of self-evolving, and thus overlapping and conflicting, discourses might be a ground for mutual recognition and also one for the ingenuous celebration of their shared inheritance.

Civility requires the minute ceremony of everyday courtesies and the solemn celebration of human achievement no less than the communal mourning of human loss. To join common persons, hence, demands addressing them in a certain manner, with a certain tone. To hear the schoolchild say from memory the words of Lincoln at the dedication of a battlefield at Gettysburg as a national cemetery for those who had fallen there, to hear the echo of the way that the president transmuted the horrific cries of the original consecration of that fateful place into his own simple, arresting utterances, is to be lifted out of thoughtless everydayness and to be inserted into the historical present. It is to be reminded of what a particular day partly means and, hence, of what our actual place actually is. It is to join a discourse whose own inner dynamic drives toward continuous engagement with irreducible otherness; and, in turn, a discourse in which the self's entanglements with others, time and again, forces the self back upon itself, demands of the self to account for itself—to others but also to itself. The centripetal movement of our self-evolving discourses is inseparable from their centrifugal movement; their self-evolving character is inseparable from the vulnerabilities to which they expose the self. Herein we find no prison-house of language (Jameson 1972); or safe refuge in which the human spirit might dwell without fear of mortal enemy. We find here nothing more—but also nothing less—than human beings trying to become what they are, mortal animals bound by a monumental history to give absolute worth to their transitory lives. We can deny our mortality. We can also reject the authoritative claim of this monumental history or even the status of this history as monumental. We can, for example, make of this history the stuff of parody. But, in doing so what have we made of ourselves? After these desecrations, what can we make of ourselves? Perhaps something noble, a step beyond our putrid ancestors and thus one toward a distant *Übermensch*. But how could we ever be in the position to access the nobility of our self-transformation, the worth of our-self-overcoming? Is not the dream of the *Übermensch* one more act of impiety? But then it was deliberately conceived as such an act. Far more to the point, is it not an instance of infidelity to the earth itself, to the here and now? Is it not the confession of one weary with life, though a confession made in such a way that the object of one's weariness is misidentified:

> Here is precisely what has become a fatality for Europe—together with the fear of man we have also lost our love of him, our reverence for him, our hopes for him, even the will to him. The sight of man now makes us weary—what is nihilism today if it is not *that*?—We are weary *of man*. (Nietzsche 1967, vol. 1, no. 12)

But Nietzsche, the author of the lines just quoted, could also stress that "artful and enthusiastic *reverence* and devotion" as "the regular symptoms of an aristocratic way of thinking and evaluating" (1966a, nos. 260, 208; emphasis added). He could even acknowledge the historical value of reverence for what he found was in his time so worthy of ridicule and contempt:

> The way in which reverence for the *Bible* has on the whole been maintained so far in Europe is perhaps the best bit of discipline and refinement of manners that Europe owes to Christianity: such books of profundity and ultimate significance require some external tyranny of authority for their protection in order to gain those millennia of *persistence* which are necessary to exhaust them and figure them out. (Ibid., nos. 263, 213)

Miller would hesitate to speak of tyranny but not of the force required to maintain the order of rational discourse as well as that of civil engagement. Those who refuse to let others speak might have to be removed forcibly so that rational discussion might have a local habitat and thus a fighting chance. In opposition to any fanatical positivists who are inclined to take the closing lines of Hume's *Enquiry* as a literal program for direct action, the only rational course would be to use all the force one could marshal to stop the book burners. Thus, the difference between Nietzsche and Miller cannot be stated in terms of a willingness to rely on force to enforce the conditions in which rationality or nobility can take root and grow. Both do not shrink from accepting force as a condition for rationality. The most fundamental difference concerns whether we can say with complete assurance that some particular inheritance is an exhausted resource, a quarry from which nothing valuable can be any longer mined. Both acknowledge our consciousness of our world and of ourselves to be a historically derived consciousness. Both deny the possibility of constructing genealogies that trace a trail to a point outside of the historical: the historical present has only historical antecedents, those antecedents themselves only have historical antecedents. It is, for Nietzsche as well as for Miller, history all the way down. But Nietzsche often supposes that, from within history, he can pronounce which parts of his inheritance have been completely exhausted and which parts yet deserve to be revered and thus preserved. But this, too, is an old story; for he would be the father whose sin of impiety would be visited upon the heads of his children, in the form of a spiritual impoverishment and personal narrowness of the most ignoble dimensions. If he proves to be successful in convincing us that we have, at long last, outgrown the Sacred Scriptures of the Judeo-Christian traditions and also the Platonic dialogues, he will have bequeathed a world in which his own appearance would be a miracle; for he would have effectively eliminated some of the most important systematic antagonists by which his own naturalistic historicism actually took shape. Apart from the opposition provided by such antagonisms, his own vision of humanity and nature could only degenerate into something amorphous.

The monumental ruins of human history, including the textual monuments of the Torah and the Gospels, are sites to be preserved because of our abiding need to revisit them, again and again. If the most effective form of critique is immanent critique, the most humane form of parody is self-parody. But the bitter, hence humorless ridicule of others is a sign that humor has no place because the self and its placements have only a tenuous and desperate status for the joyless self. Emerson, whom Nietzsche admired perhaps even more than Miller did, offers an important clue for deciphering the contemptuous soul. It is significant that this clue is found in "Plato; or, The Philosopher," a deeply appreciative essay. Here Emerson notes: "If the tongue had not been framed for articulation, man would still be a beast in the forest" (Emerson 1950, 474). He goes on to suggest:

The same weakness and want, on a higher plane, occurs daily in the education of ardent young men and women. 'Ah! you don't understand me; I have never met with any one who comprehends me': and they sigh and weep [or denounce and ridicule], write verses and walk alone—fault of power to express their precise meaning. In a month or two, through the favor of their good genius, they meet some so related as to assist their volcanic estate, and, good communication being once established, they are thenceforward good citizens. It is ever thus. (Ibid. 474–75)

But never for long. For the relationship might break off in such a bitter way that the ardent poet renounces the desire to find a contemporary worth talking to: he or she prides himself or herself that he or she possesses a cleverness for more subtle, more refined ears, ones yet to be born. Is it possible, however, that the refusal to join one's contemporaries is of a piece with the jettisoning of one's inheritance or at least significant portions of one's monumental past? Put positively, is it possible that the felt need to join one's actual compatriots, rather than to dream of a faraway audience, is rooted in the equally felt need to celebrate one's conjoint heritage, that cluster of discourses by which the self is joined, *here and now,* to others? Apart from joining such discourses, is there any possibility of being actually faithful to the earth?

Foucault on Heterotopia:
From Conjoining Discourses to Disinherited Places

Foucault, one of the most Nietzschean of all contemporary authors, writes compellingly of sacred space, just as Nietzsche himself writes without irony about the noble character of some reverential attitudes. In "Of Other Spaces," Foucault suggests that

> despite all the techniques for appropriating space, despite the whole network of knowledge that enables us to delimit or to formalize it, contemporary space is perhaps still not entirely desanctified (apparently unlike time, it would seem, which was detached from the sacred in the nineteenth century). To be sure a certain theoretical desanctification

of space (the one signaled by Galileo's work) has occurred, but we may still not have reached the point of the practical desanctification of space. And perhaps our life is still governed by a certain number of oppositions that remain inviolable, that our institutions and practices have not yet dared to break down. (Foucault 1986, 23)

As examples of such oppositions, Foucault notes those "between private space and public space, between family space and social space, between cultural space and useful space, between the space of leisure and that of work." From even just the texts here cited, it is evident that, for him, we take to be sacred that which we hold to be inviolable. The reason he contends the oppositions just noted "are still nurtured by the hidden presence of the sacred" is that they are ones most of us most of the time are committed to keeping inviolable.

To join common women and men is to join them in the task of maintaining the inviolable distinctions by which we articulate concretely our dwelling here, if not also joining them in maintaining some designated places as themselves sacred ground (Pieper 1991, chap. 3). The transformation of our earthly abode into nothing but a standing reserve is, according to Heidegger at least, an eventuality having the force of a fatality: we arrived at this point because our ancestors more or less unwittingly sent us here. To make of nature nothing more than stuff to be tapped whenever human ingenuity conspires with human "need" to put us in the position to harness natural powers for human purposes—to make of nature only what we can or eventually will make of her—is clear evidence of a practical desanctification of our earthly dwelling.

In "Of Other Spaces" Foucault introduces the suggestive notion of *heterotopias*, one to which his title alludes. Whereas utopias "are sites with no real place" (Foucault 1986, 24), heterotopias (a word framed by analogy with utopia) "are real places—places that do exist and that are formed in the very founding of society—which are something like counter-sites, a kind of effectively enacted utopia in which the real sites, all the other sites that can be found within the culture, are simultaneously represented, contested, and inverted" (ibid.). Foucault contends that heterotopias "are outside of all place, even though it may be possible to indicate their location in reality [or, as Miller would say, in actuality]" (ibid.).

It is surprising that, in his list of examples, Foucault does not include the university as a heterotopia. It may certainly be that he did not suppose that this institutional ground actually offered *other* ground in the sense he wanted to convey by his neologism. But this ground does appear to fit both the general meaning of and the specific principles governing heterotopias. Foucault asks his readers to imagine "a sort of systematic description . . . that would, in a given society, take as its object of study, analysis, description, and 'reading' . . . of these different spaces, of these other places" (ibid.). This description could be called "heterotopology"; it would involve nothing less than "a sort of simultaneously mythic and real contestation of the space in which we live" (ibid.). The principles governing this discourse are:

1. The apparent ubiquity of heterotopias: "[T]here is probably not a single culture in the world that fails to constitute heterotopias. That is a constant of every human group" (ibid.). Of course such constancy is compatible with the varied forms actually assumed by these other places. Even so, "two main categories" might help deal with what would otherwise be an overwhelming variety. First, there are *crisis heterotopias*. While prominent in so-called primitive societies, they are disappearing in the technological societies of late modernity. Second, there are in many societies today replacements for crisis heterotopias, places taking the form of *heterotopias of deviation*.
2. The functional transformability or revisability of heterotopias: "a society, *as its history unfolds,* can make an existing heterotopia function in a very different fashion" than its original function (ibid.; emphasis added). Foucault's example is that of how "the strange heterotopia of the cemetery" has come to function quite differently in our time than in immediately preceding ones (cf. Wills 1992).
3. The complex, even contradictory character of heteroptopias: "The heterotopia is capable of juxtaposing in a single real place several spaces, several sites that are in themselves incompatible" (Foucault 1986, 25). Foucault gives as examples the theater, the cinema, and (perhaps as the oldest example of this) the garden. Given the em-

phasis of our discussion, it is worth recalling that his observation that: "The traditional garden of the Persians was a sacred space that was supposed to bring together inside its rectangle four parts representing the four parts of the world, with a space still more sacred than the others."

4. The temporal linkage of heterotopias: "Heterotopias are most often linked to time—which is to say that they open onto what might be termed, for the sake of symmetry, heterochronies" (ibid., 26). A heterotopia begins to function at the height of its power only when it ruptures ordinary time, only when via its evocations humans arrive at "a sort of absolute break with their traditional time." Heterochronicity in its accumulative function is manifest in museums and libraries, in its ephemeral celebration is evident in fairgrounds and circuses.

5. The accessibility and impenetrability of heterotopias: "Heterotopias always presuppose a system of opening and closing that both isolates them and makes them penetrable" (ibid., 26). In general, however, ready accessibility is not the rule: "the heterotopic site is not freely accessible like public space." Entry is either compulsory or only permitted to those willing "to submit to rites and purifications."

Foucault concludes this essay by noting what he calls the last, perhaps ultimate, function of these other spaces, a function concerned with their "relation to all the space that remains." The function of these other places is either "to create a space of illusion that exposes every real space, all the sites inside of which human life is partitioned, as still more illusory"; or else "to create a space that is other, another real space, as perfect, as meticulous, as well arranged as ours is messy, ill constructed, or jumbled" (ibid., 27). The creation of a space of illusion having the function of exposing the ultimately illusory character of alleged more real places is one function of heterotopias; the creation of heterotopias of compensation (as Foucault himself calls them) is a distinct, but related function. One of his examples for such a place of compensation is (though he does not use this expression) the city on the hill established by the Pilgrims, that is, "the Puritan societies that the English had founded in America."

It would seem, then, that in order to know where we are we need more than maps and chronicles, more than even cultural geography and genealogical narratives: we also need heterotopological analyses of those other places that we occasionally inhabit and, of equal or perhaps greater significance, that themselves are functional objects with respect to all human sites. What the yardstick is to physical space, these heterotopias are to human place: they define the boundaries and partitions within the historical sites of human dwelling and also reveal the complex, dense, even contradictory character of these sites.

For one who was so closely associated with the university, it is curious that Foucault nowhere in this essay mentions the university nor (to the best of my knowledge) does he in his discussions of the university characterize the university as a heterotopia. But this place would certainly seem to fit very well his description. The commonplace expression that the university is a place apart suggests as much. Moreover, that the university has been a site of contestation and one in which other places are called into question (e.g., the holy places of traditional religion and the authoritative fora of instituted government) makes it a heterotopia. It is also one of the actual places in which both Foucault and Miller refined their respective understandings of genealogy, critique, and discourse. The radicalism of Foucault and the revisionism of Miller are closely linked to the way each inserted himself within educational institutions and, beyond this, the way each conceived the relationship between such institutions and their sponsoring agencies, in particular, the state.

The University and Its Discontents, the Nation and Its Dissidents

Foucault took to the barricades, often with bullhorn in hand. He visited the bathhouses in San Francisco, with the ideal of limit-experiences in mind. What Miller observed in the last decade of his life was the dissident discourse, the Dionysian heteroglossia, into which Foucault in the first decade of his career threw himself. The image of Foucault being far away from the scene of battle but listening to its sounds being transmitted by a telephone held up to the window by a friend so as to catch the struggle between the Parisian police and the rioting students (Miller 1993) is the image of a political dissident soon to be born.

Miller has little respect for "revolutionaries" who mounted deliberate assaults on traditional institutions such as the government and the university but then demanded to be treated as citizens of the one and as students of the other. He thinks that to declare oneself the enemy of one's "own" government and, then, to act on this declaration in ways that were disruptive or destructive can only mean that one has forfeited one's rights as a citizen. The representatives of the state might be wise to ignore or to treat mildly those whose revolutionary activity is little more than adolescent rebellion, when it is not simply such rebellion. But it is of course sometimes difficult to discern when the immature are merely playing the role of revolutionaries and when they actually identify themselves with this role to the point of actually being a serious threat to civic places and ordinary citizens. When those possessing actual weapons issue explicit threats, a human utterance of a genuinely revolutionary import seems to have been sounded. But, here as elsewhere, the question is, Has a person actually spoken and spoken in such a way that that individual's utterance is not only an act but, as an act, an immediacy launching or intensifying the continuum in which the act is certified or even unintelligible? (*PC,* 159). "Any continuum appears as the momentum of an immediacy. The momentous immediacy is the act. Only the act has consequences" (*MS,* 119). But the act only has consequences as part of the very continuum its own momentum establishes or constitutes. To demand to be taken seriously—to be taken at one's word and for one's deeds—but then to object that the demand has been honored is, at best, inconsistent and, at worst, evidence of cowardice, of lacking the courage to stand by what one has said and done. The right to dissent as the political right of a citizen within a constitutionally established order is one thing, the right to engage in revolution quite another.

Here as in so many other contexts Miller reveals himself to be in the tradition of Hegel. As Stephen Houlgate points out, the principal lesson to be drawn from Hegel's acute analysis of ethical life *(Sittlichkeit)* and its institutional embodiments "is that true reform of a society entails above all the engendering of *a deeper sense of civility* " (Houlgate 1991, 104; emphasis added). It is all too likely that, in claiming one's own rights or in leveling one's moral criticisms of some specific feature of the political order in its actual functioning, one acts "in such a way as to destroy the bonds of civility." The destruction of these bonds is also the destruction of the possibility of freedom; for the result of destroying "the possibility of *trust* between people and between individuals and the state" can only be that "the essential core of human freedom" is lost. It might be only lost temporarily and regained in a more vital, adequate form. Thomas Jefferson's remarks apropos of Shay's Rebellion suggest that only those generations that have actually fought for freedom can appreciate it. But permanent revolution, or revolution renewed with each generation, is either hyperbole or nonsense, and nonsensical because hyperbolic: it so stretches the term "revolution" that it trivializes not only the meaning of the word but also the actions and courage of those who in deed far more than word were actually revolutionaries.

In at least two places Miller proposes a radical revision of the Cartesian cogito. On one occasion he suggests: "As one may say, 'I rake, therefore I am,' my amendment of Descartes. His world had no rake, nor any 'tool'" (JWM, 22:14). On another, he juxtaposes two quite different self-affirmations: (1) Descartes: "I think, therefore I am" (cogito); (2) Miller: "I vote, therefore I am" *(suffrago)*. His own gloss on this contrast is instructive:

> The *"cogito"* appears in a search for cognitive assurance. One has been "deceived." The thinking self was the "reality" which was the premise of other realities. One can draw the portrait of our times in terms of the demoralization consequent upon a cognitive premise. This is a great historical movement and is a fatality in the true sense of inherent confusion, of a collapse of function, of local control, consequently of the sacred and the revelatory. (JWM, 17:15)
>
> The "suffrago" is [in contrast] a declaration of an action. The person appears as agent, and is so recognized by others.
>
> Corollary: If no vote, then no *presence* as a *person*. The slave had no vote. He was in Roman Law a "vertical dead man."
>
> The State is the organization of voters—one, a few, many, never all.
>
> On any other basis, the State (and History) is an episode in an a-Political (and a-Historic) "reality." (PL, 515)

How one stands in the historical present turns in large part on how one accredits one's actual past, or whether one accredits it at all. "You get a line on a man when he tells you what past he respects or whether he respects any past" (PL, 433 [July 20, 1969]). The *via media* being proposed by Miller is simply but forcefully expressed in a letter written while witnessing the political turmoil in the last years of the last decade of his own life. On one hand, there are those who respect only "a static past which resists reform"; on the other, those who "repudiate any past as authoritative."[11] But Miller strenuously insists that it is of the first importance for a free society that "there be an authoritative past." This past itself was historically derived; nonetheless, it permits and even requires "revision on its own terms."

> The past is what we cannot neglect if we are to allege a present act rather than a childish explosion of desires. I am suspicious of people whose ancestors were all very stupid and very wicked. It seems unlikely that such ancestors could have produced genius and virtue. For the barbarians [for those willing to lay destructive hands on historical monuments], every moment is a fresh start. So one finds them "startling," as one might pun. I am wary of the fresh innocent in politics, the man unsullied by past errors who represents himself as an angel of light. . . . We have them, alas. (PL, 433)

Miller went so far as to claim that the theogony of a free people is its history (PL, 432). But the tendency to hold up as exemplary only disruptive agents—or agents only in their dramatic gestures of societal disruption—and not hold up as well those committed to the maintenance of civility offers an impoverished and, thus, debilitating theogony. Without some monument, there simply is no past (PL, 431). But to grant monumental status to such texts as "Common Sense" and "On the Duty of Civil Disobedience" but not to the Emancipation Proclamation or the Gettysburg Address is both a sign and an aid to such impoverishment. In 1969, Miller observed:

> There is now an emphasis on persons of the past who were disturbers of the peace. not those who kept or redesigned public order. There are many references to Tom Paine and almost none to George Washington. What influence Paine had on events I do not know, but it seems agreed that it was not he who persevered at Valley Forge or could have been considered as the man to hold the Union together in 1789. Much

is made of Thoreau, but it is overlooked that he borrowed books from the library of Harvard College, a place he neither established nor held together. That Lincoln saved the Union and proclaimed Emancipation gets less notice than Nat Turner's rebellion. The effective work was Lincoln's. If any "system" has injustice—as I would maintain—it is also the case that without some system no injustice could be felt. (Ibid.)

While Miller seems to slight the importance of those who would take direct, immediate action against tyranny and other forms of injustice, this slight must be seen against a background in which the romantic glorification of the rebellious individual has completely eclipsed what might be truly called the heroes of revision. The characteristically quiet, patient, persevering heroism of those who maintain some consecrated place by revising the grounds now making effective consecration possible (*PC*, 73, 74) deserves as much honor as more dramatic forms of individual heroism.

Although democracy requires theogony, it equally requires individuals to confront squarely the actualities of their own political history. One such actuality is, in Miller's judgment, that "America began as an asylum for dogmatists" (JWM, 7:14). This has for him a direct bearing on our enduring struggles regarding the limits and, indeed, the meaning of tolerance. Because he takes our past to be an inheritance from dogmatists seeking refuge for themselves, he sees the present as a time "to take stock of the limits of tolerance" and to investigate the constitutional affirmations of the liberal state: the affirmations, formally declared and pervasively felt, by which a people institutes an order of civility and thus one of tolerance. But he is not sanguine about his immediate prospects for a favorable reception: "Just as the necessity for economic reform raised a storm of protest, so too does any suggestion that the genius of free institutions does not define the amorphous tolerance of dogmatic groups" (ibid.). There are limits to what a people ought to tolerate; in the name of tolerance itself, such limits must be clearly defined and, when necessary, vigorously defended. How the pressure of the community ought to be exerted upon those who would exploit the tolerance required by civility to shout down or close off voices to which these dogmatists are opposed is, of course, a delicate question. That a tolerant people have the moral responsibility, not simply the moral right, to define the limits of tolerance is a point virtually everyone grants. The substantive question concerns what kinds of acts and utterances are outside the pale, whereas the procedural question concerns how to establish criteria of judgment and means of reaffirmation that do not themselves serve as the sanctified instruments of any intolerant party. Hate speech manifestly has no place on a college campus; but speech codes might not either. This only means that such codes are inappropriate instruments for instituting and maintaining a civil place; it does not mean that civility should not be vigorously defended and intolerance or worse should not be directly denounced. The question only is how to establish such a place, not whether those committed to civility and tolerance have a "right" to do so. In response to the question "Who is to say what is tolerable?" the answer is, of course, that *we* are to say; and in response to that other question which supposedly would expose the futility or vacuity of this answer—"Who counts among the we?"—the answer can be given only in terms of place. Those who have a stake in a place need to be given a voice in the process by which the consecrated character of some determinate place is preserved. Those who have the principal responsibility for maintaining such consecrated ground have also the responsibility to establish the processes by which newcomers might learn whither they have come. Do we as professors at colleges and universities grant students who have spent virtually no time in such places the right to consecrate this ground for whatever purpose they desire? Or do we begin to initiate them into the modes of utterance (i.e., the traditions of discourse, scientific, artistic, and humanistic) with declarations of who we are and where we stand? When the formal rites of initiation are almost exclusively those imposed by upper-class students upon lower-class ones, in the subculture of fraternities and sororities, is this not a clear sign of abdication (cf. *MS,* 79)?

Although he can issue harsh judgments about the political history of his own country—such as his saying that the United States began as an asylum for dogmatists—Miller appreciates Alexis de Tocqueville because of the French observer's keen appreciation of, and explicit enthusiasm for, the vitally democratic ethos of this country. But, even in this context, there are important qualifications to be made. Above all, he is concerned to identify those particular parts of our historical inheritance that occlude the historical actuality of our national identity, often by glorifying nature, wilderness, apartness, and insularity. Miller observes that Tocqueville's praise of our return to nature shows also that we are not the heirs of what is settled in Europe. This is obvious, but I had not seen it. *America is the extension of the Europe that was breaking up. Its very discovery is part of that sweeping shift.* The Pilgrims and Puritans belong to the Reformation and [thus] had no Gothic churches to take over. We have prided ourselves on our rejection of the artificial and decadent Europe of the 18th century, with its aristocracy, caste, cruelty and privilege. But we had to work out equality in an unadorned wilderness. Nature is [however] not enough for association. It banishes the artificial, but also the sincere and passionate monuments of the mind's experience. Europe, in reform, retained older lore, much of which was sound and true to man. That is the Europe now visible which charms the traveler. If Athens had slaves, it also left the Parthenon, and now it no longer has slaves, either, while something remains of the imagination and delicacy of an older day. That man struggles and achieves in the spirit is better known there than here. (PL, 795; emphasis added)

The lure of nature, which inevitably draws us away from the polis and even less formal orders of human community, is stronger today than it was in 1954 when Miller wrote these lines in a letter. Even if this lure is not that of any actual domain of human experience, it is authoritative, compelling. I would say that, precisely as a purely imaginary homeland, the natural exerts its most powerful influence: the appeal to the natural as a way of condemning the artificial is a largely unconscious and, thus, extremely powerful ideology licensing he or she who presumes to have no need to be granted permission for anything—the natural person acting naturally, doing simply what comes naturally.[12]

The authority of this ideal, because it has the authorization of those who are antiauthoritarian and also because its operation is subterranean, is difficult to contest. When only the nullifiers exercise authority, and when they do so in a way that disguises the exercise of their own authority, those who challenge the nullifiers are cast as dogmatists and authoritarians. In this opposition, those who would challenge the nullifiers are thus handed equally undesirable alternatives: Either one pits one's own allegedly arbitrary affirmations against some fashionable desecration, some persuasive nullification, or one appears authoritarian and dogmatic whereas the nullifier appears to be generous and inclusive. Hence, the sway of this ideal has been largely destructive, not least of all destructive of the sensibility required for mature, steady self-governance. Its influence might partly account for what Miller observed to be lacking: "I do feel that the democratic *person* has not yet been developed. By a person, in this context, I mean a capacity for independence of mind, an ability to treat fortune with some reserve. We can't very well [i.e., very honestly] pose superior to our society, as if there were values and ideals 'fixed in heaven,' as Plato said. We can't be aloof" (PL, 804).

Miller's emphasis on the constitutional necessity for revision, often radical revision, puts him a far distance from the traditional conservative. But his insistence that the most effective, humane forms of critique are always immanent ones, that the self-maintenance of one's inherited institutions, practices, and discourses is the price of mature agency, and that noise about a contemporary revolution that carries no echoes of an authoritative past can only be the inarticulate expression of unarticulated motives puts Miller a far distance from traditional liberals and, indeed, those who would like to cut a more radical figure than liberal reformers. Miller's emphasis on the present was never intended to celebrate the present of absolute rupture, of ecstatic mysticism (religious, political, erotic, or otherwise); it was always aimed at authorizing the historical moment, the present at once discontinuous with yet connected to its past, not a past in general, but a determinate past with identifiable features and concrete embodiments: "It is action that holds distinct the present and the past, even as it also brings them together" (*PH,* 75). Hence, the immediacy of the actual moment and the continuity of an actual career were for him inseparable aspects of a single actuality (*PC,* 159; *MS,* 119)—the fateful history of those having proper names and local habitats. "The career of thought is bigger than the present, and one can join it one way or another without forsaking the actual" (PL, 804). But refusal to join this career is, of course, the evasion of the actual, the aloofness Miller so relentlessly castigates. The participation in and, thus, identification with this career is for Miller the sole solution to the problem of how to institute "a democratic aristocracy." Whereas both Plato and Nietzsche can only take this expression to be oxymoronic, Miller and Jefferson, James and Emerson, Dewey and Mead, all believe that one of the most powerful arguments for democratic institutions is that such institutions corrode the authority of artificial "aristocracies" and go a distance toward establishing the authority of "natural" superiority (consider Thomas Jefferson's letter to John Adams defending natural aristocracy or William James's lecture at Radcliffe defending the indispensable virtues of an intellectual class).

"If no Myth, then no History. Myth is our Past. It is a deficient organization of the Actual. History is the maintenance of the Actual" (PL, 511). If there is no authorizing narrative, then there is no effective history or responsible agency: the evasion of history does not bring freedom. Only an embrace of actuality and the enterprises concretely expressing the espousal of actuality effectively engender autonomy.

In connection with the 1963 strike of workers at the *New York Times*, Miller observes: "There seems to me an authority in an enterprise which exceeds that of its parts. So far as I can tell, the printers are not interested in the *Times* as an enterprise, or in their work as part of the enterprise. Except for inertia, they would stop printing and do something else. Offer ease, and they would take it" (PL, 864–65).

The humanists of course should not be indifferent to the lot of other human beings. "There is no use denying misery and want. Men go unfed and poorly housed. Above all, they rot inwardly because they lack jobs, and thereby become untrained in habits of social outlook and of self-confidence" (PL, 107). Daily meaning is, accordingly, as vital as daily bread.

"I think that for our time and in our tradition, the only locus of concrete freedom is the state, and the articulated modes of freedom are in constitutional law" (PL, 427). "I have to settle for lining up with the side which seems to me to express the widest good will, both within the nation and between nations. It is this affirmative aspect of the New Deal which attracts me" (PL, 677). Government is entitled to step in "when private failure comes as the result of some systematic blockage in our institutions" (PL, 678). Abuse is inevitable: "One has to carry the burden of the parasites, etc." (ibid.). "Many people clamor for tolerance when they mean by it only the denial of personal responsibility for their views and character" (PL, 607).

There are persistent, vast forces driving us in the direction of vagrancy. There are, however, equally powerful, pervasive forces working against our individuality: "[W]ant degenerates into impulse except as it is made relevant to private will." There "is a structure to the concept of want, and . . . this structure entails relevance of a particular want to a particular and personal program. It is my want because it furthers my program and for no other reason. What is the self which can assert want if not this set of purposes?" (PL, 110; cf. Royce 1901, chap. 6, on self as purpose).

The crises of authority in the courts, schools, and other cultural sites took various forms and derived from not a single source. But that an asylum for dogmatists had degenerated into a circus of skeptics should surprise no one. Yet the United States was never simply such an asylum, nor were the student rebellions in the 1960s ever just a circus of vagrants celebrating their vagrancy.[13] Democratic persons must have their dignity, and their dignity is impossible apart from power and authority. Sovereignty, democratic as well as monarchical, needs sanction, even if only the self-sanctioned, because self-sanctifying, utterances of a people committed to self-governance as the only viable form of human existence (*PC*, 73). "This sovereignty turns on the responsibility of the sovereign, and on reverence for his pronouncements" (ibid.). In the absence of such responsibility and of the reverence on which this responsibility is alone based, one does not have democracy but anarchy: we are thus reminded of the Platonic and Nietzschean critiques of the democratic ethos even more than their misgivings about a democratic polity. Democracy and nobility are, according to Nietzsche no less than Plato, mutually exclusive. But does this judgment itself not reflect an unwitting ontologizing of a contingent yet, in some respects, fateful inheritance? Certainly, one "does not escape tyranny by multiplying irresponsible and subjective arbitrariness" (ibid.); and just as certainly one multiplies such arbitrariness when one conceives and enforces the conception of government as an instrument to satisfy private desires rather than the career through which one defines personal objectives and, thus, the private spheres in which the effective realization of personal aims alone is possible. In a democracy, then, every person may be a king, "but in our time a king must have constitutional authority" (ibid.). Individuals must carry responsibility in their own person: only persons in control of their own lives can be effectively in control of the institutions of self-government. It is a great and dangerous illusion "to suppose that government will protect rights when actual individuals display nothing but desires in their wills, and nothing but opinions in their minds. Such doctrines paralyze resolve. They are degenerate, and they invite the conqueror and the despot" (ibid.).

The responsibility that individual persons in a democratic society carry within their own person takes principally not the form of the abstract conscience of Kant's *Moralität* but that of the actual practices of Hegel's *Sittlichkeit* (Westphal 1993, 254–56; Taylor 1975, 365).The morally aloof critic is all too often the self-abstracted, and thereby self-exiled, individual seduced by the thoroughly problematic ideal of the "Beautiful Soul" (an ideal so insightfully diagnosed by Hegel in his *Phenomenology*). The morally implicated critic is the historically self-conscious participant in the ongoing career of institutional self-revision.

"The 'intellectual' is under suspicion, and understandably so, when his own words and deeds invoke no systematic overthrow" (*PC*, 145). From this perspective, Foucault does not deserve to be considered suspect; for he put his body on the line. He exposed himself to radical risk and systematic overthrow. But, in speaking in behalf of the abiding need to maintain civil order as an indispensable condition for effective, deep-cutting, long-lasting transformations, Miller also exposed himself to risks of his own. He, who so deeply appreciated the classical equation of being ostracized with being nullified (to be excluded from the community was a death sentence of sorts), suffered this fate in his last years. He appeared a stick-in-the-mud to the liberals and radicals within the place where he had for over fifty years made his home.

Mugwumps, Flâneurs, *Angels of History, Sticks-in-the Mud, and Saunterers*

In 1885, James identified himself as a Mugwump in the original sense of this word, an independent Republican willing to bring one's former opponents into power in the hope of killing off the old guard (the party with which he had identified up until this point) and "its dead shibboleths"—in fact, not so much dead as deadening or destructive (Perry 1935, 2:297; cf. Strout 1990a, 88). In a more generalized sense, a mugwump is anyone who is disposed to bolt the established order in the hope of bringing it down, even if that means bringing this order down in ruins about one's own ears. The radical revisions necessitated by historical actors committed to maintaining themselves and their world have made the mugwump, Jamesian and otherwise, a familiar figure on our cultural landscape. Another such figure, also connected especially to the depth and rapidity of the changes wrought in the last one hundred and fifty years or so, is the *flâneur*. A less familiar figure is the angel of history (Benjamin 1968; Vattimo 1984, 154, 163). A familiar but, at least apparently, discredited figure is the stick-in-the-mud.[14]

Both the *flâneur* and the angel of history are figures encountered in the writings of Walter Benjamin. Benjamin himself derives the figure of *flâneur* from the texts of Charles Baudelaire, that of the angel of history from a painting by Paul Klee.[15]

In his "Theses on the Philosophy of History," Benjamin asserts: "The true picture of the past *flits* by" (1968, 255; emphasis added). As Hannah Arendt observes, such a picture is (according to Benjamin) available only to persons who themselves flit through scenes in which they are caught up but, at the same time, from which they retain a detachment. That is, the true picture of the past is available only to the *flâneur* (Arendt 1968b, 12). This is the figure of one strolling aimlessly through the often crowded streets of some vibrant city; the character of one's *flânerie* is brought home to one by its marked contrast to the hurried, purposeful activity swirling about oneself as an idle, aimless stroller. The Paris in which Benjamin was an émigré is a city that, perhaps more than any other, invites "strolling, idling, *flânerie*" (ibid., 21).[16] What Theodor Adorno criticizes as Benjamin's "wide-eyed presentation of actualities" (quoted in ibid., 11) is simply the mode of attention characteristic of the *flâneur*, conjoined with the will to record, to jot down what flits by. But immediate immersion in the present moment is transformed by this desire to jot things down, to construct an arresting statement of what is utterly ephemeral.[17] The *flâneur* with notebook and pen in pocket is one whose aimless strollings seem to have, it turns out, an overarching purpose. Moreover, the wide-eyed attention to ephemeral actualities transmits a current from these actualities themselves to the abiding configurations inevitably assumed in one's recorded recollections.

Here, too, Adorno offers a helpful observation of what underlies Benjamin's *flânerie:* "To understand Benjamin properly one must feel behind his every sentence the conversion of extreme agitation into something static, indeed, the static notion of movement itself" (quoted in ibid., 12). This is best seen in relationship to what Benjamin himself calls "the angel of history," a figure itself derived from a reflection on Paul Klee's painting "Angelus Novus" (ibid., 1213; cf. Vattimo 1984, 154; Schürmann 1984, 166). In Benjamin's description of Klee's painting, we observe "an angel looking as though he is about to move away from something he is fixedly contemplating. His eyes are staring, his mouth is open, his wings are spread" (Benjamin 1968, 257). But the *flâneur*, strolling through a museum or along the banks of a river where reproductions of art might be seen, encounters in Klee's "Angelus Novus" an arresting image of an implicated observer, itself arrested in its movements. Benjamin suggests: "This is how one pictures the angel of history. His face is turned toward the past" (ibid.). But, the contrast with human consciousness is not so much in terms of retrospective as opposed to prospective awareness (ours being turned toward the future, whereas the angel's is turned toward the past) as it is in terms of successiveness and simultaneity (see, e.g., *PH,* 87–90). "Where we perceive a chain of events, he sees one single catastrophe which keeps piling wreckage upon wreckage and hurls it in front of his feet" (Benjamin 1968, 257). The new angel turns out to be an impotent consciousness, not itself a historical agent: "The angel would like to stay, awaken the dead, and make whole what has been smashed. But a storm is blowing from Paradise; it has got caught in its wings with such violence that the angel can no longer close them" (ibid., 257–58). The fixed image of one fixedly contemplating the ruins and debris of history is, to be sure, an image of movement, though not one of self-placement: "This storm irresistibly propels him into the future to which his back is turned, while the pile of debris before him grows skyward" (ibid., 258). Benjamin closes this stunning reading of a powerful image with a remark as laconic as it is sardonic: "This storm is what we call progress" (ibid.).

But humans are no angels, of history or of anything else. Even so, the figure in Klee's painting, as glossed in Benjamin's "Theses," does suggest something valuable about a human orientation toward human history. For this figure is one of compassion, "a compassion for all that could have been and yet never was, or is no more, for all that produced no real *Wirkungen*, or historical effects" (Vattimo 1984, 154). The debris piling up at the feet of the angel "are traces of something that has lived" (ibid.). According to

Vattimo's reading of Benjamin's "Theses," the accent must fall on piety as well as compassion. Focusing on the Heideggerian notion of *Verwindung* (an overcoming that is, at once, an overcoming of the Hegelian notion of *Aufgehoben* without being itself an *Aufgehoben* and an overcoming of metaphysics as metaphysics, as the true account of the really real), Vattimo suggests that the sort of overcoming meant by Heidegger frees "metaphysical categories from precisely what made them metaphysical: the presumption of gaining access to an *ontos on*" (ibid., 159). They cease to be routes to a realm beyond time and become paths through history itself: "these categories become 'valid' as monuments, as a heritage evoking the *pietas* due to the traces of what has lived" (ibid.). In evoking piety, such "monuments" disclose to human beings their "mortality, finitude, and passing-away." Thought denies that it is (to use one of Miller's metaphors) a pensioner of eternity and acknowledges that it is "under the aegis of mortality and passing away" (ibid.). This forces on thought the realization that "the transcendental, or that which makes experience possible, is nothing less than caducity" (emphasis omitted); that what constitutes the objectivity of objects is not so much their character of standing against (*Gegenstand*) one another and also against anyone who could identify himself as a self as it is "their be-falling," their coming to be and, in some measure, to be manifest, out of what itself has come to be.[18]

In freeing metaphysical categories from their historical fixation with ahistoric fixities, *Verwindung* allows us to read the history of metaphysics in precisely the manner Miller himself proposes, as the story of the history of criticism (PL, 801), of the fateful struggles to secure adequate grounds for our moral, political, scientific, and other forms of discourse—especially insofar as these are critical discourses, ones in which the telling differences are authoritatively told. But in Benjamin's reading of Klee's painting, and also in Vattimo's appropriation of Benjamin's imagery, one suspects that the authoritative lure of the contemplative ideal so pervasive in Western history persists in these quite recent attempts to come to explicitly historical terms with what Benjamin and Vattimo accept as an essentially historical actuality. But the deepest difference between these thinkers on one side and Miller on the other perhaps resides in Vattimo's characterization of metaphysical categories as monuments and traces of what was once living.

These categories are still eloquent utterances because they are even now living.

Piety is not a form of necrophilia but a sign of living agents becoming confident enough to acknowledge the actual conditions of their most vital undertakings. How much of our railing against the past is an inadvertent confession of our own pettiness in comparison with the still authoritative achievements of ancestral actors? The traces of what is in some sense past are of momentous significance because they exhibit in themselves a contemporary vitality, a current authority or force able to arrest attention and to inspire utterances of our own (e.g., Keats on the Grecian urn); that is, because they are not irrevocably past but vitally present. The energies still resident in these monuments await renewal. Better put, our own renewal awaits our capacity to feel the force and discern the authority inherent in these traces (see, e.g., *DP*, 102).

Our shared loyalty to a cause pits us not only against those animated by rival loyalties but also against one another. Any human community that has had an extended tenure has been an ongoing argument about how the members of the community are to understand the meaning of their conjunction; and many, perhaps most, communities that have been only short lived have been ones in which such disagreements proved to be fatal. Thus, the mugwump is often one committed to being loyal to the ideals of a community with which he or she had, until the moment of dissociation, identified, for he or she judges the actual community to be a desecration of its professed ideals. Loyalty to these ideals thus demands dissociation from this actuality. To take a familiar example, the religious mugwump born into a particular tradition comes to the judgment that the message of Christ is not to be found among the sects of Christianity. So he or she stands opposed to and apart from the historical embodiments of what comes to be seen as a purely transcendent ideal. The political mugwump comes to the judgment that the ideals of justice are desecrated by the legislatures, police, courts, and other civic institutions of the country into which he or she was born, so much so that allegiance is not truly owed to these institutions. When it is more convenient than not, the show of allegiance is better than the practical disavowal of one's actual citizenship; so taxes are paid but resented. Better to pay them than to incur the penalty for acting on one's conscience that the government is stealing what is rightfully one's own.

Many come to feel that it would require more effort than it is worth to try reforming those laws and other features of their inherited political institutions that are the source of their deep estrangement from these institutions.

William James's denunciation of our invasion of the Philippines in uncharacteristically vulgar terms, saying that we have puked up our heritage, needs to be juxtaposed to another utterance in which he confesses, having been abroad for the better part of two years, "I long to steep myself in America again and let the broken rootlets make new adhesions to the native soil" (Perry 1935, 2:316). His declaration that he is "against bigness and greatness in all their forms, and with the invisible molecular moral forces that work from individual to individual, stealing in through the crannies of the world like so many soft rootlets" (ibid., 315), too, needs to be conjoined with his appreciation for cultural traditions of his own actual place, ones allowing for these "invisible molecular moral forces" to accomplish their often manifest, monumental work. Miller was infuriated by General Douglas MacArthur's public oppositional pose to the elected representatives entrusted with political power: MacArthur "declares one owes no allegiance to a temporary majority in power, but only to the Constitution. A five-star standard is carried before him as he walks out. I had never expected to witness such a temper in American life" (PL, 783; cf. 776). What angered Miller was the way MacArthur undertook a military coup, though one only of a symbolic character: he used his prestige and popularity to undermine the legitimate authority of elected officials. In actuality, allegiance to the Constitution required him as a general and also simply as a citizen to give his allegiance to those currently, if only temporarily, in power. Whereas James voiced his opposition in a manner that underscored his loyalty to the order in which this was actually voiced, MacArthur (despite appearances, i.e., despite professing allegiance to the Constitution) went some distance toward undermining the effective authority of the Constitutional order in which he struck his pose. In sum, there are mugwumps, and then there are mugwumps.

While the figures of the mugwump, the *flâneur*, and the angel of history have something to teach about how self-consciously historical agents can most effectively insert themselves into their actual place, each one by itself expresses a dangerous ideal because it is a debilitating one. The aloofness symbolized by the mugwump and the *flâneur*, figures that pride themselves on being detached, suggests an evasion of the actual; the angel of history, fixedly contemplating the amassing ruins of human history while being blown backward into the future, suggests the lure of an ideal enabling us to reduce the diachronic to the synchronic, the successive to the simultaneous.

Despite the numerous respects in which Miller's texts immediately resonate with contemporary themes, topics, and even terms such as "discourse" and "critique," his emphasis on the inherent authority in our inherited discourses will make him appear in the eyes of some as a stick-in-the-mud. But what if the stick is no severed, lifeless limb but a rooted, living stem? What if the mud is the symbol of the Earth? And what if the water allowing for the Earth to serve as soil for this stem, to make of the Earth a place in which things might grow, is history? What if the dynamism of action and history are not denied by the insistence on physical and historical rootedness but instead are only brought into clear focus when considered in this way?

Henry David Thoreau, that eloquent defender of saunterers who in their pilgrimages in effect condemn those who would preoccupy themselves with politics or business, formal schooling and other historically instituted practices, opens his essay "Walking" by avowing his intention:[19]

> I wish to speak a word for Nature, for absolute freedom and wildness, as contrasted with a freedom and culture merely civil—to regard man as an inhabitant, or a part and parcel of Nature, rather than a member of society. I wish to make an extreme statement, if so I may make an emphatic one, for there are enough champions of civilization: the minister and the school committee and every one of you will take care of that. (Thoreau 1995, 1)

But, if the *sanctum sanctorum* is to be found in the natural world, it is because this world is the matrix from which the historical world emerged (*DT*, 155); it is because only by traveling so far into nature can we catch a glimpse of how far we have traveled to our actual present as a historical achievement, of how far we have traveled as members of a species sprung from swamp or sea. But the historical saunterer will be compelled to undertake a very different pilgrimage. Like Thoreau, she will feel: "Above all, we cannot afford not to live in the present" (Thoreau 1995, 50); but unlike this champion of sauntering, he or she will move in self-evolving circles wide enough to encompass historical monuments as well as natural wilds.

Much of Miller's appeal to historical actuality can be read as a rewriting of Thoreau's appeal to a sanctifying nature. If human freedom is absolute, it is so only by its own insistence on finitude. If civilization has countless advocates, they all too often undermine what they advocate. The very terms of their advocacy—especially today when the influence of Freud, Marx, Emerson, Thoreau, and countless others has rendered appeals to the historically established order so deeply suspect—makes of it either a direct assault on the inherited orders of human utterance or at least provides the weapons for such an assault. Civility has had and still has too few defenders, especially ones who understand how to mount a defense that would be neither a dogmatic arbitrariness nor an unwitting contribution to a shiftless anarchy (*PC*, 178). The most eloquent voices in our intellectual history have often betrayed a desire to be inarticulate (e.g., James [1909] 1977), even when they rejected mysticism as "quite unsuitable to Western individualism and *its structural institutions*" (JWM, 5:3; emphasis added). In their assault upon inherited institutions, they have betrayed a desire to escape from human history; for we are what we have come to be. History is the career of institutions. The current assault in principle on the established forms of human functioning (the totality of which are, in a word, the establishment and, in another, the midworld) has many forms, all of which entail an attempt to evade actuality. "Otherworldliness has been a notable consequence of this unwillingness to be identified in the actual" (JMW, 7:15). One irony is the way a genuine earthiness can cohabitate with an enervating otherworldliness, one more instance of our divided inheritance, of a constitutional incoherence.

Conclusion

For all of his disagreements and dissatisfactions with Thoreau over the importance of political and other institutions, there are two respects, intimately connected and equally fundamental for each author, in which Miller agrees with Thoreau. Clearly, Miller rejects what he takes to be, fairly or not, Thoreau's hostility toward society and generally unqualified denunciation of human institutions, especially political ones. "Thoreau made a mistake in not seeing that nature required the society which he viewed with so much hostility" (PL, 670). He also "had his head too much in the clouds" (PL, 669). Despite this, he undeniably had his feet on the ground and, indeed, his hands in the Earth itself (ibid.). Hence, it does not serve accuracy to stress too much such disagreements, for Miller was appreciative of the robust vitality of Thoreau's actual engagements with the natural world. He takes Thoreau to confront nature not as an object but as an intimate, however dangerous or unpredictable an intimate she might prove to be: "Thoreau likes woods, streams and swamps because they are the extensions of man's life, something more than an object" (PL, 668). "Nature becomes pleasing to one only as the partner of one's effort" (PL, 670), the allied antagonist of one distinctive mode of human striving. While nature "shows no alliance with one in its wild aspect," it does yield "its fruits under our guidance. It can cooperate. Then it ceases to be strange, although not less itself" (ibid.). Somewhat surprisingly perhaps, Miller describes his predecessor as "entirely secular and yet not at all thoughtless or voluptuous" (PL, 668), one whose secularity is revealed in not taking nature to be "a sign of God's power but rather a direct part of one's own living, with all the intimacy involved in action, enjoyment." Whereas Francis Bacon sees nature as an object to be known, Thoreau approaches her as a partner in his own life. "But if nature becomes object, then man becomes rather a poor thing, *an orphan in the only home he knows.* In Thoreau, man is as lawful and also as wild as nature" (ibid.; emphasis added).

Against this background of appreciation, a twofold agreement between Miller and Thoreau can be noted. The first concerns the most proper function of the human intellect, the second the proper form of dwelling here. The human intellect is not a disembodied eye but a symbolically extended hand. It is comparable, moreover, to instruments crafted by the hand as well as designed for the hand.

> The intellect is a cleaver; it discerns and rifts its way into the secrets of things.... My head is hands and feet. I feel all my best faculties concentrated in it. My instinct tells me that my head is an organ for burrowing, as some creatures use their snout and fore paws, and with it I

would mine and burrow my way through these hills. I think that the richest vein [anywhere] is somewhere hereabouts; and so by the diving-rod and thin rising vapors I judge; and *here* I will begin to mine. (Thoreau [1854] 1980, 71; emphasis added).

In allowing us to burrow ever more deeply into the Earth (our natural place in Miller's case, our historical place in Miller's), the intellect proves itself to be an organ of placement, crucial for counteracting the annihilating effects of human displacement. Of course, these displacements have also been its own doing; but (as Hegel notes) the "hand that inflicts the wound is also the hand which heals it" (Hegel 1975, 43). We glimpse the devastation due to our displacements when we realize that:

> We are acquainted with a mere pellicle of the globe on which we live. Most have not delved six feet beneath the surface, nor leaped as many above it. *We know not where we are.* Beside, we are sound asleep nearly half our time. Yet we esteem ourselves wise, and have an established order on the surface. (Thoreau [1854] 1980, 220; emphasis added)

Our established order is such a ramshackle affair because the human hand that has crafted it does not belong to one who has spoken humanly from any great height or from any great depth of human things or of its natural habitat.

> For the most part, we are not where we are, but in a false position. Through an infirmity of our natures, we suppose a case, and put ourselves into it, and hence are in two cases at the same time, and it is doubly difficult to get out. In sane moments we regard only the facts, the case that is. (Ibid., 217)

Or, as Miller would put it, we confront our acts as parts of a continuum that they help sustain; we embrace what actually is.

What dwelling here demands of us is to plant our feet and to use our hands, when the intellect itself is taken to be an organ of placement and embrace. It demands not forsaking or forgetting the Earth, especially when these processes take themselves to be a lofty achievement, a liberating transcendence from actual conditions. The most rudimentary act of fidelity is the concerted effort to recall, time and again, just where we are. Of course, the only forms of rootedness possible for such motile organisms as ourselves are ones in which the displacements underlying any actual placement are acknowledged as well as possible. Our dwelling here demands a deeper, steadier attachment to our earthly dwelling itself—a burrowing into the soil beneath our feet.

This brings us to the second point of fundamental agreement between Miller and Thoreau, the will to meet the demand of the moment, to insert oneself passionately into one's inherited or chosen place, to husband each now in its hereness (as Scotus would say, in its *hecceity*). Some of the most arresting passages in Thoreau's *Walden* are best read as solicitations to meet this demand. "That man who does not believe that each day contains an earlier, more sacred, and auroral hour than he has yet profaned, has despaired of life, and is pursuing a descending and darkening way" (ibid., 65). That person has confessed the end of a life not yet ended, the failure any longer to make absolute demands. "To affect the quality of the day, that is the highest of arts. Every man is tasked to make his life, even in its details, worthy of the contemplation of his most elevated and critical hour" (ibid.). But, in the text perhaps best revealing the affinity between him and Miller, Thoreau observes:

> Men esteem truth remote, in the outskirts of the system, behind the farthest star, before Adam and after the last man. In eternity there is indeed something true and sublime. But all these times and places and occasions are here and now. God himself culminates in the present moment, and will never be more divine in the lapse of all the ages. (Ibid., 70)

To live in the actual moment is as difficult as it is necessary (see, e.g., *PH*, 89–90). A way out—the way of the ecstatic moment that systematically eludes historical judgment (*PH*, 85)—is continuously being proposed in the name of one or another ahistoric ideal. Despite Miller's characterization of Thoreau as "entirely secular," his judgment regarding Thoreau having his head too much in the clouds might be read as the tendency of Thoreau himself to propose the ecstatic moment (see, e.g., Thoreau [1854]

1980, 16). As with William James and Virginia Woolf, also with Emerson and Nietzsche, one can discern in Thoreau's writings and life not only an attempt to accredit absolutely the actual moment in its unstable actuality but also an inherited set of categoreal words (appearance and reality; time and eternity) that undercut this attempt. The same not merely might but must be true of Miller himself, for words can only mean what they have come to mean and can only be refashioned and revised in the gradual and ongoing undoing of this history. In Thoreau's writings, in any event, utterances proposing the ecstatic moment certainly do not cancel out those accrediting the historical moment in its absolute historicity.

But Thoreau castigates those who were preoccupied with the news (ibid., 69) and also those devoted to the exchange of letters. In contrast, Miller reflects on the metaphysical status of news in order to underscore its importance for our daily lives and democratic ethos. Also, he also wrote countless letters, often of great length (some even exceeding a hundred pages), and even repeatedly used the illustration of going to the post office as a paradigm of maintaining himself and his world. Walking to the post office meant for him at least two things: an immediate occasion for a courteous exchange with those physically present and an energetic renewal or inauguration of an intellectual exchange with those physically distant. Thoreau is a far distance from the contemptuous rantings that Nietzsche puts into the mouth of Zarathustra, but the power of his appeal might be linked to a sensibility, if not shaped by these rantings, at least unoffended by them; for example:

> Behold the superfluous! They are always sick; they vomit their gall and call it a newspaper. They devour each other and cannot even digest themselves.
>
> Behold the superfluous! They gather riches and become poorer with them. They want power and first the lever of power, much money—the impotent paupers!
>
> Watch them clamber, these swift monkeys. They clamber over one another and thus drag one another into the mud and the depth. . . . Foul smells their idol, the cold monster: foul they smell to me altogether, these idolaters.
>
> My brothers, do you want to suffocate in the fumes of their snouts

and appetites? Rather break the windows and leap to freedom. Escape from the bad smell! (Nietzsche 1966b, 50–51)

But Miller would find such disgust disgusting, such contempt itself contemptible. He would, to recall a text quoted in an earlier chapter, endorse Emerson's injunction to refrain from postponing and deferring and wishing, in order to "do broad justice where we are, by whomever we deal with, accepting our actual companions and circumstances, however humble or odious, as the mystic officials to whom the universe has delegated its whole pleasure for us" (Emerson 1951, 304). If these companions and circumstances "be mean and malignant," even perhaps if their smell is a stench to our nostrils, "their contentment, which is the last victory of justice, is a more satisfying echo to the heart" than the happiness wrought from more congenial companions and less onerous circumstances. In this context Emerson advises us to treat "men and women well: treat them as if they were real: perhaps they are" (ibid.). Miller offers the same advice, explicitly connecting this counsel with his opposition to nihilism. In response to the self-addressed question, "How do you oppose Nihilism?" Miller responds: "Not by reason," but by recourse to civility. He opposes nihilism "by treating a person as there" as though he or she were actually present in word or deed (JWM, 17:15). "Where no one speaks or has spoken with authority neither can anyone listen with critical authority. . . . It is not a question of particular errors . . . [but] the nullification of authority in the very medium in which alone error could occur or be called to account" (JWM, 25:25). Such nullification of course renders the human voice a purely illusory phenomenon, though it can only do so through some form of utterance (be it merely a contemptuous smile). It makes all phenomena into epiphenomena or, worse, into the pieces out of which an impenetrable curtain, falling between self and world, is woven.

Somewhat late in his life Miller confessed, "I had heard Voices and spoke in the continuum of utterance. But is it not a madman who hears Voices?" (JWM, 31:2). To convince others of his sanity, he insisted on "yard-sticks and hammers," but he demanded a price. "*Aria da capo*" (ibid.). Along these same lines, he notes: "[M]y folly was that I heard Voices, not so much that I spoke. I was audience before I became speaker, indeed in order to become speaker. That was my grave error. Those voices are all illusions in a Voiceless World," evidence of madness to those responsible for maintaining the silent universe (JWM 25:20). Whereas the voices Virginia Woolf heard ultimately drove her to her death, the ones John William Miller heard drove him to reaffirm his absolute commitment to everyday existence. That is, they drove him to renew his commitment, again and again, to the quotidian tasks of what, in the very discharge of these tasks, could be a radiant life.

Like Nietzsche and Woolf, who writes about what she calls the cotton wool of most stretches of everyday life, in contrast to "moments of being," and indeed like Emerson and Thoreau, Miller discerns in our characteristic modes of being or dwelling here both a lethargy extremely difficult to overcome and the uncanny attunement of our somnambulant movements to the sphere of these movements. This attunement allows us to glide through the actual without arrestingly encountering it. But unlike these others, for whom the name of eternity alone, however surreptitiously invoked (whether in the guise of a moment of being, or in the form of an eternal recurrence, or in that of the present instant itself, though only in its ability to serve as "the meeting of two eternities" (Thoreau [1854] 1980) redeems the temporality of our lives, Miller does not suppose that eternity is needed to redeem our existence. There is no need to posit a point or perspective outside of history in order to rescue the fateful transitions from one historical moment to the next from the blindness or nullity that is supposed to be the fate of agents who have no locus but history. The mistrust of time and the disqualification of history need themselves to be understood historically, so that the moment might be vibrantly lived and our transitions intelligently negotiated. The simple but difficult task confronting all of those willing to accept the challenge of Miller's historicism is the refusal as philosophers and as persons ever to lose the name of action. As philosophers, let us then grant human action categoreal status, the authority to explain not only itself but also the disclosures of the sciences, arts, and humanities, including of course philosophy. As persons, let us be willing to pay the price for self-maintenance—to confront the fatality inherent in what we have said and done, to assume the task of self-revision.

It is extremely unlikely that the pervasive nihilism of late modernity so manifest in so many diverse contexts can be traced to a single root. A vast system of tangled roots is more likely the grounding and sustaining agency here. But, in this tangle of roots, an abstracted cognitivism can be identified as itself a thick, old subsystem of tangled roots. But such cognitivism is a truly fantastic form of vegetation, for it is the progressive rootedness of what seems to be a relentless uprooting. Indeed, the drive of abstracted cognitivism is to abstract from the actuality of time-and-place, from the finite actualities of our historical placements (these placements as being the fateful consequence of prior displacements), and from the authoritative disclosures of what have historically been purported to be revelatory discourses. These discourses have today been denounced and even celebrated as so many fictions. But the celebration of a fiction does not alter the ontological status or discredited authority of what being is celebrated. And sanity may still require the ability to tell the difference between fact and fiction, between the purely imaginary and the securely actual.

Miller realizes that such cognitivism could not provide a counter to nihilism's getting ever firmer root, for it is itself one of the roots from which this spiritual crisis has grown and will continue to grow. "One can draw the portrait of our time in terms of the demoralization consequent on a cognitive premise. This is a great historical movement and is a fatality in the true sense of inherent confusion, of a collapse of function, of local control, consequently of the sacred and the revelatory" (JWM, 17:15). So he insists that, in our opposition to nihilism, our quotidian doings, our everyday lives alone are likely to be effective. To become reconciled to the actuality of our circumstances is to transcend, but only in principle, the fateful shape of unhappy consciousness. All of the details, however, remain to be worked out; nor is the transcendence of this shape of consciousness any guarantee that it has been put behind us, once and for all. It may recur and even do so in a more acute and subtle form than ever before. But, in striving to become what we are, an endeavor inevitably transforming us into what we, at any moment, actually are not, it is possible to undertake authentically the task of reconciliation with the actual conditions of human flourishing. Our life need not take the form of a despair regarding the conditions in which quite finite, but nonetheless redeeming, struggles, satisfactions, and successes are alone possible. It might affirm the necessity of history along with that of the actuality and, therein alone, find the resources for the transformations of the inherited forms of finite actuality.

Upon hearing this affirmation, the intellectually sophisticated are likely to smile contemptuously. In their expression of contempt, yet another instance of nullification issues. This is in keeping with a time when the only authority is the nullifier. But is there any story that might exhibit to persons the effective authority of their own nullifying utterances, be they only the facial expressions by which their own and others' capacity for affirmation, for owning up to their own affirmations, is discredited? When every established form of reverence is subjected to ridicule, only ridicule will be revered. Only the nullifier will wield authority, and he or she only when engaged in ridicule. But whence the power of ridicule to undermine authority? Whence the compelling authority of this antiauthoritative disposition? I do not say antiauthoritarian but rather antiauthoritative. The authoritarian is simply the dogmatist possessed of power. The authoritative presence of any human agent can never take dogmatic form for very long without engendering the skepticism that is its due.

The story by which we can own up to the authority of our utterances and other deeds is one to be taken up anew, virtually with each generation. In self-conscious modification of Plato—"What is it that is always becoming and never the same?"—Miller proposes, "it is discourse" (*DP,* 160). "The English language is always becoming. The Constitution is always being reinterpreted. History is always being rewritten. Any historic individual needs a new biography, and what he said . . . gets restated in every new epoch" (ibid; see also *MS,* 118–26). Because science and law are inherently conservative, they are constitutionally self-revisory (*MS,* 122). History is being continually rewritten because the bases and forms of authority, including those governing historiography, are being constitutionally revised.[20] This may seem to leave us with no choice but that between an arbitrary fiat or a self-nullifying doubt, that is, between the dogmatic assertion of our own approach or an arresting doubt regarding our ability to offer a reliable account of anything whatsoever. But, if we can only be sufficiently vigorous in our skepticism, a third way reveals itself, though one always attended by the possibility of lapsing into skepticism or, indeed, into dogmatism. Let me describe this *via media* in its relationship to skepticism: either the capacity for negation negates itself, but somehow sustains itself by priding itself on the honesty with which it follows the course of its own negations (and this view of itself can be more than a self-congratulatory self-deception), or the capacity for negation, through a historical narration of the fateful episodes defining its present actuality, develops as an integral part of its own self-critical capacity, the capacity to own up to the affirmations sponsoring and sustaining its negations (see, e.g., *MS*, 177).

If the capacity for negation does incorporate within itself the capacity for narration, for self-critical self-narration, then critique can avoid being simply demoralizing and disconcerting. The fortunes of telling are thus bound up with our acts of telling, both as our own and as being themselves acts. Confronting these fortunes *as* fatalities, as the inevitable consequences of our defining commitments, is to accept the necessity of history and also the necessities *in* history. We can and do learn from experience but only by learning that we meant something other than we meant to mean, or thought we meant. The pressure of experience compels us to go back to our utterance, to stand by it at least long enough to follow it through to its own inherent defeat. Such defeat also compels us to understand our own utterance in a way different than our original comprehension. So, we can help what we say, but only if we own up to and stick by what we have said and, behind this, what our predecessors said who were responsible for launching the discourses in which we now move and have our being. We can save our utterances from nonsense and confusion, but only if we own up to and work through the thickly sedimented histories inherent in our most commonplace words. Poetry allows us to discern these layers of sedimentation.

Invaluable resources for accomplishing all of these tasks can be found in John William Miller's constitutional revision of philosophical discourse. If the self-imposed task of owning up to the fateful conflicts yet reverberating in our most self-assured utterances and our most authentic self-disclosures has taught us anything, it has taught us: that the trail of the serpent is over everything (that purity is unattainable and complicity unavoidable); that our most secure possessions are only precariously held and our most assured truths only fallibly established; that dogmatism inevitably sows the seeds of skepticism and that authoritarianism always sows those of anarchy; that skepticism in turns generates a trilemma: (a) regression to dogmatism or (b) prolongation of the arrest of function—the continuing, disconcerting paralysis of articulate immediacy or (c) movement beyond dogmatism and skepticism in the form of a continuously renewed task—the self-drawn portrait of self-authorizing agency, the self-narrated genealogy of self-authenticating discourse; that self-possession demands systematic antagonism and identifiable differences require common ground; that all refusals to establish and maintain limits, ordinarily ones made in the name of freedom, lead to impotence and that self-limiting affirmations alone have a chance of being efficacious self-identities; that the only way out is through a reliving of the conflicts by which human consciousness has actually taken shape and human agency has actually established itself; and finally, that history "is the story of deeds and it is also the telling itself [in its status as] a deed," being thus "the autobiography of humankind where story and storyteller are inseparable and neither is to be found without the other" (JWM, 28:23). For those who have truly identified with these fatalities of consciousness, who have forged their identities by revisiting the sites where one endeavor after another to speak with an authoritative voice has failed (failed because in each of these attempts humans have evaded the finite actualities of their own historical inheritances by espousing the inhuman, be it the suprahuman voice of a divinity outside of history or the subhuman voice of mechanism immune to the passage of time and deaf to the utterances of humanity), it seems indeed likely that Miller's writings will be an invaluable resource. For his own approach to these fateful conflicts cuts as deep as, if not deeper than, any other post-Hegelian philosopher who ever acknowledged the force or importance of these conflicts. We ignore his writings, thus, at the danger of impoverishing ourselves. I conclude this study, as seems only appropriate given its subject (a philosopher who worked indefatigably to secure undogmatic grounds for our defining affirmations), with an affirmation of my own.[21] Speaking as one who is familiar with Miller's writings, speaking personally yet assuredly, I am confident that others will find what I have found there: epigrams comparable to those of Emerson and Nietzsche, of Santayana and Wittgenstein. Others are likely also to find in these texts a compelling case for narrative and a persuasive story about argument.

Notes

Preface

1. "For all of Miller's thirty-five years at Williams [College in Williamstown, Mass.,] he was," in the words of Joseph Fell (a student at Williams), "one of the greatest of American teachers. Yet . . . his profound influence on generations of students went largely unrecorded until 1980 when George P. Brockway published his vivid and accurate account of Miller's teaching in *The American Scholar*" (Fell 1990a, 21–22). See Brockway 1981. Fell's essay (1990a) also offers a vivid and informative portrait of his teacher and friend.

2. Of his teacher, Robert E. Gahringer recalls: Miller "consented to the publication of his essays only as he approached death, and then only as a favor to a beloved former student [George P. Brockway] who, as a publisher [at W. W. Norton], has neither written nor taught philosophy. He was even more reticent about giving public lectures. . . . He was also reluctant to travel" (Fell 1990b, 32). Gahringer is quick to point that this conduct was not a sign of timidity or insecurity. He insists, "Miller's unwillingness to participate by writing and speaking in the affairs of his profession is, as with his unwillingness to travel, best explained by his reverence for the sanctity of thought" (32–33). Brockway (1981) offers these recollections: "For forty years I tried off and on to get him to let me publish a book of his writings. Several times I thought I had persuaded him, only to have him back away. Once he even signed a contract for his dissertation, but it was clear enough that his intention—and that, too, of the founder of my firm, the late Warder Norton—was merely to boost my morale as I entered the army. At the time of his retirement I put together, with the help of a friend, a collection that contained most of the essays he ultimately published; yet still he hesitated" (163).

3. See my review of all five volumes in Colapietro 1987.

4. Miller tended to identify pragmatism with William James and John Dewey, not C. S. Peirce, G. H. Mead, or C. I. Lewis. Moreover, he interpreted Jamesian and Deweyan pragmatism as forms of reductionism. This interpretation was at the root of his opposition to pragmatism. The force of his criticism of course depends on the validity of his interpretation of pragmatism. My own sense is that Miller was closer to pragmatism, especially Dewey, than he was disposed to acknowledge.

5. For a fuller statement of this criticism, see Colapietro 1994.

6. In addition to these studies (including the individual essays contained in Fell 1990b, there are some excellent articles on J. W. Miller. Among the best are Bradford 1997; Corrington 1986; and McGandy 1995. Readers might also find it worthwhile to consult Colapietro 1989.

Chapter 1

1. Miller tended to identify this chaos with nihilism. "Of course our nihilism is itself," in his judgment, "a historical emergence. It was not original. It should be seen as history, not truth. . . . To be in history is to see the present as a historical fate, not as above or outside the momentum of the actual" (*PH*, 192). Miller's philosophy and thus my introduction to it are at bottom extended, detailed meditations on the meaning of this claim regarding our locus in history.

2. In "The Eighteenth Brumaire of Louis Bonaparte" Marx asserted, "Men make their own history, but they do not make it just as they please; they do not make it under circumstances chosen by themselves, but under circumstances directly found, given and transmitted from the past. The tradition of all the dead generations weighs like a nightmare on the brain of the living. And just when they seem engaged in revolutionizing themselves and things, in creating something entirely new, precisely in such epochs of revolutionary crisis they anxiously conjure up the spirits of the past to their service and borrow from them their names, battle slogans and costumes in order to present the new scene of world history in this time-honoured disguise and this borrowed language" (Marx 1978, 595; cf. 170, also 193).

3. We take in our world and, in the process, incorporate it into our being (cf. Freud 1989, 587). We embody our selves in persons and objects other than our selves, just as we embody others within our selves. The subject of this study—John William Miller—is important, in part, because he grasped the centrality of this dialectic of embodiment.

4. In anticipation of an important emphasis, let me point out that, for Miller, "our words come from many minds and outlooks. Our heritage is a mess and full of confusion. We inherit a confusion of symbols and a confusion of tongues" (*PH*,

187). Marx (1978, 594) recalls: Hegel remarks somewhere that all great, historical facts and personages occur twice, but forgets to add—the first time as tragedy, the second as farce.

5. Miller did not write extensively about literature in general or the novel in particular. But his own thinking appears to have been influenced by his familiarity with American and British novelists, none more important than Joseph Conrad. (The fact that Conrad inhabited the English language as one exiled from his mother tongue perhaps makes his novels even more deeply representative of the exilic consciousness characteristic of the modern period [cf. Rieff 1993].) In fact, Miller was fond of quoting a line from Conrad's *Lord Jim* ("In the destructive element immerse"). In a pivotal conversation, Stein says to Jim: "Very funny this terrible thing is. A man that is born falls into a dream like a man who falls into the sea. If he tries to climb out into the air as inexperienced people endeavor to do, he drowns—*nicht whar?* . . . No! I tell you! The way is to the destructive element submit yourself, and with the exertions of your hands and feet in the water make deep, deep sea keep you up" (Conrad [1900] 1961, 205). Submitting oneself to the destructive element is, in truth, no act of submission or relinquishment of life; indeed, it alone holds open the possibility of living one's life. This much is explicit in the exchange between Jim and Stein, for before Stein offers his advice Jim (as the narrator recalling his own words) stresses, "'Yes, . . . strictly speaking, the question is not how to get cured, but how to live'" (ibid., 204). It is, Miller contends, "no easy matter to attach oneself to the processes of time. Among philosophers—and they are the ones who study the constitution of experience—finitude has never been a 'category,' i.e., a factor in the verb 'to be.' In Conrad's *Lord Jim*, the wise old counselor Stein advises that the broken Jim lose himself in some actuality: 'In the destructive element immerse. Jim was to relinquish his romantic dreams and his enfeebling drift by joining some demanding society, giving loyalty, and receiving it. Only so, said Stein, could he pull himself together [i.e., could he *compose* himself] and act effectively in the dubious battles of a concrete imperfection. How fully Jim took this advice is a nice question [or crucial consideration]. 'He was one of us,' said Marlowe in a moving epitaph; but his ladylove said that he was false" (*PC*, 136).

6. The mode of narration characteristic of most novels concerns not only self and world—character and circumstances in their totality and immediacy—but also very often place (a topic to be explored in later chapters).

7. In Chapter 5 I contrast Miller and Henry David Thoreau. It is, thus, appropriate at the outset to underscore an affinity between these authors. Thoreau asserts in "On the Duty of Civil Disobedience" ([1854] 1980, 227): "It is not a man's duty, as a matter of course, to devote himself to the eradication of any, even the most enormous wrong [e.g., slavery or exploitation]; he may still properly have

other concerns to engage him; but it is his duty, at least, to wash his hands of it, and, if he gives it no thought longer, not to give it practically his support. If I devote myself to other pursuits and contemplations, I must first see, at least, that I do not pursue them sitting upon another man's shoulders. I must get off him first, that he may pursue his contemplations too." In making a life for myself, I am in effect maintaining a world in which such a life is possible (cf. Marx 1978, 170, 193). But does the exercise of my freedom in fashioning this life and maintaining this world undermine the capacity of others to live lives of their own? Am I living on the backs of others? Taking responsibility for our lives means paying the price for our freedom; in turn, paying this price means becoming cognizant of the extent to which we are complicit in the exploitation of others. Such cognizance is historical, since it concerns the conditions, consequences, and significance of the interwoven exertions of situated agents.

8. I am making the final revisions of this book in the aftermath of September 11, 2001. Though the effects of this event color this revision, re-reading my own words in the light of this tragedy enables me to discern more sharply than before emphases clearly at the center of Miller's thought.

9. For Miller, one of the marks of civilization is the preservation of ruins, at least certain kinds of ruins (e.g., that of an ancient temple or theater). Barbarians see the Parthenon "as an object and would use its marble to make lime. Other barbarians use words for similarly desirable purposes" (*DP*, 101). Much is made of this in later discussions, but it seems advisable to anticipate them at the outset.

10. George Brockway highlights an aspect of such compulsion when he suggests, "self-assertion requires self-maintenance. I must maintain my identity through the time of my existence. I must; I am required to do so; I am compelled to do so. This is a special and curious compulsion. It does not come from the outside, like a slave driver's whip. Nor does it come from the inside, like a neurosis. The compulsion is the same as my existence. The alternative is nonexistence, nonentity, nothingness" (1985, 37; cf. Taylor 1992).

11. In *History as a System,* José Ortega y Gasset contends, "I am free *by compulsion,* whether I wish to be free or not. Freedom is not an activity pursued by an entity that, apart from and previous to such pursuit, is already possessed of a fixed being. To be free means to be lacking in constitutive identity, not to have subscribed to a determined being, to be able to be other than what one was, to be unable to install oneself once and for all in any given being. The only attribute of the fixed, stable being in the free being is this constitutive instability" (1962, 203; cf. Conrad [1900] 1960, 204–5). But free beings have always already subscribed to a determinate mode of human existence from which they almost always struggle to twist free. Our constitutive instability is of a piece with our constituted identity,

our alterability of a piece with our inheritances. For example, our metaphors and other linguistic innovations are indicative of the capacity of our language to transform itself, of historically determinate forms to be historically transformative forces.

12. The singular significance of any human life is, ordinarily, not a solitary achievement or private consummation. Our lives are, at once, irreducibly unique (or singular) and inescapably social. Part of Miller's importance resides in his ability to do justice to both facets of our existence. My life must have significance for me, but it cannot be significant unless others register its force and worth. I must be someone not only for me but also for others. The imperative to live a life of one's own, having significance for oneself, is one hallmark of modernity; another hallmark is the inconsistent and even hesitant acknowledgment of the extent to which one's significance depends on the recognition of others. Even those who espouse traditional forms of religious identity, that is, those who live their lives for Jesus or Allah or some other traditionally identified deity, feel this imperative. Religious fundamentalism is, at once, a reaction against the imperative to craft a life for oneself and an enactment of this imperative.

13. In this respect, as in so many other ones, René Descartes is truly an iconic figure of the modern epoch. In particular, part 1 of his *Discourse on Method* (1968) can be read as a disavowal of history. His assault on tradition is, in effect, a disavowal of history in the sense foregrounded here.

14. As I point out in Chapter 2, while human history is, according to J. W. Miller, punctuated with radical revisions, it is never marked by absolute ruptures. One of his best statements of this (to which we return in later chapters) is found in *The Paradox of Cause:* "Facing the past we all have our shortcomings, and they are more grievous than ignorance. They suggest incompleteness in us, in the degree to which has objectified one's own axioms and habits. The past is historical because it is always relatively discontinuous with the present. Spengler, making it absolutely discontinuous, at least in theory, offers in the end an ahistoric account of past time. Yet, when one first meets the Greek mind or the medieval mind one may be deeply puzzled, wondering what common humanity unites our day with theirs. History, which vanishes if the discontinuous were made absolute, confronts us [nonetheless] with problems of continuity. On the other side, if the past presented no puzzle [e.g., if the Greek or medieval mind did not seem in some measure alien from our own contemporary mind] all transactions in time would appear transparent to a single perspective, and to any perspective" (*PC,* 91). Hence, seamless continuity precludes historical consciousness just as much as absolute rupture.

Although Michel Foucault's name is often invoked as an authority that has through his genealogical critiques exhibited the present time as an absolute rupture with past times, he actually stands for a quite different approach. In an interview, he once identified as "one of the most harmful habits in contemporary thought" to be the supposition that the present could ever be "a present of rupture, or high point, or of incompletion or of a returning dawn" (Foucault 1970, 188, 35). Radical transformations of existent practices are quite different from an absolute breach with one's historical past. Foucault's position is, thus, akin to Miller's; similarities and differences between these two historically oriented thinkers are explored in Chapter 5.

15. The expression "postmodern" is borrowed from William Ernest Hocking. The term "modernity" is open to a variety of interpretations. Lawrence E. Cahoone provisionally defines "modernity" as "the ideas, principles, and patterns of interpretation, of diverse kinds ranging from the philosophic to the economic, on which western and central European society and culture, from the sixteen through the twentieth centuries, increasingly found itself based" (1988, 1). This "provisional definition" can serve as our initial orientation to this complex topic.

16. Miller himself proposed a radical reform of traditional epistemology: "We need a new epistemology, one that does not shrink from giving ontological status to artifacts. The past rides on them, and they are symbols and voices" (AW, 261–62; cf. PH, 122). See also Rorty 1979; West 1986; Dewey [1917] 1980.

17. Cf. Feyerabend 1987. Almost fifty years ago, José Ortega y Gasset in *The Modern Theme* (1961, 58) wrote: "Our attitude implies, then, a new irony, of a type inverse to that of Socrates. While he mistrusted spontaneity and regarded it through the spectacles of rational standards, the man of the present day mistrusts reason and criticizes it through the spectacles of spontaneity. He does not deny reason, but rejects and ridicules its pretensions to absolute sovereignty. Old-fashioned people may perhaps consider this disrespectful. In any case it is inevitable."

18. Isaiah Berlin (1957, 1969), a thinker whose concerns and ideals overlap with those of Miller, insisted on the ineliminable incommensurability inherent in the ultimate ideals of any human culture.

19. Readers of Miller interested in the parallel between him and Croce should consult Roberts 1987.

20. In 1939, Ortega announced in a lecture in Buenos Aires: "The hour of the historical sciences is at hand. Pure reason . . . must be replaced by narrative reason. *Today* man is as he is because *yesterday* he was something else. Therefore, to understand what he is today we have only to relate what he was yesterday. . . . This narrative reason is 'historical reason'" (Ortega 1984, 118).

Collingwood, Croce, Ortega, and Miller were all anticipated by Giambattista Vico, who was in a sense the road not taken by modernity. In the early modern period, this still-ignored philosopher subjected the Cartesian to a severe critique that is, in broad outline at least, being restated today (Vico 1961).

21. In an unpublished manuscript, Miller notes, "So I am driven out of the world as described in physics. I must look somewhere else. But where? I must look to history, there and only there. For history is the sole place where actors can put in an appearance, can the 'I' as a unique and authoritative presence have a locus not obliterative of its actual status."

22. It is crucial to distinguish between egoism in Miller's sense and narcissism as I use the term here. In "The Owl of Minerva," Miller characterizes egoism as "the sense of local control" (OM, 402). "The baffling problems of egoism are a consequence of an imposed order, whatever the manner of that imposition, by whatever force. But egoism is no problem when the local is the same as the enactment of order in function, in the functioning object, whether yardstick, grammar, logic, or dialectic. In each case the actuality requires the medium [and the medium enforces a discipline and sustains a destiny]. *There* is the cure for any vagrant egoism, and it is the only cure" (402–3; emphasis added). Hence, narcissism progressively undermines our sense of others in their insistent and irreducible otherness, while egoism in Miller's sense sharpens just this sense.

Miller's espousal of egoism (though this term is, no doubt, dangerously misleading) occurred early in his life. An undergraduate paper entitled "The Response Situation" (JWM, 3:9) opens with the assertion: "To do the simplest act, or to express an opinion regarding what one considers to be a fairly obvious relation, requires a degree of egotism nothing short of amazing" (p. 1).

23. Following William Ernest Hocking, Miller links both politics and ethics to morale. Both are concerned with the demoralizing effects of contemporary commitments. See PH 19–20.

24. As a later discussion makes clear, the term "pilgrimage" is used here in a somewhat strict sense; for it designates a journey, as it were, to the various loci where human agents have tried to define and defend a realm of the sacred. If we are to be in the position to take possession of the present, then (Miller argues) we have no choice but to make such a "pilgrimage" (*PH*, 84). See also Weber 1958; Weil 1971.

25. In the following two chapters but throughout this study as well, I discuss in detail Miller's view that objects possess their status only in some form of discourse (*MS,* 64). It is, however, necessary here to anticipate that discussion. Unquestionably, the objects of common sense (e.g., tables and chairs, rocks and flowers) possess a secure status in human experience; but they do so only because of our thoroughgoing mastery of the various forms of human functioning (e.g., perception, manipulation in the etymological sense, and other modes of engagement) by which such objects are discriminated. See JWM, 25:1.

26. The status and character of action as utterance is a focal topic of the follow-

ing chapters. Suffice it to say here that action is, as we ordinarily take it to be, expressive of the agent's character and even of forces escaping the consciousness or intention of the agent.

27. Two key terms in Miller's lexicon are "disconcertment" and "composure." Disconcertment often carries the connotation of dissolution, the fate of a historical framework in the throes of a constitutional conflict. Composure often appears to be connected with composition: agents regain their composure when they are able to reclaim their capacity to compose themselves and their worlds.

28. Although Miller himself often uses "genetic" (from the Greek word *genesis*, meaning origin) to designate the sort of account he is intent on offering, it seems evident that "genealogical" fits as well. To speak of Miller's genealogical narratives invites comparison with Michel Foucault's genealogical critiques of contemporary institutions, practices, and discourses. Such a comparison can be found in Chapter 5.

29. The word "fatality" is no doubt problematic. In Miller's lexicon, it does not mean predestination or predetermination; instead it designates the sense that we cannot escape history. He tries to capture by "fatality" and other potentially misleading expressions the inescapable dimension of our historical existence.

30. His judgments regarding the events of this time could be intemperate and uncharitable, but they were rarely, if ever, the visceral reactions of a dismayed conservative. They were characteristically the judgments of a perceptive conservationist who had a sharp sense of the exacting price of free institutions (cf. Ortega 1957, 25–26). In later discussions, I read some of Miller's most basic philosophical affirmations in the light of his specific reactions to student protests and other related events. While his insistence upon civility might strike many today as quixotic, it is noteworthy that Stephen Carter and others today are calling for a recovery of this ideal.

31. "The 'real' World is Silent. It does not speak. Tales of the 'real' World are all illusion. They are 'Myths,' i.e., stories. Abandon discourse all ye that enter here" (JWM, 25:22). "This is the silent world, where no voice is heard and no word is spoken. It is the denial of the incarnate word" (*MS*, 126). "Nothing [in this world] is to be revered. There is no eloquent presence. Our orthodox world is the silent world. The midworld [from the perspective of this orthodoxy] is myth" (*MS*, 191). The difficulty is how to conceive presence and totality in such a way as to grant a status to eloquent or articulate presence without, thereby, undermining the basis for condemning a vagrant or irresponsible presence.

In a letter to Alburey Castell, Miller writes: "In the caves of the Pyrenees there are drawings of a herd of deer. A friend of mine, a lawyer, who saw them gave me a quiet but stirring account of his visit. What was it that he saw? Deer? A pretty picture? That would not have prompted his words or his manner. Nor was he commenting on the degree of intelligence of Neanderthal Man. It was rather that in those caves something was revealed. Here was a voice, an utterance, an announcement, not of any matter of fact but of the presence of men and objects. Such was the feeling my friend was trying to convey. Although a lawyer he is also a musician and a performer of uncommon delicacy, unostentatious but commanding, a man who could hear voices and give voice to the novelties in which person and world are made manifest. Those drawings were such a voice.

"Out of the silence a voice, and [out] of the darkness a light. In the story of Chaos from which the world emerged it was the generation of particulars—earth, sky, vegetation—which brought content and form. I think my friend felt he was a spectator of Creation. On what other basis could one find anything awesome in those drawings? The maker, the poet [as the Greeks, who had a name for things, called the maker], saw himself in telling what he saw. He is not represented there but presented.

"But this is the Mid-World. It does not represent, it presents. The person 'appears' in the same utterance that declares that objects have appeared. The drawings say nothing about the general cosmos; they say that the hunter is a hunter of deer, an observer of their ways, a discriminator of objects allied to their functioning. Those drawings are the original schoolbook. Children could learn from them. Attention is directed, and only so is discovered. They are the first identifiable stimulus, the particular that is continuous with other particular events, directing what is seen, where one goes, what one does. The drawing is a power, not another item of a passive consciousness which has no center, no control and is a chaos without focus, without arrest" (*DP,* 103–4; see also *JWM,* 21:1)

It is difficult to imagine a more eloquent plea for recognizing the Spoken World and rejecting the Silent World.

32. "To show that all philosophical ideas emerge from the pressures of commitment could require long exhibition in many types of philosophical study. For I do think it is at last a matter of exhibition, rather than of abstract argument" (*PC,* 86).

33. The characterization of human history as a slaughter bench is borrowed from Hegel, a thinker to whom (as later chapters reveal) Miller was deeply indebted.

34. Miller was not alone in observing that it took time, quite a bit of time, to discover history (see, e.g., *PH,* 181; *PC,* 92). Hannah Arendt, for example, notes: "The great impact of the notion of history upon the consciousness of the modern age came relatively late" (1968a, 68). One could find countless variations on this theme in the writings of Dilthey, Croce, Collingwood, Ortega, and others.

35. On one hand, Miller contends that, within our religious and intellectual

traditions, there has been a deep-seated tendency to treat time as "a cosmic stepchild of dubious parentage, and always a problem child" (*PC*, 77). On the other hand, this tendency has characteristically stopped short of disqualifying time entirely. "However attractive, and it always attracts distressed minds, this disqualification of the articulate and the temporal has never dominated Western thought. We have always found some value and truth in concern with circumstance" (*PC*, 185).

36. To repeat, Miller wanted to grant a categoreal status to human history, to make it irreducible and (in some respects) self-explanatory. If history is elevated to the status of a "category," then "the region of its concern, artifacts, or the midworld, must be accorded a place among the constitutional elements of being" (*PC*, 107). He knew, however, that in the light of our intellectual history this is no simple task: "This need of providing for artifacts [for according them a place among the constitutional elements] is the specter that haunts philosophers and their discourse. And it seems plain that one could not exorcise that perturbed spirit by further incantations" (ibid.). So Miller proposed to acknowledge the presence of this "spirit," that is, to grant a status to artifacts hitherto denied them. See n.5 above.

37. Cf. Gray 1989, 9. Also, the endeavor to make the secular, quotidian places and activities sacred links Miller with R. W. Emerson.

38. It is perhaps helpful to recall here that, for Miller, skepticism refers first and foremost to an arrest of functioning (see, e.g., *PC*, 150). As such, it is not so much an epistemological conundrum as an existential crisis. An example of such a crisis would be the person who desires to pray but is arrested in the act of praying by an intellectual conscience as powerful as his spiritual desire. The person is at war with himself; and the conflict experienced by such a self is the self at this moment of its existence. "The historical act shows the difficulty as the very man. He is the same as the difficulty. The historical act declares a world in a constitutional aspect. It is a revelation, a disclosure, a declaration" (*DP*, 149). But the very capacity of the historical act to declare a world in one of its constitutional aspects is what makes such an act able to exhibit the world in its constitutional confusion or disarray. He is the man who desires to pray but cannot; he is one arrested in an act he takes to be essential to his presence in the world no less than to the totality inclusive of his presence.

39. In "Is Nothing Sacred?" Salman Rushdie answers his titular question as follows: "We shall just have to get along without the shield of sacralization, and a good thing, too. We must not become what we oppose" (Rushdie 1992, 427).

40. This is Miller's own expression, borrowed from Ortega, by which he designated the discrediting of time and history. The name is taken "from the city in

southern Italy [Elea] where there appeared a number of men who argued, with originality and brilliance, that change, and thus time, was an illusion and not reality" (AW, 246; cf. *PC*, 130–37; also *PH*, 244–60). The supposition that intelligibility and invariance are inseparable (one way of expressing the Eleatic temper) is one with a long history and abiding allure.

Chapter 2

1. For an extended, detailed account of Miller's conceptualization of the midworld, one can do no better than McGandy 2000, chap. 2, except perhaps McGandy 1998.

2. Stephen Tyman (1993) offers an extremely illuminating interpretation of Miller as a thinker deeply rooted in the tradition of post-Kantian idealism. So, for him, Schelling and Fichte are important figures here. I offer my exposition not in opposition to Tyman's but as a complement to his study.

3. In *What Man Can Make of Man*, William Ernest Hocking (1942) asserts: "Every old mold becomes in time a mask, a misfit, a grotesque, a handicap, demanding a breach with itself; and man, to live in history, requires both capacities, fervent self-loyalty, and the capacity for self-rejection, even for revolution" (6). Hocking goes on to connect this point with Hegel in a way close to Miller's own innovative appropriation of the Hegelian approach: "This continued revision of the goals of human self-building is the deep-running 'dialectical' process of history, man's incessant argument with his own self-judgment [including the bases, strategies, and even styles of self-judgment!]. It is far more significant than the economic dialectic of Marx. It is far more intimate and verifiable than the nebulous procession of ideas which Hegel called the dialectic of history. For everyone finds in himself the discontent which moves it on" (6–7). This discontent resides at the heart of modernity. Thus, it provides a link between this chapter and the previous one: the discontent at the heart of modernity is self-discontent ("Everyone knows today, not by rumor but by introspection, that modern man is tired of himself" [Hocking 1942, 7]). This discontent, more than anything else, drives the movement beyond modernity.

4. The link between personal identity and historical inheritance is at the center of Miller's historical idealism. This link is explored in later chapters but deserves to be stressed here.

5. Of course, Kant in his own way was also concerned with the threat of physics, i.e., of a purely deterministic view in which the possibility of autonomous agency is extinguished. But he tried to resolve this by drawing an absolutely sharp distinction between phenomena and noumena.

6. This contemporary commonplace is of course due, in large measure, to the influence of Thomas Kuhn's *The Structure of Scientific Revolutions* (1970).

7. Here is one of the many places where the influence of Josiah Royce might be discerned.

8. Miller was, however, quite critical of Marx's attempt to marry materialism and dialectics. He tended to think that materialism and naturalism are reductivist approaches in which human agency and utterance are inevitably effaced.

9. It should be pointed out, however, even Miller's youthful position was far from orthodox (however closer it was to traditional idealism than his mature outlook). This becomes clear when we take seriously his characterization of this position as "concretism, a naturalistic idealism" (*DT*, 149).

10. The phrase "entangling alliances" is from an important speech by Thomas Jefferson. It is also used in the title of a book by Robert Elias (1973), one of Miller's students.

11. This characterization borders on caricature, since an important chapter in the complex history of philosophical realism is the emergence of the self-described "critical realists." This chapter points to nothing less than a radical revision of the realist position, so much so that (in Miller's judgment, at least) this revision marks an abandonment of the position. Insofar as Miller retains a robust notion of objectivity, and moreover insofar as the critical realists espouse a thoroughgoing appreciation of criticism, the distance between Miller's historical idealism and this form of realism is not as great as my discussion of realism might seem to imply.

12. The word "artifact" bears testimony to two crucial features of the artifactual in Miller's sense: (1) it is a *factum*, something made; and (2) it is the product of *ars*, of human craft and ingenuity. The act in question is an utterance. This means that the act is at once constituted and constitutive—it is made intelligible and it makes intelligible aspects otherwise indiscernible or inexplicable. Hence, the word "artifact" is (as Joseph Fell has suggested to me in conversation and correspondence) a dialectical unity of act and fact. There are no facts apart from acts; in turn, there are no acts apart from artifacts.

13. In this sense, the sciences are to be counted among the humanities.

14. These two expressions refer to two radical revisions of empiricism, Royce's attempt to show the necessity to relate finite, human experience with an enveloping, divine experience, and William James's insistence that continuities and conjunctions are among the data of experience. When Miller uses these expressions to refer to his own doctrines, he, of course, intends something quite different from James's "radical empiricism" and even Royce's "absolute empiricism."

Chapter 3

1. Like Miller, Adorno (1977, 124) supposes, "only out of the historical entanglement of questions and answers does the question of philosophy's actuality emerge precisely. . . . Every philosophy which today does not depend on the security of current intellectual and social conditions, but instead upon truth, sees itself facing the problem of a liquidation of philosophy."

2. "The broad demands of a philosophy of history require the authentication of discourse and a construction placed upon *functioning objects*. But discourse is language and it is a deed. Accordingly it is limitation" (*PC,* 118). Whereas the previous chapter focuses on the need for philosophy to turn toward history and to transform itself in turning to the finite actualities of our fateful undertakings, this one focuses on "the authentication of discourse."

3. "The anthropologist does not come upon man until he discovers the artifact, the revelation of local control. . . . Man is artisan; he makes artifacts. . . . The artifact is an awesome revelation. At hazard—it is an incorporate psyche" (*PC,* 125; cf. Colapietro 1990, 80).

4. "But, while functioning objects illuminate no hypostatized infinity, neither do they assist in giving order to that version of finitude which leaves it nominalistic. These two—an infinity which is a *fait accompli,* and a finitude without universality—are *alike* in their repudiation of actuality that is also ideal. Neither is articulate because neither accords organizing power to, or has any ontological place for, yardsticks [or other functioning objects]. Each, in its own way, can do nothing with discourse but leaves it arbitrary, and therefore non-rational. It is the functioning object that unites the particular and the universal. They are united in function, or in use, in the embodiment of form. The embodiment of form is function" (*PC,* 116–17).

5. Space is a measurable region of "simultaneous diversity," time a region of successive differentiation. Physical (or clock) time is measured in one way; historical (or dated) time is charted in another. For an illuminating discussion of the basis of the distinction between spatiality and temporality, see *PH,* 87–90.

6. "The original symbol is the body and its organs. Unless one stands off from one's body and alleges a disembodied mode of experience, one cannot quite objectify the body. It is the original instrument and actuality of experience. The body is not a physical body or object, but the condition of all knowledge of bodies. It is not known as body directly, but only as a part of a region to which it belongs and with which it is continuous" (*MS,* 155).

7. The midworld is the historical world; the historical world is the human world; and the human world is the artifactual world. All of this is, at least, implied in one

of Miller's best succinct characterizations of the midworld (worthy of quoting once again): "History deals in what has been done in one way or another. Its materials are the residue of deeds. They are *artifacts of every description*. The region of artifacts may be called the 'midworld' since it is exclusively neither the self nor the not-self, neither consciousness nor its object" (*PC*, 106; emphasis added). It encompasses not only language and all other means of symbolization but also artifacts in all of their heterogeneity.

8. When I am perceptually aware of an object, such perception encompasses a direct confrontation or engagement, no matter how complexly mediated is this perception. When I am inferentially aware of an object not "directly" perceived (e.g., when I infer from footprints on the beach the existence of another inhabitant on what I had presumed to be an uninhabited island), the actuality of the object is not directly experienced or perceived.

9. It is very likely that Miller has Royce's notion of mysticism (one of the four conceptions of being treated in Royce 1901) in mind when he is offering his own critique of cognitive immediacy. Whereas the realist institutes a dualism between knower and known, the mystic so stresses immediacy as to undermine the possibility of drawing the complex, fluid, and functional distinctions implied in our functional immediacies.

10. Miller, like Royce and Hocking, stresses the derivative character of the private world. To grant primacy to privacy would, for all three of these thinkers, would inevitably result in imprisoning the self in the confines of solipsism.

11. The word *Mitwelt* is borrowed from Heidegger 1996. Joseph Fell has informed me that, when Miller read Heidegger, he sensed an affinity with his contemporary.

12. The manner in which Dewey ([1934] 1986) and Santayana (1905–6) thematize piety is very close to Miller's own understanding of this notion. Whereas Dewey foregrounds natural piety, and Santayana both natural and historical piety, Miller tends to focus on history as the source of our being.

13. For an extremely illuminating classification of the signs and symbols on which we rely, see McGandy 1998, 243–55.

14. This returns us to where we began: for Miller no less than for Adorno, the actuality of philosophy demands a renewed actualization of critical reflection in radically altered circumstances.

Chapter 4

1. At the risk of stressing the obvious, it is important to underscore that all human outlooks are for Miller ontological in their final import. In one place, he

notes how hard it is to overlook the base degrees by which human beings have intellectually and practically reduced themselves to nonentities. Ironically, one of the ways we do this is by objectifying, that, entifying, ourselves. He notes that "we suffer from intellectual embarrassment in proposing as knowledge any story which employs an organizing vocabulary other than that suitable for the region of objects" (*PC*, 98). On one occasion Miller confesses to finding the struggle against the roots of this suffering "tedious"; the narratives functioning as counterarguments to the hegemony of objectification, nonetheless, had propriety as directly "a consequence of the objectification of utterance, of man, of nature, and [even] of the supernatural" (*MS*, 74). For such objectification was for him intolerable. But even those who were committed to objectification were in effect beyond it; for "[s]o long as any position is taken, even a denial[,] . . . one still maintains some outlook, however desperate and impoverished" (*MS*, 87). He is thus confident that "[w]e need not take too seriously the current objections to metaphysics. Anyone who looks farther than his nose may find himself wondering what lies over the horizon" (AW, 237). And anyone who exerts himself in any way whatsoever is implicated in a world. In insisting on ourselves we are insisting on our world, a world in which our presence will be felt and our status will be acknowledged. In sustaining a world in whatever form we declare necessary, we are in turn shaping our selves. Self and world are inseparable; and their inseparability concerns humanism, the topic of this chapter. "The fundamental problem addressed by contemporary humanist thought is that of the inseparability of the human subject from the world" (Soper 1986, 54). The self-world relationship as fatally subjected to a series of reconfigurations is the focus of Miller's concern (Fell 1997, 10). Given his stress on action and actuality, and thus on human agency and historical placement (including those fatal displacements punctuating human history), the correlative terms of this dialectical relationship are adequately expressed only when the self is conceived as agent and the world as an arena of action. These terms might be identified as the form(s) of the world implicated in an agent's utterances and deeds, on one side, and the form(s) of agency continuously solicited and frequently required by the actual placements of any human self (in short, by the world in its actuality). Our world and we are a mess because neither the forms of our own agency nor the inherited shapes of the actual world completely cohere. We no less than our world are in both subtle and obvious ways coming apart at the seams!

By approach in contrast to outlook, I simply mean the manner in which agents attempt to establish, accredit, maintain, and revise, whatever outlook is implicated in the forms of agency to which they are committed to maintaining. This implies reflexivity, for agents are compelled in some manner and measure to take into account not only their actual world (the world implicated in their deeds and utterances) but also the way they themselves are endeavoring to accomplish this.

2. Since philosophical antihumanism is intergenerational, stretching back to at least Nietzsche, it is a tradition. This is so even though those who are today part of this tradition tend to be highly suspicious of the rhetoric of tradition.

3. In *Humanism and Anti-Humanism*, Kate Soper (1986, 9) observes: "To most people in this country, the term 'humanism' is more or less synonymous with 'atheism.'" It is instructive to see why John Dewey, who espoused humanism but was reluctant to define it in terms of atheism (in particular the militant atheism of the first half of the twentieth century), would reject this identification (though not necessarily Soper's observation that this is the way most people today understand the term "humanism"): Such "atheism seems to me to have something in common with traditional supernaturalism. I do not mean merely that the former is mainly so negative that it fails to give positive direction to thought, though that fact is pertinent. What I have in mind especially is the exclusive preoccupation of both militant atheism and supernaturalism with man in isolation [from nature].... Militant atheism is ... affected by lack of natural piety. The ties binding man to nature that poets have always celebrated are passed over lightly. The attitude taken is often that of man living in an indifferent and hostile world and issuing blasts of defiance" (LW 9: 52–53).

In contrast to Dewey's (and also Santayana's) stress on natural piety, Miller emphasizes historical piety. In one of his most forceful assertion Miller announces that: "If we want reverence, anything sacred and so imperative, we must advance now to history.... There is the common world, the actual one" (*DP,* 151). It would be difficult to offer a better definition of piety in general than the one found in Santayana 1905–6 (5:125): "Piety ... may be said to mean man's reverent attachment to the sources of his being and the steadying of his life by that attachment." But both Santayana and Dewey are far from blind to the species of piety, so intimately linked to his embrace of the actual and recovery of the historical, with which Miller was primarily concerned. For example, Dewey writes: "There is sound sense in the old pagan notion that gratitude is the root of all virtue. Loyalty to whatever in the established environment [i.e., in the actual world] makes a life of excellence possible is the beginning of all progress" (Dewey [1922] 1983, 19). (This text makes it clear that, in certain places, Dewey comes close to endorsing piety in Miller's sense.) But the dynamic, practical union of such loyalty and gratitude is the essence of piety in its classical sense, a point made explicitly by Santayana. He was cognizant that "[I]f we wish to live associated with permanent racial interests [i.e., if we wish to be human and to join the human species in its most abiding achievements] we must plant ourselves on a broad historic and human foundation, we must absorb and interpret the past which has made us so, so that we may hand down its heritage reinforced, if possible, and in no way undermined or denaturalized. This consciousness that the human spirit is derived and responsible, that all its functions are heritage's and trusts, involves a sentiment of gratitude and duty which we may call piety" (Santayana 1905–6, 5:125). Even so, Dewey and Santayana most characteristically spoke of natural piety. But, in general, what they meant by this term is very close to, if not identical with, what Miller also meant. Cf. Steven G. Smith's "Piety's Problems" (1995).

From the perspective of traditional Western theism, Miller along with Dewey and Santayana were atheists. For he was committed to the position that "[o]ur times face the broad problems of morale without the traditional comforts of a supernatural support, or for that matter, the support of a rational order of nature.... *We are on our own"* (*PC*, 92–93; emphasis added). But we who are on our own are also in league with the historical careers of chronologically remote civilizations (see, e.g., *PH*, 134–35) and with the incredibly complex processes of our natural habitat. We as inhabitants of the Earth are the heirs of history, natural and human. So the positive importance of humanism is eclipsed by focusing too exclusively upon the claim that we are on our own (when this is taken to mean we are fated to live without God).

4. Oswald Spengler would be an important exception to this statement. Also, Miller certainly was not ignorant of Martin Heidegger. Around the middle of the past century (after noting that he was appalled to realize that in 1922, the year he received his Ph.D. from Harvard University, no one had even heard of Vico or the revolution associated with his name), he granted: "But things have moved. Some Heidegger is being translated. He is very hard to read in German, but I think he sees the role of the act and of the artifact. He unites historicism with existentialism" (quoted in Strout 1990b, 156; see Fell 1997, 24–25, n.39).

5. There is, arguably, an unresolved tension if James's thought regarding this matter. On one hand, his philosophy drives in the direction being highlighted in my appropriation of it; on the other, there is a tendency to see the human world as part of an "unseen order." But, in either case, the world is marked by finitude and temporality. So is James's God.

6. Miller argues: "No one can become a philosopher who has failed to experience the force of skepticism. Dogmatism is only the illegitimate escape from skepticism [not an advance beyond it but a reversion to a less sophisticated and defensible position], a very common procedure. Until thought finds its own features in its antagonist, dogmatism and skepticism remain the two unavoidable basic philosophies, although their forms be protean" (*PC*, 71–72). One might discern these two basic positions disguised underneath any number of extant humanisms: while

some versions of humanism are at bottom variations on skepticism, others are essentially reversions to dogmatism. Joseph P. Fell concludes "Miller: The Man and His Philosophy" (1990a) by confessing: "I know of no saner *via media* between skeptical relativism and metaphysical certitude," that is, between radical skepticism and regressive dogmatism, than Miller's philosophical outlook. While I concur with Fell's judgment, I want to show how his distinctive manner of going through the Scylla of skepticism and the Charybdis of dogmatism is the zigzag course of a dialectic. His going *through* these destructive points is a working *through* positions not immediately reducible to either a form of skepticism or one of dogmatism.

7. I was delighted to discover this judgment at least partly corroborated by one of Miller's own students. Robert E. Gahringer notes that, just because Hegel saw so clearly that our philosophical concepts are constitutional conceptions and, moreover, that philosophical controversies in their most authentic form concern constitutional conflicts, it "is no accident that Miller treated the preface to *The Phenomenology of Mind* with special reverence" (Gahringer 1990, 35). Another one of Miller's students, Walter Kaufmann, not only translated this preface but also wrote a commentary on it (see Kaufmann 1966).

8. As noted in Chapter 1, Collingwood in his *Autobiography* claims: "The chief business of twentieth-century philosophy is to reckon with twentieth-century history" (quoted in Strout 1990b, 153). Part of this reckoning must of course be a facing up to the mass destruction and systematic degradation of human beings so evident throughout the entirety of the twentieth century and so marked in the opening years of the twenty-first.

9. According to Casey 1993, we have traded place for space and, in turn, space for time; this itself is in Miller's sense a fateful series of metaphysical displacements.

10. One of the most insightful contemporary treatments of this topic with which I am familiar is Smith 1995.

11. In Miller's lexicon, *eternity* is to be sharply distinguished from *infinity*. Whereas the historical is defined in opposition to the eternal, it is conceived by Miller to be inclusive of the infinite. To be outside of time is one thing, to be inherently interminable and self-defining is quite another.

12. "In the caves of the Pyrenees there are drawings of a herd of deer. A friend of mine . . . who saw them, gave me a quiet but stirring account of his visit. What was it that he saw? Deer? A pretty picture? . . . It was, rather, that in those caves something was revealed. Here was a voice, an utterance, an announcement . . . of the *presence* of men and objects. Those drawings were a voice" (*DP,* 103). But also something was in this revelation itself concealed: this utterance was shrouded in silence and suggestive of what could never be uttered. In stressing what is concealed in disclosure and what remains silent in such utterances I am perhaps going

beyond, or going against, Miller. His own stress on our finitude, however, would suggest to me that he would find this counterbalancing stress of mine congenial.

13. Of course, self-authorization might take place at either the personal or the communal level. But no separation is implied by this distinction.

14. It, however, may be the case, as Joseph Fell notes in a comment on an earlier draft of this study, that Miller's position is closer to the sensibility expressed in Dylan Thomas's "In My Craft or Sullen Art" than that conveyed by Alice Walker (1983) in "In Search My Mother's Garden."

15. It is worthwhile to recall Strout's observation that Miller's "teaching was more like Emerson's essays than it was like traditional philosophical argument. He was brilliantly aphoristic and epigrammatic, thinking out loud in a meditative and spontaneous way, sometimes obscure and oracularly. Unlike Emerson, however, Miller had a strong feeling for institutions in general and for American ones in particular, as well as for liberal and democratic politics, freed of their contemporary materialistic, rationalistic, or sentimentally populistic tendencies" (Strout 1990b, 155). Robert E. Gahringer who also was a student of Miller's at Williams College offers this comment on his teacher: "As his model for arguing was F. H. Bradley, his model for writing was Emerson—both quite out of fashion" (Gahringer 1990, 33).

16. "The actual, that is, the midworld, carries one down to the present *as functioning*. It makes any composition historical. It is the immediacy that projects infinity" (*DP*, 98; emphasis added). "The present active participle [e.g., measuring, counting, speaking, dating] has been overlooked by philosophers" (*MS*, 65). So, too, have the functioning objects by which such doings are launched, sustained, and modified. But it is just in the immediacy of such doings that the present attains its intensity as well as immensity. Present active participles, in other words, help to identify the way in which we are carried down to the present.

17. "It is not that we must stand for this or that, but rather that we must stand for something, make some answer whether to agree or to differ, and we must make it freely" (*PC*, 29). This distinction is akin to one drawn by Emerson: "the question ever is, not, what you have done or forborne, but, at whose command you have done and forborne it" (Emerson 1951, 313). The absolute is nothing other than that for which we ultimately stand, that at whose command we are willing to suffer "the slings and arrows of outrageous fortune." We affirm this fate as part of our affirmation of our stance, of the name of the one at whose command we forbear this "fortune": if this be the price of affirmation, *so be it*. Perhaps I would desire it to be otherwise, but I cannot act otherwise (Luther at the Diet of Worms: "Here I stand; I cannot do otherwise"). We must also make such an affirmation resolutely, unqualifiedly. Miller, in effect, stresses, if one wants truly to be a person

one must assume the responsibility and, thus, the burden of affirmation. He suspects however most of us never quite mean all we affirm and, frequently, tend even to resist acknowledging our own affirmations.

The intellectual orthodoxies and fashions of his day (see, e.g., Strout 1990b, 158), much like those of our own, did little to encourage such affirmation. In fact, they prided themselves on undermining the confidence of those who might be foolish enough to make a pretense to authority, above all the authority to tell the truth when there is no going back on the realization that truth is in the telling. "The nullifier becomes the authority" (*DP,* 89), the only recognized and thus the only effective authority. So Miller confesses: "For my part, I cannot bear easily seeing young men leave college enervated in their morale or treating the areas of order as if they were incidental to the meaning of their own prospects of power and discipline" (*PC,* 187). To announce that, for example, golf holds no interest for you is of small consequence; to assert an indifference to art, however, is an indictment of your character (*PH,* 14), this being but one example of what Miller means here by an "order." All of the organized modes of human learning and the historical experience on which these modes of learning are based can be disavowed only at the expense of one's self. It is not a question of impoverishing but rather of annihilating the self.

18. Cushing Strout suggests that Miller's "philosophy united historicism with existentialism in an original voluntaristic way that was highly appropriate to his teaching of American students at a time (when I encountered him) of much weight in our history" (Strout 1990b, 157). In this paragraph I have tried to capture this unique conjunction of historicism, existentialism, and voluntarism. The voluntaristic dimension of Miller's philosophical outlook is perhaps nowhere more evident than in his uncompromising stress on "the desperate assertion of a limited and unfinished will" (*PC,* 36). But the desperate assertions of the human will allow for composure and satisfaction, not only for exertion and defeat.

19. In one sense Miller was addressing the question "What is the *story* about argument?" This story does not so much concern logically assessing the forms of arguments put forth by philosophers as it concerns dramatically exhibiting the grounds on which historical agents erect arguments in the decisive moments of their constitutional revisions. Miller goes so far as to identify philosophy with "the *actuality* of those conflicts which establish the grounds upon which arguments occur and by which they are regulated. That lies beyond argument and proof (*PC,* 74; emphasis added). In another sense, Miller was addressing the question, "What is the case for argument?" It does not lie beyond exhibition, beyond telling at least when telling takes the form of a story. The philosophical storyteller is, however, implicated in the history he or she would narrate: he or she stands nowhere but at

an actual crossroads. The case for narrative may be construed as a transcendental argument for narrative discourse (see Taylor 1995, 21–22); it tries to establish the conditions for the possibility of self-knowledge, even in those instances when the self is a scientist (i.e., when the self is one either constitutionally hostile or systematically blind to the ineliminable authority of narrative discourse, one who would privilege mechanical accounts to such an extent that they would eclipse historical narration). Thus, Miller insists: "The story *contains* argument but is not contentious in itself. It can't prove anything; it can only *show* something" (*PH*, 10). But this showing (or exhibiting) can perform the function of persuading. The case for narrative, then, is the case that narratives themselves make in persuading us to look and see (to use Wittgenstein's [1958, 1:66] expression), to quit the logic-choppers and join the history-makers.

20. In *Philosophy in the Tragic Age of the Greeks*, Nietzsche (1962, 54) writes: "The everlasting and exclusive coming-to-be, the impermanence of everything actual, which constantly acts and comes-to-be but *never is*, as Heraclitus teaches it, is a terrible, paralyzing thought. Its impact on men can most nearly be likened to the sensation during an earthquake when one loses one's familiar confidence in firmly grounded earth. It takes astonishing strength to transform this reaction into its opposite, into sublimity."

21. "Those who live in the eternal can do nothing for its own sake—neither play nor work, neither manual nor intellectual labor. There is something trivializing [indeed, something annihilative] in this inability to love or hate thoroughly. Then no poem is for its own sake, but must celebrate something else, something remote. Within time there can be no abandonment and nothing innocent" (*PH*, 182–83). In short, "history, the reality of time, can have a serious authority where time itself is unreal" (*PH*, 183). But when historical actuality is stripped of absolute authority, our historical existence is deprived of absolute worth. Thus, all transcendental outlooks are implicated in transporting the uncanny guest to the threshold of late modernity. The passage beyond modernity, then, demands the transcendence, the overcoming, of the traditional forms of our transcendent aspirations. The persistence of these aspirations cannot spell anything but the prolonged evasion of finite actuality; and this evasion cannot but continue to sow the seeds of nihilism.

22. In *The Varieties of Religious Experience*, James ([1902] 1985, 281–82) argues: "In heroism, we feel, life's supreme mystery is hidden. We tolerate no one who has no capacity whatsoever for it in any direction. On the other hand, no matter what a man's frailties otherwise might be, if he be willing to risk death, and still more if he suffer it heroically, in the service he has chosen, the fact consecrates him forever." He goes on to elaborate this point in a way that makes clear the ontological, not only ethical, import of heroically owning up to our mortality:

"The metaphysical mystery, thus recognized by common sense, that he who feeds on death that feeds on men possesses life supereminently and excellently, and meets the best secret demands of the universe, is the truth of which asceticism has been the faithful champion" (ibid., 282). But for asceticism to be something other than masochism it must be undertaken in the service of a cause other than restraint: it must be a denial rooted in an affirmation.

23. "Since . . . in the density of social reality each decision brings unexpected consequences, and since, moreover, man responds to these surprises by inventions which transform the problem, there is no situation without hope; but there is no choice which terminates these deviations of which can exhaust man's inventive power and put an end to his history. There are only advances. The capitalist rationalization is one of them, since it is the resolve to take our given condition in hand through knowledge and action. It can be demonstrated that the appropriation of the world by man, the demystification, is better because it faces the difficulties that other regimes have avoided. But this progress is bought by repressions, and there is no guarantee that the progressive elements of history will be separated out from experience and be added back in later. Demystification is also depoetization and disenchantment. We must keep the capitalistic refusal of the sacred as external but renew within it the demands of the absolute that it has abolished" (Merleau-Ponty 1973, 23). We might say here that the task before us is, in the face of inescapable, fateful disenchantment and desacralization, how are we to renew within such a world the demands of the absolute seemingly destroyed by our own "knowledge and action"?

Chapter 5

1. The totality of these, as they stand in relationships of conflict as well as support, is the midworld.

2. Whereas Plato construes the hatred of logos as a hatred of argument, of the responsibility to give reasons in support of one's assertions, Miller construes it in a more radical way: misology is the hatred of discourse as such, in all of its forms but especially in its status as utterances, as immediate acts carrying authoritative force.

3. Miller knows well that "it is risky and perhaps obscure to be affirmative. On the other hand the affirmative shows the basis of any remarks one might make about events, cause, presupposition, purpose. So, I keep reverting to my controlling affirmations. No basic affirmation is cognitive" (*MS*, 112). To exhibit, by means of storytelling, the basis of utterance—an actual rather than cognitive basis—was, of course, the overarching aim of Miller's philosophical project.

4. Miller offers his own native language as an example of this important point:

"No one person invented English speech. The language is no private state of mind. And it is also the chief actuality of controlled revision. Within linguistic coherence words have changed their meanings. What one means personally by 'good and evil,' 'true and false,' derives from prior utterance. A language is a career in utterance" (*PH*, 133).

5. While Miller tends to refer to this work as *The Phenomenology of Mind*, my own inclination is to translate *Geist* as "Spirit." When I am referring to Hegel's text, my inclination is to identify it as *The Phenomenology of Spirit*. An apparent inconsistency in my manner of referring to this text is just that—only apparent.

6. Albert Camus voices in this essay a suspicion regarding history, but this must be read in reference to those dogmatic Marxists who presumed to have a master code to human history.

7. Sartre, even the early Sartre, is better than he is portrayed here. My only excuse for offering a characterization bordering on a caricature is that my concern is less with this philosophical author than with his cultural appropriation in the United States. In "Motives for Existentialism," Miller observes that subjectivity "reappears in the measure that it is systematically excluded. It appears as scepticism, loneliness, and despair. [He might have added, also as rebellion, negation, and mortality.] It asserts the reality of finitude. This is the core of Existentialism" (*ME*, 4). Insofar as existentialism asserts the actuality of finitude, espouses the finite actualities of human existence, Miller senses a kinship with this movement; insofar as Kierkegaard, Sartre, and other representatives of this movement retreat within interiority and, from the innermost recesses of a solitary consciousness, launch a romantic rebellion against the modern world, he took it to be symptomatic of an evasion of actuality. As is so often the case, Kierkegaard, Sartre, and other existentialists are better than their critics suspect; but, ironically, the flaws magnified by these critics, especially when offsetting insights are left unacknowledged, can be the very reasons why these thinkers are attractive. Sartre's existentialism is severed from his Marxism, his early analysis of consciousness read apart from his mature consideration of institutions and collectivities, leaving us with an impoverished depiction of a complex achievement. My admiration for Sartre's accomplishments is, thus, not in the least conveyed by my use of him as a foil in this chapter. Some tendencies in his own text do invite using him in this way; to a far greater degree, the appropriation of him by thinkers and teachers in this country suggest this role.

8. While it is clear that Miller strenuously rejects the ahistoric, it is perhaps not at all evident that he is opposed to the trans-historical. It is certainly true that he argued for a form of transcendence but this was transcendence *in* history, by an ongoing, critical engagement with our actual past. Even temporally invariant truths

(e.g., 2+2 = 4) have grown out of temporal and bodily activities of counting. The transcendence of time is a temporal achievement, an accomplishment by historical actors ineluctably caught up in a temporal flux. Hence, such transcendence can only be provisional and perspectival; even so it is real, or better, actual.

9. This is true of the early Sartre, not of his later position. The author of the *Critique of Dialectical Reason* is much closer to Miller than is the author of *Being and Nothingness*.

10. The context of these assertions is a discussion of Ortega.

11. Five years later, he wrote, again to his son Eugene, that: "I think it not too much to say that our troubles reflect the lack of status for a Historical World. So we have the moralizers and their eternal verities, or else no verities at all. Whatever the truth may be, do not suppose you can *tell* it. Nothing that has been told is the truth. The telling condemns it" (PL, 539).

12. The desired return to nature is, however, a pressure felt within history: it is part of the tradition of antitraditionalists. This desire is a fatality within the history of those who can in some respects acknowledge their historicity, but blunt the force of this acknowledgment by imagining a pure, unadulterated nature (either in the form of a recovered environment or, more often, that of a reclaimed spontaneity) as their actual home. Such children of nature live among the trappings of civilization as exiles.

13. The student rebellions in the United States at this time are not immediately comparable to those in France. My principal concern is with Miller's assessment of the assault on the institutions in this country, not elsewhere. A liberal or perhaps even a radical unwilling to contribute unnecessarily to a culture of ineffectual irony and debilitating cynicism might have much to learn from Miller's position.

14. Of course, other images of historical insertion, of personal placement, are available—e.g., Antonio Gramsci's notion of the organic intellectual, Foucault's notion of the specific intellectual, and Cornel West's typology of types of intellectuals.

15. Baudelaire's *flâneur* seems close to, if not identical with, Emerson's eyeball.

16. "Without considering this background of the city which became a decisive experience for the young Benjamin one can hardly understand why the *flâneur* became the key figure in his writings" (Arendt 1968, 21). Here is another example of the importance of place, not as an abstract anywhere but as a determinate actuality—Paris rather than any other place.

17. After making some observations about Europe vis-à-vis his own country, Miller wrote: "Well, just the thoughts of a traveler. *But one would like to know what*

one has seen, and I'm sure it isn't a chaos of quite private expression" (PL, 797–98; emphasis added).

18. Vattimo goes so far as to say that: *"Pietas* may be another term which along with *Andenken* and *Verwindung* could characterize the weak thought of post-metaphysics." By *il pensiero debole* (weak thought), Vattimo means a form of thinking resolute in its refusal to seek absolute ground or immutable structures.

19. Thoreau contends that those who understand "the Art of walking have a genius for sauntering, which word is beautifully derived from idle people who roved about the country, in the Middle Ages, and asked charity, under the pretense of going *à la Sainte Terre,* to the Holy Land, till the children exclaimed, 'There goes a *Sainte-Terrer,'* a Saunterer, a Holy-Lander. They who never go to the Holy Land in their walks, as they pretend, are indeed mere idlers and vagabonds; but they who do go there are saunterers in the good sense, such as I mean" (Thoreau 1995, 12). "When I would recreate myself, I seek the darkest wood, the thickest and most interminable and, to the citizen, most dismal, swamp. I enter a swamp as a sacred place, a *sanctum sanctorum.* There is the strength, the marrow, of Nature" (ibid., 30).

20. "From a humane standpoint our study of history is still all too primitive. It is possible to study a multitude of histories, and yet permit history, the record of the transitions and transformations of human activities, to escape us" (Dewey [1922] 1983, 78–79).

21. Philosophy is itself "the actuality of those conflicts which establish the grounds upon which arguments occur and by which they are regulated. That lies beyond argument and proof" (*PC,* 74; cf. Wittgenstein 1972). It resides in the finite actualities of our historical inheritances and in the ongoing *re*appropriation of these fateful inheritances.

References

Adorno, Theodor. 1977. "The Actuality of Philosophy." *Telos* 31 (spring): 120–33.
———. 1984. "The Idea of a Natural History." *Telos* 60 (summer): 111–24.
Allan, George. 1986. *The Importances of the Past: A Meditation on the Authority of Tradition*. Albany: SUNY Press.
Arendt, Hannah. 1958. *The Human Condition*. Chicago: University of Chicago Press.
———. 1968a. *Between Past and Future*. New York: Viking.
———. 1968b. Introduction to *Illuminations: Walter Benjamin—Essays and Reflections*. New York: Schocken.
Bacon, Francis. 2000. *Novum Organum*. Edited by Lisa Jardine and Michael Silverthorne. Cambridge: Cambridge University Press.
Baeten, Elizabeth. 1996. *The Magic Mirror: Myth's Abiding Power*. Albany: SUNY Press.
Barthes, Roland. 1977. *Image, Music, Text: Essays Edited and Translated by Stephen Heat*. New York: Hill & Wang.
Benjamin, Walter. 1968. *Illuminations: Walter Benjamin—Essays and Reflections*. Translated by Harry Zohn. New York: Schocken.
Berlin, Isaiah. 1957. *The Hedgehog and the Fox: An Essay on Tolstoy's View of History*. New York: Simon & Schuster.
———. 1969. *Four Essays on Liberty*. New York: Oxford University Press.
Bernstein, Richard J. 1971. *Praxis and Action: Contemporary Philosophies of Human Activity*. Philadelphia: University of Pennsylvania Press.
———, ed. 1985. *Habermas and Modernity*. Cambridge, Mass.: MIT Press.
———. 1992. *The New Constellation: The Ethical-Political Horizon of Modernity/Postmodernity*. Cambridge, Mass.: MIT Press.
Blumenberg, Hans. 1985. *The Legitimacy of the Modern Age*. Translated by Robert Wallace. Cambridge, Mass.: MIT Press.

Bradford, Judith. 1997. "Telling the Difference: Feminist Philosophy and Miller's Actualist Semiotics." *Journal of Speculative Philosophy* 11:297–314.
Brockway, George B. 1981. "John William Miller." In *Masters: Portraits of Great Teachers*, edited by Joseph Epstein. New York: Basic Books. First published in *American Scholar* 49 (spring 1980): 236–40.
———. 1985. *Economics: What Went Wrong, and Why, and Some Things We Can Do about It*. New York: Harper & Row.
Burckhardt, Jacob. 1943. *Force and Freedom: Reflections on History*. Boston: Beacon Press.
Butler, Judith. 1990. *Gender Trouble: Feminism and the Subversion of Identity*. New York: Routledge.
———. 1997. *The Psychic Life of Power: Theories in Subjection*. Stanford: Stanford University Press.
Cahoone, Lawrence E. 1988. *The Dilemma of Modernity: Philosophy, Culture, and Anti-Culture*. Albany: SUNY Press.
Camus, Albert. 1970. *Lyrical and Critical Essay*. Edited by Philip Thody. Translated by Ellen Conroy Kennedy. New York: Vintage Books.
Carr, David. 1986. *Time, Narrative, and History*. Bloomington: Indiana University Press.
———. 1994. "Modernity, Post-Modernity, and the Philosophy of History." In *Reason in History: 1994 Annual ACPA Proceedings* 67:45–57.
Casey, Edward. 1993. *Getting Back into Place: Toward a Renewed Understanding of the Place World*. Bloomington: Indiana University Press.
Colapietro, Vincent M. 1987. Review of Miller's five books. *Journal of Speculative Philosophy* 1 (3): 239–56.
———. 1989. "Reason, Conflict, and Violence: John William Miller's Conception of Philosophy. *Transactions of the Charles S. Peirce Society* 25 (spring): 175–90.
———. 1990. "Human Symbols as Functioning Objects: A First Look at John William Miller's Contribution to Semiotics." In *The Philosophy of John William Miller*, edited by Joseph P. Fell. Lewisburg, Pa.: Bucknell University Press.
———. 1994. Review of Stephen Tyman's *Descrying the Ideal: The Philosophy of John William Miller* (1993). *Transactions of the Charles S. Peirce Society* 30:1033–45.
Collingwood, R. G. 1939. *An Autobiography*. Oxford: Oxford University Press.
Conrad, Joseph. [1900] 1961. *Lord Jim*. New York: Dell.
Corrington, Robert S. 1986. "John William Miller and the Ontology of the Midworld." *Transactions of the Charles S. Peirce Society* 22 (spring): 165–88.

———. 1990. "Finite Idealism: The Midworld and Its History." In *The Philosophy of John William Miller*, edited by Joseph P. Fell. Lewisburg, Pa.: Bucknell University Press.

Danto, Arthur C. 1985. *Narrative and Knowing*. New York: Columbia University Press.

Davidson, Donald. 1991. "Three Varieties of Knowledge." In *A. J. Ayer Memorial Essays*, edited by A. Phillips Griffiths. Royal Institute of Philosophy Supplement 30. New York: Cambridge University Press.

Derrida, Jacques. 1974. *Of Grammatology*. Translated by Gayatri Chakravorty Spivak. Baltimore, Md.: Johns Hopkins University Press.

———. 1981. *Positions*. Translated by Alan Bass. Chicago: University of Chicago Press.

———. 1992. "Force of Law: 'The Mystical Foundation of Authority.'" In *Deconstruction and the Possibility of Justice*, edited by Drucilla Cornell, Michel Rosenfeld, and David Carlson Grey. New York: Routledge.

Descartes, René. 1968. *Discourse on Method and The Meditations*. Translated by F. E. Sutcliffe. New York: Penguin.

Dewey, John. [1917] 1980. "The Need for a Recovery of Philosophy." In *The Middle Works, 1899–1924*, edited by Jo Ann Boydston, vol. 10. Carbondale and Edwardsville: Southern Illinois University Press.

———. [1922] 1983. *Human Nature and Conduct*. In *The Middle Works, 1899–1924*, edited by Jo Ann Boydston, vol. 14. Carbondale and Edwardsville: Southern Illinois University Press.

———. [1927] 1984. *The Public and Its Problems*. In *The Later Works, 1925–1953*, edited by Jo Ann Boydston, vol. 2. Carbondale and Edwardsville: Southern Illinois University Press.

———. [1929] 1984. *Individualism Old and New*. In *The Later Works, 1925–1953*, edited by Jo Ann Boydston, vol. 5. Carbondale and Edwardsville: Southern Illinois University Press.

———. [1930] 1984. "From Absolutism to Experimentalism." In *The Later Works, 1925–1953*, edited by Jo Ann Boydston, vol. 5. Carbondale and Edwardsville: Southern Illinois University Press.

———. [1934] 1986. *A Common Faith*. In *The Later Works, 1925–1953*, edited by Jo Ann Boydston, vol. 9. Carbondale and Edwardsville: Southern Illinois University Press.

———. [1925] 1988. *Experience and Nature*. In *The Later Works, 1925–1953*, edited by Jo Ann Boydston, vol. 1. Carbondale and Edwardsville: Southern Illinois University Press.

Diefenbeck, James A. 1990. "Acts and Necessity in the Philosophy of John William Miller." Pages 43–58 in *The Philosophy of John William Miller*, edited by Joseph P. Fell. Lewisburg, Pa.: Bucknell University Press.

Eco, Umberto. 1983. *The Name of the Rose*. Translated by William Weaver. New York: Harcourt, Brace, Jovanovich.

Elias, Robert H. 1973. *"Entangling Alliances with None": An Essay on the Individual in the American Twenties*. New York: W. W. Norton.

Eliot, T. S. 1934. *Selected Poems*. New York: Harcourt, Brace & World.

Emerson, R. W. 1950. *Selected Writings of Emerson*. Edited by Brooks Atkinson. New York: Modern Library.

———. 1951. *Emerson's Essays: First and Second Series*. Edited by Irwin Erdman. New York: Harper & Row.

———. 1982. *Ralph Waldo Emerson: Selected Essays*. Edited by Larzer Ziff. New York: Penguin.

Fell, Joseph P. 1979. *Heidegger and Sartre: An Essay on Being and Place*. New York: Columbia University Press.

———. 1990a. "Miller: The Man and His Philosophy." In *The Philosophy of John William Miller*, edited by Joseph P. Fell. Lewisburg, Pa.: Bucknell University Press.

———, ed. 1990b. *The Philosophy of John William Miller*. Lewisburg, Pa.: Bucknell University Press.

———. 1997. "John William Miller and Nietzsche's Nihilism." Roy Wood Sellars Lecture at Bucknell University, Lewisburg, Pa., October 23, 1996. *Eidos: The Bucknell Academic Journal*.

Findlay, J. N. 1964. "Can God's Existence Be Proven?" In *New Essays in Philosophical Theology*, edited by Antony Flew and Alasdair MacIntyre. New York: Macmillan.

Flynn, Thomas. 1994. "The Future Perfect and the Perfect Future: History Has Its Reasons." *Reason in History: 1994 Annual ACPA Proceedings* 67:1–15.

Foucault, Michel. 1970. *The Order of Things: An Archaeology of the Human Sciences*. New York: Random House. First published as *Les Mots et les choses* (Paris: Editions Gallimard, 1966).

———. 1977. *Language, Counter-Memory, Practice: Selected Essays and Interviews*. Edited by Donald F. Bouchard. Ithaca, NY: Cornell University Press.

———. 1984. *The Foucault Reader*. Edited by Paul Rabinow. New York: Pantheon.

———. 1986. "Of Other Spaces." Translated by Jay Miskowiec. *Diacritics* 16 (1): 22–27. An alternative translation of this lecture to the Architectural Studies Circle (March 14, 1967) appears under the title "Different Spaces" in *Aesthet-*

ics, Method, and Epistemology: Essential Works of Michel Foucault 1954–1984. Edited by James Faubion. New York: New Press, 1998. 2:174–85.

Frankfurt, Harry. 1970. *Demons, Dreamers, and Madmen: The Defense of Reason in Descartes' Meditations.* Indianapolis: Bobbs-Merrill.

Freud, Sigmund. 1989. *The Freud Reader.* Edited by Peter Gay. New York: W. W. Norton.

Frost, Robert. 1995. *Collected Poems, Prose, and Plays.* Edited by Richard Poirier and Mark Richardson. New York: Library of America.

Gadamer, Hans-Georg. 1975. *Truth and Method.* Edited by Garrett Barden and John Cumming New York: Seabury Press. First published as *Wahrheit und Methode.*

———. 1976. *Philosophical Hermeneutics.* Edited and translated by David E. Linge. Berkeley and Los Angeles: University of California Press.

Gahringer, Robert. 1990. "On Interpreting J. W. Miller." In *The Philosophy of John William Miller*, edited by Joseph P. Fell. Lewisburg, Pa.: Bucknell University Press.

Gray, Rockwell. 1989. *The Imperative of Modernity: An Intellectual Biography of José Ortega y Gasset.* Berkeley and Los Angeles: University of California Press.

Gutting, Gary. 1989. *Michel Foucault's Archaeology of Scientific Reason.* Cambridge: Cambridge University Press.

Halperin, David M. 1995. *Saint Foucault: Towards a Gay Hagiography.* New York: Oxford University Press.

Hegel, G. W. F. 1956. *The Philosophy of History.* Translated by J. Sibree. New York: Dover.

———. 1967. *The Phenomenology of Mind.* Translated by J. B. Baillie. New York: Harper & Row.

———. 1975. *Hegel's Logic: Being Part One of the Encyclopaedia of the Philosophical Sciences (1830).* Translated by William Wallace. Oxford: Clarendon.

———. 1977. *Phenomenology of Spirit.* Translated by A. V. Miller. Oxford: Oxford University Press.

Heidegger, Martin. 1977. "Letter on Humanism." In *Basic Writings*, edited by David F. Krell. New York: Harper & Row.

———. 1996. *Being and Time.* Translated by Joan Stambaugh. Albany: SUNY Press. First published as "Sein und Zeit" in *Jahrbuch für Phänomenologie und phänomenologische Forschung* 8 (1927).

Hocking, William Ernest. 1926. *Man and the State.* New Haven, Conn.: Yale University Press.

———. 1942. *What Man Can Make of Man.* New York: Harper & Brothers.

———. 1959. *Types of Philosophy.* 3d ed. New York: Charles Scribner's Sons.
Hodges, Michael, and John Lachs. 1999. *Thinking in the Ruins: Wittgenstein and Santayana on Contingency.* Nashville, Tenn.: Vanderbilt University Press.
Houlgate, Stephen. 1991. *Freedom, Truth, and History: An Introduction to Hegel's Philosophy.* New York: Routledge.
Howard, Michael. 1991. *The Lessons of History.* New Haven, Conn.: Yale University Press.
Husserl, Edmund. 1965. *Phenomenology and the Crisis of Philosophy.* Translated by Quentin Lauer. New York: Harper & Row.
Hussey, Mark. 1986. *The Singing of the Real World: The Philosophy of Virginia Woolf's Fiction.* Columbus: Ohio State University Press.
James, William. [1897] 1958. *The Will to Believe and Other Essays in Popular Philosophy.* New York: Dover.
———. [1905] 1975. *The Meaning of Truth.* Cambridge, Mass.: Harvard University Press.
———. [1907] 1975. *Pragmatism.* Cambridge, Mass.: Harvard University Press.
———. [1912] 1976. *Essays in Radical Empiricism.* Cambridge, Mass.: Harvard University Press.
———. [1909] 1977. *A Pluralistic Universe.* Edited by Frederick Burkhardt. Cambridge, Mass.: Harvard University Press.
———. 1977. *The Writings of William James: A Comprehensive Edition.* Edited by John J. McDermott. Chicago: University of Chicago.
———. [1890] 1981. *The Principles of Psychology.* Cambridge, Mass.: Harvard University Press.
———. [1902] 1985. *The Varieties of Religious Experience.* Cambridge, Mass.: Harvard University Press.
Jameson, Frederic. 1972. *The Prison-House of Language.* Princeton, N.J.: Princeton University Press.
Jardine, Alice. 1985. *Gynesis: Configurations of Women and Modernity.* Ithaca, New York: Cornell University Press.
Jefferson, Thomas. 1963. "Letter to Isaac A. Tiffany." In *Social and Political Philosophy: Readings from Plato to Gandhi,* edited by John Somerville and Ronald E. Santoni. Garden City, N.Y.: Anchor.
Johnstone, Henry W. Jr. 1990. "The Fatality of Thought." In *The Philosophy of John William Miller,* edited by Joseph P. Fell. Lewisburg, Pa.: Bucknell University Press.
Kant, Immanuel. 1965. *Critique of Pure Reason.* Translated by Norman Kemp Smith. New York: St. Martin's.

Kuhn, Thomas. 1970. *The Structure of Scientific Revolutions*. 2d ed., expanded. Chicago: University of Chicago Press.

Lacan, Jacques. 1981. *The Language of the Self: The Function of Language in Psychoanalysis*. Translated with notes and commentary by Anthony Wilden. Baltimore, Md.: Johns Hopkins University Press.

Lachs, John. 2001. "Both Better Off and Better: Moral Progress and Continuing Carnage." *Journal of Speculative Philosophy* 15 (3):173–83.

Langer, Suzanne K. 1957. *Philosophy in a New Key: A Study in the Symbolism of Reason, Rite, and Art*. 3d ed. Cambridge, Mass.: Harvard University Press.

Lauer, Quentin. 1987. *A Reading of Hegel's Phenomenology of Spirit*. New York: Fordham University Press.

Lyotard, Jean François. 1984. *The Postmodern Condition: A Report on Knowledge*. Translated by Geoff Bennington and Brian Massumi. Minneapolis: University of Minnesota Press. First published as *La Condition postmoderne: Rapport sur le savoir* (Paris: Les Editions de Minuit, 1979).

MacIntyre, Alasdair. 1980. "Epistemological Crises, Dramatic Narrative, and the Philosophy of Science." In *Paradigms and Revolutions: Appraisals and Applications of Thomas Kuhn's Philosophy of Science*, edited by Gary Gutting. Notre Dame, Ind.: University of Notre Dame Press. First published in *Monist* 60 (1977): 453–71.

Macmurray, John. 1957. *The Self as Agent*. London: Faber & Faber.

Margolis, Joseph. 1991. "Prospects for a Theory of Radical History." *Monist* 74 (2): 269–91.

———. 1993. *Flux of History and the Flux of Science*. Berkeley and Los Angeles: University of California Press.

———. 1995. *Interpretation Radical But Not Unruly: The New Puzzle of the Arts and History*. Berkeley and Los Angeles: University of California Press.

Marx, Karl. 1978. *The Marx-Engels Reader*. Edited by Robert C. Tucker. New York: W. W. Norton.

McGandy, Michael J. 1995. "John William Miller's Metaphysics of Democracy." *Transactions of the Charles S. Peirce Society* 31 (3): 598–630.

———. 1998. "The Midworld: Classifications and Developments." *Transactions of the Charles S. Peirce Society* 34 (1): 225–64.

———. 2000. "John William Miller's Actualism: A Metaphysics of Democracy." Ph.D. diss., Fordham University.

Merleau-Ponty, Maurice. 1973. *Adventures of the Dialectic*. Translated by Joseph Bien. Evanston, Ill.: Northwestern University Press.

Miller, James. 1993. *The Passion of Michel Foucault*. New York: Simon & Schuster.

Murdoch, Iris. 1989. *Sartre: Romantic Rationalist.* New York: Penguin.
Nietzsche, Friedrich. 1962. *Philosophy in the Tragic Age of the Greeks.* Translated by Marianne Cowan. Chicago: Henry Regnery.
———. 1966a. *Beyond Good and Evil: Prelude to a Philosophy of the Future.* Translated by Walter Kaufmann. New York: Vintage.
———. 1966b. *Thus Spoke Zarathustra: A Book for All and None.* Translated by Walter Kaufmann. New York: Viking.
———. 1967. *On the Genealogy of Morals.* Translated by Walter Kaufmann and R. J. Hollingdale. New York: Vintage.
Novak, Michael. 1965. *Belief and Unbelief: A Philosophy of Self-Knowledge.* New York: Macmillan.
Ortega, José y Gasset. 1957. *Man and People.* Translated by Willard R. Trask. New York: W. W. Norton.
———. 1961. *The Modern Theme.* New York: Harper & Row, 1961.
———. 1962. *History as a System and Other Essays Toward a Philosophy of History.* New York: W. W. Norton.
———. 1984. *Historical Reason.* Translated by Philip Silver. New York: W. W. Norton. First published as *Sobre la razón histórica.*
Peirce, Charles Sanders. 1931–58. *The Collected Papers of Charles Sanders Peirce,* vols. 1–6 edited by Charles Hartshorne and Paul Weiss, volumes 7 & 8 edited by Arthur W. Burks. Cambridge, Mass.: Harvard University Press.
Perry, Ralph Barton. 1935. *The Thought and Character of William James.* 2 vols. Boston: Little, Brown.
Pieper, Josef. 1962. *A Guide to Thomas Aquinas,* translated by Richard and Clara Winston. New York: Random House.
———. 1964. *Scholasticism: Personalities and Problems of Medieval Philosophy.* Translated by Richard and Clara Winston. New York: McGraw-Hill. First published as *Scholastic* (Munich: Koesel Verlag).
———. 1991. *In Search of the Sacred.* Translated by Lothar Krauth. San Francisco: Ignatius Press. First published as *Was Heisst 'Sakral'?* (Stuttgart: Schwabenverlag, 1988).
Popper, Karl. 1963. *Conjectures and Refutations.* New York: Harper & Row.
———. 1966. *The Open Society and Its Enemies.* 2 vols. Princeton, N.J.: Princeton University Press.
Ricoeur, Paul. 1965. *History and Truth.* Translated by Charles Kelbley. Evanston, Ill.: Northwestern University Press.
———. 1970. *Freud and Philosophy: An Essay on Interpretation.* Translated by Denis Savage. New Haven, Conn.: Yale University Press.

———. 1974. *The Conflict of Interpretations.* Edited by Don Ihde. Evanston, Ill.: Northwestern University Press. First published as *Le Conflict des interpretations* (Paris: Editions du Seuil, 1969).

———. 1984. *The Reality of the Historical Past.* Milwaukee, Wis.: Marquette University Press.

———. 1988. *Time and Narrative.* Vol. 3. Translated by Kathleen Blamey and David Pellauer. Chicago: University of Chicago Press.

———. 1989. *The Narrative Path: The Later Work of Paul Ricoeur.* Edited by T. Peter Kemp and David Rasmussen. Cambridge, Mass.: MIT Press.

Rieff, David. 1993. "Homelands." *Salmagundi* 97 (winter): 3–9.

Roberts, David D. 1987. *Benedetto Croce and the Uses of Historicism.* Berkeley and Los Angeles: University of California Press.

Rorty, Richard. 1979. *Philosophy and the Mirror of Nature.* Princeton, N.J.: Princeton University Press.

———. 1982. *Consequences of Pragmatism.* Minneapolis: University of Minnesota Press.

———. 1989. *Contingency, Irony, and Solidarity.* Cambridge: Cambridge University Press.

Royce, Josiah. 1901. *The World and the Individual.* Vol. 2. Nature, Man, and the Moral Order. New York: Macmillan.

———. 1908. *The Philosophy of Loyalty.* New York: Macmillan.

———. [1913] 1968. *The Problem of Christianity.* 2 vols. Chicago: Henry Regnery.

———. 1998. *Metaphysics: His Philosophy Course of 1915–1916.* Edited by William Ernest Hocking, Richard Hocking, and Frank Oppenheim. Albany: SUNY Press.

Rushdie, Salman. 1992. *Imaginary Homelands: Essays and Criticisms, 1981–1991.* New York: Penguin.

Said, Edward. 1999. "Humanism?" *MLA Newsletter* (fall): 3–4.

———. 2000. "Humanism and Heroism." 1999 Presidential Address to Modern Languages Association. *PMLA* 115 (3): 285–91.

Santayana, George. 1905–6. *The Life of Reason.* Vol. 3. New York: Charles Scribner's Sons..

Schmitz, Kenneth. 1995. "What Happens to Tradition When History Overtakes It." *Reason in History: 1994 Annual ACPA Proceedings* 68:59–72.

Schürmann, Reiner. 1984. "Deconstruction Is Not Enough: On Gianni Vattimo's Call for 'Weak Thinking.'" *Graduate Faculty Philosophy Journal* 10 (1): 165–77.

Smith, John E. 1995. *Quasi-Religions: Humanism, Marxism, and Nationalism.* New York: St. Martin's.
Smith, Steven G. 1995. "Piety's Problems." *Scottish Journal of Religious Studies* 16 (spring): 5–24.
Soper, Kate. 1986. *Humanism and Anti-Humanism.* La Salle, Ill.: Open Court.
Strout, Cushing. 1990a. *Making American Tradition: Vision and Revision from Ben Franklin to Alice Walker.* New Brunswick, N.J.: Rutgers University Press.
———. 1990b. "When Truth Is in the Telling." In *The Philosophy of John William Miller,* edited by Joseph P. Fell. Lewisburg, Pa.: Bucknell University Press.
Taylor, Charles. 1985. *Philosophy and the Human Sciences: Philosophical Papers.* Vol. 2. Cambridge: Cambridge University Press.
———. 1989. *Sources of the Self: The Making of the Modern Identity.* Cambridge, Mass.: Harvard University Press.
———. 1993. "Engaged Agency and Background in Heidegger." In *The Cambridge Companion to Heidegger,* edited by Charles Guignon. Cambridge: Cambridge University Press.
Thoreau, Henry David. [1854] 1980. *Walden and Civil Disobedience.* New York: Signet Classic.
———. 1995. *Walking.* New York: Penguin.
Tillich, Paul. 1936. *The Interpretation of History.* Pt. 1, translated by N. A. Rasetzi. Pts. 2–4, translated by Elisa L. Talmy. New York: Charles Scribner's Sons.
Tyman, Stephen. 1993. *Descrying the Ideal: The Philosophy of John William Miller.* Carbondale and Edwardsville, Ill.: Southern Illinois University Press.
Vattimo, Gianni. 1984. "Dialectics, Difference, and Weak Thought." *Graduate Faculty Philosophy Journal* (New School for Social Research) 10 (1): 151–63.
———. 1991. *The End of Modernity: Nihilism and Hermeneutics in Postmodern Culture.* Translated by Jon R. Snyder. Baltimore, Md.: Johns Hopkins University Press. First published in Italian in 1985.
Vico, Giambattista. 1961. *The New Science of Giambattista Vico.* Translated by Thomas Goddard Bergin, and Max Harold Fisch. Ithaca, N.Y.: Cornell University Press. Published as *Scienza nouva,* 3d ed. (1744).
Walker, Alice. 1983. *In Search of Our Mothers' Garden: Womanist Prose.* New York: Harcourt Brace Jovanovich.
Weber, Max. 1958. *The Protestant Ethic and the Spirit of Capitalism.* Translated by Talcott Parsons. New York: Scribner's.
Weil, Simone. 1971. *The Need for Roots.* Translated by Arthur Wills. New York: Harper & Row.

West, Cornel. 1986. *The American Evasion of Philosophy: A Genealogy of Pragmatism*. Madison: University of Wisconsin Press.

Westphal, Kenneth. 1993. "The Basic Context and Structure of Hegel's *Philosophy of Right*." Pages 234–69 in *The Cambridge Companion to Hegel*, edited by Frederick Beiser. Cambridge: Cambridge University Press.

Westphal, Merold. 1990. *History and Truth in Hegel's Phenomenology*. Atlantic Highlands, N.J.: Humanities Press International.

Whitehead, Alfred North. [1925] 1967. *Science and the Modern World*. New York: Macmillan.

———. [1933] 1967. *Adventures of Ideas*. New York: Free Press.

Wills, Garry. 1992. *Lincoln at Gettysburg: The Words That Remade America*. New York: Simon & Schuster.

Wittgenstein, Ludwig. 1958. *Philosophical Investigations*. Translated by G. E. M. Anscombe. New York: Macmillan.

———. 1972. *On Certainty*. Edited by G. E. M. Anscombe and G. H. von Wright. Translated by Denis Paul and G. E. M. Anscombe. New York: Harper & Row.

Woolf, Virginia. [1929] 1981. *A Room of One's Own*. New York: Harcourt Brace Jovanovich.

Name Index

Abraham, 90
Adams, John, 253
Adorno, Theodor, 86, 256, 285n.1, 286n.14
Alcibiades, 51–53
Allan, George, 3
Aquinas, Thomas, 10, 78, 154
Arendt, Hannah, xiv, 212–13, 164, 256, 281n.34, 296n.16
Aristotle, 26, 49, 78, 120–21, 204, 229
Athene, 80
Augustine of Hippo, 78

Bacon, Francis, 5, 10, 11, 213, 231, 263,
Baeten, Elizabeth, 14
Barthes, Roland, 7
Baudelaire, Charles, 256, 296n.15
Benjamin, Walter, 153, 256–57, 258, 296n.16
Bergson, Henri, 188
Berkeley, George, 13
Berlin, Isaiah, 278n.18
Bernstein, Richard J., 9, 111, 225
Bloch, Ernst, 135
Blumenberg, Hans, 14
Bohr, Niels, 211
Bradford, Judith, 2, 274n.6
Bradley, F. H., 210, 291n.15

Brockway, George P., xiv, xv, 2, 48, 50, 273n.2, 276n.10
Burckhardt, Jacob, 2
Butler, Judith, 129

Cahoone, Lawrence E., 4, 278n.15
Camus, Albert, 108, 216–17, 218, 295n.6
Carr, David, 9
Carter, Stephen, 280n.30
Casey, Edward, 290n.9
Castell, Alburey, xv, 20, 280n.31
Cicero, 154
Cohen, Morris Raphael, xiv
Colapietro, Vincent, 273n.3, 274n.5, 276n.6, 285n.3
Collingwood, R. G., 9, 33, 278n.20, 281n.34, 290n.8
Comte, Auguste, 83
Conrad, Joseph, 24, 275n.5, 276n.11
Copernicus, 35
Corrington, Robert S., 114, 276n.6
Croce, Benedetto, 9, 33, 278n.18, 278n.20, 281n.34

Darwin, Charles, 78
Derrida, Jacques, 5, 7, 128–29
Descartes, René, 5, 10, 11, 46, 118–19, 171, 204, 228–29, 230, 247, 277n.13

311

Dewey, John, xiv, 11, 43, 114, 116, 134, 160, 252, 274n.4, 278n.16, 286n.12, 288n.3, 297n.20
Dickinson, Emily, 157, 159
Diefenbeck, James A., 178
Dilthey, Wilhelm, 33, 281n.34

Echo, 139
Eco, Umberto, 81, 210
Einstein, Albert, 90, 101, 211
Elias, Robert H., 284n.10
Eliot, T. S., 230
Emerson, Ralph Waldo xiv, 176–77, 182, 198, 208, 234–35, 240, 252, 262, 266–68, 272, 282n.37, 291n.15, 291n.17, 296n.15
Epstein, Joseph, xiv

Fell, Joseph, xiii, xiv, 131, 273n.1, 274n.6, 284n.12, 286n.11, 290n.6, 291n.14
Feyerabend, Paul, 5, 278n.17
Fichte, Johann Gottlieb, xiv, 209, 283n.2
Findlay, J.N., 160
Flynn, Thomas, 225
Foucault, Michel, 5, 134–35, 220–26, 237, 241–45, 255, 277n.14, 296n.14
Frankfurt, Harry, 201
Freud, Sigmund, 35–36, 63, 76, 90, 112, 262, 274n.3,
Frost, Robert, 22

Gadamer, Hans-Georg, 157
Gahringer, Robert E., 212, 273n.2, 290n.7, 291n.15
Galileo, 35, 90, 242
Gibson, James Jay, 152
Goethe, Johann Wolfgang von, 25
Gramsci, Antonio, 296n.14
Gray, Rockwell, 282n.37
Gutting, Gary, 220

Habermas, Jürgen, 9, 22
Halperin, David M., 225
Hegel, G. W. F., xiv, 29, 31, 38, 41–45, 140, 143, 149–51, 171, 180, 193, 195–97, 204, 209, 212, 246, 255, 264, 275n.4, 281n.33, 283n.3, 290n.7, 295n.5
Heidegger, Martin, 90, 134–35, 137, 157, 165–66, 215, 217, 242, 258, 286n.11, 289n.4
Heisenberg, Werner, 35
Heraclitus, 78, 204, 293n.20
Herodotus, 67
Hocking, William Ernest, xiii, xiv, 1, 5, 10, 16, 111, 175, 197, 200, 209, 278n.15, 279n.23, 283n.3, 286n.10
Hodges, Michael, 3
Holt, E. B., xiii
Homer, 49, 80, 193
Houlgate, Stephen, 246
Howard, Michael, 176
Hume, David, 55, 73, 142, 239
Husserl, Edmund, 125, 135, 137–38
Hussey, Mark, 179

Isaac, 90

Jacob, 90
Jacques, T. Carlos, 226
James, William, xiv, 4, 90, 106, 107, 135–36, 138–40, 182–83, 185, 188, 252–53, 255, 260, 266, 274n.4, 284n.14, 289n.5, 293n.22
Jameson, Frederic, 78, 238
Jardine, Alice, 222
Jefferson, Thomas, 120, 213, 247, 252–53, 284n.10
Jehovah, 80
Johnson, Samuel, 13
Johnstone, Henry W. Jr., 17, 61

Name Index 313

Kant, Immanuel, 26, 29, 31–33, 37, 43, 45, 49, 84, 171, 193–94, 197, 204, 209, 213, 255, 283n.5
Kaufmann, Walter, 290n.7
Keats, John, 259
Kepler, Johannes, 35
Kierkegaard, Soren, 91, 295n.7
Klee, Paul, 256–58
Kuhn, Thomas, 187, 284n.6

Lacan, Jacques, 135, 200
Lachs, John, 3, 5
Lauer, Quentin, 40
Lewis, C. I., xiii, 274n.4
Lewis, C.S., xiv
Lincoln, Abraham, 68, 73, 213, 238, 249
Locke, John, 204
Luther, Martin, 73, 291n.17
Lyotard, Jean-François, 5, 8

MacArthur, Douglas, 260
MacIntyre, Alasdair, 9
Macmurray, John, 1
Marcel, Gabriel, 90
Margolis, Joseph, 9
Marx, Groucho, 214
Marx, Karl, 42, 151, 264, 274n.2, 275n.4, 276n.7, 283n.3, 284n.8
McGandy, Michael J., xiv, 95–96, 276n.6, 283n.1, 286n.13
Mead, George Herbert, 252, 274n.4
Mead, Margaret, xiv
Merleau-Ponty, Maurice, 90, 294n.22
Miller, Eugene, 296n.11
Mink, Louis, 9
Moore, G. E., 204, 210
More, Thomas, 142
Murdoch, Iris, 217–18, 219

Nagel, Thomas, 151
Narcissus, 139
Newton, Isaac, 78, 90, 101

Nietzsche, Friedrich, 135, 182, 184–85, 222, 231, 239–41, 252, 266–68, 272, 288n.2, 293n.20
Novak, Michael, 218

Ortega, José y Gassett, 1, 4, 9, 50, 54, 91, 125, 170, 276n.11, 278n.17, 278n.20, 281n.34, 282n.40, 296n.10

Paine, Thomas, 284
Parmenides, 78
Peirce, Charles Sanders, xiv, 215, 234–35, 274n.4
Perry, Ralph Barton, xiii, 59, 106, 255, 260
Pieper, Joseph, 5, 198, 242
Plato, 49, 64, 75, 78, 83, 121, 154, 180, 191, 193, 204, 207, 209, 210, 222, 252, 270, 294n.2
Popper, Sir Karl, 231
Pratt, James Bissett, xiii
Protagoras, 229
Ptolemy, 80

Ransom, John Crowe, xiv
Richards, I. A., xiv
Ricoeur, Paul, 8
Rieff, David, 2, 200
Roberts, David D., 278n.19
Rorty, Richard, 80, 163, 180, 278n.16
Royce, Josiah, xiv, 46, 106, 157, 197, 209, 284n.7, 284n.14, 286n.9, 286n.10
Rushdie, Salman, 200, 282n.39
Russell, Bertrand, 134, 210

Saint-Exupéry, Antoine de, 216
Santayana, George, xiv, 57, 116, 154, 272, 286n.12, 288n.3
Sartre, Jean Paul, 90–91, 217–18, 220, 295n.7, 296n.9
Schelling, F. W. J., 283n.2
Schmitz, Kenneth, 6

Schürmann, Reiner, 257
Scotus, Duns, 10, 265
Searle, John, 59
Shakespeare, William, 173, 209
Shelley, P. B., 200, 232
Skinner, B. F., 27, 35–36, 63, 90
Smith, John E., 290n.10
Smith, Stephen G., 289n.3
Socrates, 52, 154–55, 157, 210, 229–30
Soper, Kate, 288n.3
Spengler, Otto, 277n.14, 289n.4
Strout, Cushing, 9, 66, 213, 255, 290n.8, 291n.15, 292n.17, 292n.18

Taylor, Charles, 1, 15, 139, 149, 276n.10, 293n.19
Thales, 204
Thomas, Dylan, 291n.14
Thoreau, Henry David, xiv, 158, 176, 249, 261–65, 268, 275n.7, 297n.19
Tillich, Paul, 298–99

Tocqueville, Alexis de, 250
Turner, Nat, 249
Tyman, Stephen, xiv, 283n.2

Vattimo, Gianni, 135, 137–38, 256–58, 297n.18
Vico, Giambattista, 278n.20, 289n.4

Walker, Alice, 174, 291n.14
Washington, George, 248
Watson, John B., 112
West, Cornel, 278n.16, 296n.14
Westphal, Merold, 4
Whitehead, Alfred North, xiv, 155, 175
Whitman, Walt, xiv
Wittgenstein, Ludwig, 272, 293n.19, 297n.21
Wordsworth, William, 178
Woolf, Virginia, 153, 173, 179, 266, 268
Wundt, Wilhelm, 35

Subject Index

absolute, 28, 79, 106, 136, 165, 184, 195–96, 291n.17
absolute empiricism, 72, 284n.14
absolute idealism, 44
absolute pragmatism (Josiah Royce), 106
accidental, 72
action, 13, 16–17, 19, 21, 25, 33, 36, 46, 50, 52, 58, 61, 73–74, 77, 89, 91–93, 98–99, 103, 192, 207, 210, 216, 219, 235, 279n.26, 282n.38, 284n.12, 287n.1
actual, 15, 17, 23, 29, 41, 43, 45, 48, 46, 86–87, 89–90, 101, 112, 125, 131, 145, 161, 164, 166, 168, 172, 174–75, 178, 180, 183, 185, 188, 193, 195, 197, 203, 207, 214–18, 221, 224, 232, 242, 246–47, 279n.22, 287n.1, 291n.16, 292n.19, 297n.21
actual world, 12–14, 23–24, 27, 34, 42, 68, 81, 84, 99, 101, 105, 178, 181, 186, 192, 219, 261, 296n.11
affirmation(s), 23–24, 86–87, 125, 129, 135, 146, 169, 187, 192, 217, 230, 291n.17, 294n.3
affordance, 152
agency, 13, 23, 33, 35–36, 44, 54, 58, 68, 70, 89–90, 95–96, 100, 104, 107, 110, 113, 116, 118, 123, 140, 144, 166, 169–70, 201–2, 205, 208, 218, 227, 234–35, 253, 268, 280n.27, 287n.1
ahistoric, 168–69, 184, 295n.8
America, 121, 213, 218, 244, 249–51, 295n.7, 296n.13
American democracy, xiv-v, 213
anachronism, 67
anarchy, 18, 254, 262
ancestor(s), 90, 175, 201, 227
angel of history, 256–57, 260
animism, 200, 202
annihilation, 132, 163, 176, 179, 182, 268
antagonist, 41, 79, 92–94, 112, 263
anti-hero, 80
anti-humanism, 135, 185, 288n.2
appearance, 17, 88, 90, 99–100, 104–5, 136, 166, 192, 283n.5
archaeology of knowledge, 134
aristocracy, 252–53
art, 49, 180–81, 187, 192, 205–7, 213–14
articulation, 54, 188, 190, 192, 281n.31
artifact, 23, 34, 38, 61, 84, 87, 89, 95–96, 99, 122, 130, 205, 233, 282n.36, 284n.12, 285n.3, 286n.7
artist, 186
asceticism, 294n.22
atheism, 114, 288n.3
Athens, 107, 121, 154–55, 180, 251

315

Aufgehoben, 248
Auschwitz, 180, 216
authoritarian versus authoritative, 28, 47, 54, 203, 208, 248, 270
authority, 13–15, 20–22, 28, 35, 43, 47, 54, 58, 63–65, 76, 92, 99, 101, 111, 142, 160, 165–67, 172, 189–90, 198, 206–7, 232–33, 248, 251, 254, 253, 262
authorization (*see also* self-authorization), 22
authorship, 56

back to nature, 115
barbarism, 155, 166, 276n.9
Bible, 239
body, 96, 122, 125, 152, 172, 207–8, 285n.6
calibanism, 16
capitalism, 217–18, 294n.23
career, 212, 289n.3, 295n.4
categoreal words (also see constitutional words), 266, 282n.36
categories, 72–73, 123, 194–95, 258, 266, 282n.36
chaos, 98, 281n.31
Chartres, 207
Christianity, 185, 239, 259
circles (self-evolving), 243
City of God (Augustine), 42
Civil War, 12
civility, 153–55, 159, 166, 238, 246, 249, 262, 267, 280n.30
clock time, 172, 222, 285n.5
clock(s), 52, 96, 127, 172, 190, 193, 195
cogito, 119, 171, 223, 247
cognition, 102, 125–26
cognitivism, 193, 228, 269
commitment(s), 3, 19, 21, 23, 28, 91, 141–42, 145, 175, 178, 180, 215
common sense, 12, 58, 128, 131, 139, 279n.25, 294n.22

commonplace, 2, 131, 177
communication, 62, 111–12
communism, 217–18
community, 12, 48, 80, 91, 156–57, 214–15, 217, 222, 259
compassion, 258
composition, 105
composure, 14, 31, 40, 205, 280n.27
compulsion, 3, 39, 171, 276n.10
conflict, 12, 14, 39, 41, 111–12, 179, 211, 292n.19, 297n.21
Connecticut College (New London, Conn.), xiii
consciousness, 33, 64, 100, 125, 141, 145, 149–50, 218
conservative, 252
Constitution (U.S.), 12, 19, 209, 253, 260, 270
constitutional conflict, 10, 15, 19, 23–24, 81, 124, 141–42, 167, 175, 184, 196, 204–5, 211, 252, 268
constitutional incompleteness, 28, 101, 188, 204, 216
constitutional words, 189–90, 193–95, 236, 266
contemptus mundi, 185
contingency, 7, 72, 161
continuity, 74, 221, 252, 277n.14
continuum, 13, 25, 75, 79, 91–92, 94, 125, 195, 208, 214, 227, 246, 264
controls (*see also* local control), 30, 72, 93, 98, 208
cosmos, 53, 85, 98, 199
counter-memory (Michel Foucault), 222
counting, 131, 189
crisis, 17, 19, 137–38, 254
crisis of legitimation, 23, 28, 254
critique, 9, 187–88, 191, 194, 196–97, 199, 201, 211, 213, 228, 230, 261
culture, 196, 198
cynics, 223

data, 102–3, 197, 214
dated (or historical) time, 26, 67, 71, 78, 172, 222, 285n.5
decentering of the subject, 137
deconstruction, 7, 118, 129
deeds, 110, 128
democracy, 121, 159, 249–50, 252–54
democratic ethos, 121, 253–55, 266
demoralization, 18–19, 174, 269, 279n.23, 292n.17
destiny, 87
destructive element, 24, 28, 54, 275n.5
dialectic, 44, 59–60, 79, 83, 146, 149, 171, 283n.3, 284n.8
difference, 160–61
discipline, 87, 96, 116
disclosure. *See* revelation
discourse, 22, 36, 45, 61, 63, 65, 79, 99, 109–10, 127, 188–90, 192, 196, 205, 213, 215, 225, 232, 261, 270, 279n.25, 294n.2
displacement (or dislocation), 132, 140, 165, 200–201
divinity (*see also* God), 161–62, 198–99
dogmatism, 15, 18, 45, 73, 167–68, 180, 189, 194, 249, 262, 289n.6
doing (*see also* action), 35, 37, 158, 202, 208
drama, 11, 83, 142
dualism (including ontological duality), 139, 144–45, 147, 286n.9
dwelling, 132, 136, 173, 203, 263–65

earth, 136, 138, 150, 152, 154–56, 174, 185, 207, 239, 261, 263–64, 289n.3
education, 132
ego (*see also* I, self, and subjectivity), 90, 179
egoism, 50–51, 279n.22
Eleatic temper, 28, 283n.40
Elm Street, 131, 153
emancipation, 129, 248

Emancipation Proclamation, 248
embodiment, 118, 274n.3, 285n.4
empiricism, 71, 102–3, 194, 197, 284n.14
Enlightenment, 5–6, 157
entangling (or fateful) alliances, 53, 91, 94, 148, 171, 263, 284n.10
environment, 40, 65, 91, 94, 148, 171, 263, 284n.10
epistemology, 74, 99, 101, 117, 124, 278n.16
error (*see also* mistake), 59, 77
esthetics of existence, 223
estrangement, 132, 263
eternal, 180, 183, 221, 232, 290n.11, 293n.21
ethics, 131, 279n.23
Eurocentrism, 4
Europe, 137, 251, 296n.17
evasion of the actual, 17, 25, 178, 183, 191, 196, 215–16, 252–53, 295n.7
evolution, 109, 213–14
exile, 199–200
existentialism, 90, 217, 292n.18, 295n.7
experience, 39, 71–72, 86, 102, 106, 136, 178, 235, 271, 284n.12, 284n.14, 285n.6, 292n.17

fact, 58–60, 103
fanaticism, 23, 216
fantasy, 14, 93, 68, 140
fatality, 15, 17, 68, 140, 142, 153, 170, 182, 198, 205, 210, 219, 221, 228, 247, 271–72
fate, 15, 124, 181, 205, 291n.12
fateful, 1, 17, 28, 39, 55, 117, 127, 148, 164, 170–71, 181, 252, 254, 268
fateful shape of human freedom, 2, 141, 17, 198, 202, 208, 210, 252, 268–69
fidelity to the earth, 239, 241, 265
finite actuality, 21, 24, 37, 42–43, 84, 86–88, 97, 107, 130, 151, 174, 178, 180–81, 188, 219, 222, 269, 295n.7

finitude, 61, 65, 106–7, 135–36, 168
flâneur, 153, 256, 260, 296n.15
formal order, 88, 95, 103, 172
formalism, 162
freedom, 2, 16, 21, 40, 60, 62, 92, 121, 140, 146, 171, 218, 235, 253, 261, 276n.7, 276n.11
functioning, 15, 17, 19–20, 24, 34, 83–84, 98, 102–3, 119, 140, 162, 209, 236, 246, 262, 291n.16
functioning object(s), 17, 23, 26, 34, 36–38, 85, 88, 95–96, 119, 122, 125, 152, 166, 188, 192, 207–9, 245, 279n.22, 285n.2, 285n.4, 291n.16
future, 257

genealogy, 14, 221–22, 245, 280n.28
genealogy of critique, 196
German idealism, xiv, 86, 194, 197, 212, 283n.2
God, 64, 104, 116, 134, 136, 160–61, 168, 170, 183, 198–99, 210–11, 229, 265, 289n.5
gospels, 240
government, 120, 247, 253–54
Greece (Ancient), 84, 211, 216, 277n.14, 281n.31
guilt, 77–78

hammer, 87
hand, 96, 119
Harvard, xiii
hecceity, 265
Hegelian idealism, 37, 45
here and now (*see also hecceity*), 158, 170, 182
heritage, 40, 181, 274n.4
hermeneutic of explication, 8
hermeneutic of suspicion, 8
hero, 80
heroism, 185, 293n.22
heteronomy, 53

heterotopia, 241–43
heterotopology, 243, 245
Hiroshima, 216
historian, 15, 64, 70
historical consciousness, 24, 39, 110, 114, 171, 184, 198, 222
historical idealism, 44, 46, 168, 283n.4
historical moment (or present), 153, 163, 172, 182, 195, 247, 252
historical reason, 32, 278n.20
historicism, 89, 151, 168–69, 207, 268, 292n.18
historicity, 2, 136, 172, 198
historiography, 2, 188, 221, 245
history, xv, 1–3, 14, 22, 24–27, 33, 38–39, 56, 61, 65–69, 73–74, 83, 89, 114, 133–34, 136, 140, 150–51, 154, 156, 164, 166, 169, 171, 182–84, 186–87, 191, 193, 195–96, 203, 206, 209–10, 212, 216, 220, 224, 240, 252–53, 262, 268, 270, 272, 277n.13, 277n.14, 281n.33, 281n.34, 286n.7, 293n.19, 293n.21, 295n.6, 297n.20
home, 107–8, 147, 202
homeless, 199
humanism, 23, 129–31, 133–36, 149, 151, 164, 166, 168, 181–83, 185, 207, 289n.6
humanist, 207–8, 253
humanities, 62, 64, 156, 192, 205–7, 213–14
humanity, 186–87, 191, 193, 201, 209
Humean empiricism, 32

ideal(s), 5, 176, 183, 218
idealism, 31, 44, 106–8, 133–34, 148, 187, 203
ideality, 88–89, 130, 218
identity, 1, 11, 176, 20, 48, 55, 81, 151, 169, 170, 180, 188, 191, 209, 211–13, 276n.10, 276n.11
ideology, 9

Subject Index 319

imagination, 16, 116, 204
immanence, 111, 138
immediacy, 54, 96–97, 101–2, 189–90, 192, 203, 214, 246, 252
impersonal, 202, 227
impiety, 215
individual, 44, 52–53, 56, 68, 77, 158, 253, 270
individualism, 160, 262
infinity, 88, 101, 130, 290n.11
inheritance, 2, 10, 40, 50, 91, 124, 127, 154, 170, 204, 213, 222, 254, 262, 269, 297n.21, 274n.4
institution(s), 6, 22, 40, 55, 41, 167, 175, 180, 205, 215, 218, 221, 234, 291n.15
intellect, 263
intellectuals, 131, 164, 220, 255, 296n.14
interiority, 143
inviolable (*see also* sacred), 241
irony, 278n.17

knowledge, 18–19, 44, 74, 79, 101–2, 123–24, 126, 139, 167

language, 61, 78, 91, 96, 111–12, 119–20, 140, 193, 215, 233, 270, 295n.4
law (Constitutional), 253, 270
learning, 123
Lebenswelt, 100
letters, 266
liberal state, 249
liberalism, 129, 252, 255
life, 58, 183–85, 276n.7, 277n.12, 293n.19
literature, xiv, 275n.5
local control, 36, 52, 95, 130, 152, 209, 279n.22
logos, 84, 210–11, 294n.2
London, 173
Lord Jim, 24, 275n.5
loyalty, 259, 288n.3

madness, 50, 144, 192, 267–68
magic, 193
maps, 172, 245
marginality, 4
Marxists, 220, 295n.7
master and slave dialectic, 146
materialism, 107
measuring, 12, 17, 34, 77, 102, 172, 207–8
mechanism, 19, 35, 118, 137, 202
medieval, 5, 277n.14
metanarrative, 8
metaphysics, xiv, 75, 117, 124, 127, 131, 237, 258
midworld, 23, 28–29, 37–38, 45, 84, 86–89, 97–98, 105, 113, 116–17, 123, 127, 130, 172, 174, 176, 187–89, 192, 197, 203, 205, 214, 232, 281n.31, 285n.7, 291n.16, 294n.1
mind, 89, 97, 121, 203
misologists, 191, 233, 278n.17
mistakes (*see also* errors), 117, 123, 126, 208
Mitwelt, 112, 227, 232, 286n.11
modernity, 5, 9, 11, 23–24, 28–29, 81, 113, 133, 135, 175, 268, 278n.15, 283n.3
monument(s), 27, 55, 70, 88, 121, 155, 166, 174, 205, 209
Moralität (Immanuel Kant), 255
morbidity, 91
mourning, 238
mugwump(s), 259–60
mysticism, 117, 196–97, 206, 286n.9
myth (*see also* story), 80, 94, 109–10, 210–11, 253, 280n.31

Nagasaki, 216
narcissism, 11, 279n.22
narrative, 8, 36, 41, 73, 82, 110, 143, 165–66, 196, 202–3, 210, 212, 228–29, 245, 271–72, 278n.20

natural piety, 114, 116, 288n.3
natural science, 109
naturalism, 88, 137, 202
naturalistic idealism, 284n.3
nature, 11, 33, 64, 80, 84, 87, 93, 109, 114, 116, 125, 143, 159, 160, 175, 177, 188, 196, 201, 207, 209, 251, 261, 263, 289n.3, 296n.12, 297n.19
negation(s), 21, 130, 142, 146, 167–68
New Deal, 253
news, 158–59, 253, 266
Newtonian physics, 33
nihilism, 15, 17, 20, 21, 28, 81, 131, 163, 165, 167–68, 182, 184, 230, 239, 267–69, 274n.1
nouns, 212
novel, 2, 207, 275n.5
Novum Organum (Francis Bacon), 213
nullification, 18, 50, 53, 103, 132, 179, 216, 251, 267–68, 292n.17

object(s), 13, 18, 30, 36, 45, 87–88, 95, 103, 111, 125, 128, 196, 214, 258, 279n.25, 286n.8
objective idealism, 37, 45
objectivity, 35, 61, 66, 88, 111, 137–39
obscurantism, 78, 193
order, 20, 37, 53, 68, 72, 101, 107, 189, 192–93, 195, 205, 207, 221, 229, 264
ordinary language, 120
organism (*see also* body and embodiment), 96, 119, 207–8
original sin, 154
orthodoxy, 174, 210, 280n.31, 284n.9, 292n.17
other(s), 60, 146
Owl of Minerva, 41, 279n.22

Paris, 256, 296n.16
parrésia, 224
Parthenon, 76, 155, 209, 276n.9
passion, 209

past, 14, 25, 65, 67, 70–72, 74, 126, 161, 176, 218, 221, 247–48, 253, 257, 274n.2, 277n.14
perception, 12
person, 11, 22, 94, 113, 153, 227, 292n.17
personal, 35, 101
personal identity, 10
personal realism, xiii
phenomenology, 39, 41, 99, 104, 139–40, 165
philosopher, 134, 158, 188, 289n.6
philosophy, 9, 22, 24–25, 27–29, 40, 56, 58, 62, 76–77, 81–82, 86, 151, 175, 192, 201, 204–5, 214, 233, 285n.1, 189n.5, 290n.8, 292n.18, 297n.21
philosophy of history, 36, 64, 124, 285n.2
physics, 32, 89, 172, 206, 279n.21, 283n.5
piety, 54–55, 75–76, 114, 116, 154, 157, 166, 190–91, 215, 258–59, 286n.12, 288n.3, 297n.18
pilgrimage, 11, 25–26, 41, 55, 279n.24, 297n.19
pilgrims, 244, 251
place, 132–33, 136, 140, 151–52, 158, 165–66, 172, 196, 205, 241, 260, 296n.16
Platonic dialogue(s), 76, 191, 229
play, 92–93, 139, 220, 237
pluralism, 57
poem, 178, 205, 207
poet, 19
poetry, 193, 232, 271
poiesis, 16
polis, 53, 84, 213, 251
politics, 212–13, 279n.23
post office, 158, 176, 266
postmodern, 4, 8, 278n.15
postmodernism, 7
power, 115
pragmatism, 117, 119

presence, 14, 20, 31, 37, 47, 52, 54, 102–3, 112, 188, 270, 280n.31
present, 14, 19, 67, 72, 198, 216, 218, 221, 224, 249, 252
present active participle(s), 17, 22, 96, 104, 190, 291n.16
present moment, 23, 25, 51, 64, 67, 107, 169, 175–77, 183–85, 247, 256, 265
privacy, 93, 197, 286n.10, 295n.7
progress, 5, 288n.3, 294n.23
promethean humanism, 160, 183
promethean self, 67
provincialism, 157
psyche, 84, 285n.3
psychology, 32, 76, 89, 112, 183
Puritans, 251
purpose, 34, 97
pyramids, 155
Pyrenees, 207, 290n.12

quantification, 95
quotidian, 154

radical empiricism, 72, 284n.14
radicals, 230, 255
rationality. *See* reason
reader, 7
realism, 45, 57, 59–60, 99, 104, 194, 197, 286n.9
reality, 17, 46, 59, 88, 90, 97–99, 100, 104–5, 166, 192–93, 198, 247, 280n.31, 283n.5
reason, 5–6, 8, 16, 20, 32, 66, 103, 112–13, 116, 137, 213, 219, 278n.17
rebellious individual, 180, 217
recognition, 146, 148
reductionism, 274n.4
reflexivity (*see also* self-authorization, etc.), 287n.1
reformation, 251
religion, 140, 170, 182–83
Republic (Plato), 42

res gestae, 74
responsibility, 18, 40, 56, 110–11, 164, 179, 180, 190, 253, 276n.7, 292n.17
return of the same, 134
revelation, 85, 117, 174, 187, 192–93, 195, 198–99, 203, 233, 269, 290n.12
reverence, 26, 55, 75, 175, 180, 186, 198, 222, 239, 254, 290n.7
revision, 24, 37, 38, 69, 117, 124, 127, 132, 184, 186–87, 192, 271
revolutionaries, 246
Romantic rationalism, 219
Romanticism, 114, 217, 219
Rome, 121
roots (rootedness), 237, 265
ruins, 3, 156, 173, 276n.9
ruptures, 7, 74, 278n.14

sacred, 26–27, 160–61, 180, 186, 242, 265, 269, 282n.39
sacred scripture, 198, 206
sadomasochistic eroticism, 237
saunterer(s), 261, 297n.19
scholar, 181, 186
science, 33, 35, 49, 63, 67, 109, 167, 181, 187, 205–7, 209, 213–14, 219, 235, 270, 284n.13
scientific naturalism, 168
scientism, 207
scientist, 19, 53, 71, 167, 186, 188, 206
secular, 26–27, 263
self, 11, 18, 39, 60, 67, 75, 90–91, 94, 96, 125, 144–45, 254, 267, 286n.7, 292n.17
self-authorization, 169, 214, 253, 291n.13
self-consciousness, 39, 69, 76, 140–42, 146
self-criticism, 67, 124, 127, 187, 196
self-definition, 54, 61, 69, 90, 123, 144, 168, 180, 290n.11
selfhood, 179–80, 211, 213, 224, 228, 254, 267

self-identification, 208, 213–14, 228
self-limitation, 78
self-maintenance, 77, 125, 144, 180, 184, 186–88, 190, 205, 221, 227, 283n.3
self-nullification (*see also* nullification), 189
self-overcoming, 175, 179, 185, 235
self-possession, 219, 228, 230
self-regulation, 60
self-revision, 56, 68–69, 71, 76–77, 120, 144, 179, 188, 192, 196, 203–4, 227, 252, 271
self-transcendence, 179
semiotics, 128–29
Shay's Rebellion, 247
signs, 112, 127, 194, 194, 286n.3
silent universe (or world), 19, 53, 103, 175, 191–92, 199, 268, 280n.31
simultaneity, 257, 261
Sittlichkeit (Hegel), 246, 255
skeptical empiricism, 194
skepticism, 15, 30, 45, 55, 73, 79, 117, 140–42, 144, 167, 171, 174–76, 180, 189, 197, 203, 211, 223, 229, 289n.6
solidarity, 91, 217
solipsism, 286n.10
solitude, 91
soul, 153
sovereignty, 218
Soviet Union, 218
space, 88, 119, 149, 155, 172, 195, 205, 241, 285n.5, 290n.9
speaking, 12, 189, 193, 216
spectator, 12, 64–65, 72, 100
spirit (*Geist*), 38, 137
spiritualism (*see also* animism), 200, 202
sticks-in-the-mud, 256
Stimmung, 163
stoicism, 140–41, 142, 143, 144, 149
story, 14, 36, 80, 100, 143, 202, 292n.19, 293n.19
storyteller, 36, 228, 292n.19, 294n.3

students, 192
subjectivism, 60, 175
subjectivity, 35, 61, 89, 110–11, 117, 121, 123, 137, 149, 171, 211, 213, 295n.7
successiveness, 257, 261
sundial, 97
symbol, 28, 88, 89, 96, 122, 125–26, 130, 172, 193, 195–97, 233, 278n.16, 285n.6, 286n.13
Symposium (Plato), 52

talk, 128–29
teaching, 292n.15
technology, 113, 137, 231
telling, 16, 79–80, 110, 160, 164, 232, 271, 292n.19, 296n.11
The Definition of the Thing, 56
The Structure of Scientific Revolutions (Thomas Kuhn), 187
theogony, 146, 148, 156
theology, 32, 89, 206
thing, 57, 103, 108
thought, 6, 54, 87, 141, 234
time, 26, 52, 71, 74, 88, 107, 153, 160, 162, 165, 169, 172, 195, 268, 283n.40
timelessness, 169, 184
tolerance, 249, 253
tool(s), 87, 89, 96–97, 113
topos, 133
Torah, 240
totality, 2, 14, 20, 24, 31, 37, 45, 103, 112, 188, 202
tradition(s), 6, 78, 240, 274n.2, 277n.13, 288n.2, 296n.12
transcendence, 22, 107, 269, 295n.8
transcendental signified, 127
transhistorical, 7, 171, 213
travel, 273n.2, 296n.17
Treaty of Versailles, 210
triumphalism, 164, 166

truth, 16, 45, 76, 81, 124, 160, 162, 166, 168, 172, 236
tyranny, 186, 254, 270

Übermensch, 185, 231, 238
unhappy consciousness, 146, 148, 174–76, 185, 200, 269
Unheimlichkeit, 172, 182
United States, 12, 19, 250
unity, 107
universal, 52–53, 56, 97, 157
universalism, 157
universe, 107, 183
university, 155–56, 243, 245
utopia, 184, 242
utterance(s), 18, 36, 47–50, 54, 68, 78–79, 94, 98, 113, 119–20, 187, 191–93, 205, 216, 219, 233, 284n.12, 287n.1

vagrancy, 21, 51, 53, 98, 103, 179, 190, 253, 262
vagrant, 51, 153, 163, 165, 279n.22
verbs, 83, 131, 212, 214
violence, 122–23
Vir, 234
voiceless world. *See* silent world

voices, 44, 94, 126, 191–92, 236, 267, 278n.16, 281n.31
voluntarism, 292n.18

Walden (H. D. Thoreau), 158, 265
walking (or sauntering), 266
want(s), 254
western culture, 4, 171, 229, 262
western philosophy, 26, 29, 139, 188, 229
western technology, 218, 231
western tradition, 10, 171, 229
wilderness, 251, 261
Williams College, 164, 291n.15
Williamstown, Mass., 157
wonder, 204–5
word(s), 40, 47, 49, 50, 76, 84, 88, 189–90, 192–93, 236
working through, 174, 290n.6
world, 3, 20, 40, 49–50, 52, 75, 85, 87, 92, 94, 98–99, 108–9, 111–12, 128, 132, 144–45, 148, 150, 164, 178–79, 181, 183, 186, 195–97, 199, 205, 233, 261, 267, 280n.31, 296n.11
World War I, xiii, 210

yardstick, 23, 45–46, 87, 96–97, 102, 127, 190, 193, 195, 207

www.ingramcontent.com/pod-product-compliance
Lightning Source LLC
Chambersburg PA
CBHW030909040526
R18240000001B/R182400PG44116CBX00012B/11